Sustainable Finance

Sustainable Finance is a concise and authoritative reference series linking research and practice. It provides reliable concepts and research findings in the ever growing field of sustainable investing and finance, SDG economics and Leadership with the declared commitment to present the theories, methods, tools and investment approaches that can fulfil the United Nations Sustainable Development Goals and the Paris Agreement COP 21/22 alongside with de-risking assets and creating triple purpose solutions that ensure the parity of profit, people and planet through choice architecture passion and performance. The series addresses market failure, systemic risk and reinvents portfolio theory, portfolio engineering as well as behavioural finance, financial mediation, product innovation, shared values, community building, business strategy and innovation, exponential tech and creation of social capital. Sustainable Finance and SDG Economics series helps to understand keynotes on international guidelines, guiding accounting and accountability principles, prototyping new developments in triple bottom line investing, cost benefit analysis, integrated financial first plus impact first concepts and impact measurement. Going beyond adjacent fields (like accounting, marketing, strategy, risk management) it integrates the concept of psychology, innovation, exponential tech, choice architecture, alternative economics, blue economy shared values, professions of the future, leadership, human and community development, team culture, impact, quantitative and qualitative measurement, Harvard Negotiation, mediation and complementary currency design using exponential tech and ledger technology. Books in the series contain latest findings from research, concepts for implementation, as well as best practices and case studies for the finance industry.

Karen Wendt • Bernd Villhauer
Editors

Sustainable Wealth Management

Directing Capital Towards Sustainability

Springer

Editors
Karen Wendt
CEO
President Sustainable Finance
Cham, Zug, Switzerland

Bernd Villhauer
Weltethos-Institut
Tübingen, Baden-Württemberg, Germany

ISSN 2522-8285 ISSN 2522-8293 (electronic)
Sustainable Finance
ISBN 978-3-031-55504-6 ISBN 978-3-031-55505-3 (eBook)
https://doi.org/10.1007/978-3-031-55505-3

This Springer imprint is published by the registered company Springer Nature Switzerland AG
The registered company address is: Gewerbestrasse 11, 6330 Cham, Switzerland

Paper in this product is recyclable.

Contents

About the Authors

Stefan Brunnhuber MD PHD CMO, Medical Director, Chair Sustainability HSMW, Trustee World Academy of Art and Science, Full Member Club of Rome, Member European Academy of Science and Arts, Member Lancet-Commission on 'Post covid and green recovery', Member Friends of the Earth, German Liberal Party (FDP), Federal Council on 'Sustainable Finance' of the current German government, contact: www.stefan-brunnhuber.de

Martin Buchner CFA, CESGA, joined Metzler in 2020. He is a Portfolio Manager in the team Asset Allocation & Fixed Income and is responsible for multi-asset mandates and asset allocation. Prior to joining Metzler, Buchner earned a master's degree in business administration from Goethe University in Frankfurt/Main, Germany. Alongside his studies, he worked for Metzlers Asset Allocation & Fixed Income team in a supportive role for two years. He also gained practical experience in internships at ING- DiBa AG and Deutsche Börse AG in Frankfurt/Main. From 2008 to 2011, Buchner completed an apprenticeship in banking at VR-Bank in Landau an der Isar, Germany.

Shidi Dong received her PhD degree from University of South Australia. She is currently working in the School of Management, Shenyang University of Technology (SUT) in north China. She has diverse interests in accounting research, including corporate social responsibility (CSR), environmental accounting and reporting, green finance, and ESG. So far, she has published in the high-ranking academic journals, such as *Sustainability Accounting*, *Management and Policy Journal*, *Meditari Accountancy Research*, etc. while accumulating rich experience in supervising graduate students.

Stefan Klauser is CEO of Aisot Technologies, the next-generation AI for Asset Management provider. Before founding Aisot, Stefan worked as Project Lead Finance 4.0 at ETH Zurich. He is co-author and editor of a number of books at the intersection of fintech and sustainability. Stefan holds an MA from the University of Zurich and postgraduate certificates in Leadership as well as Entrepreneurship & Innovation Management from the London School of Economics and Political Science LSE and in Fintech and the Future of Markets from MIT.

His notable speeches include: World Web Forum, Web Summit, Finance Fair Zurich, Rise London, Google Zurich, Realvision Daily Crypto Show, World Innovation Economics.

Kai Lessmann leads the research group on Public Economics and Climate Finance at the Potsdam Institute for Climate Impact Research. He holds a degree in Applied System Science from the University of Osnabrück and a doctoral degree from the Technical University of Berlin. His research agenda addresses the implementation of climate policies, ranging from game-theoretic analysis of climate agreements to the analysis of national climate policy instruments, often in second-best settings, for example with consideration of technology externalities or distributional implications. More recently, his research has shifted to questions of mobilizing private finance and aligning climate policy with frictions in the financial system.

Marcel Malmendier Profession: Asset manager and insurance broker, founder of two companies in the field of sustainable investment, Qualitates GmbH and Investmentkontor RheinRuhr GmbH, Managing Director of Investmentkontor RheinRuhr.

Areas of Expertise: Sustainable and ethical investments, risk management, change management and organizational design, personnel development.

Ron McIver is Lecturer in Financial Planning and Finance and Deputy Director of the Policy and Regulation stream of the Centre for Markets, Values and Inclusion (CMVI)—positions located within the University of South Australia's Business School, UniSA Business, in the City of Adelaide.

In addition to his academic roles Ron is actively engaged with industry, being a Senior Associate of the Financial Services Institute of Australasia (FINSIA) and an Academic Affiliate of the Financial Advice Association of Australia (FAAA).

Ron's research and teaching interests encompass the broader areas of business education, corporate governance, financial institutions, financial markets, and personal financial planning, the latter focusing personal investment and personal risk management. His empirically oriented research currently addresses the corporate performance and disclosure impacts of corporate social responsibility (CSR) and environmental, social, and governance (ESG) factors, green financial policy, and institutional and regulatory reform; the value of personal financial advice; and identification and analysis of financial spillovers and spillover networks.

Ron has produced a wide variety of scholarly publications, including, among others, recent papers in *Accounting Auditing and Accountability Journal*, *Accounting and Finance*, *Business and Society*, *Energy Economics*, *Journal of Commodity Markets*, and *Meditari Accountancy Research*.

B. Tobias Peylo is Professor of Business Administration and Finance and Deputy Head of the Institute of Internationalization at Hochschule Kempten University of Applied Sciences, Germany. His research and teaching focuses on green finance, sustainability management, and portfolio/risk management.

Daniel Sailer CESGA, heads the Sustainable Investment Office at Metzler Asset Management. In this position, he and his team are responsible for the further development of the comprehensive sustainability strategy and coordinate its implementation. Before joining Metzler, he worked for nine years at MSCI Inc. in Frankfurt am Main. He was responsible for expanding the ESG research presence in the DACH region—most recently in a management position. From 2007 to 2010, Sailer worked at LBBW, Stuttgart, in the Derivatives Sales & Marketing department as Sales Manager. From 2004 to 2007 he worked at LBBW and studied part-time at the Baden-Württemberg Cooperative State University and the Open University of London. Sailer graduated as Diplom-Betriebswirt (BA) and Bachelor of Arts in Business Administration.

Franziska Schütze is a Research Associate in the climate policy department at DIW Berlin since 2019 and coordinator of the project "sustainable finance research platform." She has been working in the field of sustainable finance for more than 10 years. She has worked on several EU and national research projects, aiming at understanding economic implications of climate and energy policies and the role of the financial sector. This includes the assessment of climate-related risks and opportunities and the assessment of green fiscal policies and financial market regulation. Prior to DIW, she worked at the Global Climate Forum e.V. and obtained her PhD at the University of Potsdam. She holds an MSc in International Economics and Business from Utrecht School of Economics, including one semester at Lund University and Copenhagen Business School. After her studies, she worked as an analyst for a venture capital fund for sustainable businesses in the area of renewable energy, e-mobility, natural resources, and green IT.

Na Shen is an Associate Professor in the Department of Business Administration, Hong Kong Shue Yan University. Her research interests include corporate finance, family business, emerging markets, etc. She has published a lot of papers in reputable journals such as *Journal of Corporate Finance* and *Asia Pacific Journal of Management* and has published several book chapters. She was awarded the Endeavour Fellowship and served as a visiting scholar at the University of South Australia. She also serves as director of The Hong Kong Association of Overseas-Returned Scholars and committee member in Greater Bay Area Youth Innovation and Entrepreneurship Foundation.

Dirk Soehnholz is owner and CEO of Soehnholz ESG GmBH, a B2B provider of rules-based portfolios focusing on pure ESG and SDG, and of Soehnholz Asset Management GmbH, the advisor of an Article 9 (SFDR) mutual fund. He is also an Honorary Professor of Asset Management at Leipzig University, Germany.

Karl Weinmayer is Assistant Professor of Finance at the Department of International Management at Modul University Vienna, Austria. His research interests include sustainable finance, sustainability disclosure, portfolio modeling, and efficiency analysis.

Helge Wulsdorf doctorate in social ethics, graduate theologian, banker, since 2003 Head of Sustainable Investments at Bank für Kirche und Caritas eG in Paderborn (www.bkc-paderbon.de), board member of Forum Nachhaltige Geldanlagen e. V. (2004–2022), lecturer at EBS Business School (2019–2023) and member of the Sustainable Finance Advisory Board of the German Federal Government (2019–2021), also deputy chairman of the Supervisory Board of Bischöfliche Kommission Aktion Adveniat e. V., numerous specialist publications on business ethics and sustainable issues in the financial sector.

Lei Xu holds a PhD in Finance from the University of South Australia, while also bringing to his teaching and research practical experience in banking, including roles at the Bank of China and China Merchants Bank. The combination of academic and practical experience enables Dr. Xu to bring unique and practical perspectives to his teaching and research, as he can draw on his wealth of experience to provide valuable insights into the field of finance.

Dr. Xu's research interests are diverse and encompass a range of topics in finance, including banking, corporate governance, financial markets, financial systems, and FinTech. As testament to his research skills and expertise, Dr. Xu has over 50 high-quality authored and co-authored publications. His reputation as an active researcher in the field is further cemented by his role as Editor-in-Chief of *Economics & Politics*, an ABDC A/ABS 2-ranked journal. Dr. Xu is frequently invited to present at international conferences and seminars, to review for quality peer-reviewed journals publishing in the areas of accounting, corporate governance, economics, finance, and management, and to undertake contract research.

Guodong Yuan is a Senior Lecturer in Finance and Financial Planning at UniSA Business, University of South Australia.

With extensive teaching and research experience across both Australia and China, Dr. Yuan's expertise spans finance, accounting, and taxation. His research interests include the market valuation effects of financial behavior and regulatory events, taxation policies, market structure, and corporate governance. Dr. Yuan's work has been widely published in book chapters, international journal articles, and conference proceedings.

In addition to his academic roles, he is actively engaged with the industry and the community, serving as a member of CPA Australia and an academic member of the Financial Advice Association of Australia (FAAA).

Chapter 1
Learn or Lose: Challenges and Perspectives in Sustainable Wealth Management

Karen Wendt, and Bernd Villhauer

You can't predict, you can prepare.

(Howard Marks, The most important thing)

2022 has been a catastrophic year for wealth management. The ongoing Covid pandemic, war in Ukraine, and rising inflation rates have all made it very hard to grow or even protect wealth. At the end of the year,[1] the *Financial Times* quoted Renaud de Planta, Senior Partner of the Pictet Group: "This year is one of the most significant years of wealth destruction in nearly 100 years," he said, and added: "Looking at it rather simply, many private investors could have lost more than a quarter of their real inflation-adjusted wealth."

It is estimated that the US billionaires alone lost 660 billion US Dollars in 2022. While some (like Elon Musk) made questionable investments, the majority lost money simply because of the gravity of the global situation. All ships went down with the ebb.

Looking at wealth management in 2023 and beyond, strategic planning will not be possible without bearing these crises and falling tides in mind. We must nevertheless continue to ask what the positive aspects of truly sustainable wealth management might be in this uncertain future.

Is "sustainability" just a fair-weather strategy, something "nice to have" in good times? I would argue that Sustainable Wealth Management (SWM) ought, by

[1] 30.12.2022.

K. Wendt (✉)
Sustainable Finance, Cham, Switzerland
e-mail: karen@sustainablefinance.io

B. Villhauer
Weltethos-Institut, Tübingen, Baden-Württemberg, Germany
e-mail: villhauer@weltethos-institut.org

K. Wendt, B. Villhauer (eds.), *Sustainable Wealth Management*, Sustainable Finance,
https://doi.org/10.1007/978-3-031-55505-3_1

definition, to provide frameworks for investment in times of crisis. The very concept of sustainable investment is an expression of a new will to understand and mitigate global crises and to provide useful navigation tools for economic storms. Nassim Taleb's definition of "antifragility" as "beyond resilience or robustness" is particularly apt here: "The resilient resists shocks and stays the same; the antifragile gets better."[2]

It makes sense to describe the new wealth management in these antifragile terms. One possible definition of SWM is that it balances traditional investing with environmental, social, and governance-related (ESG) insights to improve long-term outcomes. It integrates wealth protection, asset planning, estate planning, tax planning, succession planning, and family governance with ESG criteria.

1.1 Main Challenges and the Special Role of Risk Management

There are two main factors that define the difference between conventional wealth management and SWM: a new understanding of risk management and a convincing description of impact factors (including a better understanding of sustainable business models) for ecological and social transformation. Both elements require more ESG research and valid data.

A recent issue of the journal *Sustainability*[3] shows that a new understanding of risk management is essential for the description of impact-driven sustainability strategies in finance. Other articles (Krysiak, 2009) explain how longtermism is highly dependent on new risk management paradigms. Against this background of new risk models, we present a future vision of SWM in our handbook.

This future, however, is approached from a variety of different angles:

- Marcel Malmendier ("Sustainability as an Information Challenge in Asset Management") provides an analysis of informational flows in SWM, where the accessibility, availability, reliability, and interpretability of data are crucial. Malmendier compares four types of asset management (quantitative, qualitative, single investment, and rule-based asset management), all of which are shaped by the new imperative of innovative data management in the framework of a sustainability strategy.
- Tobias Peylo and Christian Nuß ("Two Sides of the Same Coin: ESG Risk and Opportunity Management in the Investment and Lending Business") offer a pragmatic approach to an inclusive, coherent, and structured manner of ESG risk and opportunity management. They particularly describe how ESG factors can have a very positive impact on the financial performance of solvency.
- Dirk Söhnholz ("Custom ESG Indexing: How Direct ESG Indexing Can Solve Many Responsible Investing Problems") presents a practioner's toolkit for sustainable portfolio selection. Describing instruments for rule-based ESG

[2] Taleb (2012).

[3] Garcia Benau et al. (2021).

investments, Söhnholz helps both professional wealth managers and self-directed investors to find sustainable solutions.

- Helge Wulsdorf ("Values and Norms in Sustainable Finance") emphasizes the importance of a value-driven investment style. This becomes even more important in times of widespread disagreement concerning rules and norms for ethical investment. The less common norms are accepted, Wulsdorf argues, the more values are needed. This is particularly true in the case of wealthy private investors who want to see their values realized in their investment strategies.
- Lessmann et al. ("Can the Financial Sector Protect the Climate? The Potential of Sustainable Finance") review three key mechanisms of sustainable finance to show how SF can buttress climate policy: (1) by providing investors with the necessary information to factor climate risk into their decisions; (2) by building awareness of sustainable investing by differentiated means; and (3) by addressing the cost of capital as an obstacle to low-carbon investments. Taking this idea one step further, we need also to talk about the infrastructure of the market and how it can support sustainability. In his article Emerging Structure of Sustainable Finance. Tobias Peylo is discussing just that.
- Dong et al. ("Environmental Information Disclosure Quality, Institutional Pressure, and the Cost of Debt: Evidence from China's Heavy Polluters") guides us through environmental information disclosure: quality, institutional pressure, and the impact on the cost of debt.
- Daniel Sailer and Martin Buchner ("Sustainability Across Different Asset Classes – Integration in a Multi-Asset Portfolio") explore a study that shows how ESG criteria for institutional investors can be aggregated and documented in the context of private banking to build sustainable multi-asset portfolios via strategic asset allocation (SAA).
- Lei Xu ("Towards a Digital and Sustainable Economy: A Review of Recent Fintech Policies and Developments in China") provides some key insights into the Chinese investment scene. With its Fintech Development Plan (2022–2025), China is choosing a different sustainability path than the West. After numerous cryptocrashs in the West and the breakdown of essential parts of the global financial ecosystem in 2022, it is particularly important to understand China's growing role in the global investment landscape of the future. Likewise, Lei opens the procedures on reflecting on Sustainable FinTech.
- Na Shen and Lei Xu ("Internet Finance, Private Firm Financing and Investment: Evidence from China") paint an ambivalent picture of the role of Chinese Internet finance and fintechs. With a regional focus, Na and Lei show how the financial behavior of private firms in China is changing—a phenomenon of the utmost relevance for globally orientated wealth managers in the post-Covid era. A new topic not to be missed is the emergence of Artificial Intelligence (AI) in investment strategies and even full offers of AI driven wealth management platforms. Stefan Klauser CEO of such platform company AISOT is discussing his interesting topic here.

Dr. Karen Wendt dives into portfolio engineering, showing SDG-aligned portfolios with a systematic positive selection strategy applying a theory of change, she demonstrates how SDG aligned portfolios can be created using a systematic model and a strict scientific approach.

Karl Weinmayer investigates the impact of SRI efficiency screening intensity on portfolio performance.

> The contribution also put a special focus on what is happening in China, with various contributions stretching from Internet finance, private firm financing, and investment (Na Shen), Impact of Corporate Tax Reform on Firm Share Price (Yuan, McIver and Xu), Overinvestment, internal control, and government intervention (Yuan, McIver and Xu), to Exploring financial institutions environmental disclosures (Dong)

Out of these diverse contributions, a common view of the transformative role of SWM nevertheless emerges. Perhaps above all, the book casts new light on the nature of *cyclical challenges* in modern finance.

1.2 Cycles

Most SWM investment decisions (as well as conventional ones) are based on cyclical models. This includes macro- or microeconomic cycles as well as the traditional wealth management cycles for individuals or families. In the case of families, this cycle is often described in four stages: accumulation, transition, reaping, and intergenerational transfer. Every stage comes in a short-term and a long-term version. Long-term thinking automatically again leads to cycle-based investment philosophies that consider the broader economic picture.

Cycles in wealth management are sometimes only fashions or an expression of a change in investment strategy. Such cyclical models are important, however, for the growth of individual and family wealth, and they may also help us understand important macroeconomic changes. Sometimes, they reflect the situation in the real economy, but very often they are driven by dynamics of their own. Financial markets are, in any case, highly influenced by cyclical developments. For the practical thinker, it is clear: "Most things prove to be cyclical."[4]

One important example of cyclical thinking connects economic and political history, although not coming from a philosopher or an economist: "Hard times create strong people, strong people create good times, good times create weak people, weak people create hard times…"[5]

This description of cyclical development is about learning processes. One generation learns from the other and is shaped by its experiences. It may be possible, however, to escape the determinist trap via active learning. And one of the key areas of future learning is the field of ecological transformation.

1.3 SWM Learning

Which specific learning processes are important in SWM? What skills and capabilities will be required for such learning? What are the important topics? We will name some:

---

[4] Marks, H., The most important thing, p. 67.

[5] G. Michael Hopf, author of postapocalyptic books like "The End" or "The Long Road."

- Customers
- Markets
- Assets

Customers demand new forms of investment, especially sustainable investment—and at the same time stability in turbulent times. Safe havens and transformation areas are both needed; SWM must show where the two overlap. An NBER working paper (Pastor et al., 2020) explains how Green Assets outperform others when positive shocks influence the ESG factor, which captures shifts in customer taste for green products and investor taste for green holdings. Sustainable Success in Finance is made by the expectations and hopes of a new generation of investors.[6] Customer needs and demands define the framework for new strategies. Also, 71% of respondents think that companies with good sustainability strategies make good investments.[7] New generations, in particular, are highlighting the green impact. In the wealth management area particularly, it is crucial to recognize and answer the expectations of the heirs.

Markets have changed as well. We have more and more "political" markets—influenced by ecological concerns and political interventions. These are set in a partly deglobalizing world with few big players dominating their spheres. We should carefully watch the influence of the central banks, who feel obliged to play a defining role in the climate crisis discussion.

The plurality of *assets* has also been growing immensely. New forms of alternative investments have arisen in quick time, proving both technologically (e.g., crypto/blockchain) and ecologically (e.g., climate compensations) disruptive. There are more and more products that can be offered by wealth managers, more and more options to diversify portfolios.

Considering all of this, we have to ask: What are the "weak" people or the "good times" in a cyclical understanding of investment history? Are the "hard times" only about the losses of the rich? What can we say about the probable length and structure of future crises? And is a certain sensibility for sustainability-related questions in this area a strength or a weakness? In any case, the current situation in wealth management inspires a lot of innovative and disruptive strategies from SWM, considering new customer demands, new markets, and new assets.

We identify some recent trends in the following areas and connect these to the sustainability paradigm:

- New risk management
- Innovative impact models
- Retail revolution and neobrokers
- Digital innovations
- New elites in developing states
- Regulatory changes
- Ultra-high net worth individuals ("neo-Feudalism")

These are megatrends that not only cause changes but also frame the entire discussion around future developments. These trends influence each other and are

[6] Everling and Lampe (2014).

[7] Charles Schwab, UK online survey in 2022.

therefore interdependent puzzle pieces in a holistic investment strategy. And as we know:

> Successful investing requires thoughtful attention to many separate aspects, all at the same time. Omit any one and the result is likely to be less than satisfactory.[8]

1.4 It's Not the Technology, Stupid!

In recent debates, technological innovation is sometimes overrated. Technology is seen as the one moving and deciding factor. Thus, it is not taken into account that there are many cultural and psychological requirements for the application or incorporation of technological innovations. You need particular cultural preconditions for the application of technology.

The debate about robo-advisory or the use of artificial intelligence/machine learning has a lot of important implications for the future of wealth management.[9] This relevance should be understood in human resource development as well as organization development and business development. Technological innovation must be embedded both psychologically, and culturally. Read the fascinating artile of AI wealth management platform co-founder Stefan Klauser here. The construction of AI wealth management of course includes a new understanding of firm culture and a hightened level of team spiriat together with the creation of an ecosystem where values are aligned. Embedmement of AI pschologically and culturally. allow us to leverage the advantages of AI without overemphasizing its dangers. Studies from other industries[10] show how important this connection is. The impact of national and international regulation is obvious, especially when one considers that the role of machine learning in the global economy is set to increase exponentially over the coming years. In a survey of the World Economic Forum of 2020, 77% of the financial institutions anticipate that it will be of high or very high overall importance to their businesses.[11]

1.5 Bipartisan Investment and the Importance of Values

One element for the use of technological innovations is a common understanding of basic political and economic issues. Technological or economic innovations must be discussed rationally in an atmosphere of respect, mutual curiosity, and understanding—this may sound overly idealistic, but we will face severe problems if the preconditions for such a dialogue are destroyed. In the USA, we are witnessing the development of a highly politicized and polarized climate of public discourse, in which it becomes more

[8] Howard Marks, The most important thing, p. ix.

[9] Villhauer (2021).

[10] Roberts et al. (2021).

[11] WEF 2020.

and more difficult to harness the innovations of sustainable investment. In this heated discussion, facts and rational arguments are more and more left aside.

When confronted with criticism that ESG criteria threaten financial success or follow a political agenda, investment managers need to show that sustainability is not only a reason for rentability and can provide excellent returns, but also a precondition for further learning about optimization in wealth management.

The personal aspect of SWM connects it to the value-driven or value-oriented approach. SWM—like all wealth management for high net worth individuals—is very personal business. You have to know what people believe and hope and then create an investment strategy based on this individual person's aspirations.

"Strong people emerging out of hard times" will best be able to learn, adapt, and develop while remaining aware of their values. Global SWM must explore the scope of shared values and the role of value-driven decisions for financial sovereignty in different countries and cultures.

1.6 Ethical Finance for the Future of Wealth Management

"Ethical finance" enables a more comprehensive concept of impact than just focusing on CO_2 emissions: climate finance is less than sustainable finance and sustainable finance is less than ethical finance. This book shows how, in the current cycle, we are now witnessing the rise of a new ethical paradigm for wealth management.

Recently, financial institutions have increasingly been accused of causing or worsening economic, ecological, and humanitarian crises. Where the financial sector is seen only as part of the problem, however, the call for regulation becomes louder and louder, and the freedoms of financial institutions get curtailed. As soon as such regulation proves inefficient, calls for deregulation are heeded, with imprudent speculation returning. To exit this vicious circle, a new conception of the "freedom of finance" is needed that views open markets and the liberties of financial institutions rather as "part of the solution." SWM is therefore part of a larger effort: how can we ethically enhance finance?

A moral revolution in the exercise of financial freedom requires that two conditions be met. (1) The globality of financial markets needs to be matched with a worldwide acceptable ethics of financial freedom. (2) The moral orientation of this ethics must be both inspired from and consonant with the (spiritual as well as nonspiritual) ethical traditions of humanity, as they are potent drivers of human conduct. Thus, we can hope to arrive at a conception of financial freedom that provides a useful orientation for current efforts in impact investing and socially responsible investment (SRI).

The research remaining to be carried out in this field can be summarized as: (1) the formulation of an inter-cultural meta-ethics of finance; and (2) an enrichment of a global financial ethos via contact with the "practical wisdom" retained in the moral traditions of humanity. Whereas the former would be a conceptual and rather centralized endeavor, the latter would encompass intensive and extensive intercultural exchange on behalf of globally participating researchers and practitioners. Research on cross-cultural and diachronic case studies would showcase both theoretical alternatives to the present *status quo* and best practice models for improvement in the spirit of the motto "reality proves possibility."

Motivation to engage in this important work should be amply provided by two major contemporary challenges: rapid technological change and the accelerating ecological crisis.

Although socially responsible investment (SRI) has become an important element of finance discussions around the world, the outcome in terms of investment effects and products is still very much that of a niche strategy. In particular, in German-speaking countries, many investors are yet to be convinced about the effects.

Another important concern is the polarization and politicization of ESG-oriented investment. In the USA in particular, this has become an important issue, blocking important bipartisan decisions for ethical finance in the institutional investment scene. This is partly due to fuzzy definitions of sustainability.

Today, sustainable investment in Germany covers only 2.8% of overall assets invested.[12] The potential of such investment, however, is significant, and decision-makers in wealth management have begun to understand and react to the new demands of their customers. There is still a long way to go: mainstreaming these new strategies with SWM is an ongoing process. However, the challenge in question requires more than an SDG-related change of perspective or the adoption of sustainability slogans: finance itself will have to be substantially reconceptualized. The longtermism inherent in sound wealth management makes it a key area for the ecological transformation of the financial industry. Nevertheless, there is still a lot to do to provide the necessary innovation for a truly future-orientated strategy.

References

Everling, O., & Lampe, J. (2014). *Rating von Vermögensverwaltungen* (Vol. 2014). Springer Gabler.

Garcia Benau, M., Gambetta, N., & Sierra, C. (2021). Financial risk management and sustainability. *Sustainability, 13*. https://doi.org/10.3390/su13158300

Krysiak, F. C. (2009). Risk management as a tool for sustainability. *Journal of Business Ethics, 85*, 483–492.

Pastor, L., Stambaugh, R. F., & Lucian, A. (2020). *Sustainable investing in equilibrium*. Taylor NBER working paper no. 26549 December 2019, Revised June 2020 JEL No. G11,G12.

Roberts, R., Flin, R., Millar, D., & Corradi, L. (2021). Psychological factors influencing technology adaption: A case study from the oil and gas industry. *Technovation, 102*, 102219.

Taleb, N. N. (2012). Antifragile. In *Things that Gain from Disorder* (p. 430). Random House.

Villhauer, B. (2021). Machine learning in finance. In K. Wendt (Ed.), *Theories of change*. Springer.

[12] FNG (2017), p 32.

Chapter 2
From ESG to Impact Investing, Taxonomies, and Sustainable Development Goals

Karen Wendt

Since the economic crisis triggered in 2008, the concept of impact investing emerged. Impact investing has initially been a term coined by the Rockefeller Foundation. Impact creation was necessary "because governments, charities, philanthropists alone were no longer capable of dealing with the twenty-first century's social and environmental challenges. Focussing on the act of charitable giving rather than on achieving social outcomes and a dependence on unpredictable funding hindered many charitable organisations from realizing their full potential concerning innovations, effectiveness and scale" (Brandstetter & Lehner, 2015). The World Economic Forum recently acknowledged the role the investment and finance sector can play in creating solutions to social problems and stated: "Given the nature of how resources are distributed in the world, private investors may have a special role and responsibility in addressing social challenges" (World Economic Forum, 2013). Yet apart from a small number of specialized forms of impact investing like social impact bonds, green bonds, and mission-related philanthropic investments, little is known about the complex interplay between entrepreneurs or organizations, intermediaries, investor regulations, and the successful use of instruments in the field. Glänzel and Scheuerle (2016) use the term social impact investing to clearly distinguish from finance first approaches of impact investing that have a stronger commercial orientation. Hummels (2014) places impact investing in the wider category of responsible investing, considering it just one component. Hebb (2013), Pretorius and Giamporcaro (2012), Viviers and Firer (2013), and Viviers et al. (2011) view impact investing as "responsible investing." Shulman and George (2012) consider impact investing as a form of Socially Responsible Investing (SRI).

K. Wendt (✉)
Sustainable Finance, Cham, Switzerland
e-mail: karen@sustainablefinance.io

K. Wendt, B. Villhauer (eds.), *Sustainable Wealth Management*, Sustainable Finance,
https://doi.org/10.1007/978-3-031-55505-3_2

Geobey and Weber (2013) highlight a distinction: SRI screens out investments for social, environmental, or governance reasons, while impact investing assumes that investments can create financial returns and address social and environmental challenges simultaneously. Impact investing is also included by many authors in the social finance landscape (Suetin, 2011; Geobey & Weber, 2013; Geobey et al., 2012; Mendell & Barbosa, 2013; Weber, 2013, 2016).

According to Barille et al. (2018), sustainability has been shaped by corporate social responsibility. In a traditional view stemming from the Corporate Social Responsibility World, the inevitable consequence of wanting to compress sustainability operational rules in an ideal direction has resulted in the definition of three dimensions that specify sustainability (description according to Barille et al. (2018)):

Economic sustainability is the ability to efficiently use the available resources to assure economic growth.

Social sustainability is the ability to ensure conditions of stability, democracy, participation, respect for human rights and international labor laws, equal access to education and justice, and the possibility to guarantee that human welfare conditions (safety, health) are equally distributed among classes and genders. These requests were found first in a compulsory manner in Prof. Ruggies Protect, Respect, Remedy Framework, which he produced as an advisor to the UN.

Environmental sustainability is the ability to maintain the quality and reproducibility of natural resources. This requirement was first found by Carlowitz (1680) in his use only what you can reproduce approach.

The idea of the triple bottom line was first expressed by John Elkington in his famous book Partnership from Cannibals with Forks. However, Elkington himself acknowledged the need for a reevaluation of the triple bottom line in a recent rewrite, recognizing its reductionist nature and failure to adequately capture the intricate interplay among the three dimensions it aims to address. In his reassessment this year, Elkington advocates for an overhaul and a shift to a new paradigm that better reflects the complex interactions and interdependencies inherent in the triple bottom line concept.

In order to understand the synergies, interplay, and dynamics between the dimensions, we need to understand how the synergetic energy flows among these dimensions—which can be either positive or negative—resulting in the growth or diminishment of these dimensions. According to the intersection between the considered dimensions determines the conditions of development that can be defined as viable (environment and economic), equitable (social and economic), and bearable (environment and social). Drawing from system theory and the viable system organization model, posit that "These dimensions appear to be preliminary but are also necessary and sufficient for a full implementation of a commonly shared approach to sustainability." The interplay between these three dimensions is depicted in Fig. 2.1.

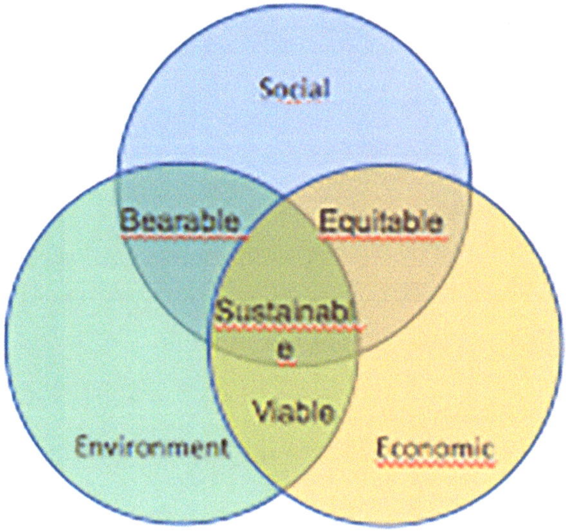

Fig. 2.1 Own representation drawing from Barille et al. (2018)

2.1 Viable System Model

With this interpretation, Barille et al. (2018) provide a more dynamic approach to sustainability, as they take an integrated dynamic look at the three dimensions and do not treat them as separate pillars. Thereby, they allow us to analyze the interplay and the process of how the desired intersection of the three dimensions can be achieved, constructed, and maximized.

Jaeggi et al. (2018) seek to provide frameworks that help understand better how sustainable finance can be disseminated both within and beyond the financial sector. There are two fundamentally different understandings of "sustainable": first, the long-standing notion of long-term stability, financial or political, including extra-financial risks from the environmental and social sphere and, second, the more modern use in the context of sustainable resource use and sustainable development (Jaeggi et al., 2018). The second definition is more pro-active and future oriented as its ambition is to shape the world through sustainable development, an expression stemming from development finance organizations (Jaeggi et al., 2018). It is important to differentiate between the two views, as they cover largely different issues, might aim for divergent objectives, and require different strategies.

The economic sphere is described as containing companies and the assets that they own, whereas society and natural environment are treated as externalities (Fig. 2.2).

Whereas the traditional definition of sustainability sees the environment as an externality (and consequently includes it in the sphere of market failure), the emerging definition is looking into the system dynamics and overlap between financial

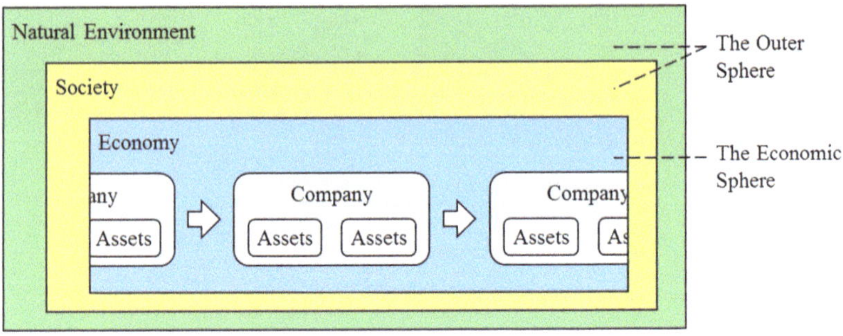

Fig. 2.2 Own representation based on Jaeggi et al. (2018)

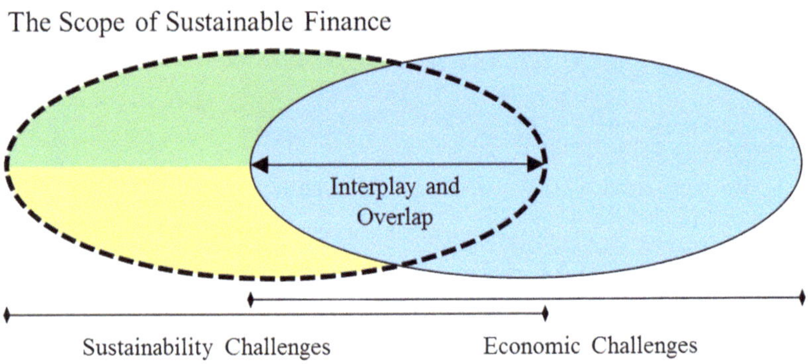

Fig. 2.3 Scope of sustainable finance

and eco-social issues and return. When discussing sustainability in the traditional model, the discussions primarily focus on the outer sphere, and on how the sustainability challenges that are observed in the outer sphere might affect or be affected by the economic sphere and the entities it contains (Jaeggi et al., 2018).

Figure 2.3 explains the emerging approach, which concentrates on the interplay between the dimensions and has been further evolved in the viable system approach.

In this approach, sustainability challenges and economic challenges overlap. It therefore matters which objectives are strategically relevant and whether they focus—in the words of Mc Nelly—on impact or risk mitigation essentially. The difference between the two views requires different strategies as they cover largely different issues and aim for divergent objectives.

Impact investing, in its most consistent form, follows an "impact first" approach as delineated in the EVPA Spectrum (2018) and operates within the Sustainable Development Goals. Thereby, it can be delineated from ESG, and negative screening approaches subsumed under "finance first." Probably, the most common denominator is the proactive pursuance of social and/or environmental goals in the investment strategy instead of a passive strategy such as negative screening. In the portfolio engineering industry, passive investment approaches cover 96% of all investments. In a passive investment approach, there is no space for active pursuance of eco-social goals as the primary business objective. In addition, passively managed funds try to minimize the tracking error against the standard they use as a blueprint. This limits the leeway for integrating companies that focus on impact. Therefore, impact investing can be found mainly in the actively managed alternative asset classes like private equity, venture capital, and seed (Dinnen et al., 2018). Furthermore, the investment evaluation in impact investing almost always incorporates an elaborative impact assessment as a basis for additional impact reporting like the Social Reporting Standard SRS.

The impact analysis is core to any impact investment. The proactive approach of understanding if and how impact is generated by a venture is a key differentiator from environmental, social, and governance (ESG) screening approaches used in the traditional sustainability models. As part of the due diligence process, the insights from the impact analysis are crucial to the ultimate investment decision. Furthermore, the analysis identifies social key performance indicators (KPIs) in order to achieve measurability and traceability of the impact created.

Whereas ESG screening stems from the sources of so-called sustainability rating agencies like Bloomberg, Sustainalytics, ISS Ethics, and RobecoSam, to name a few, that build the ESG scores on the Global Reporting Initiative framework, using self-reported company sustainability reports and top it up with management interactions, impact analysis stems from two different approaches: the theory of change and the logic model approach. According to Rauscher et al. (2012, p. 7), who build upon Weiss (1998), "[…] the logic model reflects what is to be achieved […], the theory of change focuses on the question how and under what preconditions specific effects are to be achieved […]." Moreover, they highlight the importance of empirical evidence upon which the assumptions for a systematic change through certain interventions are built. The main elements of an impact analysis, which is investment decision relevant, encompass two key aspects. First, there is a need for a comprehensive understanding and analysis of the eco-social challenge at hand. This involves reducing complexity, for instance, by using the Cynefin framework. The goal is to uncover and expose causal links inherent in the challenge, while interpreting the venture activities in the context of the SDGs and the societal challenges it aims to address. Second, after describing the societal issue and the causal links addressed by a social venture's business activities, a summary is provided. This includes an outlook on what is expected to be achieved, utilizing the IOOI-Logic-Model (IOOI = Input, Output, Outcome, Impact).

2.2 The Emerging Role of Taxonomies

Using the EU Action Plan for Sustainable Growth, the EU with its proactive approach of defining target industries and target technologies and its intention to redirect capital to sustainable growth, the EU decided for an impact-based approach rather than a risk-based approach using the emerging model of sustainability. The

EU has published Its EU Action Plan containing a green, a brown, and a social taxonomy, the EU Green Bond, two climate benchmarks, the Sustainable Finance Disclosure Regulation (SFDR), and the Social Economy Action Plan in 2019–2021. According to the EU definition, an asset is only sustainable when it fulfills one of the environmental or social objectives defined by the EU the green taxonomy or the social taxonomy enshrined in the directives (with a social taxonomy currently in progress). Importantly, the asset should not adversely affect other eco-social objectives, adhering to the principle of Do No Significant Harm (DNSH), and must adhere to good governance practices as per the OECD norms-based screening. This latter art is the risk assessment part; however, the main focus (key objectives plus DNSH) is on the key objectives to be achieved in the future and only then rounded up by an ESG screening (OECD norms based) and has its basis in creating an eco-social impact. As Fig. 2.4 depicts a three-step sustainability assessment mandated by the EU. The initial step involves ensuring that the asset meets the criteria for positive impact on the environment or social impact, as stipulated by the EU Green taxonomy and its classification criteria. In the second step, it has to be ensured that there is no harm provided by the activities of this asset, company, or project to other environmental or social goals, and finally there has to be a screening on fulfilling ESG criteria.

The EU has been working on its taxonomies for more than 5 years and got advice from a counsel of asset providers, asset managers, and civil society organizations and universities, the so-called High-Level Expert Groups. However, it is not just the EU that is developing its taxonomy. Taxonomies have come to be developed and are emerging as sustainable finance classification systems all around the world. Market-based efforts have reflected a sectoral and project-based methodology in line with the approach of the sustainable finance market. Many countries, so the political official sector, have developed taxonomies, in some cases based on identifying green and/or sustainable activities building on classification systems developed for statistical and economic analysis purposes. Official sector taxonomies may incorporate additional considerations beyond classification purposes, such as requirements to consider multiple sustainable objectives or to avoid conflicting aims (e.g., the EU "do no significant harm" requirement), as well as to take into account social criteria.

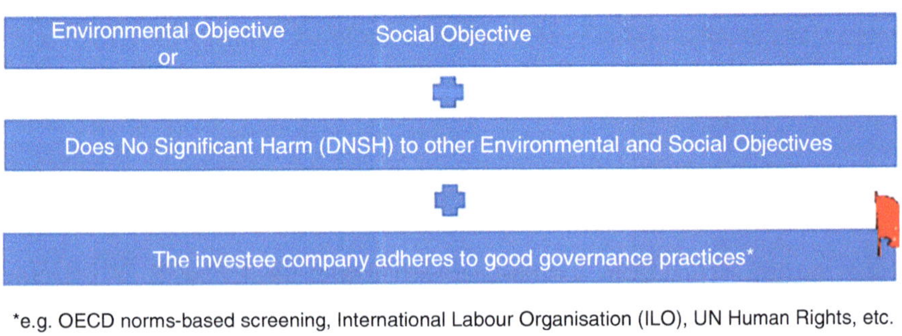

Fig. 2.4 Own representation: definition of sustainability

The International Capital Market Association (ICMA), as a main market player, has likewise developed requirements for successful taxonomies.

They propose some key success factors for taxonomies with the objective of promoting international consistency and market usability. Taxonomies should be:

- Targeted in their purpose and objectives.
- Additional in relation to existing international frameworks.
- Usable by the market for all intended purposes.
- Open and compatible with complementary approaches and initiatives.
- Transition-enabled incorporating trajectories and pathways.

Taxonomies define and explain how to develop them to provide clear guidance to the market on what activities, assets, and/or projects are eligible as green (and increasingly as transitional) and or social. The progress made on the EU Taxonomy further accelerated the discussion about taxonomies all over the world.

A "taxonomy" is a classification system identifying activities, assets, and/or project categories that deliver on key climate, green, social, or sustainable objectives with reference to identified thresholds and/or targets. Some introduce eligibility criteria that can be quantitative (e.g., absolute and relative performance thresholds) or qualitative and process based. Others only list and describe the projects, assets, and activities based on an assessment of their sustainability.

The author herewith provides an overview of these taxonomies with the aim to catalyze whether they might be helpful in streamlining impact investing.

2.3 The EU Action Plan and Taxonomy

The EU Action Plan Financing Sustainable Growth (hereafter Action Plan) is the 2018 Action Plan centered on developing the *EU Taxonomy*, putting in place disclosure regimes, in particular, the Sustainable Finance Disclosure Regulation (SFDR), and developing tools for the market to develop sustainable investment solutions and prevent greenwashing

It includes the introduction of two climate benchmarks, the SFDR accounting, and the consideration of sustainability in the supervisory regulations for banks and insurance companies, which includes the "Green Supporting Factor." At its heart is a unified classification system of economic activities, called a taxonomy, which aims to end the fragmentation, fraying and fragmentation of the concept of sustainable or green investments. The taxonomy defines a methodology, as well as quantitative and qualitative screening criteria. The Taxonomy has now developed such screening criteria for 67 activities in 7 key sectors. Taxonomy lists technical criteria and defines requirements for sustainable companies, investments, projects, and funds. It contains a clear description of which investments, companies, projects, and assets are to be considered sustainable in the sense of the EU sustainability definition. So far, the basic framework of the technical taxonomy is in place, as well as a well-developed Green Bond Standard, which contains the requirements for registration as an "EU Green Bond." Taxonomy, Green Bond Standard, and climate benchmarks and climate accounting is completed. An important part of the package is the governance structure. The agreement provides for an independent platform for sustainable finance (Platform for Sustainable Finance) to develop and maintain the full taxonomy. The EU has launched the International Platform for Sustainable Finance (IPSF) with third countries and plans to establish the stand-alone Sustainable Infrastructure Europe by the end of 2020. The taxonomy is flanked by the Disclosure Regulation, which applies from 2021 onward. According to the EU Commission's Green Infrastructure Strategy, ecosystems and biodiversity must be preserved. Ecosystems provide services for the benefit of society. The approach has evolved in international fora from biodiversity to preservation of ecosystem services. This will be implemented by the EU according to its Green Infrastructure Strategy through Sustainable Infrastructure Europe.

In order to meet the EU's climate and energy targets for 2030 and reach the objectives of the *European green deal*, the EU regards it vital to direct investments toward sustainable projects and activities.

With the taxonomy, climate benchmarks, and supporting mechanisms, the EU wants to create a single market for sustainable finance and a uniform classification system for environmentally sustainable economic activities. The EU defines six objectives in its green taxonomy: climate change mitigation, climate adaptation risk mitigation, sustainable use of water and marine resources, circular economy, pollution prevention, and healthy ecosystems (see Fig. 2.5).

The eligibility criteria required for the CCM (climate change management) objective under Annex 1 of the Climate Delegated Act are very diverse. Some low-carbon (e.g., renewable energy generation from solar and wind) and enabling activities (e.g., manufacturing of low-carbon technologies) are considered eligible and substantially contributing to the CCM by their very nature and without performance thresholds, but indeed subject to the Do No Significant Harm (DNSH) objective. For other activities, especially the transitional ones, the Substantial Contribution depends on the satisfaction of GHG performance thresholds and/or various process-based requirements (due diligence and verification).

Regarding the climate change activity (CCA) objective, an activity needs to provide an adaptation solution either for itself or enable the adaptation of people,

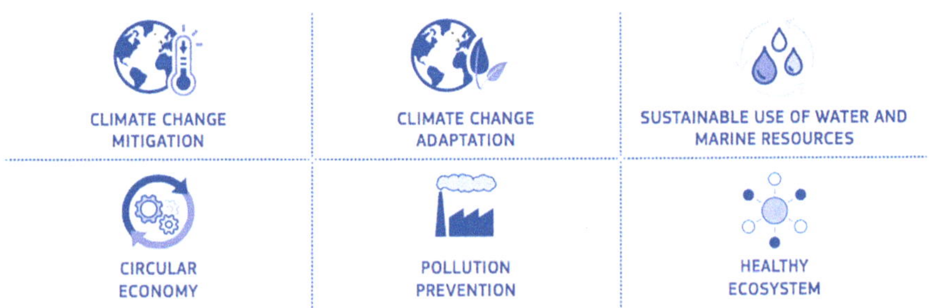

Fig. 2.5 EU Green Deal Targets as the basis for the green taxonomy

nature, or assets. This approach is comparable with the Climate Bonds Initiative Climate Resilience Principles, where the adaptation can be asset-focused or system-focused. The location and context-specific nature of climate adversities and avoiding adverse impacts on other activities, people, nature, and assets also need to be considered. The Substantial Contribution for CCA under Annex 2 of the Climate Delegated Act, on the other hand, is qualitative and quite standard across most activities. These require the implementation of physical and non-physical solutions that substantially reduce the material physical risks based on the identification of the latter from an indicative list of climate-related hazards (included as an appendix) and with an assessment that is proportionate to the scale and expected lifespan of the activity. Also, among other requirements, nature-based, green, or "blue" adaptation solutions should be favored to the extent possible, and consistency with overarching adaptation efforts and regular monitoring of solutions should be ensured. It is also important to note that Annex 2 on the CCA includes some specific adaptation-enabling activities (e.g., engineering, financial and insurance services, etc.) as well as activities that provide essential services and solutions like health, education, and arts.

The green taxonomy is complemented by the forthcoming social taxonomy (report on social taxonomy expected by the end of 2022), a uniform classification system for socially sustainable activities, and the Social Economy Action Plan. Together with the brown taxonomy and the SFDR reporting, they form the EU Taxonomy of sustainable activities.

On July 6, the European Commission published *its Strategy for Financing the Transition to a Sustainable Economy*, the successor of the EU's Sustainable Finance Action Plan, which launched in 2018. The strategy focuses on transforming the financial system and financing transition plans, building on the 2018 Action Plan, which centered on developing the *EU Taxonomy*, putting in place disclosure regimes, and developing tools for the market to develop sustainable investment solutions and prevent greenwashing.

The new strategy identifies four main areas for action for the financial system to fully support the transition to a sustainable economy:

1. *Financing the transition*: tools and policies to finance transition plans and reach climate and other environmental goals
2. *Inclusiveness*: access to sustainable finance for individuals and small and medium companies
3. *Financial sector resilience and contribution*: support the financial sector to contribute to meeting the EU's Green Deal targets, becoming resilient, and combat greenwashing
4. *Global ambition*: collaborating globally and promoting an ambitious global sustainable finance agenda

Together with the new strategy, the Commission also published the rules for how and when companies ("non-financial undertakings") and financial institutions ("financial undertakings") need to do their Taxonomy-related reporting, the Delegated Act for Taxonomy Regulation in particular articles, 7, 8, and 9. The EU

Taxonomy also promotes the life cycle assessment of activities wherever possible and requires compliance with a social dimension by undertakings with reference to international texts and conventions. The usability of the EU Taxonomy is a major topic of debate given that it is cross-referenced in many other regulations and policies, and the International Platform on Sustainable Finance (IPSF) has a dedicated group working on the subject. First, companies subject to the Non-Financial Reporting Directive (NFRD) in Europe, generally large public companies, will disclose to what extent their business activities align with the EU Taxonomy in terms of turnover, CapEx, and OpEx as of 2022 for the CCM and CCA objectives. Asset managers will also disclose the proportion of alignment of their sustainability-focused products. Second, the EU Taxonomy will become the main reference for regulated sustainable financial products in Europe, like the EU Green Bond.[1]

Through this new strategy and the unified classification system creating a standard and classification, it might be possible in the future to apply eco-social dimensions as listing criteria on an impact stock exchange or an impact segment on a traditional stock exchange. For instance, the IPSF has currently a dedicated workstream led by the EU and China to develop a "Common Ground Taxonomy." The outcome of this workstream is expected to be released in 2021.

2.4 Asian Taxonomies

In China, the official sector guidelines on eligible projects for green bonds can be traced back to 2015 when two sets of standards prevailed in the market. The Green Bond Endorsed Project Catalogue (2015 Edition) ("2015 Project Catalogue") published by the China Green Finance Committee, an organization supported by the People's Bank of China (PBOC), applied to all types of green bonds in China,[2] except green enterprise bonds which were regulated by the National Development and Reform Commission (NDRC)'s Guideline for Issuing Green Bonds referred to as "2015 Guideline"(China National Development and Reform Commission). In 2019, People's Bank of China and the national energy administrator published a catalogue of green industries, the Green Industry Guidance Catalogue 2019 Edition, i.e., the "2019 Industry Catalogue" (China National Development and Reform Commission). As the name indicates, the 2019 Industry Catalogue identifies a concise list of industries considered green in China. Following this achievement in harmonizing domestic definition of green, the three regulators—PBOC, NDRC, and CSRC—announced in April 2021 that they will work on creating standards for

[1] The EU explains the application of the classification criteria in its Green Bonds Usability Guide: https://ec.europa.eu/info/sites/default/files/business_economy_euro/banking_and_finance/documents/200309-sustainable-finance-teg-green-bond-standard-usability-guide_en.pdf

[2] See footnote 1.

climate finance and striving for international harmonization of green bond standards as the next steps.

Malaysia's central bank, Bank Negara Malaysia (BNM), issued a discussion paper on Climate Change and Principle-based Taxonomy in December 2019 and finalized it as a guidance document in April 2021, creating a classification system for assessing economic activities that promote transition toward a low-carbon and climate-resilient economy.

The taxonomy will apply to licensed banks, investment banks, Islamic banks, insurers and reinsurers, operators, and prescribed development financial institutions under the supervision of BNM. Malaysia's taxonomy is principally designed for financial institutions to classify the assets in their lending and investment portfolios, measure climate-related risks and exposure, and report to BNM for internal risk management and supervisory purposes. It provides a framework for Financial Institutions to classify their assets into categories related to climate transition (see flowchart below). The level of climate-friendliness ranges from category C1 ("climate supporting") to C2 and C3 ("transitioning") to C4 and C5 ("watchlist"). It begins with guiding questions to determine whether the facility contributes positively or negatively to climate change or climate change mitigation measures. If the answer is affirmative, a DNSH provision is applied, and, if applicable, an examination of the remedy measures the facility has taken to reduce the negative impacts is conducted.

By whichever lens you see it, the shift to theories of change and positive selection schemes is daunting.

References

Barille et al. (2018). Sustainability and the viable systems approach: Opportunities and issues for the governance of the territory. *Sustainability 10*(3). https://doi.org/10.3390/su10030790

Brandstetter, L., & Lehner, O. M. (2015). Opening the market for impact investments. The need for adapted portfolio tools. *Entrepreneurship Research Journal, 5*(2), pp. 87–107.

Carlowitz (1680). *Nachhaltigkeit in der Forstwirtschaft*. https://www.nachhaltigkeit.info/artikel/nachhaltigkeit_i_d_forstwirtschaft_1725.htm

Geobey, S., & Weber, O. (2013). Lessons in operationalizing social finance: The case of Vancouver City savings credit union. *Journal of Sustainable Finance and Investment, 3*(2), 124–137.

Geobey, S., Westley, F. R., & Weber, O. (2012). Enabling social innovation through developmental social finance. *Journal of Social Entrepreneurship, 3*(2), 151–165.

Glänzel, G. & Scheuerle, T. (2016). Social Impact Investing in Germany: Current Impediments from Investors' and Social Entrepreneurs' Perspectives. Voluntas: International Journal of Voluntary and Nonprofit Organizations, vol. 27, no. 4, 2016, pp. 1638–68. JSTOR. Retrieved from http://www.jstor.org/stable/43923250. Accessed 4 Dec. 2022.

Hebb, T. (2013). Impact investing and responsible investing: What does it mean? *Journal of Sustainable Finance and Investment, 3*(2), 71–74.

Hummels, H., & de Leede, M. (2014). The emergence of impact investments: The case of microfinance. In Socially responsible investment in the 21st century: Does it make a difference for society? (pp. 91–115). Bingley: Emerald Group Publishing Limited.

Jaeggi et al. (2018). Sustainable Finance. In K. Wendt (Ed.), *Positive Impact Investing*. Springer.

Mendell, M., & Barbosa, E. (2013). Impact investing: A preliminary analysis of emergent primary and secondary exchange platforms. *Journal of Sustainable Finance and Investment, 3*(2), 111–123.

Pretorius, L., & Giamporcaro, S. (2012). Sustainable and responsible investment (SRI) in South Africa: A limited adoption of environmental criteria. *Investment Analysts Journal, 75*, 1–19.

Shulman, J. M., & George, B. (2012). Growing jobs and getting returns: Impact investing through entrepreneurs. *Journal of Global Business Management, 8*(1), 123–132.

Suetin, A. (2011). Post-crisis developments in international financial markets. *International Journal of Law and Management, 53*(1), 51–61.

Viviers, S., & Firer, C. (2013). Responsible investing in South Africa – A retail perspective. *Journal of Economic and Financial Sciences, 6*(1), 217–242.

Viviers, S., Ratcliffe, T., & Hand, D. (2011). From philanthropy to impact investing: Shifting mindsets in South Africa. *Corporate Ownership and Control, 8*, 25–43.

Weber, O. (2013). Impact measurement in microfinance: Is the measurement of the social return on investment an innovation in microfinance? *Journal of Innovation Economics and Management, 11*, 149–171.

Weber, O. (2016). Impact investing. In O. M. Lehner (Ed.), Routledge handbook of social and sustainable finance. Routledge.

Weber, O., & Feltmate, B. (2016). Sustainable banking: Managing the social and environmental impact of financial institutions. Toronto: University of Toronto Press

World Economic Forum. (2013). From ideas to practice, pilots to strategy – Practical solutions and actionable insights on how to do impact investing. Retrieved from http://www3.weforum.org/docs/WEF_II_SolutionsInsights_ImpactInvesting_Report_2013.pdf.

Part I
Climate Change and Climate Risk

Chapter 3
Can the Financial Sector Protect the Climate? The Potential of Sustainable Finance

Kai Lessmann, Franziska Schütze, Angelika von Dulong, Daniel Engler, Gunnar Gutsche, Achim Hagen, Christian Klein, Andrew McConnell, Oliver Schenker, Marie Theres von Schickfus, and Boyan Yanovski

3.1 Introduction

Key instruments in the implementation of the ambitious climate protection goals set by both the European Union and Germany are aimed at making emission-intensive activities more expensive than climate-friendly economic activities. This includes carbon pricing (through emissions certificates in the EU ETS or Germany's carbon tax), price and purchase guarantees (e.g., Germany's Renewable Energy Act, EEG), and minimum requirements for products, production facilities, and processes. The carbon price, for instance, ensures that the environmental impact of fossil fuels such

K. Lessmann (✉)
Potsdam-Institut für Klimafolgenforschung, Potsdam, Germany
e-mail: lessmann@pik-potsdam.de

F. Schütze
Deutsches Institut für Wirtschaftsforschung (DIW Berlin), Berlin, Germany

A. von Dulong · A. Hagen
Humboldt-Universität zu Berlin, Berlin, Germany

D. Engler · G. Gutsche · C. Klein
Universität Kassel, Kassel, Germany

A. McConnell
Pollination Group, Sydney, NSW, Australia

O. Schenker
ZEW-Leibniz-Zentrum für Europäische Wirtschaftsforschung, Mannheim, Germany

M. T. von Schickfus
ifo Institut & LMU München, Munich, Germany

B. Yanovski
Magnolia Consulting GmbH, Hamburg, Germany

K. Wendt, B. Villhauer (eds.), *Sustainable Wealth Management*, Sustainable Finance,
https://doi.org/10.1007/978-3-031-55505-3_3

as coal, oil, or gas is also reflected in a lower return for investors in emission-intensive projects or businesses.

The profitability of such investments also depends on the costs of financing. If the cost of raising capital is different for emission-intensive and climate-compatible investments, financing conditions can reinforce the aims of climate policy. Sustainable finance measures that reduce the cost of raising capital for climate-friendly alternatives and make emission-intensive investments more costly in comparison thus serve to support the energy transition.

Emission pricing and the assessment of the climate compatibility of investments are thus two incentives that steer investors and capital markets to favor low-emission economic activities or move away from high-emission activities. We argue that the following prerequisites are needed to allow financial actors to make well-informed investment decisions:

Transparency: Investors need reliable information as to what extent their investments are affected by climate policy measures to factor the impact of climate policy into their investment decisions. Thus, investors need to create a demand for quantitative data, especially for more reliable forward-looking data. To be able to secure long-term returns on their investments, companies and financial institutions must gear their strategic planning toward the goal of climate neutrality and report on it accordingly.

Information requirements of different investor groups and their preferences: Unlike institutional investors, retail investors cannot be expected to acquire knowledge and expertise for interpreting and understanding information on sustainability. Thus, retail investors need to be provided with this information in order to sensitize them to the topic of sustainable investment. Institutional investors play an important role in making sustainability information available and comprehensible to retail investors.

Frictionless capital markets: It is essential to identify market failures that distort the pricing of capital. Distortions in capital allocation result in failure to achieve the targeted level of investment volume for climate-compatible projects. Investors and banks can support this by integrating climate-related risks and opportunities into the pricing of investment and into all financing decisions.

The role of sustainable finance is also influenced by the quality of climate policy measures. If measures such as carbon pricing, funding programs, and minimum standards are sufficiently ambitious to achieve climate policy objectives, the role of sustainable finance is to address the remaining distortions. The main priority is then to provide and use the required information to assess investments in terms of their climate risk.

If climate policy is not ambitious enough, sustainable finance can support the achievement of climate policy goals by (i) factoring expected policy measures in the medium term into financing conditions early on and (ii) adding additional incentives for climate-compatible investments, for instance, through the differentiation of capital buffers.

Fig. 3.1 Key links between climate policy and sustainable finance. (Source: PIK Potsdam)

This chapter provides an overview of the current knowledge regarding the relationship between climate policy and sustainable finance. The chapter focuses on the challenges of directing capital flows to climate-compatible investments. In the following three subsections, we will discuss instruments that can be used to create the necessary information to facilitate a proper assessment of sustainability risks and opportunities, to ensure that different classes of investors are addressed in a manner tailored to the specific classes, as well as removing any capital market disruptions (Fig. 3.1).

3.2 Reporting as an Instrument for Communication

For companies, sustainability reporting is an important communication and planning instrument for achieving climate neutrality. Investors need reliable information about the extent to which their investments are exposed to the effects of climate policy to factor climate-related risks and opportunities into their investment decisions.

3.2.1 How Corporate Reporting Helps Mitigate Climate Change

By reporting on how they contribute to climate change mitigation, companies are playing an important role in achieving the aims of the Paris Climate Agreement. This applies in both a negative (CO_2 emissions) and a positive sense (saved CO_2 emissions) and requires that companies make the relevant information publicly accessible, particularly to capital market actors.

Several thousand companies worldwide voluntarily disclose their CO_2 emissions through the CDP,[1] for instance. Moreover, in Europe, larger, capital market-oriented corporations with more than 500 employees are obliged to report on ESG topics (environmental, social, governance) in accordance with the *Non-financial Reporting Directive* (NFRD).[2] In a revision process of the NFRD, which culminated in the *Corporate Sustainability Reporting Directive* (CSRD), this reporting obligation was significantly expanded and now covers more than 50,000 companies rather than the 11,000 it had originally included. In the USA, the *Sustainability Accounting Standards Board* (SASB) has identified climate change and companies' contribution to climate change as financially relevant risks in almost all sectors of the economy. This proves that sustainability is a relevant topic for almost all companies.

Today, most institutional investors and asset managers are already using climate-relevant information. The biggest asset managers worldwide are urging firms to do more to confront the risks posed by climate change. That said, there are a variety of barriers that continue to prevent capital market players from using climate-related information more widely. One particular problem hindering the effective use of this information is that the majority of companies that have produced sustainability reports so far have done so on a voluntary basis. The lack of a mandatory framework or standard implies that not all firms provide climate-related information and also has a negative impact on the comparability and quality of the available data, as the information provided voluntarily is often not very precise or reliable. As a result, although investors are aware of the information, they do not always adequately take it into account in their investment decisions. This means that companies lack the incentive to undertake any genuine improvements in this area. One way of improving comparability would be to develop a uniform definition of sustainability. The EU is attempting to achieve this objective with its *EU Taxonomy* for sustainable activities, a document that is an integral part of the EU Sustainable Finance Action Plan. Another way is that investors demand more quantitative and comparable data from companies and hence create a strong demand for such information.

Only in a few exceptional cases, company-level reporting on CO_2 emissions is mandatory. Recent research shows, however, that introducing such mandatory reporting for individual production locations of a company, as stipulated in the *US Greenhouse Gas Reporting Program* (GHGRP), for example,[3] has positive effects on the companies' environmental performance. Companies participating in the GHGRP have improved their CO_2 efficiency (Bauckloh et al., 2023) and, at the same time, have reduced their emissions in the respective production locations (Tomar, 2019). That being said, this type of reporting obligation barely has any

[1] Formerly *Carbon Disclosure Project*, see information on the CDP website: https://www.cdp.net/en/info/about-us/what-we-do

[2] The requirements of the CSR Directive Implementation Act were incorporated into paragraphs 289b ff of the German Commercial Code (HGB) in 2017.

[3] *Greenhouse Gas Reporting Program*: https://www.epa.gov/ghgreporting

impact on a company's total emissions. The *UK Companies Act 2013*,[4] in contrast, has introduced mandatory climate reporting for British firms, which has resulted in overall emission reductions in the reporting companies (Downar et al., 2021).

However, the obligation to provide information alone will not necessarily mean that investors and other capital market operators will be any better at using this information effectively. Investors need to ensure that sustainability information is considered in daily investment and financing decisions. Although the European NFRD is binding, a study published by the *Alliance for Corporate Transparency* shows that the quality of the reports produced is alarmingly poor (Alliance for Corporate Transparency, 2019). This might be because the NFRD itself does not provide any specific details on certain aspects of content (such as, for example, the key metrics that must be reported), instead requiring only very generally that companies publish, for instance, "the most important non-financial performance indicators, which are of relevance for the business activity concerned", suggesting that firms should refer to national, EU, or international frameworks. In reality, in NFRD reporting, only around 22% of companies provide their sustainability indicators in a quantitative format that can be compared with financial indicators (Alliance for Corporate Transparency, 2019). These figures are especially important, however, as financial market operators need them to assess their products according to other EU regulations, such as the *Sustainable Finance Disclosure Regulation* (SFDR). Harmonization of requirements when it comes to reporting according to the different EU regulations is therefore needed. When it comes to climate change, up to 90% of companies only report on general voluntary commitments or objectives but neglect to mention any specific measures, targets, or progress.

Recent research identifies five problem areas when it comes to using climate-related information in the investment process (Atalay et al., 2021):

1. The investors themselves lack know-how. They recognize the importance of climate change as well as the risks it poses, but they do not have access to the requisite information and therefore cannot take proper account of climate change and the associated risks.
2. The parallel existence of primary data from businesses, on the one hand, and secondary data captured by rating agencies, on the other, makes it more difficult for investors to properly evaluate individual investment opportunities.
3. The "historical" information, which has so far been the typical form provided by companies, only provides insight into the company's past. It does not provide any kind of guidance regarding the company's strategic orientation and any adjustments to their business model.
4. Most incentive schemes for investors are based on a short-term time horizon. Bonuses or short-term dividend targets are, however, not compatible with the long-term impact of climate change.

---

[4] *The Companies Act 2006 (Strategic Report and Directors' Report) Regulations 2013*: https://www.legislation.gov.uk/uksi/2013/1970/pdfs/uksi_20131970_en.pdf

5. Both companies and investors are aware that climate data are not yet comprehensive enough. Investors complain about the poor quality of the data available and see this as an obstacle to using them effectively.

At the same time, companies do not believe the high costs and effort of reporting are justified because there is simply not enough demand for this type of sustainability data. A mandatory regulation could serve as an important impetus to overcome these teething problems and make reporting beneficial for both sides. Additionally, investors themselves can create the demand for this data.

3.2.2 Forward-looking Reporting to Break the Tragedy of the Horizon

Mark Carney (2015) described climate change as a "tragedy of the horizon". More specifically, he saw this tragedy as being rooted in the short-term horizon of the financial markets conflicting with the long-term horizon of climate change. Climate change is often regarded as a systemic risk, which can trigger rapid and strong reactions in the financial markets following a landmark event (Battiston et al., 2017). Individual financial institutions have only a limited interest in fully taking into account the risks that accompany the desired structural change, as they fear being at a competitive disadvantage to other operators. To avoid transferring future risks to the general public, all financial institutions must factor these into their decision-making at an early stage. To facilitate key players in both the financial and the real economy to effectively mitigate the impacts and risks of climate change, they must align their business strategies to take account of long-term climate scenarios. Future-oriented, forward-looking reporting has a key role to play here.

Financial market regulation is already increasingly calling for financial institutions to disclose the emissions from their loan and investment portfolios and to integrate climate-related risks in their analyses (see "ECB Guide on Climate-Related and Environmental Risks"[5] and the "BaFin Guidance Notice on Dealing with Sustainability Risks"[6]). Given that companies' current reporting provides insufficient information about their strategy on climate change, investors are forced to generate their own projections on the basis of historical emissions or climate

[5]The ECB Guide for Banks on Climate-Related and Environmental Risks was published in November 2020: https://www.bankingsupervision.europa.eu/ecb/pub/pdf/ssm.202011finalguideonclimate-relatedandenvironmentalrisks~58213f6564.en.pdf

[6]The Federal Financial Supervisory Authority (BaFin) Guidance Notice was published in December 2019: https://www.bafin.de/SharedDocs/Downloads/EN/Merkblatt/dl_mb_Nachhaltigkeitsrisiken_en.html

scenarios. The latter are provided by central banks, for instance.[7] This could result in companies that operate in emission-intensive sectors being excluded from financing in the future and thus also preventing important investments in the transition. Since this information is provided by external actors and is not company specific, investors are not aware of the type of transition a company has started to or is seeking to implement. In recent years, there have been a number of initiatives looking at the extent to which corporate strategies are compatible with the Paris targets for 2030 and 2050 and/or with a 1.5 °C or 2 °C climate path.[8] The comparability and coverage of these strategies remain a major challenge, however.

The international *Task Force on Climate-related Financial Disclosures* (TCFD)[9] is urging companies to provide forward-looking information, such as concrete emissions targets. The German government's *Sustainable Finance Committee* (SFB)[10] calls for mandatory forward-looking reporting in accordance with TCFD recommendations for large companies. To date, there has been very limited literature on how to apply the TCFD recommendations. Demaria and Rigot (2021) studied 40 companies and found that reporting was increasing but with major differences within individual sectors. Bingler et al. (2021) examined the TCFD reporting of 800 companies and concluded that the information they provided was far from robust.

A study shows how scenario analyses can help factor in the risks and opportunities associated with climate change and identify the necessary investments for a climate-neutral economy (Fujimori et al., 2021). To date, however, there is only very scant literature on how scenario analysis can help companies and investors and make a positive contribution to the regulatory framework (Kempa et al., 2021). It is important to bear in mind here that even in the very narrowly defined (disaggregated) sectors, the emissions of individual companies can sometimes vary considerably (Lyubich et al., 2018).

A standardized, forward-looking system of reporting and the use of a uniform climate neutrality scenario would allow both companies and financial institutions to identify the risks and opportunities of an ambitious climate policy at an early stage. This would help eliminate the tragedy of the horizon and better align investments with long-term climate targets.

---

[7] The *Network for Greening the Financial System* (NGFS) provides access to different climate scenarios via a data portal: https://www.ngfs.net/ngfs-scenarios-portal/

[8] The most recent *Transition Pathway Initiative* (TPI) report examines 401 companies worldwide: https://www.transitionpathwayinitiative.org/publications/82.pdf?type=Publication. In addition, companies such as right.based on science GmbH also provide temperature ratings of companies: https://www.right-basedonscience.de/

[9] In 2015, the TCFD was established by the *Financial Stability Board* and has since developed recommendations on climate-related financial disclosures: https://www.fsb-tcfd.org/

[10] The Sustainable Finance Committee was created in June 2019 and presented its final report in February 2021: https://sustainable-finance-beirat.de/

3.2.3 Recommendations

We would like to highlight four recommendations we believe are the most important:[11]

- Empirical studies show that, in contrast to voluntary standards, mandatory reporting has a considerable impact and companies begin to improve their emissions after introducing such a reporting system. As a matter of principle, therefore, mandatory requirements should set out what aspects of sustainability reporting should be considered by the various different sectors.
- Extending reporting obligations to include other companies would be an important step toward increasing the availability and comparability of data and also toward providing small and medium-sized enterprises (SMEs) with access to sustainable financing instruments. The reporting obligations should be adapted for SMEs bearing in mind the cost implications. For example, an SME might only be obliged to report on those issues that are seen as material for that company (and/or within that specific sector).
- The (raw) data generated from corporate climate reporting must be made easily accessible. Creating a centralized and publicly accessible database would make a substantial contribution to achieving this objective. This is also reflected in the CSRD proposal, which refers to the establishment of a *European Single Access Point* (ESAP).
- Forward-looking reporting will be particularly important in breaking the tragedy of the horizon. In their reports, companies should disclose how more ambitious climate targets, such as achieving climate neutrality significantly before 2045, would impact their business. In order to provide for comparability of results and incorporate long-term thinking, a standardized scenario should be specified.

By disclosing sustainability information, companies allow external actors to verify whether their investment and/or financing decisions are in line with their own climate objectives. Policy measures fostering and indeed stipulating this transparency thus improve the range and availability of such information. Additionally, investors can play a more active role by creating the demand for comparable sustainability information and by integrating it into everyday financing and investment decisions.

[11] These recommendations build on earlier recommendations from the Sustainable Finance Committee of the German government (SFB), to which some of the authors have contributed to.

3.3 Investor Demand for Sustainability Information

To provide effective information, it is important to know how it is used by investors: How does sustainability information affect investment decisions and what type of information do investors take into account? What are the obstacles to accessing the information and what measures would improve the flow of information most effectively?

It is useful to distinguish at least two groups of investors. Professional investors can be assumed to have adequate resources available to obtain the relevant information (financial resources) and to analyze and interpret that information with respect to their investment decision (time and human resources). This applies to institutional investors who manage large assets, in particular. The portfolios of retail investors are usually comparatively small portfolios; thus, the costly acquisition and analysis of sustainability information is harder to justify. For this group of investors, it is therefore especially important to provide easy-to-understand and trustworthy information, e.g., by providing a standardized sustainability label.

3.3.1 *Institutional Investors Are Taking the Lead*

Institutional investors such as investment funds, pension and retirement funds, and insurance companies are becoming increasingly interested in assessing their assets in terms of sustainability. Membership in organizations such as *Institutional Investors Group on Climate Change* (IIGCC) or the *UN-convened Net-Zero Asset Owner Alliance* indicates this increased awareness. Both of these alliances have substantial amounts of assets under management (49.6 trillion US dollars and 9.3 trillion dollars, respectively, with significant overlap among the two alliances). This corresponds to a share of 48% or 9% of globally managed assets (103.1 trillion US dollars in 2020 according to STATISTA 2021).

In a representative survey of institutional investors, "climate risk" was classified as a relevant risk by almost all those surveyed, even though it was only ranked fifth in terms of importance: the top two positions were taken by financing risk and operational risks (Krueger et al., 2020). The same study also examined how institutional investors factor climate risks into their investment decisions. Almost all investors surveyed reported having already undertaken some measures to manage climate risks. A key instrument (mentioned most frequently) was the analysis of CO_2 emissions from the companies in their portfolios (the *carbon footprint*). Moreover, the risk of a company losing its value due to climate policy (*stranded asset risk*) and implementing measures to reduce both carbon footprint and stranded asset risk play an important role.

This emphasizes the key role of disclosure (reporting) and transparency and is an indication of the demand for and use of sustainability information. Consequently, lack of disclosure is cited by the investors surveyed as one of the reasons why integrating climate risks into their decision-making processes remains a challenge. Moreover, it is difficult to include climate risks in company evaluations or to apply traditional risk management tools to climate risks in investment portfolios (lack of hedging instruments). Finally, investors pointed out that climate risks are (at least partially) systemic risks, which make them difficult to counter by means of portfolio management. Institutional investors therefore go beyond portfolio management by seeking to influence companies' strategic orientation (engagement), for example, by voting accordingly at shareholder meetings or entering direct dialog with managers (Krueger et al., 2020). The scholarly literature suggests that a high share of institutional investors leads to improved ESG ratings and lower CO_2 emissions (Dyck et al., 2019; Azar et al., 2020). That said, an impact of institutional investors on green innovation—which would be a more forward-looking characteristic—cannot yet be shown unambiguously (Cui et al., 2021; von Schickfus, 2021).

Interest in climate risks is, however, not exclusively motivated by financial benefits, such as reduced portfolio risk or a higher rate of return. In fact, the investors surveyed reported three other motivations to incorporate climate risks in their investment decisions more frequently than purely financial motivation: (a) the effect on their reputation, (b) moral/ethical considerations, and (c) fiduciary duty (Krueger et al., 2020).

3.3.2 *Risk of Retail Investors Being Overchallenged*

A substantial share of retail investors has a strong preference for sustainable investment strategies (Gutsche & Ziegler, 2019; Bauer et al., 2021). Relevant studies on the basis of survey data (Nilsson, 2008; Gutsche et al., 2019), investment experiments (Gutsche et al., 2020; Lagerkvist et al., 2020), customer data (Døskeland & Pedersen, 2016), or a combination of these (Riedl & Smeets, 2017) show that these preferences are driven by both financial and non-financial motives. Beyond expected returns or risk perceptions, there is thus an important role in investment decisions for social preferences (Riedl & Smeets, 2017), political ideology, attitude toward the environment (Gutsche & Ziegler, 2019), trust (Nilsson, 2008; Gutsche & Zwergel, 2020), factors relating to social context (Gutsche et al., 2019), the warm glow feeling (Heeb et al., 2021), and financial literacy (Rossi et al., 2019; Gutsche et al., 2020). It is likely that these findings translate to the specific case of climate-friendly investments, but empirically this remains an open question as studies on this topic are still rare (some exceptions are Bassen et al., 2019; Heeb et al., 2021). The preliminary findings of survey experiments carried out in five European countries do suggest, however, that the aforementioned factors are also important for making climate-related investment decisions.[12] That said, the relevance of these

[12] The survey was conducted as part of the BMBF joint project IF "Investment Funds for Low-Carbon Infrastructure."

motives seems to vary across different countries. The extent to which retail investors take specific climate risks into account in their investment decisions remains unclear, however. However, the preliminary findings clearly show that the level of knowledge among retail investors about sustainable investments and, for example, investment strategies that exclude fossil fuel investments is very limited. Nevertheless, retail investors in all five European countries considered slightly prefer narrower climate-related investment strategies over broader ESG strategies.

Even less is known about whether additional sustainability-related or climate-related information discourages retail investors from investing. Only a few studies directly address potential (information) barriers that dissuade retail investors from deciding on sustainable investments (Gutsche & Zwergel, 2020) or consider possible ways of dismantling these barriers, e.g., by analyzing preferences for different labels for sustainable financial products (Bassen et al., 2019). Importantly, the availability and incorporation of additional (potentially contradictory) sustainability-related or climate-related information makes differentiating and deciding between different financial products more complex for individuals. For individuals, acquiring and processing information is associated with high psychological costs (Hirshleifer, 2015). Hence, retail investors could instead apply to simplify heuristics and deliberately choose not to know, despite the information they need to make such decisions being readily available, a phenomenon referred to as "homo ignorans" or information avoidance (Hertwig & Engel, 2016). Overall, the availability of climate-related information could, in fact, make it more difficult for retail investors to reconcile their financial objectives (e.g., secure retirement provision) with available investment products, which is no simple task for retail investors to begin with (Campbell, 2006). These aspects have, however, not been studied in detail, and whether the provision of additional climate-related information or regulatory measures (e.g., EU Taxonomy) would foster the further development and acceptance of sustainable or climate-related investments among retail investors or whether it would, in fact, lead to unintended problems remains yet unclear.

3.3.3 Recommendations

The analysis of retail investors shows substantial potential for sustainable investments, which, in addition to mobilizing further capital, could also have a positive impact on investors and their acceptance of climate policy. That said, suitable investment products, as well as information about them, are still scarce.

We would like to highlight several measures that address these shortcomings:[13]

- The development of a straightforward and easy-to-understand classification system to make the sustainability of an investment transparent for retail investors,

[13] These recommendations build on earlier recommendations from the Sustainable Finance Committee of the German government (SFB), to which some of the authors have contributed to.

for instance, on a scale of one to five. For retail investors, it is especially important that the classification is implemented by a trusted organization. But since nowadays significantly less than half of all retail investors go to their bank in person to make their investments and/or get information from the bank before investing, the information for classification must be designed to be easily understandable without further explanations. Moreover, it should be ensured that the classification system does not conflict with other sustainability classifications (e.g., the EU Taxonomy) but that they are integrated.

- Similarly, it is important to improve information and explanations about the sustainability of investment products given by customer advisers. However, these advisers can only reach retail investors who still seek personal contact. This could be countered by an educational information campaign, which aims to systematically improve sustainable financial and sustainability literacy across society.

3.4 Mobilizing Investment for the Energy Transition

Two important cornerstones for mobilizing the required capital have now been discussed: improved transparency (Sect. 3.2) and encouraging various groups of investors to invest sustainably (Sect. 3.3). This section discusses how the design of climate policy instruments and the resulting financial conditions affect climate-friendly investment.

3.4.1 Carbon Pricing Signals Do Not Always Reach Investors

Over the last 20 years, carbon pricing has been a key component of climate policy. By reducing the rate of return on projects that use fossil inputs, carbon pricing can steer investors away from fossil fuels and toward sustainable investments. To achieve this, a sufficiently high price of carbon is necessary, and financial markets need to accurately incorporate current and future carbon prices in their evaluations of companies and investments according to their dependence on CO_2 emissions. However, the effectiveness of carbon pricing can, in practice, be impaired by political uncertainty, lack of international coordination on climate policy, and other market failures. Hence, additional supportive measures might be needed to establish a strong signal to investors (Koch et al., 2016; Fuss et al., 2018).

For instance, a carbon price is less effective if exemptions are granted to important industries to ensure their international competitiveness. A key example is the raw materials industry, whose products are tradable internationally. In the event of a domestic carbon price, there is a risk that production will be relocated to other countries that do not have a carbon price. To prevent the relocation of CO_2 emissions away from the EU, some of these sectors received emission certificates free of charge as part of the EU ETS. However, this distorts the price signal and weakens investment incentives. Moreover, carbon pricing may not suffice as an incentive to avoid emissions by utilizing and recycling materials more efficiently (Neuhoff & Ritz, 2019; Chiappinelli et al., 2021). Levying a climate tax on producing and importing raw materials might provide the necessary additional incentives (Pollitt et al., 2020). In addition, *Contracts for Difference* (CfD) can be used as instruments for mitigating risk from price volatility, particularly for investments in industry decarbonization (*Carbon Contracts for Difference*, CCfD). In CCfDs, the government and the companies agree on a (target) carbon price. If the agreed price is higher than the current carbon price, the government subsidizes the project proportional to the difference, which can significantly reduce investment risks (Neuhoff et al., 2018; Richstein & Neuhoff, 2019).

That said, even a strong and credible carbon price might not influence investors if the financial markets fail to reflect this price signal. Analyses conducted by asset managers (Schulten et al., 2021) and the International Monetary Fund (IMF, 2020) show that investments that are highly exposed to climate and transition risks are generally traded at a lower price than the risk of them being affected by climate change or climate policy would lead us to expect. This mispricing could be caused by a combination of several factors. For example, since capital markets are incomplete (e.g., there are only limited markets for futures trading of emissions certificates), there are also limits to pricing climate risks. Moreover, investors often rely on outdated methods of risk assessment. Furthermore, short-term decision horizons, financing limitations, and uncertainty and inflation constraints are widespread (Campiglio, 2016; Hafner et al., 2020; Lessmann & Kalkuhl, 2024; Condon, 2021). To be able to design policy measures that solve these market failures and thus promote the necessary green investments, a solid understanding of the interaction between carbon price and other climate policy instruments is key (Mercure et al., 2019; Steffen & Schmidt, 2021).

3.4.2 Financing Costs Have a Greater Impact on Green Sectors

Developing the infrastructures and technologies needed for a climate-friendly economy will require substantial investment. Essentially, there are three ways of financing this investment: bank loans, market bonds, and equity capital. In each case, the financing costs must be raised by the project or firm to be financed. In the case of loans and bonds, this is the interest paid; in the case of equity capital, it is the return on investment expected by the investor. These financing costs differ markedly depending on the country, the sector and the project. For larger climate-friendly investment projects, in particular, financing costs can be an obstacle, even with a reasonable carbon price. The possible reasons for this include information asymmetries, the volume of collateral to be secured, political uncertainty, immature markets and technologies, and investors' expectations.

Financing costs include the operational costs to financial institutions of assessing creditworthiness and managing associated risks. In principle, financial intermediation facilitates the flow of money from investors to investment projects (e.g., through banks or investment funds) and significantly reduces the risks and associated information costs. It is nevertheless important to take the remaining costs of intermediation into account. Financing costs are also increased from the imperfect competition among intermediaries and their pursuit of profit (Lessmann & Kalkuhl, 2024). In terms of climate policy objectives, high intermediation costs and thus higher capital costs may counteract any reduction in emissions (Hirth & Steckel, 2016).

This may mean considerably overshooting a climate target that would otherwise have been met. Lessmann and Kalkuhl (2024) estimate that a 10% point increase in capital costs would result in an additional temperature rise of 0.3 °C relative to a 2 °C policy. To compensate for these effects, the price of carbon would have to be increased by 50%. In addition, their study shows that the problem of imperfect competition in the financial sector can be overcome by subsidizing loans or capital income.

Likewise, financing costs are affected by the amount and quality of the collateral a debtor can provide. In general, the more assets the borrower can make available to the creditors as collateral and the lower the credit risk for the creditor, the lower the interest rates on the loan and thus the cost of capital. Collateral is, therefore, an important indicator of a company's ability to raise funds. This is relevant for climate policy when the collateral of climate-friendly companies has a lower value. Access to credit is thus reduced for new and small companies since lenders are not familiar with neither the companies nor their business models. A carbon price alone is not enough to resolve these information asymmetries between borrowers and lenders (Haas & Kempa, 2023). The problem is exacerbated by the fact that new companies in the emerging low-carbon industry have a relatively low net worth as they start out and therefore little collateral. Creditors demand higher interest rates from these firms, driving up capital costs and delaying climate-friendly investments or projects. Investment subsidies or government guarantees for green loans are policy options that might help overcome the issue of collateral holding back the climate transition. However, banks themselves need to adequately price the future climate-related risks to high-carbon companies, as the collateral can become a stranded asset if climate policy measures are being extended.

Differences in the cost of capital or financing costs for climate-friendly versus carbon-intensive investments thus have substantial implications on the implementation of climate policy. Empirically, the differences between green and brown financing costs are still substantial (Steffen, 2020); however, risk perceptions are changing as information becomes more widely available. For example, recent growth in green knowledge has led to an increase in green investments (Cojoianu et al., 2020). Using global microdata on individual loans, Kempa et al. (2021) found that renewable energy firms face relatively higher borrowing costs when technologies and markets are young and immature. However, this cost disadvantage seems to disappear as low-carbon technologies and markets mature and their business risks are better understood (Egli et al., 2018).

3.4.3 Policy Signals Could Improve Financing Conditions

Recent findings suggest that policymakers could encourage this reduction in financing costs in two ways (Kempa et al., 2021). First, ambitious yet credible environmental targets would strengthen lenders' confidence in the long-term viability of green business models and technologies. Environmental policy measures not only have a positive effect on expected corporate profits but can also have an important risk-mitigating effect. This suggests that consistent environmental policies, regardless of their direct impact on profitability, send a valuable signal to lenders. Second, there is a strong statistical link between the level of development of a country's financial institutions and how high the costs of borrowing are for renewable energy companies. Improving the capability of financial institutions to assess and manage the risks of investments in new and immature low-carbon technologies could therefore be a key contributor to attracting investment.

The study further shows that previously higher capital costs for renewable energies are now in fact lower than those for fossil energies in some countries. However, the financing of renewable energy remains a challenge because of its much greater capital intensity (Hirth & Steckel, 2016; Best, 2017), which implies that the return on investment for renewable energy is lower than for fossil energies. This has important implications for the capital structure of the energy sector, as the comparatively low profits rule out financing the accumulation of capital through retained earnings and do little to mobilize further capital for renewable energy. In contrast, more reliance on external financing has implications for financial stability and is likely to become more costly as its role in the transition increases. Yanovski and Lessmann (2021) examined the effects of these relationships on climate policy. Since carbon pricing improves the profitability of renewable energy only relative to its fossil alternatives but not in absolute terms, its impact on capital mobilization and accumulation is limited by the necessity to borrow large amounts of funds. Technology subsidies, government guarantees for green loans, or capital injections can support capital accumulation in renewable energy more directly to a speedy transition, but their benefit must be weighed against potential rebound effects and political lock-in into support schemes.

Empirical evidence shows that investors in the stock market are aware of the risks of climate policy and price investments accordingly, particularly when they receive new information on regulatory measures or risks (Ramiah et al., 2013; Griffin et al., 2015). Specifically, the election of Donald Trump and the signing of the Paris Agreement were cited as events with a potential impact on climate policy expectations (Ramelli et al., 2018; Monasterolo & de Angelis, 2020; Seltzer et al., 2021). A study by Bolton and Kacperzyk (2021) found that investors are demanding higher returns from carbon-intensive industries to compensate for the additional risks associated with climate policy events. These findings are supported by Donadelli et al. (2020), who found that the value of companies using fossil fuels has fallen significantly due to increased climate awareness. In the corporate bond market, Seltzer et al. (2021) showed that the Paris Agreement has increased debt costs for companies with poor environmental performance, especially in countries with more ambitious climate policies. These findings suggest that investors expect climate policy developments to impact their profits and are therefore increasingly factoring them into asset valuations. This appears to be the case, irrespective of whether these climate policy developments are vague or specific.

Sen and von Schickfus (2020) provide further evidence for the significance of climate policy measures for investors. However, they find that policies need to be very carefully designed to affect investor expectations as intended. Using stock market data from the companies in question, the authors trace the impact of a climate policy proposal in Germany in three stages: first, carbon taxes that imply a loss in profits, second, financial compensations for decommissioned power plants, and third, legal challenges to the compensation plan. Interestingly, investors only responded negatively when the German compensation policy was challenged by EU State Aid Regulation, i.e., by an independent supranational body. The findings indicate that investors in the stock market are aware of and expect political processes, including potential compensations for companies experiencing losses due to climate policy. They therefore continue to rate companies highly even if companies face high exposure to climate policy risks because they ultimately expect these risks to be absorbed by the state. If a large number of investors expose themselves to climate policy in this way, this creates a path dependency that may necessitate even greater compensation in the future in order to avoid major shocks on the financial markets.

Hagen et al. (2019) extend this argument to governmental bailouts. They study the possibilities of financial instability and economic dislocation caused by a bursting "carbon bubble," which might trigger government intervention. Both a strong, credible climate policy and legislation that excludes this kind of a bailout are potential policy solutions that could reinforce investments being reallocated away from carbon-intensive assets. However, the devil is in the details: Carattini and Sen (2019) examined stock exchange pricing for carbon-intensive assets after the public voted on two different carbon tax proposals in Washington state. The difference between the tax proposals was how the tax revenue was to be used: either revenue neutral (by reducing other taxes) or earmarked to promote environmental and social goals. The reduced financial burden on polluting companies under the revenue-neutral regime was anticipated by stock markets, resulting in a much weaker impact for this proposal.

3.4.4 Recommendations

The frictions and barriers resulting from the costs of raising capital discussed in this section hamper the financing of green projects, thereby counteracting the aims of climate policy to redirect funds from carbon-intensive to climate-compatible investments. Measures to reduce these financing costs can be implemented at various levels.

For example, climate-friendly projects can be made more attractive through state funding of (some of) the financing costs, for instance, by means of preferential loans or interest rate subsidies (Steckel & Jakob, 2018). An indirect way of influencing the costs of financing might be to regulate the capital buffers that financial institutions are required to set up. Capital buffer requirements are used by financial regulators to ensure that financial institutions remain solvent in the event of a loan default. Different capital buffers for climate-friendly versus fossil fuel investments would be reflected in the financing costs. Differentiating between capital buffers might be justified if climate policy is not adequately priced due to failures of the financial markets, with the result that financial institutions are unknowingly exposed to a transition risk. This would justify the tightening of capital requirements for institutions with a high proportion of emission-intensive exposures.

Other measures can reduce financing costs by minimizing the risk that is reflected in financing costs ("de-risking"), for example, state guarantees for climate-compatible loans. Here, the state guarantees that the amount of the loan (or part of it) is to be reimbursed in the event of the debtor becoming insolvent. This would reduce both the premium required for collateral and the risk premium for green investments, thus lowering the cost of raising capital. Credit guarantees that apply specifically to climate-friendly investments make these investments more attractive than fossil fuel alternatives (Steckel & Jakob, 2018). Loan guarantee programs implemented in the past have been shown to reduce default rates and increase the revenues and assets of companies in question (Brault & Signore, 2020), e.g., when used to support the economy during the COVID-19 crisis, leading to higher borrowing and lower financing rates for participating companies (ECB, 2020). Supranational and national development banks will play a crucial role in financing and de-risking green projects because of their scope and size. As part of the European Green Deal, a large share of the one trillion euros in investments to be made by 2030 will be managed by the European Investment Bank. At the national level, 58% of the commitments made by Germany's state-owned investment and development bank KfW in 2018 related to climate and environmental protection. Furthermore, the empirical analysis mentioned above suggests that, in the case of renewable energies, financing costs are particularly low when capital is brokered via modern, well-developed financial systems and when governments pursue ambitious and credible environmental policies. Investors and banks can support this by integrating climate-related risks and opportunities into all financing decisions in a forward-looking manner, even if climate policy measures are currently insufficient. Collateral can become a stranded asset if climate policy measures are being extended.

3.5 Conclusion

To achieve the goal of climate neutrality—at the EU level through the European Green Deal and in Germany by tightening up regulations in the Climate Protection Act—will require rapid decarbonization of the economy. Sustainable finance, i.e., specifically considering or promoting long-term investments in sustainable economic activities and projects, will play an important role in this transformation. Sustainable finance can make a substantial contribution if sustainability reporting can create transparency about the progress companies make in achieving this transformation, if investors utilize this type of information in their investment decisions, and if targeted government measures help to overcome investment barriers.

Reporting on sustainability thus becomes an essential prerequisite. It is a vital tool for financial market players to align their portfolios with climate targets. In recent years, there has been a clear trend toward more reporting. However, the (mostly voluntary) standards currently in use lack uniformity and comparability, and mandatory standards such as the Non-financial Reporting Directive remain too vague regarding the required content. The new Corporate Sustainability Reporting Directive (CSRD) and the respective European Sustainability Reporting Standards (ESRS) are expected to improve the reporting quality. Studies on the UK Companies Act 2013 and the US Greenhouse Gas Reporting Program show that mandatory reporting with well-defined and harmonized specifications (on the current status of emissions) actually leads to a reduction in emissions for the companies concerned. In recent years, there has also been a considerable increase in the disclosure of information relating to future events, such as climate neutrality targets and emission pathways. But here, too, standards and hence comparability are lacking. Financial institutions are required to disclose the emissions from their loan and investment portfolios and to integrate climate-related risks into their analyses. So far, financial institutions often work with information on the sectoral level. This could make it more difficult for companies in emission-intensive sectors to access financing in future thus preventing important investments being made in their transformation. Therefore, investors need to create the demand for more comparable quantitative data at company level, especially for more reliable forward-looking data.

Investors are already using sustainability information to assess the climate risk of their investment and portfolio decisions. These risks are already considered in the investment decisions of most institutional investors, who pay particular attention to key data such as carbon footprints or stranded asset risk. Institutional investors are reported to be more motivated by the potential impact on their reputations and moral considerations than any financial advantages gained. Retail investors are also known to have both financial and non-financial motives for choosing sustainable investment strategies. It is not yet fully clear to what extent more and better information about sustainability would turn these preferences into investment decisions since the increasing complexity that comes with all the additional information makes investment decisions difficult, especially for retail investors. Hence, institutional investors play an important role in making sustainability information available and comprehensible to retail investors.

The effectiveness of traditional climate policy, e.g., carbon pricing, on the flow of investments into renewable energies may be hindered by various barriers. These include incomplete capital markets, reliance on outdated methods of risk assessment, short-term decision-making horizons, financing constraints, and uncertainty. Two aspects, in particular, were examined in more detail in this chapter: First, carbon pricing via the markets (e.g., through the EU ETS system) leads to a volatile

CO_2 price. This is a problem for risk-averse investors. Second, capital costs have a greater impact on renewable energy than on fossil fuels. While green technologies are often more capital intensive, companies involved in this sector tend to be smaller and less established and, therefore, have less collateral at their disposal. Such barriers could be overcome through tailored measures to encourage investments in renewable energy sources combined with credible political signals about future climate policies. Investors and banks can support this by integrating climate-related risks and opportunities into all financing decisions in a forward-looking manner, even if climate policy measures are currently insufficient.

Acknowledgments This chapter is based on the report "Der Finanzsektor als Klimaschützer? Das Potenzial von Sustainable Finance" (Lessmann et al., 2022). We have benefited from feedback by Kai Dombrowski, Gernot Klepper, Matthias Kopp, Karsten Neuhoff, Menglu Neupert-Zuang, and Frank Schiemann. We thank Bastian Tittor for carefully editing our text. Funding by the German Federal Ministry of Education and Research (BMBF) as part of the QTFINANZ project [grant number 01LA1909A and 01LA1909B] is gratefully acknowledged.

References

Alliance for Corporate Transparency. (2019). *Research report – An analysis of the sustainability reports of 1000 companies pursuant to the EU Non-Financial Reporting Directive*. https://www.allianceforcorporate- transparency.org/assets/2019_Research_Report%20_ Alliance_for_Corporate_Transparency.pdf

Atalay, N., Hahn, R., & Foese, D. (2021). *Trend report*. https://www.climate-reporting.hhu.de/fileadmin/redaktion/Fakultaeten/Wirtschaftswissenschaftliche_Fakultaet/Sustainability/2021_Trendreport.pdf

Azar, J., Duro, M., Kadach, I., & Ormazabal, G. (2020). The big three and corporate carbon emissions around the world. *SSRN Electronic Journal*. https://doi.org/10.2139/ssrn.3553258

Bassen, A., Gödker, K., Lüdeke-Freund, F., & Oll, J. (2019). Climate information in retail investors' decision-making: Evidence from a choice experiment. *Organization & Environment, 32*(1), 62–82. https://doi.org/10.1177/1086026618771669

Battiston, S., Mandel, A., Monasterolo, I., Schütze, F., & Visentin, G. (2017). A climate stress test of the financial system. *Nature Climate Change, 7*(4), 283–288. https://doi.org/10.1038/nclimate3255

Bauckloh, T., Klein, C., Pioch, T., & Schiemann, F. (2023). Under pressure? The link between mandatory climate reporting and firms' carbon performance. *Organization & Environment, 36*(1), 126–149.

Bauer, R., Ruof, T., & Smeets, P. (2021). Get real! Individuals prefer more sustainable investments. *The Review of Financial Studies, 34*(8), 3976–4043. https://doi.org/10.1093/rfs/hhab037

Best, R. (2017). Switching towards coal or renewable energy? The effects of financial capital on energy transitions. *Energy Economics, 63*, 75–83. https://doi.org/10.1016/j.eneco.2017.01.019

Bingler, J. A., Kraus, M., & Leippold, M. (2021). Cheap talk and cherry-picking: What ClimateBert has to say on corporate climate risk disclosures. *SSRN Electronic Journal*. https://papers.ssrn.com/sol3/papers.cfm?abstract_id=3796152

Bolton, P., & Kacperczyk, M. (2021). Do investors care about carbon risk? *Journal of Financial Economics, 142*(2), 517–549. https://doi.org/10.1016/j.jfineco.2021.05.008

Brault, J., & Signore, S. (2020). *Credit guarantees in the COVID-19 crisis – Relevance and economic impact*. SUERF policy note 176. https://www.suerf.org/policy-notes/14869/www.eif.org

Campbell, J. Y. (2006). Household finance. *The Journal of Finance, 61*(4), 1553–1604. https://doi.org/10.1111/j.1540-6261.2006.00883.x

Campiglio, E. (2016). Beyond carbon pricing: The role of banking and monetary policy in financing the transition to a low-carbon economy. *Ecological Economics, 121*, 220–230. https://doi.org/10.1016/j.ecolecon.2015.03.020

Carattini, S., & Sen, S. (2019). *Carbon taxes and stranded assets: Evidence from Washington State*. CESifo working paper no. 7785. https://papers.ssrn.com/sol3/papers.cfm?abstract_id=3434841

Carney, M. (2015). *Breaking the tragedy of the horizon – Climate change and financial stability*. Lloyd's of London. https://www.bankofengland.co.uk/-/media/boe/files/speech/2015/breaking-the-tragedy-of-the-horizon-climate-change-and-financial-stability.pdf

Chiappinelli, O., Gerres, T., Neuhoff, K., Lettow, F., de Coninck, H., Felsmann, B., Joltreau, E., et al. (2021). A green Covid-19 recovery of the EU basic materials sector: Identifying potentials, barriers and policy solutions. *Climate Policy, 21*. https://doi.org/10.1080/14693062.2021.1922340

Cojoianu, T. F., Clark, G. L., Hoepner, A. G. F., Veneri, P., & Wójcik, D. (2020). Entrepreneurs for a low carbon world: How environmental knowledge and policy shape the creation and financing of green start-ups. *Research Policy, 49*(6), 103988. https://doi.org/10.1016/j.respol.2020.103988

Condon, M. (2021). Market Myopia's climate bubble. *SSRN Electronic Journal*. https://doi.org/10.2139/ssrn.3782675

Cui, J., Qi, S., Xu, J., & Zeng, S. (2021). Institutional investors and corporate environmental innovation. *SSRN Electronic Journal*. https://doi.org/10.2139/ssrn.3706637

Demaria, S., & Rigot, S. (2021). Corporate environmental reporting: Are French firms compliant with the Task Force on Climate Financial Disclosures' recommendations? *Business Strategy and the Environment, 30*(1), 721–738. https://doi.org/10.1002/bse.2651

Donadelli, M., Grüning, P., & Hitzemann, S. (2020). *Understanding macro and asset price dynamics during the climate transition*. Bank of Lithuania discussion paper no. 18/2019. https://doi.org/10.2139/ssrn.3801562

Døskeland, T., & Pedersen, L. J. T. (2016). Investing with brain or heart? A field experiment on responsible investment. *Management Science, 62*(6), 1632–1644. https://doi.org/10.1287/mnsc.2015.2208

Downar, B., Ernstberger, J., Reichelstein, S., Schwenen, S., & Zaklan, A. (2021). The impact of carbon disclosure mandates on emissions and financial operating performance. *Review of Accounting Studies, 26*(3), 1137–1175. https://doi.org/10.1007/s11142-021-09611-x

Dyck, A., Lins, K. V., Roth, L., & Wagner, H. F. (2019). Do institutional investors drive corporate social responsibility? International evidence. *Journal of Financial Economics, 131*(3), 693–714. https://doi.org/10.1016/j.jfineco.2018.08.013

ECB. (2020). Economic and monetary developments. *Economic Bulletin*. Issue 6/2020. https://www.ecb.europa.eu/pub/pdf/ecbu/eb202006.en.pdf

Egli, F., Steffen, B., & Schmidt, T. S. (2018). A dynamic analysis of financing conditions for renewable energy technologies. *Nature Energy, 3*(12), 1084–1092. https://doi.org/10.1038/s41560-018-0277-y

Fujimori, S., Krey, V., van Vuuren, D., Oshiro, K., Sugiyama, M., Chunark, P., Limmeechokchai, B., et al. (2021). A framework for national scenarios with varying emission reductions. *Nature Climate Change, 11*(6), 472–480. https://doi.org/10.1038/s41558-021-01048-z

Fuss, S., Flachsland, C., Koch, N., Kornek, U., Knopf, B., & Edenhofer, O. (2018). A framework for assessing the performance of cap-and-trade systems: Insights from the European Union Emissions Trading System. *Review of Environmental Economics and Policy, 12*(2), 220–241. https://doi.org/10.1093/reep/rey010

Griffin, P. A., Jaffe, A. M., Lont, D. H., & Dominguez- Faus, R. (2015). Science and the stock market: Investors' recognition of unburnable carbon. *Energy Economics, 52*, 1–12. https://doi.org/10.1016/j.eneco.2015.08.028

Gutsche, G., & Ziegler, A. (2019). Which private investors are willing to pay for sustainable investments? Empirical evidence from stated choice experiments. *Journal of Banking & Finance, 102*, 193–214. https://doi.org/10.1016/j.jbankfin.2019.03.007

Gutsche, G., & Zwergel, B. (2020). Investment barriers and Labeling schemes for socially responsible invest-ments. *Schmalenbach Business Review, 72*(2), 111–157. https://doi.org/10.1007/s41464-020-00085-z

Gutsche, G., Köbrich León, A., & Ziegler, A. (2019). On the relevance of contextual factors for socially responsible investments: An econometric analysis. *Oxford Economic Papers, 71*, 756–776. https://doi.org/10.1093/oep/gpy051

Gutsche, G., Wetzel, H., & Ziegler, A. (2020). *Determinants of individual sustainable investment behavior: A framed field experiment.* MAGKS joint discussion paper series in economics no. 33-2020. http://hdl.handle.net/10419/234838

Haas, C. & Kempa, K. (2023). Low-Carbon Investment and Credit Rationing. *Environmental and Resource Economics, 86*, 109–145. https://doi.org/10.1007/s10640-023-00789-z

Hafner, S., Jones, A., Anger-Kraavi, A., & Pohl, J. (2020). Closing the green finance gap – A systems perspective. *Environmental Innovation and Societal Transitions, 34*, 26–60. https://doi.org/10.1016/j.eist.2019.11.007

Hagen, A., Jaakkola, N., & Vogt, A. (2019). The interplay between expectations and climate policy: Compensation for stranded assets. In *IAEE energy forum* (pp. 29–31) https://www.iaee.org/en/publications/newsletterdl.aspx?id=844

Heeb, F., Kölbel, J. F., Paetzold, F., & Zeisberger, S. (2021). *Do investors care about impact?* SSRN working paper. https://ssrn.com/abstract=3765659

Hertwig, R., & Engel, C. (2016). Homo ignorans: Deliberately choosing not to know. *Perspectives on Psychological Science, 11*(3), 359–372. https://doi.org/10.1177/1745691616635594

Hirshleifer, D. (2015). Behavioral finance. *Annual Review of Financial Economics, 7*(1), 133–159. https://doi.org/10.1146/annurev-financial-092214-043752

Hirth, L., & Steckel, J. C. (2016). The role of capital costs in decarbonizing the electricity sector. *Environ-mental Research Letters, 11*(11), 114010. https://doi.org/10.1088/1748-9326/11/11/114010

IMF. (2020). *Global financial stability report: Markets in the time of COVID-19*. Physical risk and equity prices- Online Boxes 5.1–5.3. International Monetary Fund. https://www.imf.org/en/Publications/GFSR/Issues/2020/04/14/global-financial-stability-report-april-2020#Chapter5

Kempa, K., Moslener, U., & Schenker, O. (2021). The cost of debt of renewable and non-renewable energy firms. *Nature Energy, 6*, 135–142. https://doi.org/10.1038/s41560-020-00745-x

Koch, N., Grosjean, G., Fuss, S., & Edenhofer, O. (2016). Politics matters: Regulatory events as catalysts for price formation under cap-and-trade. *Journal of Environmental Economics and Management, 78*, 121–139. https://doi.org/10.1016/j.jeem.2016.03.004

Krueger, P., Sautner, Z., & Starks, L. T. (2020). The importance of climate risks for institutional investors. *The Review of Financial Studies, 33*(3), 1067–1111. https://doi.org/10.1093/rfs/hhz137

Lagerkvist, C. J., Edenbrandt, A. K., Tibbelin, I., & Wahlstedt, Y. (2020). Preferences for sustainable and responsible equity funds – A choice experiment with Swedish private investors. *Journal of Behavioral and Experimental Finance, 28*, 100406. https://doi.org/10.1016/j.jbef.2020.100406

Lessmann, K., & Kalkuhl, M. (2024). Climate finance intermediation: Interest spread effects in a climate policy model. *Journal of the Association of Environmental and Resource Economists, 11*, 213–251.

Lessmann, K., Schütze, F. et al. (2022). Der Finanzsektor als Klimaschützer? Das Potenzial von Sustainable Finance. Hintergrundpapier zum 11. Forum Klimaökonomie.

Lyubich, E., Shapiro, J., & Walker, R. (2018). Regulating mismeasured pollution: Implications of firm hetero-geneity for environmental policy. *AEA Papers and Proceedings, 108*, 136–142. https://doi.org/10.1257/pandp.20181089

Mercure, J. F., Knobloch, F., Pollitt, H., Paroussos, L., Scrieciu, S. S., & Lewney, R. (2019). Modelling innovation and the macroeconomics of low-carbon transitions: Theory, perspectives and practical use. *Climate Policy, 19*(8), 1019–1037. https://doi.org/10.1080/14693062.2019.1617665

Monasterolo, I., & de Angelis, L. (2020). Blind to carbon risk? An analysis of stock market reaction to the Paris agreement. *Ecological Economics, 170*, 106571. https://doi.org/10.1016/j.ecolecon.2019.106571

Neuhoff, K., & Ritz, R. A. (2019). *Carbon cost pass-through in industrial sectors*. EPRG working paper 1935. https://www.jstor.org/stable/resrep30282

Neuhoff, K., May, N., & Richstein, J. C. (2018). *Renewable energy policy in the age of falling technology costs*. DIW Berlin discussion paper no. 1746. https://ssrn.com/abstract=3227734

Nilsson, J. (2008). Investment with a conscience: Examining the impact of pro-social attitudes and perceived financial performance on socially responsible investment behavior. *Journal of Business Ethics, 83*(2), 307–325. https://doi.org/10.1007/s10551-007-9621-z

Pollitt, H., Neuhoff, K., & Lin, X. (2020). The impact of implementing a consumption charge on carbon-intensive materials in Europe. *Climate Policy, 20*(sup1), S74–S89. https://doi.org/10.1080/14693062.2019.1605969

Ramelli, S., Wagner, A. F., Zeckhauser, R. J., & Ziegler, A. (2018). *Investor rewards to climate responsibility: Evidence from the 2016 climate policy shock*. NBER working paper 25310. https://doi.org/10.3386/w25310

Ramiah, V., Martin, B., & Moosa, I. (2013). How does the stock market react to the announcement of green policies? *Journal of Banking & Finance, 37*(5), 1747–1758. https://doi.org/10.1016/j.jbankfin.2013.01.012

Richstein, J. C., & Neuhoff, K. (2019). *CO2-Differenzverträge für innovative Klimalösungen in der Industrie*. DIW aktuell no. 23. https://www.diw.de/documents/publikationen/73/diw_01.c.679524.de/diw_aktuell_23.pdf

Riedl, A., & Smeets, P. (2017). Why do investors hold socially responsible mutual funds? *The Journal of Finance, 72*(6), 2505–2550. https://doi.org/10.1111/jofi.12547

Rossi, M., Sansone, D., van Soest, A., & Torricelli, C. (2019). Household preferences for socially responsible investments. *Journal of Banking & Finance, 105*, 107–120. https://doi.org/10.1016/j.jbankfin.2019.05.018

Schulten, A., Bertolotti, A., Hayes, P., & Madaan, A. (2021). Getting physical: Scenario analysis for assessing climate-related risks. In J. W. Dash (Ed.), *World Scientific Encyclopedia of climate change* (pp. 211–217). Black Rock Financial Institute. https://doi.org/10.1142/9789811213960_0027

Seltzer, L., Starks, L. T., & Zhu, Q. (2021). *Climate regulatory risks and corporate bonds*. Nanyang Business School research paper no. 20-05. https://doi.org/10.2139/ssrn.3563271

Sen, S., & von Schickfus, M.-T. (2020). Climate policy, stranded assets, and investors' expectations. *Journal of Environmental Economics and Management, 100*, 102277. https://doi.org/10.1016/j.jeem.2019.102277

Steckel, J. C., & Jakob, M. (2018). The role of financing cost and de-risking strategies for clean energy investment. *International Economics, 155*, 19–28. https://doi.org/10.1016/j.inteco.2018.02.003

Steffen, B. (2020). Estimating the cost of capital for renewable energy projects. *Energy Economics, 88*, 104783. https://doi.org/10.1016/j.eneco.2020.104783

Steffen, B., & Schmidt, T. S. (2021). Strengthen finance in sustainability transitions research. *Environmental Innovation and Societal Transitions, 41*, 77–80. https://doi.org/10.1016/j.eist.2021.10.018

Tomar, S. (2019). *CSR disclosure and benchmarking-learning: Emissions responses to mandatory green-house gas disclosure*. Working paper. https://doi.org/10.2139/ssrn.3448904

von Schickfus, M.-T. (2021). *Institutional investors, climate policy risk, and directed innovation*. Ifo working paper no. 356. http://hdl.handle.net/10419/235243

Yanovski, B., & Lessmann, K. (2021). *Financing the fossil fuel phase-out*. https://ssrn.com/abstract=3903026

Chapter 4
Environmental Information Disclosure Quality, Institutional Pressure, and the Cost of Debt: Evidence from China's Heavy Polluters

Shidi Dong, Lei Xu, Ron McIver, and Ning Huang

4.1 Introduction

China's remarkable economic success over recent decades has imposed tangible pressure on its natural resources, environment, and social harmony. Achieving the path to sustainable growth is now at the top of the largest emerging economy's national agenda. For example, the 19th CPC National Congress in 2017 promulgated adherence to harmonious coexistence between man and nature and promoted China's development of an ecological civilization. However, severe environmental accidents, such as the Defeng Chemical Co. water pollution (China Environment News, 2021) and Hailan Co. chemical dumping (People's Daily, 2021) incidents, suggest that China still has a long way to go if it is to achieve its environmental targets.

Recognition of the environmental pollution imposed by its heavy polluters and the long-term presence of protection of the natural environment as part of its national agenda imply that corporate environmental responsibility has become a focus for Chinese society. Environmental reporting, an essential part of the corporate environmental responsibility system, has become a key information channel for stakeholders, including creditors, in evaluating firm environmental risk and in their investing and financing decision-making (Thompson & Cowton, 2004; Wu & Xu, 2022). Under the influence of green credit and green value chain practices, the relationship between environmental protection and corporate debt financing has become closer in recent years, reflecting an increased sensitivity of financial institutions to

S. Dong · N. Huang
School of Management, Shenyang University of Technology, Shenyang, China
e-mail: dongshidi@sut.edu.cn; huangning@sut.edu.cn

L. Xu (✉) · R. McIver
UniSA Business, University of South Australia, Adelaide, SA, Australia
e-mail: lei.xu@unisa.edu.au; ronald.mciver@unisa.edu.au

K. Wendt, B. Villhauer (eds.), *Sustainable Wealth Management*, Sustainable Finance,
https://doi.org/10.1007/978-3-031-55505-3_4

corporate environmental issues (Wang et al., 2019). Nevertheless, due to the potential negative externalities associated with reporting environmental problems, a reliance on public pressure to change firms' willingness to voluntarily disclose environmental information has proved insufficient, suggesting a need to use economic incentives and institutional arrangements as complementary forces (Cormier et al., 2005).

During the last decade, the Chinese government has issued successive policies and regulations promoting environmental protection and environmental reporting to actively encourage firms to disclose environmental information. For example, the 2015 revision of the Environmental Protection Law[1] enhanced punishment levels and increased obligations for polluters to truthfully disclose environmental information. The 2020 "Guiding Opinions on Building a Modern Environmental Governance System"[2] and 2021 "Reform Plan of Environmental Information Disclosure System"[3] support the construction of an environmental disclosure system by firms in China. However, at present, convergence in the level of firm environmental information disclosures and their quality remains low. Additionally, creditors' difficulties in using this information to assist in making effective economic decisions have seen creditors gradually shift their attention from the "quantity" to "quality" of environmental disclosures. Therefore, whether environmental disclosure quality can affect corporate debt financing and how and whether institutional pressures can effectively promote improvement in the quality of firm environmental information disclosures and play a moderating role in debt financing remain worthy of study.

Using the institutional context of China, this study has selected "A-Share" firms in heavy-polluting industries listed on the Shanghai and Shenzhen stock exchanges from 2012 to 2019 as the research sample. Based on institutional and information asymmetry theories, it investigates the impact of the quality of environmental information disclosure and the moderating effects of institutional pressures on the cost of corporate debt. In addition, it also examines the influences of different types of environmental information on the cost of debt in heavy-polluting industries. The study makes several potential contributions to the prior literature. First, in the Chinese setting, empirical evidence is provided for a longer study period on the relationship between the quality of environmental disclosures and the cost of debt. Second, institutional pressures are examined in terms of coercive, normative, and mimetic pressures to determine their influence on the cost of debt. Finally, this study originally examines the influences of different types of environmental disclosures, namely "soft disclosures" and "hard disclosures," on corporate cost of debts in the Chinese context.

The rest of the paper is organized as follows. Section 4.2 presents a review of the literature on the economic consequences of environmental disclosures, including the cost of debt. The literature on the influences of institutional pressures on environmental disclosures is also reviewed. Section 4.3 discusses the theoretical

[1] https://www.mee.gov.cn/ywgz/fgbz/fl/201404/t20140425_271040.shtml

[2] http://www.gov.cn/zhengce/2020-03/03/content_5486380.htm

[3] https://www.mee.gov.cn/xxgk2018/xxgk/xxgk03/202105/t20210525_834444.html

framework and hypotheses. Section 4.4 describes the research methods, and Sect. 4.5 presents the results and discussion. Section 4.6 provides the conclusion, research limitations, and directions for future research.

4.2 Literature Review

4.2.1 Economic Consequences of Environmental Disclosures

The economic consequences of environmental reporting have been studied for decades, with prior studies examining its consequences for such areas as corporate financial performance, firm value, and cost of equity. Generally, past studies have confirmed that firms' active disclosures of environmental information can improve their financial performance, increase firm value, and decrease the cost of equity. In the context of a set of African countries, Khlif et al. (2015) identify that there is a significant positive relationship between the level of environmental disclosure and financial performance. Qui et al. (2016), taking firms within the FTSE350 index as their research sample, find that the disclosure of environmental information can positively influence firm ROA. In the context of Malaysia, Nor et al. (2016) conclude that active environmental disclosures can attract investors and therefore play a significant positive role in improving corporate profit margins and financial performance.

In the Chinese context, Li et al. (2017) select a 2012–2014 sample of energy-intensive Chinese listed firms with a total of 1179 firm-year observations. Based on institutional theory, they confirm that the more active a company's environmental responsibility performance, the better its financial performance. Using "A-share" listed firms on Shanghai and Shenzhen stock exchanges, Wang et al. (2020) also conclude that corporate environmental information disclosure has a direct and significant positive impact on firm financial performance. However, analyst coverage and liquidity can moderate this relationship. Wang et al. (2021) reveal that the positive effect of environmental disclosure on high-polluting industries' firms' financial performance is consistently significant in China, although a structural break exists in 2015 due to the implementation of the new Environmental Protection Law.

Firms with good environmental information disclosure usually have higher internal information transparency and stronger market competitiveness and therefore can attract more investors and improved corporate value (Yang et al., 2020). When studying the impact of environmental disclosures on firm value, Gozali et al. (2002) conclude that with investors' increasing demand for environmental information, environmental disclosures can enhance corporate value. Focusing on the quality of environmental information, Marshall et al. (2009) identify that firm value can increase corresponding with the quality of environmental information disclosed, with Iatridis (2013) showing that good quality environmental information can change investors' opinions and decisions to a certain extent. Using firms in Taiwan as the research sample and applying the Olson valuation model, Wang (2016) provides differing results, identifying that total environmental disclosures and mandatory government information have a negative relationship with firm valuation. However, voluntary environmental information has a positive influence on firm valuations, although the relationship is not established for non-environmentally sensitive industries.

Corporate financing includes equity and debt financing, with many prior studies concluding that environmental disclosures can ease investors' risk estimation and thus reduce the cost of equity capital. Villiers and Staden (2011) identify that environmental information can not only improve corporate environmental reputation but also alleviate information asymmetry, and thus reduce firm cost of capital. In the Chinese setting, Yao and Liang (2019) identify that environmental disclosure has a moderating effect that determines how analyst following influences the cost of equity. Moreover, this interaction is more significant in heavy-pollution industries and following the issue of the new environmental policy in China. Selecting the key A-shares in the Shanghai stock market over 2016–2018, Su and Zhang (2019) analyze the relationship between the quality of environmental information and cost of equity financing. Their study concludes that the quality of environmental information disclosure and the cost of equity capital have a negative association and the degree of impact differs across industries.

4.2.2 Environmental Disclosures and Corporate Cost of Debts

Among the economic consequences examined above, such as financial performance, firm value, and cost of equity, the influence of environmental disclosures on corporate debt financing has attracted considerable attention from researchers, particularly in the Chinese setting. Sengupta's (1998) study provides some early evidence on corporate disclosure quality and the cost of debt. It argues that creditors and investors will consider the quality of information disclosure of a company when assessing default risk. Timely, detailed, and high-quality information disclosure can reduce their estimate of the default risk of a publicly traded firm, thus reducing its debt financing cost. Through a questionnaire survey and semi-structured interviews, Thompson and Cowton (2004) provide insights into the environmental information used or desired by banks when making lending decisions that take account of environmental issues. The study finds evidence of interest by banks in firm environmental information, including some desire for features of the available information to be improved beyond current practice. Specifically, bankers are interested in measuring aspects such as externalities and periodic net social contribution. Sharfman and Fernando (2008) examine the impact of environmental risk management on the cost of capital of US firms and find that improved environmental risk management can reduce debt financing costs and increase tax benefits. In the Chinese setting, Zhao et al. (2014) examine the impact of environmental information disclosure on the cost of debt in the utilities industry. The results identify that although environmental information disclosure in the utilities industry is increasing, the overall level is still low and, in this industry, full disclosure of environmental information can effectively reduce the cost of debt. Fonseka et al. (2019) identify that energy firms with a higher level of environmental information disclosure and use of cleaner products can obtain loans from banks at a lower cost.

In addition to the above, several studies have provided evidence for heavy-polluting industries in China. Using fixed effects panel data, Luo et al. (2019) conclude that, in heavy-polluting industries, there is a negative relationship between the quality of environmental information and the cost of debt financing. High-quality environmental information disclosures can not only promote corporate reputation but also alleviate information asymmetry with creditors and, therefore, reduce the cost of financing.

However, in the Chinese setting, research on the relationship between environmental disclosures and debt financing starts later than in Western countries and whether institutional pressures can moderate the relationship has not been investigated extensively, given that institutional pressures tend to have a significant impact on Chinese firms' reporting behavior (Dong et al., 2014; Li et al., 2020, 2022).

4.2.3 Environmental Disclosures and Institutional Pressures

Following institutional theory's introduction and application in the field of social and environmental accounting research (e.g., DiMaggio & Powell, 1983), empirical studies have focused on investigating the relationship between institutional pressures and environmental information disclosure. Buhr and Freedman (2001) find that the promulgation of government policies related to environmental protection can affect the attitude to and performance of firms in disclosing environmental information. Kothari et al. (2009) finds that enhanced government supervision plays a positive role in promoting corporate environmental information disclosure, which can assist firms in improving internal information transparency and obtaining more financial support. Trevlopoulos et al. (2021) collect the environmental information disclosed in 100 sustainable development reports released by 25 firms in the metal products sector over 4 years and find that the degree of compliance with environmental regulations of firms positively affects their environmental performance. This implies effective environmental regulations can force firms to actively disclose environmental information and strengthen environmental management. In the Chinese context, several studies have investigated the influence of government policies on corporate information disclosures. Wei and Peng (2014) identify that the implementation of environmental information disclosure policies and the intensity of environmental regulations can have a significant impact on firms' environmental information disclosure in the non-ferrous metals industry. Using a quasi-natural experiment, Tu et al. (2019) conclude that government regulation plays a crucial role in environmental improvement while public participation plays a complementary role. Moreover, the results show that the positive impact of public participation on pollution reduction is found mainly in the eastern region of China. Overall, the previous studies confirm that pressure from the government can play a significant role in environmental regulation and environmental reporting. This is by formulating policies and regulations to restrict firms' environmental behavior, issuing incentives and subsidies triggering firms to attach importance to environmental protection, and improving the content and quality of environmental disclosures (Chen et al., 2022; Xu et al., 2021). However, a few studies have found that institutional pressures, such as the green financing policies issued by the Chinese government, have an insignificant role in environmental information disclosure. Wang et al. (2019) find no significant positive correlation between environmental information disclosure and green finance policy, as measured by the implementation of green credit policy. The results imply that the implementation effect of green credit policy is still weak and has failed to become a decision-making tool for banks to conduct environmental risk assessment in the Chinese context.

Previous studies generally confirm that external institutional pressure can affect firms' environmental disclosures. However, there are still some limitations to and gaps in previous studies. First, studies on the economic consequences of environmental disclosure focus mainly on firm value, financial performance, and the cost of equity capital. Few studies focus on debt financing. Second, the moderating effects of institutional pressures on the relationship between environmental reporting and firm cost of debt have not been studied fully, particularly in the Chinese setting. Previously, studies focused on the direct impact of institutional pressures on environmental disclosures rather than the moderating effect. Third, when examining institutional pressures, most previous studies examine these as a whole and focus on the role of government regulations and policies. Therefore, to fill gaps in the prior literature, this study aims to examine the influence of environmental disclosures on the cost of corporate debt in heavy-polluting industries and, further, to examine the moderating effect of institutional pressures on this relationship in the Chinese context.[4] Specifically, this study selects "A-Share" listed firms in heavy-polluting industries over 2012–2019. In this study, the institutional pressures examined are coercive, normative, and mimetic pressures. Environmental disclosures are investigated based on their information content, including "soft" and "hard" disclosures. Therefore, this study contributes to the extant literature by comprehensively providing empirical evidence on the influences of the quality of environmental disclosures on the cost of corporate debt, examining the influences of different types of institutional pressures on environmental disclosures in the Chinese context, and examining the influences of different types of environmental disclosures on the cost of debt.

[4]The classification of "heavy-polluting industries" is based on the Guidance on Industry Classification of Listed Companies issued by the China Securities Regulatory Commission (CSRC) in 2012 and includes Coal and Consumable Fuel, Metals and Mining, Textile and Leather, Papermaking, Oil and Gas, Pharmaceutical, Chemical, and Thermal power industries.

4.3 Theoretical Analyses and Hypothesis Development

4.3.1 The Impact of Environmental Information Disclosure on Cost of Debts

Previous studies have provided consistent results on the relationship between environmental disclosures and the firm's cost of debt both in the context of Western countries and China. As environmental accidents occur frequently, lenders and creditors have gradually realized that a company's environmental risks have become a key factor affecting their future financial status and solvency, which, in turn, determines whether creditors can recover their investment in time (Sengupta, 1998). In the Chinese setting, due to the concealment of environmental problems, and the imperfect disclosure mechanisms on corporate environmental performance in China, the information asymmetry between creditors and firms is significant (Luo et al., 2019). To safeguard loan performance, creditors tend to add restrictive terms into contracts with firms, including a higher cost of interest. Therefore, to reduce their financing constraints, firms are likely to undertake initiatives, such as environmental disclosure, to meet creditors' demands for environmental information. Based on information asymmetry theory, firms' active disclosure of environmental information can improve the transparency of internal information so that creditors can better understand the environmental performance of firms and evaluate their environmental default risk, effectively alleviating the "adverse selection" problem. On the other hand, firms with higher-quality environmental information disclosures are often viewed by creditors as having better environmental performance and correspondingly less environmental risks (Hamrouni et al., 2019; Wu & Xu, 2022). Therefore, these firms gain creditors' trust and so obtain a cost advantage in debt financing, lowering the cost of debt. Based on the above analysis, hypothesis 1 is developed as follows:

H1: In the Chinese setting, the higher the quality of environmental information disclosure by heavy-polluting firms, the lower their cost of debt

4.3.2 The Impact of Institutional Pressures on the Quality of Environmental Disclosures

4.3.2.1 Coercive Pressure

Coercive pressure refers to formal and informal pressure from government agencies, mainly through the policies and regulations issued by the government and relevant regulatory agencies (DiMaggio & Powell, 1983). In the Chinese setting, the new "Environmental Protection Law" has been implemented since 2015, while the "Reform Plan for the Legal Disclosure System of Environmental Information" was issued in 2021. The introduction of environmental protection policies and the continued improvement in China's environmental information disclosure requirements have, undoubtedly, brought significant mandatory pressure on firms regarding their environmental performance. From an institutional theory perspective, an organization's adoption of specific management practices, such as environmental disclosures, is a way of responding to coercive pressures in its institutional setting. Ding et al. (2019) conclude that environmental administrative regulations have improved firms' environmental information disclosure levels in China in the manufacturing industry. Jiang et al. (2020) confirm that implementation of the amendment to the new Environmental Protection Law significantly improved firms' disclosures of environmental information.[5] Thus, based on institutional theory, firms in heavy-polluting industries will be more likely to disclose high-quality environmental information under this institutional setting to meet legal requirements. Based on the above analysis, hypothesis 2a is developed as follows:

H2a: Coercive pressure has a positive impact on the quality of environmental information disclosures by heavy polluters in China.

4.3.2.2 Normative Pressure

Under institutional theory, normative pressures can be used to motivate firms to implement legitimate organizational activities that are perceived to be conforming (Zhu & Zhang, 2015; Dong et al., 2020, 2023). DiMaggio and Powell (1983) define normative isomorphism as the collective struggle of members of an occupation to "define the conditions and methods of their work," to control the production of producers, and to "establish a cognitive base and legitimization for their occupational autonomy." Normative pressure comes mostly from NGOs, such as industry associations and other organizations and social groups that use moral standards and social norms to guide firms' environmental performance, including evidencing this through environmental disclosures. In the Chinese setting, these NGOs, acting as the main form of social supervisor, could play an effective supervisory role by increasing public awareness of environmental protection, and thus motivating firms to fulfill their environmental responsibilities through public reporting (Dong et al., 2014). Therefore, based on the above analysis, hypotheses 2b is developed as follows:

H2b: Normative pressure has a positive impact on the quality of environmental information disclosures by heavy polluters in China.

[5] Written in Chinese.

4.3.2.3 Mimetic Pressure

According to DiMaggio and Powell (1983), mimetic isomorphism refers to a standard response to the uncertainty embedded in organizational operations and involves organizations seeking to emulate or improve upon the institutional practices of other organizations, often for reasons of competitive advantage in terms of legitimacy (Deegan, 2006). Mimetic pressures come mainly from competitive behavior within the same industry and exist in the form of homogeneity and imitation (Meyer & Rowan, 1977). In complex and uncertain environments, firms are more inclined to observe and imitate the behaviors of their industry peers to gain legitimacy to operate in the industry (Cormier et al., 2005). According to previous studies, imitation is a phenomenon that exists in the environmental information disclosure of listed firms in China (Liu et al., 2010; Dong et al., 2014; Dong & Xu, 2016; Yao & Li, 2018). When considering their long-term survival, firms are more likely to disclose environmental information to shape their "green image" and achieve competitive advantages in the sector. Consequently, when some firms in the industry actively disclose environmental information, especially after benefiting from it, other peers in the same industry are more likely to follow and disclose environmental information in terms of quantity and quality. Based on the above analysis, hypothesis 2c is developed as follows:

H2c: Mimetic pressure has a positive impact on the quality of environmental information disclosures by heavy polluters in China.

4.3.3 *The Moderating Effects of Institutional Pressures on the Relationship Between Environmental Information Disclosure Quality and Corporate Cost of Debt*

The moderating effects of institutional pressures on the relationship between environmental reporting and firm cost of debt have not been studied fully in previous studies, particularly in the Chinese setting. Catalyzed by multiple external institutional pressures, creditors have an incentive to re-examine the transactional risks associated with firms' environmental problems and will endeavor to increase capital security by reducing loan scale, shortening loan term, and increasing the cost of debt. To alleviate creditors' concerns, firms under financing pressures have strong incentives to improve the quality of environmental information disclosure and reduce their financing constraints. Based on institutional theory, the presence of institutional pressures may influence the quality of environmental information disclosures, reducing the information asymmetry faced by creditors. In turn, environmental disclosure may influence firms' cost of debt. Based on the above discussion, the following hypotheses are developed (Table 4.1):

Table 4.1 Summary of hypotheses

	Hypothesis	Direction
H1	In the Chinese setting, the higher the quality of environmental information disclosure by heavy-polluting firms, the lower their cost of debt.	*Negative*
H2a	Coercive pressure has a positive impact on the quality of environmental information disclosures by heavy polluters in China.	*Positive*
H2b	Normative pressure has a positive impact on the quality of environmental information disclosures by heavy polluters in China.	*Positive*
H2c	Mimetic pressure has a positive impact on the quality of environmental information disclosures by heavy polluters in China.	*Positive*
H3a	Coercive pressure can significantly enhance the negative correlation between the quality of the environmental information disclosure of heavy polluters and their cost of debt.	*Positive moderating*
H3b	As compared to coercive and mimetic pressures, normative institutional pressure has a greater moderating effect on the relationship between the environmental information disclosures of heavy polluters and their cost of debt.	*Positive and stronger moderating*
H3c	Mimetic pressure can significantly enhance the negative correlation between the quality of environmental information disclosure and the cost of debt of heavy-polluting firms.	*Positive moderating*

H3a: Coercive pressure can significantly enhance the negative correlation between the quality of the environmental information disclosure of heavy polluters and their cost of debt.

H3b: As compared to coercive and mimetic pressures, normative institutional pressure has a greater moderating effect on the relationship between the environmental information disclosures of heavy polluters and their cost of debt.

H3c: Mimetic pressure can significantly enhance the negative correlation between the quality of environmental information disclosure and the cost of debt of heavy-polluting firms.

4.4 Methodology

4.4.1 Sample Selection and Data Sources

As the production and operating activities of heavy-polluting industries have significant direct impacts on the natural environment, they should embrace more environmental responsibilities and disclose relevant environmental information to different stakeholders. In China, environmental protection policies and regulations are more targeted at heavy-polluting industries. For example, in 2012, the issue of the "Green Credit Guidelines by the China Banking and Insurance Regulatory Commission (CBIRC)" has more closely linked firms' environmental disclosures and banks' financing decisions. Furthermore, in 2016, seven government departments including the People's Bank of China, the Ministry of Finance, and the Ministry of Environmental Protection (MEP), jointly issued the "Guiding Opinions on Establishing a Green Finance System." The "Guiding Opinions" emphasize that eco-friendliness is embodied in green credit, green securities, green funds, and environmental insurance and requires financial institutions to incorporate corporate environmental risks into their decision-making processes (MEP, 2016). In such an institutional setting, firms in heavy-polluting industries' financing activities are more obviously affected by institutional pressures.

This study selects firms listed on the Shanghai (SSE) and Shenzhen (SZSE) stock exchanges belonging to heavy-polluting industries as classified by the exchanges from 2012 to 2019, including the Coal and Consumable Fuel, Metals and Mining, Textile and Leather, Papermaking, Oil and Gas, Pharmaceutical, Chemical, and Thermal power industries. The sample excludes firms in the Financial industry, "Special Treatment" firms, and firms with missing data. Finally, the sample includes a total of 365 heavy-polluting firms, resulting in a total of 2920 year-firm observations across an 8-year period. The financial data in this study are collected from CSMAR,[6] and data on the quality of environmental disclosure are collected from the CSMAR "Environmental Research database."[7] Additionally, this study involves content analysis of environmental disclosures through manual sorting and analyses (Table 4.2).

4.4.2 *Variables and Measurements*

4.4.2.1 Dependent Variables

The dependent variable used in this study is the corporate cost of debt, which is measured by interest expenses as a percentage of average total liabilities. Interest expenses include all detailed items under "financial expense" in the notes to corporate financial fillings, and average total liabilities are calculated by taking the average of the beginning and ending total liabilities in the current year. The dependent variable is measured as

$$\text{Cost of debt} = \text{interest expenses} / \text{average total debts}$$

[6] CSMAR is short for the China Stock Market & Accounting Research database, and it is widely used for collection of financial data for China-based economic and financial research. Therefore, the financial data used in this study are collected from CSMAR.

[7] Since 2015, CSMAR has launched a new sub-database, the "China Listed Firm's Environmental Research Database," which provides both general and detailed data on Chinese listed companies' environmental performance, environmental disclosures, and environmental investment.

Table 4.2 Sample composition 2012–2019

Industry	Number[a]
Coal and consumable fuel	125
Metals and mining	930
Textile and leather	146
Papermaking	112
Oil and gas	72
Pharmaceutical	523
Chemical	721
Thermal power	281

[a]Company-year observations (2012–2019)

4.4.2.2 Independent Variable

The independent variable is environmental disclosure that is measured through content analysis, the most used research methodology for analyzing sustainability or social and environmental disclosures in social accounting research over the last century. Content analysis involves codifying qualitative and quantitative information into defined categories to derive patterns in the presentation and reporting of information (Guthrie et al., 2004), and the core activity in performing content analysis is to develop a classification scheme with well-defined disclosure categories and decision rules (Hackston & Milne, 1996). In this study, environmental disclosure is measured by a scoring index using content analysis. Firstly, a classification scheme with well-defined environmental disclosure categories is developed based on the requirements for environmental information disclosure measures under the "Environmental Information Disclosure (Trial),"[8] "Guidelines for Environmental Information Disclosure of Listed Companies of Shanghai Stock Exchange,"[9] and "Guidelines for Environmental Information Disclosure of Listed Companies (Draft)"[10] issued in China. Second, 28 specific indicators are developed. Third, according to the indicators, each sentence of environmental disclosure is scored using the following procedures: (1) if the relevant information is disclosed separately in the social responsibility report, environmental report, or sustainable development report, "2" points are assigned; if the environmental information is disclosed separately in the annual report but not in the independent report, "1" point is assigned; (2) in accordance with the indicators, if the related environmental information is disclosed as qualitative information, "1" point is assigned; if the related information is disclosed as quantitative information, "2" points are assigned; otherwise, "0" points are given. The following table presents the classification scheme and scoring procedures for content analysis of the environmental disclosures by heavy-polluting industries (Table 4.3).

---

[8] http://www.gov.cn/ziliao/flfg/2007-04/20/content_589673.htm

[9] http://www.sse.com.cn/aboutus/hotandd/ssenews/c/c_20121024_51173.shtml

[10] http://www.dongmi.org.cn/index.php?m=content&c=index&a=show&catid=14&id=17

Table 4.3 Scoring index for environmental information disclosures

Classification dimensions	Indicators	Scoring criteria
Environmental management	Environmental protection concept	0 points for failure to disclose, 1 point for disclosure
	Environmental targets	
	Environmental protection management system	
	Environmental education and training	
	Special action on environmental protection	
	Environmental protection emergency mechanism	
	Environmental honors and awards	
	"Three simultaneous" system	
Environmental regulation and certification	Pollutant discharge standards	
	Sudden environmental accident	
	Environmental violations	
	Environmental letters and visits	
	Whether it has passed ISO14001 certification	
Environmental performance and governance	Exhaust gas emission reduction management situation	Non-disclosure 0, qualitative 1, qualitative and quantitative 2
	Treatment of wastewater emission reduction	
	Dust control situation	
	Utilization and disposal of solid waste	
	Noise, light pollution, radiation, etc.	
	Implementation of cleaner production	
Environmental liabilities	Wastewater discharge	
	COD emissions	
	SO_2 emissions	
	CO_2 emissions	
	Smoke and dust emissions	
	Production of industrial solid waste	
Energy consumption	Energy consumption	
Environmental protection investment	Environmental investment	
Disclosure channel	Independent reports and annual reports	2 marks for independent report, 1 mark for annual report only

4.4.2.3 Moderating Variables

Institutional pressures are measured using the following procedures. Coercive pressure is measured by the China Pollution Source Regulatory Information Disclosure Index (PITI), which is issued by the Institute of Public & Environmental Affairs (IPE).[11] The PITI is a quantitative and composite score based on daily monitoring, self-monitoring, reporting responses, emissions data, and environmental impact assessment information (EIA) of major Chinese cities (IPE, 2018). The PITI index score reflects the information openness and transparency of environmental protection departments and therefore, the higher the PITI index is, the stronger the local government's environmental supervision. Therefore, the PITI index provides a proxy of coercive pressures to which firms are exposed by the government. Normative pressure mainly comes from the public and environmental protection organizations. Environmental Non-Governmental Organizations (NGOs) refers to voluntary social groups, social organizations, or non-government associations that support or deal with environmental issues. Normative pressures on firms will increase as the number of environmental NGOs increases in a particular region (Xiao et al., 2016). Therefore, in this study, normative pressure is measured by the number of environmental NGOs in the region where the heavy-polluting company operates. Mimetic pressures faced by firms mainly come from peers and competitors in the same industry. Therefore, the more concentrated an industry is, the stronger the degree of market competition, and the greater the mimetic pressure faced by its firms. Therefore, based on Li and Zhang (2016), this study adopts the Herfindahl–Hirschman Index (HHI) of the industry where the company operates to measure mimetic pressure. The HHI is calculated as:

$$\mathrm{HHI} = \Sigma\left(X_i / X\right)$$

X_i is the operating income of a company, and X is the total operating income of the industry where the company is operating. Therefore, the ratio of X_i/X measures the industry market share of the company, namely, the square sum of the ratio of the operating income of each company in the industry to the total operating income of the industry.

4.4.2.4 Control Variables

Consistent with the prior literature, this study uses company size, financial leverage, profitability, fixed assets, liquidity, firm age, size of the supervisory committee, industry, and year of listing as control variables. The variables used in this study are summarized in Table 4.4.

[11] The Institute of Public & Environmental Affairs (IPE) is a non-profit environmental research organization registered and based in Beijing, China. Since its establishment in June 2006, IPE has dedicated itself to collecting, collating, and analyzing government and corporate environmental information to build a database of environmental information.

Table 4.4 Variable definition and measurements

Variable		Symbol	Measurement
Dependent variable	Cost of debt	Debt	Interest expense/total average liabilities
Independent variable	Environmental disclosure	EDI	Content analysis
Moderating variables	Coercive pressure	PITI	China Pollution Source Regulatory Information Disclosure Index
	Normative pressure	NGO	Number of registered environmental NGOs
	Mimetic pressure	HHI	Herfindahl–Hirschman Index
Control variables	Financial leverage	Lev	Average total liabilities/average total assets
	Profitability	Roa	Return on total assets = net profit/ average total assets
	Company size	Size	Take the logarithm of total enterprise assets
	Fixed asset ratio	Fixass	Total fixed assets/total assets
	Current ratio	Ration	Current assets/current liabilities
	Firm age	Age	Company listing years
	Size of supervisory board	Bos	Number of supervisors
	Industry	Industry	Industry classification

4.4.2.5 Models

Based on the hypotheses developed in the preceding sections, the main regression models are summarized as follows. Model (4.1) examines the relationship between environmental disclosure quality and corporate cost of debts. Models (4.2)–(4.4) examine the influence of three types of institutional pressures on environmental disclosures. Models (4.5)–(4.7) examine the moderating effects of institutional pressures on the relationship between environmental disclosures and the cost of debts. The fixed-effect panel data regression is applied to estimate model coefficients and is controlled for year and industry.

$$\begin{aligned}\mathrm{Debt}_{i,t} &= \beta_0 + \beta_1\mathrm{EDI}_{i,t} + \beta_2\mathrm{Lev}_{i,t} + \beta_3\mathrm{Size}_{i,t} + \beta_4\mathrm{Roa}_{i,t} + \beta_5\mathrm{Fixass}_{i,t} \\ &+\beta_6\mathrm{Ration}_{i,t} + \beta_7\mathrm{Age}_{i,t} + \beta_8\mathrm{Bos}_{i,t} + \varepsilon_{i,t}\end{aligned} \tag{4.1}$$

$$\begin{aligned}\mathrm{EDI}_{i,t} &= \beta_0 + \beta_1\mathrm{PITI}_{i,t} + \beta_2\mathrm{Lev}_{i,t} + \beta_3\mathrm{Size}_{i,t} + \beta_4\mathrm{Roa}_{i,t} + \beta_5\mathrm{Fixass}_{i,t} \\ &+\beta_6\mathrm{Ration}_{i,t} + \beta_7\mathrm{Age}_{i,t} + \beta_8\mathrm{Bos}_{i,t} + \varepsilon_{i,t.}\end{aligned} \tag{4.2}$$

$$\begin{aligned}\mathrm{EDI}_{i,t} &= \beta_0 + \beta_1\mathrm{NGO}_{i,t} + \beta_2\mathrm{Lev}_{i,t} + \beta_3\mathrm{Size}_{i,t} + \beta_4\mathrm{Roa}_{i,t} + \beta_5\mathrm{Fixass}_{i,t} \\ &+\beta_6\mathrm{Ration}_{i,t} + \beta_7\mathrm{Age}_{i,t} + \beta_8\mathrm{Bos}_{i,t} + \varepsilon_{i,t}\end{aligned} \tag{4.3}$$

$$\begin{aligned}\mathrm{EDI}_{i,t} &= \beta_0 + \beta_1\mathrm{HHI}_{i,t} + \beta_2\mathrm{Lev}_{i,t} + \beta_3\mathrm{Size}_{i,t} + \beta_4\mathrm{Roa}_{i,t} + \beta_5\mathrm{Fixass}_{i,t} \\ &+\beta_6\mathrm{Ration}_{i,t} + \beta_7\mathrm{Age}_{i,t} + \beta_8\mathrm{Bos}_{i,t} + \varepsilon_{i,t}\end{aligned} \tag{4.4}$$

$$\text{Debt}_{i,t} = \beta_0 + \beta_1\text{EDI}_{i,t} + \beta_2\text{EDI} * \text{PITI} + \beta_3\text{Lev}_{i,t} + \beta_4\text{Size}_{i,t} + \beta_5\text{Roa}_{i,t} + \beta_6\text{Fixass}_{i,t} + \beta_7\text{Ration}_{i,t} + \beta_{87}\text{Age}_{i,t} + \beta_9\text{Bos}_{i,t} + \varepsilon_{i,t} \tag{4.5}$$

$$\text{Debt}_{i,t} = \beta_0 + \beta_1\text{EDI}_{i,t} + \beta_2\text{EDI} * \text{NGO} + \beta_3\text{Lev}_{i,t} + \beta_4\text{Size}_{i,t} + \beta_5\text{Roa}_{i,t} + \beta_6\text{Fixass}_{i,t} + \beta_7\text{Ration}_{i,t} + \beta_8\text{Age}_{i,t} + \beta_9\text{Bos}_{i,t} + \varepsilon_{i,t} \tag{4.6}$$

$$\text{Debt}_{i,t} = \beta_0 + \beta_1\text{EDI}_{i,t} + \beta_2\text{EDI} * \text{HHI} + \beta_3\text{Lev}_{i,t} + \beta_4\text{Size}_{i,t} + \beta_5\text{Roa}_{i,t} + \beta_6\text{Fixass}_{i,t} + \beta_7\text{Ration}_{i,t} + \beta_8\text{Age}_{i,t} + \beta_9\text{Bos}_{i,t} + \varepsilon_{i,t} \tag{4.7}$$

4.5 Results and Discussion

4.5.1 Descriptive Analyses

The data in Table 4.5 identify that the minimum value of environmental disclosure quality is 0.022 and the maximum value is 0.622, with a difference of 0.6 between the two, indicating that the quality of environmental information disclosure of listed firms in China's heavy-polluting industry is uneven and the disclosure levels vary significantly. At the same time, the overall sample mean for environmental disclosure quality is only 0.259, and the median is 0.244, indicating that the overall level is low, with a majority of firms having disclosures below the industry average. The average value of corporate debts is 0.028, the minimum value is 0.004, and the maximum value is 0.050, indicating that the cost of debt for the sample listed firms in heavy-pollution industries has a wide range. Some heavy polluters face more financing pressure than others.

4.5.2 Correlation Analyses

In this study, a Pearson correlation coefficient matrix is used to present the correlation coefficients between variables (Table 4.6). The results show that the correlation coefficient between the quality of environmental disclosure and the cost of debt is −0.038 and significantly correlated at the 5% level, indicating that the quality of environmental information disclosure has a negative impact on the cost of debt. Therefore, hypothesis 1 is supported. Meanwhile, the correlation coefficients between variables in the model are all less than 0.8, indicating that there is no serious multicollinearity between variables. In addition, the VIF value is far less than 10, which supports the fact that there is no serious multicollinearity among the variables used in the model.

Table 4.5 Descriptive analyses

Variable	*N*	Mean	Median	SD	Min	Max
Debt	2920	0.028	0.029	0.013	0.004	0.050
EDI	2920	0.259	0.244	0.177	0.022	0.622
Lev	2920	0.457	0.462	0.172	0.163	0.740
Roa	2920	0.039	0.032	0.040	0.033	0.126
Size	2920	22.640	22.444	1.175	20.890	25.080
Fixass	2920	0.323	0.308	0.154	0.092	0.632
Ration	2920	1.551	1.245	0.997	0.439	4.084
Age	2920	12.110	12.000	6.322	1.000	27.000
Bos	2920	3.908	3.000	1.303	1.000	10.000

Table 4.6 Correlation analysis

	Debts	EDI	Lev	Roa	Size	Fixass	Ration	Age	Bos
Debt	1								
EDI	0.038**	1							
Lev	0.441***	0.161***	1						
Roa	0.326***	0.034*	0.456***	1					
Size	0.130***	0.465***	0.480***	0.047**	1				
Fixass	0.292***	0.157***	0.374***	0.183***	0.288***	1			
Ration	0.406***	0.141***	0.770***	0.388***	0.409***	0.499***	1		
Age	0.013	0.249***	0.345***	0.045**	0.428***	0.231***	0.330***	1	
Bos	0.062***	0.163***	0.304***	0.092***	0.346***	0.178***	0.253***	0.284***	1

Notes: * Significant at the 10% level; ** significant at the 5% level; *** significant at the 1% level

4.5.3 *Regression Analyses*

The regression results for this study are presented in Table 4.7. Hypothesis 1 is tested according to model (4.1). The regression results are given in Column (1) of Table 4.7. The coefficient on environmental disclosure quality is −0.052, which is significant at the 1% level, indicating that the quality of environmental disclosure is significantly negatively related to the cost of debt, supporting that hypothesis 1 be accepted. Disclosure of high-quality environmental information by heavy polluters can effectively improve the transparency of their internal information, help creditors understand the internal environmental performance of firms, effectively ease their estimation of the environmental default risk of firms, and thus reduce the firm cost of debt.

Hypotheses 2a, 2b, and 2c are tested under models (4.2)–(4.4), with regression results shown in columns (2)–(4) of Table 4.7. The coefficient of coercive pressure measured by the PITI is 0.054, which is significant at the 1% level, while the coefficient of normative pressure measured by the number of NGOs is 0.029, which is

Table 4.7 Regression results

	Hypothesis 1	Hypothesis 2			Hypothesis 3		
Variable	(1)	(2)	(3)	(4)	(5)	(6)	(7)
EDI	−0.052***				−0.050***	−0.048***	−0.048***
	(2.86)				(2.73)	(2.60)	(2.60)
PITI		0.054***					
		(2.60)					
NGO			0.029*				
			(1.72)				
HHI				0.058			
				(1.14)			
EDI*PITI					−0.029*		
					(1.92)		
EDI*NGO						−0.051***	
						(3.72)	
EDI*HHI							−0.030*
							(1.90)
Lev	0.295***	0.012	0.014	0.016	0.294***	0.292***	0.295***
	(9.59)	(0.44)	(0.51)	(0.58)	(9.57)	(9.52)	(9.61)
Roa	0.130***	0.056***	0.059***	0.061***	0.129***	0.131***	0.132***
	(7.15)	(3.11)	(3.28)	(3.36)	(7.09)	(7.23)	(7.28)
Size	0.079***	0.389***	0.386***	0.392***	0.080***	0.089***	0.081***
	(3.21)	(18.24)	(18.01)	(18.34)	(3.28)	(3.62)	(3.32)
Fixass	0.126***	0.142***	0.145***	0.142***	0.128***	0.127***	0.122***
	(5.61)	(7.03)	(7.10)	(7.01)	(5.71)	(5.69)	(5.42)
Ration	0.120***	0.057**	0.058**	0.057**	0.121***	0.121***	0.122***
	(3.72)	(2.31)	(2.34)	(2.28)	(3.76)	(3.77)	(3.79)
Age	0.095***	0.033*	0.032	0.032	0.096***	0.098***	0.096***
	(4.49)	(1.67)	(1.63)	(1.60)	(4.55)	(4.65)	(4.58)
Bos	0.063***	0.067***	0.066***	0.063***	0.063***	0.068***	0.063***
	(3.78)	(3.73)	(3.71)	(3.53)	(3.79)	(4.10)	(3.79)
Constant	0.136	0.085	0.093	0.155	0.139	0.110	0.122
	(1.56)	(0.87)	(0.96)	(1.41)	(1.59)	(1.26)	(1.38)
Industry	Control	Control			Control		
Year	Control	Control			Control		
Adj-R^2	0.320	0.322	0.321	0.321	0.321	0.323	0.321
The F value	51.79	56.06	55.85	55.86	50.70	50.72	50.94

Notes: * Significant at the 10% level; ** significant at the 5% level; *** significant at the 1% level. *t*-statistics in parentheses

also significant at the 10% level. These results indicate that both mandatory and normative pressures can improve the quality of environmental disclosures by heavy-polluting firms. That is, both mandatory and normative pressure have significant positive associations with the quality of environmental disclosures, supporting acceptance of hypotheses 2a and 2b. The coefficient of mimetic pressure measured by the HHI is 0.058, but statistically insignificant. Thus, mimetic pressure is not identified as being statistically significant in improving the quality of environmental information disclosure, and hypothesis 2c is rejected. This could be because firms choose to hide environmental information to avoid losing environmental competitiveness. For example, exposing advanced environmental technologies and other information after sensing the imitation of competitors in the same industry.

Hypotheses 3a, 3b, and 3c are tested in models (4.5)–(4.7). The empirical results are shown in columns (5)–(7) of Table 4.7. The coefficients on environmental disclosure quality are negative and statistically significant, while the coefficients of interaction terms EDI*PITI, EDI*NGO, and EDI*HHI are all negative, and significant at the 10%, 1%, and 10% levels, respectively. These results imply that coercive, normative, and mimetic pressure can play a significant role in strengthening the negative relationship between environmental information disclosure quality and corporate cost of debt. As shown in Table 4.7, the coefficient of normative pressure is −0.051, which is greater in absolute terms than the coefficients on coercive and mimetic pressures. Therefore, normative pressures have a stronger moderating effect than other pressures. Acceptance of hypotheses 3a, 3b, and 3c is supported.

In the Chinese setting, the increasingly severe environmental situation has led to a substantial increase in external institutional pressures on firms in relation to their environmental risks. Creditors must deal with the potential threat of environmental default risk by setting financing constraints. Under the impetus of institutional pressures, this study finds that the quality of environmental disclosures has a negative relationship with debt financing risks and, therefore, the cost of debt. Heavy polluters have strong motivation to actively improve the quality of their environmental disclosures based on their financing needs. Additionally, coercive and normative pressures are identified as having stronger moderating effects than mimetic pressure on the impact of environmental disclosure quality on the cost of debt in the Chinese setting.

4.5.4 Further Analyses

To further investigate the influence of environmental disclosures on the corporate costs of debts, this study classifies environmental disclosures into two categories: "soft" disclosures and "hard" disclosures. Based on the study of Yao and Li (2018), soft disclosures include vision and strategy, environmental measures, and public welfare activities related to the environment; hard disclosures include environmental management systems, reliability and credibility of environmental information, expenditure on environmental technology and investments, resource consumption and pollution control, importance of environmental problems and types of influence, and improvement of environmental performance. Soft information is easy for peers to imitate, but hard information is usually difficult for these same peers to imitate. Our focus is on whether the disclosures of different types of environmental information have similar or different effects on the cost of debt. To examine this, the sample is divided into a "soft disclosure" group and a "hard disclosure" group. Regression results are presented in Table 4.8. The coefficient on softEID is −0.059, significant at the 1% level, indicating that the higher the quality of soft disclosures, the lower the cost of debt. In other words, the quality of soft disclosures has a significant negative relationship with the cost of debt. The coefficient on hard environment information disclosure quality (hardEID) is −0.046, significant at the 1% level, indicating that firms actively disclose hard information and the higher the quality of disclosure, the lower the cost of debt. Therefore, the quality of "soft disclosures" and "hard disclosures" are each significantly negatively related to the cost of corporate debt.

The above results may be because, at present, China's environmental information disclosure is still in a semi-mandatory state of "no disclosure or explanation." A unified and standardized disclosure system has not been established, so firms have substantial autonomy in the disclosure of environmental information. "Soft disclosure," such as environmental philosophy, or vision of environmental protection, is positive information. This provides firms with incentives to prefer to disclose this more qualitative information, with improvements in the overall level of environmental information disclosure potentially being biased toward enhancing the quality of "soft disclosure" to improve creditors' opinions. "Hard disclosure" content on enterprise environmental performance will include environmental litigation, environmental violations, fines, and other negative information. Too much of these types of disclosure may potentially endanger the enterprise, as it may suggest the presence of excessive environmental risk to creditors.

The above identifies that for firms in heavy-polluting industries with good environmental performance, quantitative information disclosure in the "hard disclosure"

Table 4.8 Regression results of the relationship between the different types of environmental disclosures and corporate cost of debts

	Soft disclosure		Hard disclosure	
Variables	Coefficients	*t*	Coefficients	*t*
softEID	−0.059***	−3.19		
hardEID			−0.046***	−2.59
Lev	0.294***	9.52	0.296***	9.61
Size	0.079***	3.29	0.076***	3.10
Roa	−0.131***	−7.20	−0.131***	−7.17
Fixass	0.128***	5.67	0.125***	5.55
Ration	−0.122***	−3.79	−0.120***	−3.72
Age	−0.094***	−4.47	−0.095***	−4.51
Bos	−0.063***	−3.82	−0.063***	−3.80
Constant	−0.149*	−1.70	−0.132	−1.51
Industry	Control		Control	
Year	Control		Control	
Adj-R^2	0.321		0.320	
F value	51.81		51.74	

Notes: * Significant at the 10% level; ** significant at the 5% level; *** significant at the 1% level

indicator set may provide a competitive advantage in winning the trust of creditors and obtaining debt financing at a lower cost. This reflects that such information is more verifiable than "soft disclosure" information, and so imitation is difficult for peers.

4.5.5 Robustness Tests

Robustness tests are also performed to ensure the reliability of regression results. First, the ratio of interest expense to total ending debt is used as a substitute for the original cost of debt variable and used in the retest in the regression model. Second, lagging values of independent and control variables are used, given that there may be a reverse causality problem in the impact of the quality of corporate environmental disclosure on the cost of debt. Therefore, the explanatory and control variables are regressed again with a lag period of 1-year. The results of these tests confirm the robustness of the original empirical results, and endogeneity problems do not appear to have a material impact on the relationship between environmental disclosure quality, institutional pressures, and the corporate cost of debt.

4.6 Conclusions

This study selects listed firms in heavy-polluting industries in China and investigates the influence of environmental disclosures on the corporate cost of debt over the 2012–2019 period. Additionally, it examines the moderating effects of institutional pressures in this relationship, given that China has a unique institutional setting. The study first concludes that the quality of environmental disclosure has a negative relationship with the cost of debt. By disclosing high-quality environmental information, heavy polluters can effectively reduce creditors' concerns about environmental risks, enhance creditors' trust, and help firms to achieve the objective of obtaining low-cost financing. Second, the study concludes that coercive, normative, and mimetic institutional pressures play significant roles in promoting the quality of corporate environmental disclosures. However, normative pressures are found to have a stronger influence on improving the quality of environmental disclosures, while mimetic institutional pressures only promote the quality of corporate environmental information disclosure to a limited extent. Third, institutional pressure can also moderate the negative relationship between environmental disclosure quality and the cost of debt. Normative institutional pressure is also found to play a more significant positive moderating role.

In summary, the existence of external institutional pressure can trigger increases in firms' environmental risk disclosures. Specifically, external institutional pressures can motivate firms in heavy-polluting industries to alleviate creditors' concerns about corporate environmental behavior. By improving the quality of their environmental disclosures, these firms may influence creditor financing decisions, improving their ability to gain debt financing and reducing their cost of debt. However, to allow the loan market to efficiently price firm environmental risk and encourage a focus on verifiable environmental performance outcomes, policymakers and regulators may need to tighten the rules on firm EID to encourage greater hard EID disclosure.

References

Buhr, N., & Freedman, M. (2001). Culture, institutional factors and differences in environmental disclosure between Canada and the United States. *Critical Perspectives on Accounting, 12*(3), 1–322.

Chen, X., Li, X., & Huang X Y. (2022). The impact of corporate characteristics and external pressure on environmental information disclosure: A model using environmental management as a mediator. *Environmental Science and Pollution Research, 29*, 12797–12809. https://link.springer.com/article/10.1007/s11356-020-11410-x

China Environment News. (2021). *Defeng chemical company sentenced with 5.5 million RMB yuan penalty*. Dated 18 January. https://cenews.com.cn/legal/202101/t20210118_968277.html (in Chinese).

Cormier, D., Magnan, M., & Velthoven, B. V. (2005). Environmental disclosure quality in large German companies: Economic incentives, public pressures or institutional conditions? *European Accounting Review, 14*(1), 3–39.

Deegan, C. (2006). *Financial accounting theory*. McGraw-Hill.

DiMaggio, P. J., & Powell, W. W. (1983). The iron cage revisited: Institutional isomorphism and collective rationality in organizational fields. *American Sociological Review, 48*(2), 147–160.

Ding, X. G., Qu, Y., & Shahzad, M. (2019). The impact of environmental administrative penalties on the disclosure of environmental information. *Sustainability, 11*, 1–24.

Dong, S., & Xu, L. (2016). The impact of explicit CSR regulation: Evidence from China's mining firm. *Journal of Applied Accounting Research, 17*(2), 237–258.

Dong, S., Burritt, R., & Qian, W. (2014). Salient stakeholders in corporate social responsibility reporting by Chinese mining and minerals companies. *Journal of Cleaner Production, 84*, 59–69.

Dong, S., Xu, L., & McIver, R. (2020). China's financial sector sustainability and 'green finance' disclosures. *Sustainability Accounting Management and Policy Journal, 12*(2), 353–384.

Dong, S., Xu, L., & McIver, R. (2023). Sustainability reporting quality and the financial sector: Evidence from China. *Meditari Accountancy Research, 31*(5), 1190–1214.

Fonseka, M., Rajapakse, T., & Richardson, G. (2019). The effect of environmental information disclosure and energy product type on the cost of debt: Evidence from energy firms in China. *Pacific-Basin Finance Journal, 54*, 159–182.

Gozali, N. O., How, J. C., & Verhoeven, P. (2002). *The economic consequences of voluntary environmental information disclosure*. International Congress on Environmental Modelling and Software, 263, pp. 483–489.

Guthrie, R. P., Yongvanich, K., & Ricceri, F. (2004). Using content analysis as a research method to inquire into intellectual capital reporting. *Journal of Intellectual Capital, 5*(2), 282–293.

Hackston, D., & Milne, M. J. (1996). Some determinants of social and environmental disclosures in New Zealand companies. *Accounting, Auditing & Accountability Journal, 9*(1), 77–108.

Hamrouni, A., Boussaada, R., & Toumi, N. B. F. (2019). Corporate social responsibility disclosure and debt financing. *Journal of Applied Accounting Research, 20*(4), 394–415.

Iatridis, G. E. (2013). Environmental disclosure quality: Evidence on environmental performance, corporate governance and value relevance. *Emerging Markets Review, 14*, 55–75.

Jiang, Y., Wang, Y. R., & Jiang, H. (2020). New environmental protection law, information disclosure and value effect. *China Economic Studies, 4*, 32–46. (Written in Chinese).

Khlif, H., Guidara, A., & Souissi, M. (2015). Corporate social and environmental disclosure and corporate performance. *Journal of Accounting in Emerging Economies, 5*(1), 51–69.

Kothari, S. P., Shu, S., & Wysocki, P. D. (2009). Do managers withhold bad news. *Journal of Accounting Research, 1*, 45–52.

Li, H., & Zhang, X. Y. (2016). A study on the relationship between managerial competence and corporate environmental responsibility: Based on the moderating effects of imitative pressure and coercive pressure. *East China Economic Management, 30*(8), 139–146. (Written in Chinese).

Li, D. Y., Gao, C. C., & Zhang, L. (2017). Effects of corporate environmental responsibility on financial performance: The moderating role of government regulation and organizational slack. *Journal of Cleaner Production, 166*, 1323–1334.

Li, B., Xu, L., McIver, R., Wu, Q., & Pan, A. (2020). Green M&A, legitimacy, and risk-taking: Evidence from China's heavy polluters. *Accounting & Finance, 60*, 97–127.

Li, B., Xu, L., McIver, R., Liu, X., & Pan, A. (2022). Mixed-ownership reform and private firms' corporate social responsibility practices: Evidence from China. *Business & Society, 61*(2), 389–418.

Liu, X., Liu, B., Shishime, T., Yu, Q., Bi, J., & Fujitsuka, T. (2010). An empirical study on the driving mechanism of proactive corporate environmental management in China. *Journal of Environmental Management, 91*, 1707–1717.

Luo, W. B., Guo, X., & Zhong, X. H. (2019). Environmental information disclosure quality, media attention and debt financing costs: Evidence from Chinese heavy polluting listed companies. *Journal of Cleaner Production, 231*, 268–277.

Marshall, S., Brown, D., & Plumlee, M. (2009). *The impact of voluntary environmental disclosure quality on firm value*. Academy of Management Annual Meeting Proceedings, 1, pp. 1–6.

Meyer, J. W., & Rowan, B. (1977). Institutionalized organizations: Formal structure as myth and ceremony. *The American Journal of Sociology, 83*(2), 340–363.

Ministry of Environmental Protection of the People's Republic of China (MEP). (2016). *The guiding opinions on establishing a green finance system*. Available at: http://www.mep.gov.cn/gkml/hbb/gwy/201611/t20161124_368163.htm

Nor, N. M., Bahari, N. A., & Adnan, N. A. (2016). The effects of environmental disclosure on financial performance in Malaysia. *Procedia Economics and Finance, 35*, 117–126.

People's Daily. (2021). *A Zhejiang Company is sentenced to pay over 3 million RMB yuan*. Dated 7 January. http://gs.people.com.cn/n2/2021/0107/c396711-34515784.html (in Chinese).

Qui, Y., Shaukat, A., & Tharyan, R. (2016). Environmental and social disclosures: Link with corporate financial performance. *The British Accounting Review, 48*, 102–116.

Sengupta, P. (1998). Corporate disclosure quality and the cost of debt. *The Accounting Review, 73*(4), 459–474.

Sharfman, M. P., & Fernando, C. S. (2008). Environmental risk management and the cost of capital. *Strategic Management Journal, 29*, 569–592.

Su, L. P., & Zhang, H. M. (2019). *Environmental information disclosure quality and equity financing cost*. Advances in Economics, Business and Management Research, 109, pp. 116–121.

The Institute of Public & Environmental Affairs (IPE). (2018). *Pollution information transparency index*. https://wwwoa.ipe.org.cn//Upload/201904190423050506.pdf

Thompson, P., & Cowton, C. J. (2004). Bringing the environment into Bank lending: Implications for environmental reporting. *The British Accounting Review, 36*, 197–218.

Trevlopoulos, N. S., Tsalis, T. A., Evangelinos, K. I., et al. (2021). The influence of environmental regulations on business innovation, intellectual capital, environmental and economic performance. *Environmental Systems and Decisions, 41*, 163–178.

Tu, Z. G., Hu, T. Y., & Shen, R. J. (2019). Evaluating public participation impact on environmental protection and ecological efficiency in China: Evidence from PITI disclosure. *China Economic Review, 55*, 111–123.

Villiers, C. D., & Staden, C. J. (2011). Where firms choose to disclose voluntary environmental information. *Journal of Accounting and Public Policy, 30*(6), 504–525.

Wang, M. C. (2016). The relationship between environmental information disclosure and firm valuation: The role of corporate governance. *Quality and Quantity, 50*, 1135–1151.

Wang, F., Yang, S. Y., & Reisner, A. (2019). Does green credit policy work in China? The correlation between green credit and corporate environmental information disclosure quality. *Sustainability, 11*(3), 733.

Wang, S. Y., Wang, H. L., & Wang, J. (2020). Does environmental information disclosure contribute to improve firm financial performance? An examination of the underlying mechanism. *Science of the Total Environment, 714*, 1–11.

Wang, D. Q., Li, X. M., & Tian, S. H. (2021). Quantifying the dynamics between environmental information disclosure and firms' financial performance using functional data analysis. *Sustainable Production and Consumption, 28*, 192–205.

Wei, X. B., & Peng, J. (2014). An empirical study on impacts of environmental regulation on environmental information disclosure of listed companies of China: Based on researches on listed companies in nonferrous metal industry. *Canadian Social Science, 10*(2), 113–123.

Wu, L., & Xu, L. (2022). Bank loans and firm environmental information disclosure: Evidence from China's heavy polluters. *Australian Economic Papers, 61*(1), 42–71.

Xiao, H., Zhang, G. Q., & Li, J. F. (2016). Institutional pressure, executive characteristics and environmental information disclosure. *Business Management Journal, 38*(3), 168–179. (Written in Chinese).

Xu, L., Wu, L., & Dong, S. (2021). Internal mechanism and quality of CSR disclosure: Evidence from China. In K. Wendt (Ed.), *Green and social economy finance: A review* (pp. 49–70). Taylor & Francis.

Yang, Y. L., Wen, J., & Li, Y. (2020). Impact of environmental information disclosure on the firm value of listed manufacturing firms: Evidence from China. *International Journal of Environmental Research and Public Health, 17*, 1–20.

Yao, S., & Li, S. Y. (2018). Soft or hard information? A trade-off selection of environmental disclosures by way of peer imitation and geographical distance. *Applied Economics, 50*(30), 3315–3330.

Yao, S., & Liang, H. T. (2019). Analyst following, environmental disclosure and cost of equity: Research based on industry classification. *Sustainability, 11*, 1–19.

Zhao, X., Zhan, L. K., & Song, Y. W. (2014). Environmental information disclosure of listed company study on the cost of debt capital empirical data: Based on thermal power industry. *Canadian Social Science, 10*(6), 88–94.

Zhu, Q., & Zhang, Q. (2015). Evaluating practices and drivers of corporate social responsibility: The Chinese context. *Journal of Cleaner Production, 100*, 1–10.

Part II
Sustainability and Environmental Social Governance (ESG) in Asset Management

Chapter 5
Values and Norms in the Sustainable Finance Debate: Similarities, Differences, and Perspectives for Sustainable Investment

Helge Wulsdorf

Sustainability has its core consideration in finance. One undisputed reason for this, if not the main one, is European regulation. In 2018, its legislative package “Financing Sustainable Growth” ignited a dynamic on the capital markets that is unparalleled. Whereas until then each financial market participant was largely able to determine for itself how sustainable its products and services were, this role is increasingly being taken on by the regulator. It determines what is sustainable and what is not. However, the regulator-driven concentration on the binary code “sustainable”/“non-sustainable” means that financial market participants are primarily concerned with fulfilling, as far as possible, what they are required to do by regulation. In contrast, the strategic opportunity to actively position themselves as responsible sustainable finance players and to make ambitious contributions to sustainable development beyond legal requirements is seen and used by only a few.

The financial sector is therefore waiting in the wings to implement what the regulatory authorities prescribe so that it can declare its products and services to be “sustainable.”

Although sustainability has thus reached the core of financial market activities, this still does not mean that they meet the individual sustainability requirements of investors, let alone reflect their value orientations. Wealthy investors in particular increasingly expect tailored investment strategies that take into account not only their financial return expectations but also their sustainability and value orientations. Wealth management must meet this demand. It is therefore much more than just managing assets and advising on investments. It stands for holistic wealth coordination, which will have to increasingly address the individual sustainability and value preferences of investors beyond the purely regulatory sustainability requirements.

H. Wulsdorf (✉)
Bank für Kirche und Caritas eG, Paderborn, Germany
e-mail: helge.wulsdorf@bkc-paderborn.de

K. Wendt, B. Villhauer (eds.), *Sustainable Wealth Management*, Sustainable Finance,
https://doi.org/10.1007/978-3-031-55505-3_5

5.1 Norms and Values as the Hallmarks of Sustainable Finance

The development of the financial sector toward sustainable finance shows that sustainability is currently defined predominantly by regulatory measures, for example, in the normative requirements of the Taxonomy and Disclosure Regulation of the European Union (EU), the European Green Deal, in international target agreements such as the Sustainable Development Goals (SDGs) of the United Nations (UN), the Paris Climate Agreement, UN human and labor rights, and other social-ecologically relevant UN conventions. Beyond these normative regulatory measures and frameworks, individual sustainability and value preferences of investors play a role, but their importance for sustainable finance has so far only been a marginal note. Consequently, it is not only norms that give sustainability its face in finance, but also values. The distinction between norms and values makes it clear that financial market participants who believe that they comprehensively represent sustainability by implementing regulatory requirements only represent a partial area of sustainability, which does not necessarily cover the individual sustainability requirements and values of customers.

The financial industry has long distinguished between values and norms. It recognizes "values-based" and "norms-based" investment approaches (Swiss Sustainable Finance, 2022), which can be implemented using various building blocks or instruments of sustainable investment, primarily exclusion criteria, but also positive/negative screening and engagement (Wulsdorf, 2018, pp. 142–147). While norms-based investments map enumerated international and national sustainability standards, values-based investments are based on the respective religious, political, ideological, or personal beliefs of the capital owners. Especially for the latter, values-based investment approaches are profile-building. This means that they need financial service providers who can translate their value orientations into tailor-made investment solutions. Although exclusion criteria are usually at the forefront of values-oriented investors' investment behavior, their own values can also be implemented through the two building blocks of positive/negative screening and engagement. Broad-based and high-quality sustainability approaches pursue a combination of different building blocks and implementation strategies of sustainable investment. They are not only concerned with preventing investments in controversial business models and activities through exclusions and avoiding negative effects on people, society, and the environment but also and in particular with promoting positive impact effects for sustainable development and change, for example, through targeted ESG engagement activities (CRIC, 2020). The latter impact effects are intended to make positive contributions based on investors' values and at the same time achieve positive effects for sustainable development in the sense of the so-called "Great Transformation" (Schneidewind, 2018).

5.1.1 The Holistic Claim to Action of Ethical Investors

Not only wealthy retail customers in private banking but also institutional investors expect more from their investments than just that normative minimum requirements regarding sustainability are met. They want their individual values to be reflected in a holistic way, both in the way they realize their purpose and in the way they invest their assets. In terms of their intentions, they are predominantly intrinsically motivated regarding sustainability in investment. In addition to family offices, these include in particular foundations, the sponsors of the church, Caritas and Diakonie, and increasingly pension funds. Church institutions explicitly see themselves as ethical investors, characterized by the fact that they invest the financial resources set aside for their purposes in such a way that they do not conflict with their mission and fields of activity (Wulsdorf, 2022, pp. 26–30). From their point of view, as is the case with all values-oriented investors, the use of earnings and the generation of earnings must be continuously reconciled in the sense of a holistic fulfillment of the organizational purpose.[1]

Ethical investors are aware of the leverage effect of sustainable finance for achieving the social and ecological goals of sustainable development. They also want to use their assets to fulfill their mandate to create more sustainability and justice. For their financial managers, this raises the question of which investment objects can and should be used to generate financial returns as an economic necessity, at best in harmony with, but at least not in contradiction to, their own purpose fulfillment. With ethically sustainable investments, values-oriented investors secure and strengthen their claim to holism in any case. They share the insight that there are neither values-free nor ethically neutral investments. This means that they know that their investments always have positive and negative effects on people, society, and the environment. It should be noted that this realization applies to all investments, regardless of whether they are conventionally managed, investments that meet regulatory sustainability requirements, or investments that reflect specific values. Their responsibility for people, society, and the environment also and especially requires ethical investors to be able to account for the socio-ecological consequences of their investments in terms of the respective organizational purpose beyond the financial return.

[1] Beyond wealth management clients, values-oriented investors include church banks, church insurers, the public Sector, and financial service providers specializing in sustainability. Last but not least, the entire field of Islamic banking should be mentioned in this context.

5.1.2 Churches as Ethical Investors

The Catholic and Protestant churches in Germany are a good example of how ethical investors operate. Like other values-oriented investors, the churches are classified by the financial industry as values-based investors. On the one hand, they have to face the requirements and framework conditions of the capital market just like all other investors. For this reason, they cannot avoid evaluating the financial and sustainability risks of their investments and generating corresponding returns for the fulfillment of their mission. Unlike other investors, the churches do this, on the other hand, with the self-committed claim of wanting to make contributions to a more just and sustainable world in general and a more just and sustainable financial system in particular with their financial investments, based on the Christian faith. Although church investment strategies are values-motivated, i.e., Christian values should characterize their financial conduct, these are first and foremost the starting point for their financial behavior, but not their sole goal.

The churches do represent Christian values. However, these values do not exclusively determine their actions as social institutions. In their financial actions, for example, both churches refer in their respective documents on ethically sustainable investments to national and international sustainability standards, including the above-mentioned fundamental social-ecological UN standards (DBK & ZdK, 2021, pp. 15–18; EKD, 2023, p. 8f). The churches are thus always socially located and anchored in their actions. In other words, they do not operate in a special or parallel world. As part of society, they want to help shape society from their Christian faith with different emphases. Christian values shape all their services and activities. The financial resources required for this are therefore always part of this work in and for society. The churches know that they can not only make a difference in terms of their values, but can also have a significant leverage effect on sustainable development. Church financial conduct, like the other fields of action of its mission, must therefore be accorded a testimonial character.

5.1.3 Church Investment with Values- and Norms-Based Approaches

As civil society actors, the churches must position themselves in the field of tension between their Christian value claim and general norms-related sustainability requirements in such a way that they take account of both their own claims and those of society. They thus invest in a values-based manner regarding their own values and at the same time in a norm-compliant manner regarding the sustainability requirements of society as a whole, whereby the specifically Christian values are initially placed before the general sustainability standards. It can be said that the churches act in conformity with both values and norms - or, to use the terminology of the financial sector, in a values- and norms-based manner. For them, the one-sided classification of churches as values-based investors made by the financial sector thus represents a truncated view that does not necessarily correspond to their (self-)understanding and investment behavior. The same applies to other ethical investors because they also act in accordance with values and norms.

5.2 Values and Norms: Differences and Mutual Conditionality

The example of churches as ethical investors shows that the distinction in finance between values-based and norms-based investments raises questions for a practical allocation of investors. In the sustainable finance discussion, however, these have not been addressed much so far, as the distinction is rather a side issue. They do, however, call for a differentiated view of what values and norms are in general and what significance they have specifically for sustainable finance.

5.2.1 *On the Relationship Between Values and Norms in General*

Whereas values generally indicate points of orientation or targets for individual and collective action, norms are measures or regulations that permit, prohibit, or deem actions to be required. In other words, norms contain "in their form and content rules for morally good, because morally correct or even required action" (Lutz-Bachmann, 2021, p. 261).[2] Accordingly, they are restrictive, that is, they have a function of limiting the freedom of action of the individual for the sake of the freedom of others. They are supposed to apply to the point, at least for the designated scope. Norms are originally anthropologically rooted and fundamental to social coexistence. Values, on the other hand, are attractive; that is, they are an expression of successful life. They are identity-, meaning-, and community founding and are justified religiously, politically, ideologically, or personally. In the sense of superordinate control parameters, they can be understood as "orientation directives" (Krijnen, 2002, p. 528) that provide guidelines for individual or collective behavior. The latter aspect is relevant for communities and organizations since values create a sociocultural sense of belonging.

Modern Western societies are characterized by a certain value pluralism, which largely enables individuals to develop their personal value profiles systemically in different forms of community, organization, and life within the valid legal system.

[2]According to Möllers (2018, p. 14), norms "refer to a possible state or event. Making the impossible the confession of a norm is meaningless. Positively marking a possibility indicates that it is to be realized."

Particularly with regard to international sustainability norms, their possibility and marking in space and time are of central importance, which must be constantly reflected upon and evaluated.

The values lived by each individual according to his or her profile represent his or her basic moral stance, i.e., his or her religiously, ideologically, or otherwise based view of life. Values are therefore located on a different level than behavior that conforms to norms, which does not ask about the attitude of the person concerned and does not necessarily have this as its basis.

Despite the distinctive features that have been pointed out, the reciprocal relationship between values and norms must not be lost sight of. Norms are always an expression of value preferences (Lutz-Bachmann, 2021, p. 260f). Every norm is usually accompanied by a set of values that makes it concrete and legitimizes it. Conversely, values can also be assigned certain norms that make values manageable in the sense of rules of conduct. The value of justice, for example, stands for the norms that all people are equal before the law, have equal opportunities, and are able to participate in social processes. Honesty stands for the prohibition of false statements (lies), the environment or creation for environmental protection and the realization of the most equal life chances possible for present and future generations, life for the prohibition of killing, peace for solutions that are as non-violent as possible, whereby the value listed in each case does not have to be the only one that can be assigned to a norm. In summary, the identity of individual and collective actors is articulated "through values and in norms" (Lutz-Bachmann, 2021, p. 277). Values set the framework for action at the micro, meso, and macro levels (Wilhelms & Wulsdorf, 2017, pp. 25–32). Due to their overarching orientation character as steering parameters, they implicitly always already have a normative effect, which ensures that their general validity is ultimately formulated in behavioral or legal norms in a socially differentiated manner at various levels. For such norms, collective values in particular have a legitimizing character in that they justify social rules and regulations, for example, by conforming to the constitution or as an expression of the community of values.

5.2.2 The Importance of Values and Norms for Sustainable Finance

The distinction made by the financial industry between values-based and norms-based investment approaches does not, strictly speaking, allow investors (groups) to be clearly assigned to just one of the two categories, as illustrated by the example of churches. Another difficulty is that the financial distinction only focuses on possible differentiating features between the two categories of values and norms, but does not take into account their mutual interdependence. However, values-oriented investors in particular cannot ignore this, because they are aware of the close interplay between values and norms. For them, the two variables cannot be implemented separately in their fields of activity. If they base their investments on international and national sustainability standards, they are norms-based investors whose content and requirements can also be derived from their religious, political, ideological or personal values, basic attitudes and convictions. For them, norms-based investments are thus always also values-based investments, both of which usually arrive at similar, if not virtually identical, results in terms of sustainable investment criteria.

It is hardly reflected that, due to the close interplay of norms and values, norms-based investments can be values-based investments at the same time. After all, social-ecological sustainability norms are always based on values such as the protection of human life, the environment, biodiversity and the climate, as well as freedom, equality, democracy and peace. The fact that the latter values correspond to and legitimize the aforementioned norms is a blind spot in the sustainable finance debate. For the normative sustainability requirements of the UN, EU and other institutions, the underlying values may have become so self-evident, even common property of (world) society, that there seems to be no need for explicit justification of their norms by higher-level values. Many norms, especially in the Western hemisphere, are based on the ideals of Christianity—as laid down by the Church, for example, in the conciliar process "Peace, Justice and the Integrity of Creation"—which concretize social values, but do not explicitly address them or reflect on them further. It is tacitly assumed that those affected by the norms accept and support them as a community of values.[3] The distinction between values-based and norms-based investments is thus at least questionable, if not invalid, due to their mutual conditionality. It suggests different investment styles which, arguing from different starting points, nevertheless mostly pursue the same goals.

5.2.3 *The Importance of Values and Norms for Church Investors*

As has been seen, the churches are investors who want to implement further Christian values in their investments beyond general sustainability requirements, which are not readily expressed in generally accepted norms of society. They therefore check whether their values are reflected in the investments, or at least whether they are not significantly violated. If the investments are largely in line with their ethical values and basic moral attitudes, the churches look to see whether and to what extent their investments make additional positive contributions to the fulfillment of international and national sustainability standards. From the churches' perspective, Christian values sharpen the focus on concrete social and/or ecological transformational contributions to such sustainability norms. Although church values are often not directly evident, international norms, such as human and labor rights, the SDGs, and other UN conventions conform to fundamental Christian values, such as those found in the topoi of the aforementioned conciliar process "Peace,

[3] If the value basis is called into question due to divergent value portfolios, different value hierarchies or conflicting world views, the consensus on norms can become fragile. In the worst case, this leads to a "clash of civilizations" (Huntington, 1998), which in turn can result in the division of society.

Justice and Integrity of Creation." For example, the churches understand the SDGs or the Paris Climate Agreement as a "secular" translation of their values (DBK & ZdK, 2021, p. 15; EKD, 2023, p. 8f). For the churches, investments that conform to norms are therefore at the same time investments that conform to values, since the normative societal requirements for sustainability are based on genuine Christian values.

For the churches, moreover, investments that conform to Christian values are always based on norms, such as Christian commandments that regulate religious and social life or protect human and non-human creation. In addition to biblical messages, Christian norms are based above all on church documents in the form of memoranda, (social) encyclicals, and other pronouncements, with which the churches, as civil society actors, exert some influence on the development of social norms.[4] These documents set out and justify rules of conduct that are fundamental to the success of human life in community. From the church's point of view, investments that conform to values are therefore always investments that conform to norms. Although there is a very large overlap between "ecclesiastical" and "secular" sustainability norms, the churches are also characterized by special values. In the Catholic sphere in particular, they are concretized in specific norms, i.e., commandments, such as the ban on abortion, the ban on embryonic stem cell research, and the ban on pornography and cloning of human genetic material (DBK & ZdK, 2021, p. 29), which do not conform to general social sustainability requirements.[5] If investments in these segments are not excluded from the outset, there are reputational risks for investors, especially in the Church and Caritas, which they have to face in their investments. Particularly in the case of reputational risks, it is not a question of whether value or norm are decisive for the investment, but of general investment guard rails that should take Christian values and norms into account.

For the churches, their investments, which conform to Christian values, do not merge with investments of the global society that conform to norms.[6] They have their own ethical- sustainable value profile, which is reflected in various combinations in the three building blocks of sustainable investments mentioned above. Their large overlap with norms-conforming sustainability investments makes it clear that the churches also make positive and negative impact contributions to the

[4] Christian norms and values regulate human interaction from a religious-political perspective. However, both the 10 Commandments (OT) and the Sermon on the Mount (NT), for example, are not suitable as political action programs, let alone as ethical value criteria sets that can be implemented one-to-one in capital investments. They must be transformed into ethical and sustainable investment criteria that conform to values and norms.

[5] "Classic" exclusions in the evangelical sphere include gambling, tobacco, alcohol, and pornography (EKD, 2023, p. 39).

[6] The fact that church investments are not completely absorbed into norms-based investments has to do with the relationship between church and society. The churches act in society, but also in relation to it. In other words, as part of society, they support its ideas and actively promote them. As religious communities, however, they also set themselves apart from society with certain values and live these out in their ministries and works while recognizing the existing legal system, which is why there is no complete congruence between Christian values and secular norms.

"social-ecological transformation" (Wulsdorf, 2022, p. 33f), as the two churches interpret the "Great Transformation," with their financial investments. It becomes apparent that the value conformity of financial investments is not only a matter for more or less obviously values-oriented investors, but ultimately for all capital investors. In other words, the value aspect cannot be attributed unilaterally and solely to selected investor groups such as the churches. It affects the entire investor landscape.

5.3 Values and Norms as the Basis of Every Financial Investment

All institutional investors embody values more or less consciously. Organizations in business, society, and politics stand for certain values with their respective realizations of purpose. These values go beyond the requirements of generally accepted sustainability standards but are seldom reflected in one's own financial investments—regardless of whether they are motivated by political, sociocultural, or other factors. Anyone who, as an organization in the financial sector, acts or invests exclusively on the basis of norms and does not want to reflect his or her own values in his or her investments, acts like many, probably most, other investors or competitors only on the basis of general normative framework conditions—no more and no less. Institutional investors are thus depriving themselves of the strategic opportunity to sharpen their own value profile as sustainability actors by living their organizational values in addition to the general sustainability standards in their own investments or in their core business as a whole and sharing them with their customers.[7] For organizations, dealing with values and norms with regard to their investments is a question of consistency. In other words, to what extent should the organization's own values be reflected coherently in its investments alongside norms-based sustainability requirements.

The question of values- and/or norms-based investments also arises in the retail business. As already mentioned in the section on values, everyone has an individual value profile of which they are more or less aware. Depending on the context in which they live and the depth of their reflection and abstraction, they may want to implement these values in their actions. In particular, people who attach importance to sustainable consumption, for example, expect their investments to reflect their personal values in the social and ecological spheres as far as possible. For them, this is part of a coherent, i.e., consistent, life plan that is as free of contradictions as possible. Accordingly, it is the task and challenge of customer advisory services to offer appropriate investments. The sustainability preference survey (MiFID II), which will be mandatory from summer 2022, offers the opportunity not only to simply offer customers sustainable products if they express a positive opinion, but also to

[7] Even then, if you only resort to general norms, you are acting in a values-oriented manner, whether you like it or not, because these are ultimately based on social values.

pick up on their personal value preferences and place them in the context of sustainability. This would give customer loyalty a new intellectual quality and depth. Financial service providers specializing in sustainability are aware of this added value for their customers and have therefore been playing the "value card" in both institutional and private customer business for some time. Up to now, however, it has also been apparent when it comes to the topic of money that consumers' self-perceptions and external perceptions often diverge, and that thinking and acting are consequently inconsistent. The self-perception of wanting to live (more) sustainably is therefore not yet reflected in the volumes of sustainable investments.

5.4 On the Practice of Values and Norms in Monetary Investments

The fact that their investments are always based on values and norms is not necessarily something that many, if not most, investors—whether institutional or private customers—have in mind. The sustainability preference survey, which will be mandatory for advisory meetings from summer 2022, will at least raise awareness of the implementation of sustainability standards in financial investments. The question of the extent to which applied sustainability standards in the areas of environmental, social, and good corporate governance (ESG investment criteria) match one's individual value preferences may come up for some investors. Various international norms, such as human and labor rights, the UN Convention on Biological Diversity and the Paris Climate Agreement, illustrate that general sustainability requirements and individual value preferences are often in harmony. However, certain investment topics can also lead to different results with regard to the implementation of values and norms. One example is the issue of nuclear energy. Another investment criterion that has moved onto the agenda of the debate on values and norms in investment as a result of the war of aggression on Ukraine is armaments and the military. The three investment criteria of human rights, nuclear energy, and armaments and the military will be used to illustrate the investment results that can be achieved on the one hand by a values-oriented and on the other by a norms-oriented argumentation.

5.4.1 Investment Criterion Human Rights Violations

Even though none of the 17 UN Sustainable Development Goals has human rights explicitly in its title, many of them are about respecting them, as SDG 1 (no poverty), SDG 2 (no hunger), SDG 3 (health), SDG 4 (education), SDG 5 (equality), all the way to SDG 16 (peace, justice, and strong institutions) show. The international human rights charter is the normative basis for the social dimension of sustainability. This means that sustainable development is not possible without lasting respect for human rights. Investors with a sustainability preference will therefore want to have the permanent and systematic violation of human rights activated as an exclusion criterion in their financial investments. Among the top ten exclusion criteria in German-speaking countries for sustainable assets, human rights violations rank third (FNG, 2022, p. 33). They are thus among the standard exclusions of sustainable investment. The norms-oriented argumentation is underpinned by further normative provisions such as the German Act on Corporate Due Diligence to Prevent Human Rights Violations in Supply Chains, or Supply Chain Act for short, the National Action Plan for Business and Human Rights, as well as the UN Global Compact and the UN Guiding Principles on Business and Human Rights.

Just like the norms-oriented argumentation, the oriented argumentation comes to the conclusion that human rights violations are a central exclusion criterion for values-based investments. As normative guidelines for global society, they protect universally valid values that are intended to enable fulfilled life worldwide and must therefore be observed at all costs in the sense of drawing boundaries. This view can be illustrated by the argumentation of the churches, which, as seen, act as ethical investors on the capital market. "Human rights are (...) granted indivisibly by the church to all people on the basis of their intrinsic dignity and without distinction of person" (DBK & ZdK, 2021, p. 39; EKD, 2023, p. 37; 40; 46). Persistent and systematic human rights violations therefore lead to exclusions of both companies and states. The churches, like other values-oriented investors, know only too well that the recognition and observance of human rights are central indicators of future-oriented and sustainable development worldwide. Freedom, justice, democracy, and peace, as well as environmental, biodiversity, and climate protection, cannot be realized as central basic values of the world community without human rights. Compliance with these values is therefore a central investment guideline for values- and norms-based investments.

5.4.2 *Nuclear Energy as an Investment Criterion*

While both a norms-based and a values-based argumentation may lead to divestments in the case of fossil fuels such as coal due to its high CO2 emissions, norms and values may lead to different results in the case of uranium and gas and, as a result, different investment options may be preferred. This is clearly illustrated by the discussion on the EU taxonomy, which can be used as a normative basis for sustainable economic action and investment. Despite significant opposition from some member states, the European Commission advocated in a supplementary delegated taxonomy act at the beginning of 2022 that nuclear energy and fossil gas be included in the EU taxonomy under precisely defined conditions (EU, 2022). In its compromise, the EU Commission considers nuclear energy and fossil gas as a stability reserve for the transition to a renewable and CO2 -free energy economy. If the draft submitted becomes law, investments in nuclear energy could be classified as "sustainable." That is, the norms-based argumentation would classify nuclear energy as a "sustainable" investment at the European level. In Germany, contrary to the EU compromise, the norms-based argument can be based on the national nuclear phase-out adopted by a large majority in the German Bundestag and enshrined in the amended Atomic Energy Act.

In German-speaking countries, nuclear energy is rated differently from the EU Commission. Nuclear energy ranks ninth among the top ten exclusion criteria and has thus established itself as the standard for sustainable assets (FNG, 2022, p. 33). Nuclear energy is a high-risk technology with a remaining "residual risk" that can become a serious threat to the lives of humanity through potential accidents and consequential effects. The Catholic Church, as a Christian community of values, therefore excludes nuclear energy.[8] It argues as follows: "The residual risk of nuclear energy does not only refer to the operation of nuclear reactors and possible accidents that have massive effects on the human and natural environment. The still unanswered question of the final storage of radioactive waste also represents a legacy burden that places a mortgage on future generations in particular that is difficult to calculate and is therefore incompatible with the idea of intergenerational justice" (DBK & ZdK, 2021, p. 21; EKD, 2023, p. 37; 40). Especially from the point of view of intergenerational justice, the Church does not see the value of protecting people living now and in the future through nuclear energy as guaranteed. Although energy security is an important social value, for the Church it does not cancel out the guarantee of life chances for future generations. Moreover, uranium causes non-negligible CO2 emissions, if one considers its entire value chain. Nuclear energy is thus an investment criterion that can lead to different investment results depending on the values- or norms-based argumentation.

5.4.3 Armaments and Military Investment Criterion

Armaments and the military are an investment criterion that has come into the focus of sustainable investments due to the war in Ukraine. From a defense perspective, the need for weapons of war and military technology is hardly ever seriously questioned. The discussion has also been fueled by the special fund of 100 billion euros set aside for the German armed forces. The Federal Association of the German Security and Defense Industry (BDSV) explicitly claims to be "sustainable." Its claim is: "Security is the mother of all sustainability" (BDSV, 2022). Whether the defense industry can so easily hijack the term sustainability for its own purposes is almost certainly debatable beyond the limits of sustainable finance. Even if there is no legal definition of sustainability—everyone thus thinks they can continue to interpret and use the term for their own purposes—this does not mean that both values-based and norms-based arguments support the BDSV's claim. Particularly

[8] The disagreement between France and Germany, for example, on the assessment of nuclear energy in relation to sustainable development shows that the European Union, unlike the Catholic Church, does not act as a unified community of values.

when it comes to the investment criterion of armaments and the military, an extremely differentiated view is therefore required in order to be able to form an investment judgment. Numerous normative requirements outlaw specific categories of weapons in some cases and are thus not investable for norms-based investors. These include the Nuclear Non-Proliferation Treaty, the Biological Weapons Convention, the Chemical Weapons Convention, the Convention on Prohibitions or Restrictions on the Use of Certain Conventional Weapons, the Ottawa Convention on the Prohibition of Anti-Personnel Mines, and the Oslo Convention on the Prohibition of Cluster Munitions with the respective protocols. Given that certain conventional weapons are internationally outlawed, categorizing weapons based on distinctions such as heavy, light, controversial, weapons of mass destruction, and dual-use items may not be readily useful. This is particularly true as all armaments can be utilized not only for defense purposes but also for offensive purposes. So far, little attention has been paid to the fact that wars are not only about real warfare but increasingly also about cyber warfare, which can also pose a threat to people, society, and the environment, and for which state-of-the-art defense technologies are needed. The fact that weapons are viewed critically for social development is evidenced, for example, by the SDGs. Sustainable Development Goal 16 Peace, Justice, and Strong Institutions advocates in its sub-goals for arms regulation to significantly reduce all forms of violence, violence-related mortality, and illicit arms flows (SDG 16.1 and 16.4). Also, in the first recommendations for the structure and content of the EU social taxonomy, armaments are not among the activities that contribute positively to the Sustainable Development Goals. They are classified there as non-social. From a normative point of view, therefore, there is nothing to be said in favor of giving the investment criterion of armaments and the military a sustainability coating.

For values-oriented investors, the exclusion criterion of armaments and the military is part of the standard for sustainable investments. On the list of the top ten, the criterion is ranked sixth for the German-speaking region (FNG, 2022, p. 33). For the Catholic Church, all acts of war constitute crimes against God and man. From the Church's point of view, arms races are no guarantee for peace—on the contrary, excessive armament prevents the development of man and society. The Catholic Church's orientation guide states: "In Article 51 of the Charter of the United Nations, the community of states has established a right of self-defense, which gives each member state the right to defend itself against an armed attack. However, a progressive arms race and uncontrolled armament do not secure peace. Moreover, financial resources that flow into arming armed forces are lacking for investments in other areas, such as education, health care, or infrastructure" (DBK & ZdK, 2021, p. 40; EKD, 2023, p. 38; 47; 50).[9] In addition to the production of outlawed, ABC, and conventional armaments as well as their strategic components, values-oriented investors also exclude the distribution of small arms as this is, in their view, required

[9] From an ecumenical-Christian point of view, it will be interesting to see how the Russian Orthodox Church and the Ukrainian Orthodox Church will react to the investment criterion of armaments and the military after the war in Ukraine.

by the protection of the human person and civil society as well as peace, security, and justice. Furthermore, they are aware of the fact that armaments repeatedly find their way into unauthorized hands, for example, of terrorist militias, hostile or extremist groups, and are often used against the civilian population, especially in underdeveloped countries.

There is no doubt that sophisticated armaments and defense technologies are needed for national defense and geopolitical security. However, to declare these as "sustainable," for example, within the framework of the EU social taxonomy, runs counter to the goals of sustainable development. Such an endeavor shows once again that the binary code "sustainable"/"unsustainable" mentioned at the beginning is not suitable for classifying certain economic activities. For a values- and norms-based assessment of investments in armaments and the military, it is essential to make further information transparent: Are armaments and defense technologies provided exclusively for defense purposes of free democratic states? Are human rights due diligence requirements being complied with in the practice of arms exports? Are arms exports to authoritarian or dictatorial states not subject to state export licenses? To date, there is no reliable information from external data providers, such as sustainability rating agencies, that would allow us to consider whether and to what extent investments in geopolitical security measures and in weapons systems and defense technologies required for defense purposes might be possible to a limited extent under certain conditions.

5.4.4 Further Investment Criteria

In addition to the three investment criteria discussed, human rights, nuclear energy, and armaments and military, there are others that can be justified on the basis of values and norms. As with the investment criterion of human rights, values- and norms-based argumentations for the investment criteria of labor rights violations, biodiversity and environmental destruction, the death penalty, corruption, and the fossil fuel coal come to the conclusion that exclusions are activated. In addition to numerous normative requirements at both international and national levels, values-oriented investors see values such as the protection of the human person, social development, and the integrity of creation being violated. They therefore exclude investments in such corporate business practices and models as well as governmental behavior that contradicts the values mentioned. Unfair business practices, such as tax evasion, money laundering, and fraud, are further practices that can lead to exclusion based on values and norms. Addictive substances, pornography, gambling, abortion,[10] embryonic stem cell research animal testing, and green genetic

[10] The Supreme Court's decision of June 24, 2022 to repeal the right to abortion, which has been in force in the USA since 1973, is not in line with the values of large sections of the US population as a normative requirement. It therefore does not necessarily lead to a change in the investment behavior of US investors with regard to abortion.

engineering, on the other hand, are criteria that are particularly significant for values-based investors. They thus not only implement their values in their financial investments but also religious codes of conduct or internal norms of values-oriented communities.[11]

Finally, it should be pointed out in the practical part that the result of values-based and/or norms-based argumentation does not yet determine the level of detail (definition of criteria) and the degree of penetration (e.g., into the supply chains) with which the abovementioned and other investment criteria are determined, nor the turnover thresholds or degree of severity, nor the building blocks and implementation strategies for companies and/or countries with which they are applied in financial investment. The decisions on this are made by the investor, who then looks for financial products that most closely match his sustainability and/or value preference. In addition to prevention through defined exclusion criteria, investors can also promote positive effects in terms of human rights, climate, and other sustainability and value requirements through targeted investments and initiate change processes at investment objects through engagement activities. The goal is to be able to speak, judge, and act with values- and norms-based investment strategies with regard to one's own value and sustainability preferences in financial investments.

5.5 Values as a Further Materiality Dimension

Different materialities determine investments. In the meantime, no financial market participant seriously doubts that sustainability materiality plays a central role beyond financial materiality. This connection is expressed in the concept of double materiality, which has become one of the cornerstones of sustainable finance. It states that ESG sustainability criteria have an influence on the financial materiality of investment objects—the so-called outside-in perspective—and that investment objects have positive and negative effects on sustainability, i.e., on people, society, and the environment—the so-called inside-out perspective. The explanations have shown that values also influence the materiality of investments. Since values- and norms-based arguments can lead to different investment decisions, value materiality and sustainability materiality cannot be equated. Value materiality is therefore to be understood as an independent materiality dimension, which has so far hardly been taken into account in the sustainable finance discussion. In particular, for values-oriented investors, the question is how do their values impact financial materiality (outside-in perspective), and vice versa, what do their financial investments pay on their values (inside-out perspective). There is a lack of transparency on the interplay of potential value performance with financial and sustainability performance and, to

[11] In terms of religious policy, it proves problematic when different religious values clash and insurmountable differences emerge between religiously based investment criteria, for example, between Islam and Christianity with regard to investments in states that systematically violate human rights and practice the death penalty.

date, a lack of sensitivity to the value issue in sustainable investing. The idea of any kind of value performance as an additional valuation indicator for values-oriented investors needs to be developed.

The challenges of a value approach are likely to be similar to those in the current discussion on the ESG impact of investments: What is the state of the data on value criteria in the real and financial economy? Can value criteria be measured and evaluated in a uniform and comparable way? What do the inside-out and outside-in perspectives mean in relation to values? How can reputational risks arising from values be integrated into risk management alongside performance risks? Can greenwashing be prevented with values? Although this is not yet being discussed, it may be important not only for explicitly values-oriented investors, but also for those who may jeopardize their credibility and authenticity vis-à-vis their internal and external stakeholders if they do not also implement their values in their investments.

The sustainability rating agency MSCI ESG Research, for example, shows that the financial sector is already beginning to see the issue of values—although it has not yet penetrated it to the necessary depth. In the evaluation of fund products, the MSCI ESG Fund Rating Report has a Religious Values category divided into Catholic Values Non-Compliant (%) and Islamic Non-Compliant (%). In addition to the specifically Catholic values and norms of abortion, contraception, stem cells, and gambling, general criteria such as discrimination and guns are also applied.[12] The MSCI assessment of religious values and norms thus only implements the building block exclusions. The report does not provide any information on what positive or even negative effects on religious values are achieved with investment objects. As with many values-oriented investors, MSCI research is about preventing, not promoting or changing. What is possible for funds should not be a hurdle for other portfolio constructions because the data is available for individual investment properties. Here, too, it would be possible to determine what percentage violates religious values, knowing full well that the Religious Values indicator is always based on MSCI's interpretation of religion and not that of investors from the church, Caritas and Diakonie, who sometimes work with implementation thresholds and completely different investment criteria for the MSCI religious criteria, as the documents of the two churches on ethical-sustainable investment show.[13]

[12] The MSCI methodology provides the following explanation of Catholic values: "Catholic Values Fail (%): The percentage of portfolio's market value exposed to companies that have been flagged for one or more of the underlying USCCB exclusionary factors: abortion, contraceptives, stem cells, discrimination, adult entertainment, defense and weapons, landmines, or predatory lending" (MSCI, 2022).

[13] Since data on religious values are available from most sustainability rating agencies, it should not be a problem to create a religion score or indicator as an investment standard for churches, for example, on the basis of their documents, either denominationally or ecumenically. Although the commonalities are emphasized in church investments, the differences between the religions have not yet been systematically worked out. Nor is there any evidence on where the dividing lines between values-oriented religious and non-religious investing lie and how these affect investment behavior. In terms of religious policy, the question also needs to be addressed of the extent to which the churches can (and do) consciously exert influence on cultural policy ("missionary"), for example, through engagement activities, with values-compliant investments on the basis of well-founded ethical value judgments.

5.6 Conclusion and Outlook

The issue of values is likely to become increasingly important if there is no normative legitimation in the sense of generally accepted norms for exclusion for certain investment criteria, even though there is a broad social consensus, as is the case with the criterion of nuclear energy in the German-speaking world. If the issue of values is to be strengthened in sustainable finance, further methodological considerations are necessary. This is not only a matter of preventing by means of exclusion criteria, but also of promoting, so that capital can be mobilized for those investment objects which, from the investor's point of view, contribute to his specific values in addition to the sustainability goals. Above all, transparency must be created as to how values and norms are interpreted in financial products and with which goals they are implemented. The term "ethical-sustainable investment" chosen by the churches speaks in favor of combining value materiality (ethical) and sustainability materiality (sustainable), i.e., implementing them consistently in one's own investments. The ESG score, which stands for the three sustainability dimensions, i.e., the "sustainable" dimension, must be disclosed in addition to the religion score (generally known as the value score for values-oriented investors), which shows the value dimension, i.e., the "ethical" dimension[14] of the investment. Together, the two scores provide information on how investors are positioned in terms of values and norms and what contributions they make, on the one hand, to their values and, on the other, to sustainable development. Sustainable Wealth Management will not be able to escape this trend if it wants to live up to its high-quality standards vis-à-vis its customers.

Literature

BDSV. (2022). https://www.bdsv.eu/themen/nachhaltigkeit-61.html. Accessed 30.05.2022.

CRIC e.V (Ed.). (2020). *Nachhaltige Finanzen: Durch aktives Aktionärstum und Engagement Wandel bewirken*. Springer Gabler.

DBK, ZdK (Ed.) (2021). *Ethisch-nachhaltig investieren: Eine Orientierungshilfe für Finanzverantwortliche katholischer Einrichtungen in Deutschland* (2nd ed.). German Bishops' Conference.

EKD (Ed.). (2023). *Leitfaden für ethisch-nachhaltige Geldanlage in der evangelischen Kirche* (5 act. ed.). Church Office of the EKD.

EU. (2022). https://ec.europa.eu/commission/presscorner/detail/de/ip_22_711. Accessed 30.05.2022.

[14] However, ethics is not an add on to sustainable investments. It is implicit in all financial investments. Ethics as reflected morality (Wilhelms and Wulsdorf, pp. 13–16) is particularly important for churches because, as explicitly ethical investors, they also consciously reflect their values for financial investments. Since all investments are based on basic moral attitudes and values, every capital investor acts at least as a moral investor, and depending on the degree of reflection, as an ethical investor. Accordingly, morally or ethically "neutral" actions and investments are not possible. Thus, depending on the level of reflection, the characteristic words moral and ethical are not only to be attributed to explicitly values-oriented investors, but to all capital owners, since moral basic attitudes always come into play in investments.

FNG. (2022). Marktbericht Nachhaltige Geldanlagen 2021. https://www.forumng.org/fileadmin/Marktbericht/2022/FNG-Marktbericht_NG_2022-online.pdf. Accessed 07.06.2022.

Huntington, S. (1998). *Kampf der Kulturen: Neugestaltung der Weltpolitik im 21. Jahrhundert* (5th ed.). Goldmann Verlag.

Krijnen, C. (2002). Wert. In M. Düwell, C. Hübenthal, & M. Werner (Eds.), *Handbuch der Ethik* (pp. 527–533). J. B. Metzler.

Lutz-Bachmann. (2021). Werte und Normen. In R. Forst & K. Günther (Eds.), *Normative Ordnungen* (2nd ed., pp. 249–277). Suhrkamp Verlag.

Möllers, C. (2018). *Die Möglichkeit der Normen: Über eine Praxis jenseits von Moralität und Kausalität*. Suhrkamp Verlag.

MSCI. (2022). https://esgmanager.msci.com/esgManager/ (no public access). Accessed 05/30/2022.

Schneidewind, U. (2018). *Die Große Transformation: Eine Einführung in die Kunst gesellschaftlichen Wandels* (3rd ed.). Fischer Verlag.

Swiss Sustainable Finance. (2022). *Glossary*. https://www.sustainablefinance.ch/en/glossary-_content%2D%2D-1%2D%2D3077.html. Accessed 30.05.2022.

Wilhelms, G., & Wulsdorf, H. (2017). *Verantwortung und Gemeinwohl: Wirtschaftsethik - eine neue Perspektive*. Verlag Friedrich Pustet.

Wulsdorf, H. (2018). Nachhaltige Geldanlagen: Ethisches Verständnis - Systematik - Wirkung. In M. Stapelfeldt, M. Granzow, & M. Kopp (Eds.), *Greening Finance: Der Weg in eine nachhaltige Finanzwirtschaft* (pp. 135–152). Logos.

Wulsdorf, H. (2022). Ethisch-nachhaltiges Investment: Ein Beitrag aus der Anlagepraxis der Bank für Kirche und Caritas (BKC). In *Amos international* (Vol. 16(2), pp. 26–34). Aschendorff Verlag.

Chapter 6
Sustainability as an Information Challenge in Asset Management

Marcel Malmendier

6.1 Introduction

To state my view directly and clearly: Sustainability, as ambitious as possible, is the credo of our time. The economy as it is and as it was is not an option for the future. It is the way we produce and consume goods and energy that poses the greatest and most pressing crises today. To mitigate and overcome them, we need the greatest efforts, the best of our creativity and a high willingness to change.

The broad scientific consensus that, without decisive changes, existence-threatening scenarios will occur in the form of climate crises and a decline in the resilience of ecosystems due to biodiversity loss underpins this view. Many in politics and business see the financial industry as having a key role because it is believed to be able to provide decisive impulses and incentives for this change (e.g. CRMRS, 2020; EC, 2018, 2019; SFB, 2021). In addition to the credit system, the area of asset management is considered important, as it is here that important decisions are made about the allocation of capital as a central factor of production in any economic system. Here, changes in investment preferences and actual reallocations of capital can be observed (e.g. GSIA, 2021). These developments are reflected intensively in the discourse on sustainable and climate finance, which aims to develop concepts for the practice of asset management and banking (e.g. Friede et al., 2015; Giglio et al., 2021a; Hong et al., 2020; Krueger et al., 2019; Pástor et al., 2021; Pedersen et al., 2021; Rohleder et al., 2022; Stroebel & Wurgler, 2021; Wendt, 2021).

Sustainability is not a new topic. For more than fifty years, we have been discussing the need for transformation. Today, however, the necessary changes are already underway or imminent. What is new, therefore, are a variety of practical challenges in implementing these transformation processes.

M. Malmendier (✉)
Investmentkontor RheinRhur GmbH, Bochum, Germany
e-mail: marcel.malmendier@ikrr.de

K. Wendt, B. Villhauer (eds.), *Sustainable Wealth Management*, Sustainable Finance,
https://doi.org/10.1007/978-3-031-55505-3_6

6.2 Sustainability as Information Challenge

The challenges of transformation are different in every industry. In the financial industry, whose central raw material is data and information, we face challenges in this area in particular. This is about the fundamental availability, accessibility, reliability and interpretability of data (e.g. Avramov et al., 2022; Berg et al., 2022; Chen et al., 2021; Gibson et al., 2021; Giese et al., 2021; Kalesnik et al., 2020). The aspect of the legal reliability of information to safeguard against liability cases and thus its usability vis-à-vis the public and investors is currently a central international topic (e.g. Linklaters, 2022). In the practice of asset management, we are dealing with the valuation of investment objects such as companies or projects. The challenges are therefore: first, to generate data or make existing data sources available; second, to screen, sort and check data; and third, to evaluate and discursively process data sets so that usable information can be extracted from them. I will call this challenge of data generation, data processing and the production of usable information from this data the information challenge of sustainability.[1]

The sustainability assessment of companies and projects, which has been driven by sustainability pioneers for many years, is now increasingly becoming a general regulatory requirement and a strategic point in the market. This means that data and information on the sustainability of investment objects finds its way into asset management and thus becomes part of the industry raw material.

Asset managements who take up sustainability as a topic have to develop perspectives on sustainability and corresponding patterns of assessment. This development also means that organisations need to evolve. Personal qualifications, the development or change of processes, organisational arrangements, policies and strategies and contributions to internal and sector-wide discourses that are essential for the formation of personal and cultural beliefs are important.

Part of this development of the financial industry towards sustainability are marketing strategies that flag sustainability without adequately backing this up with asset management. Such greenwashing is becoming an issue in the professional community, among regulators and in the legal system as a liability issue (Cherry & Sneirson, 2011; Mitchell & Ramey, 2011).

To understand how deeply rooted such various face-value practices are in the financial industry, a sideways glance at how international associations define "ESG integration"[2] as a sustainability strategy is instructive. One meaning of the term "integration" refers to a state or process in which a new entity emerges by bringing together several separate entities. Another meaning is a kind of inclusion (e.g.

[1] The following observations and descriptions are exclusively qualitative. Theory-based perspectives related to this topic, such as the idea of bounded rationality and decision-making (e.g. Simon, 1966) or information economics (e.g. Stiglitz, 2019), are not discussed in this chapter.

[2] In a PRI publication "ESG integration" is explained as "analysing financial information and ESG information; identifying material financial factors and ESG factors; assessing the potential impact of material financial factors and ESG factors on economic, country, sector, and company performance…" (PRI et al., 2018).

DWDS, 2022). Talking about "ESG integration" implicitly conveys both meanings, which implies the idea that sustainability and financial issues are really brought together. This contrasts with a definition that uses ESG data merely to diagnose financial risks and value drivers. Essential sustainability issues, such as transformational and ethical issues, are subordinated to classical financial analysis objectives. What we can observe here is the occupation of issues through the occupation of terms, designating and simultaneous gutting of term meanings—a well-known discursive power strategy.

Overall, adjustments to asset management practices as well as organisational developments are necessary because what I call the information challenge leads to significantly increased data and information complexity. Complexity here does not only mean an increase in the amount of data points that have to be handled. As well, perspectives and frames for the interpretation of available data on investment objects are gaining in variety. New levels of valuation are emerging, such as ethical, social or climate impact assessments, besides assessing financial data and information, management and organisational performance as well as the competitive position in a specific market segment. Each new data point, each new perspective, each new frame of interpretation and each new level of valuation have to be integrated into workflows, which, by the end of the day, must lead to decisions about investment or divestment.

If we systematise this train of thoughts about the increase in data and information complexity, we can distinguish at least four different challenges. These challenges relate to volumes of data, new and more diverse topics, new and more diverse types of data and what is known in ethics as the difference between being and ought.

1. The amount of data and information to be processed increases because of the current trend towards sustainability. This is due to developments in society, economy, financial markets and regulation.
2. New issues are emerging or, if not new as for the pioneers in sustainable finance, are becoming mandatory and therefore require at least an adaptation of data processing procedures. This means that new or modified perspectives need to be integrated into asset management approaches.
3. Descriptions and thus qualitative data and information are gaining importance in asset management. Descriptions and stories, as condensed, multi layered accounts, can contribute to a holistic view of companies and organisations and their business practices, and thus to a picture of whether they act ambitiously sustainable in the sense of avoiding harmful practices and promoting practices with positive impacts.
4. Ethical questions arise when the difference and sometimes also the experienced tension between what is and can be described (being) and what one desires or can justifiably demand under certain criteria (ought) comes into focus. In asset management, this question arises when it comes to assessing the impact of business models, products, services and value creation processes. Impact is both a question of measurement and description (question of what is) and an ethical

question, namely when it comes to whether we should promote and adopt certain practices (question of what should be).

I will take up these challenges later when describing some types of asset management. First, I would like to make some conceptual clarifications.

6.3 Facing the Information Challenge

6.3.1 Conceptual Reflection: Managed Practices, Knowledge Objects and Organisational Bubbles

In this section, I will discuss and develop some concepts in terms of intellectual tools that help to organise some more detailed observations. The approach, I use here, is both, empirically based and conceptually reflective. From an epistemological, especially phenomenological and constructivist perspective, we always see a "what" under a certain perspective, a "how". The following short remarks on central concepts serve as a brief, suggestive reflection on this "how". Of course, these remarks by no means provide a fully comprehensive account.

The remarks that follow on some empirically based types of asset management are to be understood analogously. However, we are concerned here with managed practices, i.e. with types of more or less deliberate and reflexive action in context, and not with methodological observation. Without being able to develop this analogy in detail here, it can be said that the way we act and the way we organise individual and collective action (question of how we act) opens up certain areas of possibility for what can be produced and achieved (question of what can be done). This systematic reflection on the interlacement of the questions of "how" and "what", today a self-evident part of organisational, strategic, epistemological and methodological discourses, sometimes seems to be a blind spot in finance discourses. As far as I can see, this questioning is rarely as central as the diverse quantitative analyses and their content, namely investment objects and markets, which clearly dominate journals and professional discourses.

The following questions are aimed directly at the combination of "how" and "what" in regard to managed and organised practices, here in the field of asset management. What is the essence and what are the characteristics of different asset management practices? What space of possibility is constituted by a specific asset management practice? What types of data are processed in what way and what types of information and assessments can be generated or processed on this basis? Finally, what contributions to sustainability strategies are possible and can be expected on the basis of this information?

***Concept of Management and Management Practice*[3]**

Without going into practical management and leadership talk and scientific studies in these areas at this point, we can say that the term "management" describes action that is consciously directed towards issues and goals in order to initiate and achieve certain results. As a professional practice, it is to a certain extent reflexive, i.e. it is reviewed and controlled in feedback loops with regard to the results achieved. Management is about the use of means as techniques: Methods, procedures and strategies are used in a targeted and mostly calculated way.

The main motivation to adopt a management perspective here is to find viable ideas that are ready to use and thus, to initiate and promote improvements and changes, or to maintain the status quo at a certain level.

***Concept of Practice and Action*[4]**

The sociological and philosophical term "practice" refers to all action, intentional and/or reflexive action such as management practices as well as intuitive and/or spontaneous action. Furthermore, the term "practice" refers to the empirically observable fact that actions, individual and collective, always take place in meaningful contexts and interact and are interwoven with these contexts. Contexts can be orienting, encouraging, limiting, unifying or disuniting. They can provide resources or ideas. They can objectify or emotionalise. Among other things, this involves observations that psychological and social reality is contingent and variable, i.e. could always be different, without variations being predictable. In other words, each practice has its own dynamics and is only manageable to a certain extent.

The main motivation for taking up a practice perspective here is to better understand the intrinsic dynamics of individual and collective actions and the respective contexts.[5] Such understandings may reveal starting points to initiate changes as well as resistance aimed at the preservation of existing status quos and normalities.

Combing the Ideas of Management and Practice

Combining the ideas of management and practice generates new insights. At the heart of these insights is the tension between a practice perspective that seeks to see *what is* and a management perspective that seeks to intervene and realise *what is wanted and what should be*.

- First, both perspectives have their strengths. A practice perspective is good for perceiving and understanding. A management perspective is good as a shortcut

[3] To keep the text short, I use the term "management" here for both task-oriented management and person-oriented leadership.

[4] For further information on this way of observing and reflecting social reality see Garfinkel, 1967; Geertz, 1973; Goffman, 1974; Hitzler et al., 2020; Honer & Hitzler, 2015; Malmendier, 1995, 2003, 2021; Schatzki, 1996; Schatzki ct al., 2001; Schutz, 1967, 1970; Turner 1994.

[5] Sometimes we encounter a narrow understanding, that practice and (collective) action in context would be linked to the idea of rule-governed, habitual and routine activity (e.g. Knorr Cetina, 2001 refers to this discussion). In my view, creativity and change have always been intrinsically linked to the notions of practice and action (Malmendier, 1995).

or trial to initiate something new and as a resource. In any case, understanding practice can be very fruitful for management.

- The second insight is that these views complement each other. Practices form fundamentally conservative and persistent contexts that, in order to move, keep moving, and reach a certain level, often need impulses. Such impetus can be provided by management. On the other hand, good (i.e. successful and effective) management is more about managed practices as an interaction between a management practice and a non-managed practice than about management as a method, methodology or art.[6]

When we observe asset management practices, we observe managed practices. In the following I will be talking about managed practice in the sense, that I have just described, namely an intertwining of management practices and the dynamics of managed practice.

Concepts of Knowledge Objects and Organisational Bubbles

To understand some typical aspects of asset management practices, I will develop in brief two more specific concepts. Data and information processing in the context of asset management is about research to evaluate investment objects and about investment decisions. Many asset managements are built around pragmatic forms of knowledge production. Within these practices, investment objects are considered as knowledge objects. They are not trivial objects that basically show their characteristics and peculiarities at first glance, either because these are comprehensively known or, because they have simple structures. Knowledge objects need processes and a working through of different perspectives in order to be understood and constituted within a knowledge process.[7]

Working through this requires organisational arrangements. I will figuratively refer to these as organisational bubbles. This metaphor, unlike the often negative image of bubbles bursting, which causes losses and often incomprehension among investors, is meant here in a purely descriptive way. By organisational bubbles, I mean temporary contexts that can easily be initiated and ended again or that end themselves. Bubbles are highly captivating for the actors involved, whose attention they absorb to a large extent, here in the analysis and questioning of investment objects as knowledge objects. On the inside of bubbles, we find a kind of structural openness, so that expertise can unfold and methods can be freely applied, adapted,

[6] Much of the management and leadership literature exhibits this (sometimes narcissistic) belief in feasibility, power and targeted effectiveness, that consciously making a particular difference is a matter of skill. This thinking from a practice point of view is shortening and for this very reason often damaging to the advancement and transformation of existing practices and cultures. Because this is a widespread way of thinking, I will only refer to Malik (2019) as an example, whose explanations of management I consider to be cleverly thought out and practically helpful, but whose texts also contain a strong belief in feasibility.

[7] The similar notion of "epistemic objects" is closely related to qualitative studies on practices of researching objects, specifically from the so-called laboratory studies on scientific knowledge production (Knorr Cetina, 2001). Here I prefer the notion of "knowledge objects", which is less specifically linked to scientific contexts.

changed or newly created, depending on the case and situation. Such bubbles allow open knowledge processes to be built into organisations that, in many facets, are otherwise more oriented towards routines and coordination and thus stand in the way of open and creative processes. When bubbles finally dissolve again, they leave behind a kind of image with more or less memorable results.

The main motivation for introducing these specific concepts here is to point out that the rationality of open research processes can be essential for asset management. This aspect of the openness in knowledge processes is, as far as I can see, largely underestimated in the financial literature and in the practice of asset management. This rationality of open research processes has its very own legitimacy in contrast to a machine-like and rule-based rationality, as we often find in very detailed and highly designed organisational processes.

6.3.2 Learning from Existing Managed Practices[8]

Let us take up the functionalist idea that every practice is a solution, while sometimes it is not obvious for which problem (Mauss, 1990). That's why cultural anthropologists and researchers doing qualitative field observations often ask: What problem do we have the solution for here? This idea gives us a hint that finding solutions to management challenges might primarily be about observing and learning from reality, rather than reading books or asking (so-called or self-proclaimed) experts.

By learning from practice, I don't mean simply copying certain practices. I mean rethinking them, identifying the facets of a practice, deconstructing them and then trying to develop new solutions by putting these facets together in new and different ways. This is partly what I want to convey in this text: I have asked myself what types and ways of managing assets I encounter when I invest in other asset managers strategies and what my colleagues and I have tried both successfully and unsuccessfully in building and managing our own multi-manager strategies over many years. These observations can serve as material for asset managers to create their own organisational arrangements to address key sustainability challenges, among others.

From my point of view, it has proven useful to distinguish between four general types of asset management practice. The distinction between these types results from the two questions of what specific role asset management plays in the selection and evaluation of investment objects and what methods and methodologies are used.

[8] The following qualitative descriptions are based on 15 years of experience in the establishment and supervision of multi-manager investment strategies and continuous contact with investment houses and asset managers, always with the aim of understanding how these managements act and make decisions. In the area of single investments, I designed, introduced, actively participated in and had responsibility for review processes for over 10 years.

6.3.3 Types of Asset Management Practice

In this paragraph, I will be describing these four general types of asset management practices: quantitative, qualitative, single-investment and rule-based asset management. The aim is to describe the basic characteristics of these types and thus how asset management is or can be implemented in practice. I describe these types analytically in terms of patterns of action. Two aspects are important here: First, we rarely find these types in pure form in reality. We mostly find variations and also combinations of different types. The following descriptions specifically look for distinguishing characteristics in order to emphasise certain aspects. Second, we are concerned here with patterns of action and thus precisely not with the personal styles or approaches of certain individual investors. The subject is not the personality of a concrete investor or individual abilities and attitudes. The focus is not on heads but on action and action frameworks. Therefore, books, interviews, speeches and articles in which famous investors describe or have others describe their strategies, at least the parts that are easy to communicate to the public and that they want to disclose, are not the material on which the following descriptions are based.

The subsequent paragraphs are guided by the following questions:

- What role does the asset management play in the selection and valuation of investment objects, in particular what kind of research processes are installed?
- How do these different types of asset management practices deal with the various information challenges posed by a growing amount of data, by an increasing diversity of valuation perspectives trough the sustainability discourse, by a combination of quantitative and qualitative data, and by the consideration of ethical concerns?

In order to present these four types of asset management practices in a comparable way, I have chosen to start with a general description of the managed practice, including basic considerations of how to deal with the informational challenge of sustainability in the context of each type. Then, I briefly focus on central individual aspects that I recognise in each case: the quality of the investment objects as knowledge objects, data processing mechanisms and associated complexity reduction mechanisms, main management challenges, main organisational and procedural challenges and typical possible contributions to sustainability strategies.[9] Some aspects that I understand as being similar within the different types are not presented here such as controlling and organisational learning.

[9] An overview of different ESG strategies is provides by the FNG (2022) or the SSF (2016).

6.3.3.1 Quantitative Asset Management

General Description of Managed Practice

Quantitative financial data and analysis are, as I see it, fundamental to just about all professional investment decisions. The analysis of financial ratios such as turnover, profit, leverage, cash flow, price-earnings ratio, comparisons of ratios between competitors, etc. are key and already have a longer tradition dating back at least to the first half of the twentieth century (e.g. Graham & Dodd, 2008).

Quantitative sustainability analysis uses clearly defined positive and negative investment criteria for which data is available, including estimates. Often these data are binary, i.e. they say whether a criterion is fulfilled or not, or they are about whether certain threshold values on a continuum are reached or not.

In this text, I use the terminology "quantitative asset management" in a broad methodological sense to describe approaches that aim to base investment decisions specifically on quantitative data and analysis.[10] An important development in this area has been taking place for more than 40 years. Since then, more and more managers have been using databases to process growing amounts of data, whose availability in electronic form and accessibility has increased exponentially during this time. Today such data are provided pre-packaged by professional service providers. Parallel to these developments quantitative financial science research has evolved significantly. Against the backdrop of these developments, some authors use the term in a narrower sense. Quantitative asset management for them means asset management that is based on today's data, uses IT-supported analytical tools or automated algorithms and often adopts certain financial science findings. Today, some of these algorithms use artificial intelligence (AI) technologies. To classify this larger development of AI applications, it should be added that AI today cannot be reduced to quantitative knowledge processes. Certain AI applications are capable of fulfilling tasks in the field of qualitative research, e.g. semantic analyses.

For a large group of practitioners and scholars, the argument that quantitative data and analysis in particular are reliable and offer a rational or scientific view on the financial world seems to be a strong one. We find this basic attitude especially in the analysis of investment factors (e.g. Arnott et al., 2019; Baltussen et al., 2021; Bender et al., 2013; Fabozzi, 2022; Fama & French, 1993, 2014; Giglio et al., 2021b; Harvey et al., 2015). For some quantitively oriented managers—sometimes simply called "quants" (e.g. Vescore, 2017) -, the usage of only quantitative data is even a matter of conviction. Data other than quantitative is considered subjective and not sufficiently reliable.[11] A critical stance towards qualitative data is sometimes justified by the possibility of influence in personal conversations and interview

---

[10] Overviews can be found, for example, in *The Journal of Portfolio Management* in 2021 (Fabozzi & Kocdijk, 2021) and in *The Oxford Handbook of Quantitative Asset Management* (Scherer & Winston, 2012).

[11] This epistemologically one-sided view based on the opposition of objective and subjective in relation to data and information is still quite common thinking in the financial industry. To give an example: "What is Qualitative Analysis? In business and management, qualitative analysis uses

situations. Thus, personal contact with representatives of investment objects is often reduced to a minimum.

Knowledge Object Quality of Investment Objects
Within the framework of quantitative analysis, investment objects such as companies or projects are regarded as objects whose essential structures and details can be represented by a set of measurable categories.

Data Processing and Mechanisms to Reduce Data Complexity
Quantitative financial and sustainability data are processed, specifically binary data and threshold data indicating whether a criterion or a measurable threshold on a continuum has been met or not. The main strength of quantitative data is that the complexity reduction is inherent in the data itself, so that it can be easily processed using databases and IT tools as the basis for scalable data processing procedures. Sustainability criteria can be modelled to a large extent so that they can be processed as binary data or thresholds. The same is true for ethical concerns as long as they can be translated into general standards that can be linked to measurable KPIs or simple rules. If this is not the case as in assessing controversies, quantitative research reaches its limits, and qualitative data become important as a basis for (ethical) assessments.

Main Management Challenges
In my view, three points can be made: Find and keep appropriate IT-tools. Organise and finance space and time for situations and procedures, where expertise for quantitative analysis can unfold (see my notion of organisational bubbles above in Sect. 6.3.1). Manage rising complexity and ambiguity through sustainability assessments by integrating qualitative perspectives into the concepts of assessment and providing appropriate concepts for dealing with ethical discussions as well as controversies.

Main Organisational and Procedural Challenges
The definition of a selection process can partly precede the actual decision-making process, mainly by defining investment topics and KPIs to be used. When such organisational techniques of seriality and linearity are used, the pitfalls of exclusions for later selection processes should be well observed: Earlier selections act as a veto for later selections. On the other hand, the pitfalls of 360-degree situations, where anything can become relevant to the selection, should also be well considered. Both techniques can be combined. In summary, techniques of seriality and linearity help to process and reduce large amounts of data. Techniques for 360-degree situations help to keep an open mind and to reflect on the "how" of selection procedures.

---

subjective judgements to analyse the value of a company or prospects based on non-quantifiable information..." (Smith, 2022)

Typical Contributions to Sustainability Strategies
The sustainability strategies "positive criteria" and "negative criteria" in particular can be advanced. The strategies "proxy voting" and "engagement" find a good basis in quantitative data.

6.3.3.2 Qualitative Asset Management

General Description of Managed Practice
In addition to quantitative data and analysis, there is also a qualitative research perspective, which is very common in practical asset management. In financial analysis, this perspective focuses on specific aspects of business models, management practices, competitive advantages and strategies.

Qualitative sustainability analysis examines the more complex impact chains, that cannot be stated in binary form or as a measurable position on a continuum, because we are dealing with intertwined interdependencies, and contingent cause-effect relationships.[12] These are intended and unintended social and ecological effects of business models, products, services and value creation processes for which no technical KPIs are available. At the same time, it is about the ethical assessment of such effects, in particular to find case-appropriate criteria and maxims through a multi-perspective and multi-layer understanding of a situation on the basis of which we can make such evaluations.

Qualitative perspectives in investment research are, as far as I know, only rarely used in an isolated way without quantitative perspectives. Today, even if asset managers rely strongly on qualitative analysis in their processes, in most cases they use a quantitative lens as well, combining these two basic methodological orientations. Sometimes qualitative data and analysis are seen as a complementary view and enrichment of quantitative data. Sometimes the view is vice versa, that financial data and analysis serve as a kind of corrective for qualitative assessments.

Those managers who use qualitative data and analysis are, in my impression, usually very open minded to multi-perspective views and thus for quantitative data and analysis. I suspect that qualitative discourse in general is open to the said argument of "two sides of the same coin" because of its inherent implicit constructivist epistemological assumptions: qualitative and quantitative approaches are seen as mutually enriching, very much like an understanding of qualitative and quantitative social research as complementary approaches. Interestingly and consistently, with implicit epistemologies, we do not see in qualitative perspectives the tendency to claim a principally superior position in analysis. Unfortunately, we still find this attitude in a lot of quantitative approaches, which is in contrast to modern methodological and epistemological thinking.

[12]As far as I can see, this perspective, which has been well established in sociology and social philosophy for about one hundred years, is not adequately taken up in the current discussion on "impact" and "impact investing", which leads to a shortening of the topic and, as a consequence, to possibly bad regulation.

Knowledge Object Quality of Investment Objects
Within the framework of qualitative analysis, investment objects are regarded as holistic objects whose essential structures and details can only be fully understood by multi-layer and multi-perspective observations. Measurability is often possible, but not a criterion for the validity of insights.

Data Processing and Mechanisms to Reduce Data Complexity
Qualitative financial and sustainability data are mainly processed by various forms of texts, videos and pictures containing descriptions, interviews, notes or condensed stories encompassing multiple perspectives or voices. The main strength of qualitative data is that it provides multiple impressions for a specific case. To reduce complexity in the research process, asset managers need to be highly selective when using qualitative methods as an in-depth research process. In contrast to quantitative data analysis, reading, communicating and understanding cases are main sources. Sustainability insights may be inherent in case-related material that is being scrutinised. Ethical considerations have a better basis than with only quantitative data, because the ethical question of how we should act is always at least partly a question of how general ideas and standards of good and bad can be used and applied to a concrete case.

Main Management Challenges
In my view the following points are important: Organise and finance space and time for situations and procedures in which this specific expertise can be applied (see my notion of organisational bubbles above in Sect. 6.3.1). Usually, the combination of this expertise with quantitative research is important to keep track of the markets and their investment opportunities. Develop and continuously define selection criteria for cases to go through such an in-depth research process. Provide concepts for dealing with ambiguity and ethical discussions as well as controversies.

Main Organisational and Procedural Challenges
Qualitative in-depth analysis in most cases is combined with quantitative research, which may provide an overview of the market. The discussion in this paper highlights some main purposes of these different management approaches. Defining detailed objectives based on these purposes that can be pursued in practice will set the agenda for procedural organisational designs.

Typical Contributions to Sustainability Strategies
All sustainability strategies can be advanced with qualitative asset management practices. In particular, strong ESG integration encompassing people, processes, organisations, policies, strategies, and IT systems will benefit from a strong culture of qualitative research, as an openness to ask questions and develop nuanced, new and creative perspectives require appropriate capabilities from people and organisations.

6.3.3.3 Project-Oriented Investments and Other Single Investment[13]

General Description of Managed Practice

Here, the general description is identical to that of a combined quantitative and qualitative asset management methodology, but in many cases with one significant difference. Most asset managers construct diversified portfolios. Investors or organisations bundling the participation of many investors in single investments tend to control larger shares of the investment object. Due to this fact and to risk-concerns when investing without diversification, investors tend to have stronger interests in the well-being of a single investment.

In private equity or investments in single projects this often refers to positions that formally allow a say or are dominant. Such positions tend to change the role of the investor. In such a case, the asset manager deciding on an individual investment may become a kind of external peer for the internal corporate finance manager with various, often informal, means of influence. If the asset manager has a dominant position in the corporate law sense, he may himself take on the role of a corporate finance manager and thus take the lead in financial decision-making. Or his role may contain elements of both, namely that of a traditional external asset manager and that of an internally influential person who exercises influence, for example, as a member of the board of directors on the basis of major shareholdings.

Knowledge Object Quality of Investment Objects

The same applies here as for quantitative management in combination with qualitative management. For the challenge of emotional proximity to the investment object, see the comments on procedural organisational challenges. Such proximity can lead to positive prejudice (from sympathy to fascination) and motivation for a speedy implementation of an investment, making further critical analysis seem rather superfluous.

Data Processing and Mechanisms to Reduce Data Complexity

The same applies here as for quantitative management in combination with qualitative management.

Main Management Challenges

In my view, the following points are important: Organise and finance space and time for situations and procedures, where in-depth case analysis can be exercised (see my notion of organisational bubbles above in Sect. 6.3.1). Because in some segments there is no continuous market, investments in networks to get in contact with interesting investment objects may be crucial. Provide concepts for dealing with ambiguity and ethical discussions as well as controversies.

---

[13] In my own practice of asset management, I introduced this notion of single investment to contrast possible asset management roles as well as default risks in contrast to investments in diversified portfolios. Despite a widespread use of this notion in corporate and asset management practice, my impression is that it is not a technical term in the sense I use it here.

Main Organisational and Procedural Challenges
Integrating a qualitative and quantitative case study methodology, including segmental market overviews, is key to investing in projects and individual investments. Due to the often intense relationship with the investment, issue or people, one challenge is that sympathies and emotions can interfere with analysis. Therefore, the organisation should encourage using the energies of heart and mind separately, without creating procedures where one side dominates.

Typical Contributions to Sustainability Strategies
All sustainability strategies can be advanced with single investment practices.

6.3.3.4 Rule-Based Asset Management

General Description of Managed Practice
Rule-based practices of asset management select investment objects like quantitative asset management approaches through the use of quantitative data and algorithms that apply certain KPIs and rules in the sense of if-then-relations. These can refer to a bundle of different data categories such as asset class, region, thematic focus, market capitalisation, valuation, fundamental weight or various factors such as size, value, momentum, etc. Nevertheless, it makes sense to differentiate between quantitative asset management approaches and rule-based approaches.

Quantitative management is a form of asset management and, thus, a managed practice. This means that in this approach, acting, acting in context and defining situations by trying to make sense of events are central categories. Making sense is a complex and contingent process within which applying, modifying and creating schemas is essential. The fact that many techniques and methods used are based on extensive mathematisation and on formalised insights from quantitative financial science is a matter of practical implementation. This is part of a practice. It is important to stress here, that rules and their trials in practice are seen as a means to master complex and dynamic situations in the capital market, and not as the essence of a rational approach. The individual and collective ability to frame situations and to develop schemas of interpretation is still seen as a main potential.

Rule-based investments are using predefined quantitative algorithms, often praising the advantage of a machine rationality, which will apply the highly controlled knowledge of quantitative capital market research. As I see it, there are two crucial differences to quantitative asset management that can be observed: First, the rules that are applied are in most cases of a rather general nature and are not based on current interpretations of capital market situations. Second, the research and the selection of the set of rules to determine the investment objects to be invested in, such as stocks, bonds, commodities, etc. take place some time before the investor's investment decision. Thus, both the research and the investment decision of an investor are separated in time, which is precisely not the case with other investment approaches. This can, of course, have advantages if the asset management is poorly managed and organised, but it can also have disadvantages in the opposite case.

The most famous case of rule-based investments is the usage of a predefined index, for example by using exchange traded funds and exchange traded commodities. Here, the essence of indexing is defining or selecting tested rules and applying them. In the last 20 to 30 years, other forms of rules-based investing have also become popular, such as robo-advisers and high-frequency trading. These are investments based on algorithms that automate decisions on asset allocations, diversification and the selection of specific financial instruments.

Knowledge Object Quality of Investment Objects
Here, I observe the processes of research and investment decisions. Research is outsourced in the sense described above. In investment decisions, the basic investment objects such as shares, bonds, derivatives, etc. also have no knowledge object quality.

During the research, that is necessary to set up a rule-based financial instrument itself, investment objects are treated similarly to quantitative asset management approaches as objects whose essential structures and details can be represented by a set of measurable categories.

To avoid mixing up the approaches, I would like to emphasise here that studying a rule-based financial instrument in an asset management setting is something else entirely. For this study the research approach can be quantitative, qualitative, single-investment oriented or rule-based.

Data Processing and Mechanisms to Reduce Data Complexity
This is part of the outsourced rule-based process to set up the financial instrument. The essence of this process is a quantitative research process, with some specifics in research and rule-selection, which I will not be going into in this text.

Main Management Challenges
The same applies as for data processing.

Main Organisational and Procedural Challenges
Here, too, the same applies as for data processing.

Typical Contributions to Sustainability Strategies
As with quantitative asset management, the sustainability strategies 'positive criteria' and 'negative criteria' in particular can be advanced.

6.4 Summary

If the thesis is true that the challenge of sustainability in the financial industry is primarily an informational challenge, then the accessibility, availability, reliability and interpretability of data are crucial. It is helpful to master a variety of ways to address this challenge. Quantitative approaches, as prevalent in the industry, are powerful but also limiting. The text shows that processing data and information can be done in different ways, with typically different results.

This leads to the question of how to develop or find such different types in an effective and efficient way. Here, the observation of different existing practices can be used as an inexhaustible learning programme. By the way, bionics work in the field of nature, just like practitioners who observe what people do or sociologists who do field research. Four types of asset management are described in this text: quantitative, qualitative, single investment, and rule-based asset management. These four types can be used as building blocks to enrich and further develop one's own asset management—of course with the necessary sensitivity for people, situations and organisations. In contrast to a child playing with building blocks, a good understanding of practices is important, because feedback on whether or not various practices fit together in a certain way is often detected too late in social reality. By then, a lot could have gone wrong.

Something very similar happened in the global economic system: The functioning and the intended as well as unintended consequences of the global economic system were not well understood by us. And it took a long time for the planet to send the first serious feedback. Without science, we probably wouldn't have yet noticed much of this feedbacks. Nevertheless, we have tended to look the other way for far too long and shied away from the strenuous processes of change. Now we have to make up for it.

References

Arnott, R. D., Harvey, C. R., Kalesnik, V., & Linnainmaa, J. T. (2019). *Alice's adventures in Factorland: Three blunders that Plague factor investing*. https://ssrn.com/abstract=3331680 (downloaded 20.08.2022). https://doi.org/10.2139/ssrn.3331680

Avramov, D., Cheng, S., Lioui, A., & Tarelli, A. (2022). Sustainable investing with ESG rating uncertainty. *Journal of Financial Economics, 145*(2), 642–664. https://doi.org/10.1016/j.jfineco.2021.09.009

Baltussen, G., Swinkels, L., & Van Vliet, P. (2021). Global factor premiums. *Journal of Financial Economics, 142*(3), 1128–1154. https://doi.org/10.1016/j.jfineco.2021.06.030

Bender, J., Briand, R., Melas, D., & Subramanian, R. A. (2013). *MSCI research insight*. Foundations of Factor Investing. MSCI. https://www.msci.com/documents/1296102/1336482/Foundations_of_Factor_Investing.pdf/004e02ad-6f98-4730-90e0-ea14515ff3dc (downloaded 15.01.2022)

Berg, F., Kölbel, J. F., & Rigobon, R. (2022). Aggregate confusion: The divergence of ESG ratings. *Review of Finance*, 1–30. https://doi.org/10.1093/rof/rfac033

Chen, M., von Behren, R., & Mussalli, G. (2021). The unreasonable attractiveness of more ESG data. *The Journal of Portfolio Management, 48*(1), 147–162. https://doi.org/10.3905/jpm.2021.1.281

Cherry, M. A., & Sneirson, J. F. (2011). Beyond profit: Rethinking corporate social responsibility and greenwashing after the BP oil disaster. *Tulane Law Review, 85*(4), 983–1038. https://doi.org/10.2139/ssrn.1670149

CRMRS – Climate-Related Market Risk Subcommittee. (2020). *Managing climate risk in the U.S. Financial System*. Washington, D.C.: U.S. Commodity Futures Trading Commission, Market Risk Advisory Committee. https://www.cftc.gov/sites/default/files/2020-09/9-9-20%20Report%20of%20the%20Subcommittee%20on%20Climate-Related%20Market%20Risk%20-%20Managing%20Climate%20Risk%20in%20the%20U.S.%20Financial%20System%20for%20posting.pdf (downloaded 15.04.2022).

DWDS – Digitales Wörterbuch der deutschen Sprache. (2022). Integrieren, ed. Berlin-Brandenburgische Akademie der Wissenschaften. https://www.dwds.de/wb/integrieren (downloaded 20.07.2022).

EC – European Commission. (2018). *Action plan: Financing sustainable growth*. https://eur-lex.europa.eu/legal-content/DE/TXT/PDF/?uri=CELEX:52018DC0097&from=EN (downloaded 20.05.2022).

EC – European Commission. (2019). *The European Green Deal*. https://eur-lex.europa.eu/legal-content/EN/TXT/?qid=1576150542719&uri=COM%3A2019%3A640%3AFIN (downloaded 20.05.2022).

Fabozzi, F. J. (2022). Editor's introduction for 2022 special issue on factor investing. *The Journal of Portfolio Management, Quantitative Special Issue, 48*(2), 1–6. https://doi.org/10.3905/jpm.2021.48.2.001

Fabozzi, F. J., & Koedijk, K. (2021). Editors' introduction to the special issue on investment models. *The Journal of Portfolio Management, 47*(5), 1–5. https://doi.org/10.3905/jpm.2021.47.5.001

Fama, E. F., & French, K. R. (1993). Common risk factors in the returns on stocks and bonds. *Journal of Financial Economics, 33*(1), 3–56. https://doi.org/10.1016/0304-405X(93)90023-5

Fama, E. F., & French, K. R. (2014). *A Five-Factor Asset Pricing Model*. Fama-Miller Working Paper. https://ssrn.com/abstract=2287202 (downloaded 30.07.2022). https://doi.org/10.2139/ssrn.2287202.

FNG – Forum Nachhaltige Geldanlage. (2022). *Nachhaltige Geldanlagen*. https://www.forum-ng.org/de/markt/nachhaltige-anlagestrategien (downloaded 15.08.2022).

Friede, G., Busch, T., & Bassen, A. (2015). ESG and financial performance: Aggregated evidence from more than 2000 empirical studies. *Journal of Sustainable Finance & Investment, 5*(4), 210–233. https://doi.org/10.1080/20430795.2015.1118917

Garfinkel, H. (1967). *Studies in ethnomethodology*. Prentice-Hall.

Geertz, C. (1973). Thick description: Toward an interpretive theory of culture. In C. Geertz (Ed.), *The interpretation of cultures. Selected essays* (pp. 3–30). Basic Books.

Gibson, R., Krueger, P., & Schmidt, P. S. (2021). *ESG Rating disagreement and stock returns (December 22, 2019)*. Swiss Finance Institute Research Paper No. 19–67, European Corporate Governance Institute – Finance Working Paper No. 651/2020. https://doi.org/10.2139/ssrn.3433728.

Giese, G., Nagy, Z., & Lee, L.-E. (2021). Deconstructing ESG ratings performance: Risk and return for E, S, and G by Time Horizon, sector, and weighting. *The Journal of Portfolio Management, 47*(3), 94–111. https://doi.org/10.3905/jpm.2020.1.198

Giglio, S., Kelly, B., & Stroebel, J. (2021a). Climate Finance. *Annual Review of Financial Economics, 13*, 15–36. https://doi.org/10.1146/annurev-financial-102620-103311

Giglio, S., Kelly, B., & Xiu, D. (2021b). *Factor models, machine learning, and asset pricing*. https://ssrn.com/abstract=3943284 (downloaded 30.07.2022). https://doi.org/10.2139/ssrn.3943284.

Goffman, E. (1974). *Frame analysis. An essay on the organization of experience*. Harper and Row.

Graham, B., & Dodd, D. L. (2008). *Security analysis* (6th ed.). McGraw-Hill Education.

GSIA – Global Sustainable Investment Alliance. (2021). *Global Sustainable Investment Review 2020*. http://www.gsi-alliance.org/wp-content/uploads/2021/08/GSIR-20201.pdf (downloaded 20.07.2022).

Harvey, C. R., Liu, Y., & Zhu, H. (2015). … and the cross-section of expected returns. *The Review of Financial Studies, 29*(1), 5–68. https://doi.org/10.1093/rfs/hhv059

Hitzler, R., Reichertz, J., & Schröer, N. (2020). Zwei Jahrzehnte Hermeneutische Wissenssoziologie. Ausbau und Differenzierung. In R. Hitzler, J. Reichertz, & N. Schröer (Eds.), *Kritik der Hermeneutischen Wissenssoziologie* (pp. 9–24). Beltz Juventa.

Honer, A., & Hitzler, R. (2015). Life-world-analytical ethnography. A phenomenology-based research approach. *Journal of Contemporary Ethnography, 44*(5), 544–562. https://doi.org/10.1177/0891241615588589

Hong, H., Andrew Karolyi, G., & Scheinkman, J. A. (2020). Climate Finance. *The Review of Financial Studies, 33*(3), 1011–1023. https://doi.org/10.1093/rfs/hhz146

Kalesnik, V., Wilkens, M., & Zink, J. (2020). *Green Data or Greenwashing? do corporate carbon emissions data enable investors to mitigate climate change?* https://doi.org/10.2139/ssrn.3722973 (Working Paper, downloaded 30.08.2022, removed from ssrn 12.09.2022). The Journal of Portfolio Management (in print).

Knorr Cetina, K. (2001). Objectual practice. In T. R. Schatzki, K. Knorr-Cetina, & E. von Savigny (Eds.), *The practice turn in contemporary theory* (pp. 175–188). Routledge.

Krueger, P., Sautner, Z., & Starks, L. T. (2019). *The importance of climate risks for institutional investors*. Swiss Finance Institute Research Paper No. 18-58, European Corporate Governance Institute - Finance Working Paper No. 610/2019. https://doi.org/10.2139/ssrn.3235190.

Linklaters. (2022). *Banking litigation: A look ahead.* https://www.linklaters.com/en/insights/publications/year-review-year-to-come/2021-2022/legal-topics/banking-litigation-2022-a-look-ahead (downloaded 30.08.2022).

Malik, F. (2019). *Führen Leisten Leben. Wirksames Management für eine neue Welt.* Campus.

Malmendier, M. (1995). *Selbstverständlich, adäquat, normal. Überlegungen zur Soziologie der Normalität.* Master thesis. University Bielefeld.

Malmendier, M. (2003). *Kommunikations- und Verhaltenstraining in Organisationen. Zur Interventionspraxis in der Personalentwicklung.* Campus.

Malmendier, M. (2021). About bridges and goals. On the art of change management as a bridge to the goals for a sustainable world and a world of sustainable investing. In K. Wendt (Ed.), *Theories of change. Change leadership tools, models and applications for investing in sustainable development* (pp. 13–39). Springer. https://doi.org/10.1007/978-3-030-52275-9

Mauss, M. (1990). *Die Gabe. Die Form und Funktion des Austauschs in archaischen Gesellschaften.* Suhrkamp.

Mitchell, L., & Ramey, W. (2011). Look how green I am! An individual-level explanation for greenwashing. *Journal of Applied Business and Economics, 12*(6), 40–45. https://ssrn.com/abstract=2409956 (downloaded 20.07.2022)

Pástor, Ľ., Stambaugh, R. F., & Taylor, L. A. (2021). Sustainable investing in equilibrium. *Journal of Financial Economics, 142*(2), 550–571. https://doi.org/10.1016/j.jfineco.2020.12.011

Pedersen, L. H., Fitzgibbons, S., & Pomorski, L. (2021). Responsible investing: The ESG-efficient frontier. *Journal of Financial Economics, 142*(2), 572–597. https://doi.org/10.1016/j.jfineco.2020.11.001

PRI et al – Principles of Responsible Investment and CFA Institute. (2018). *ESG in equity analysis and credit analysis. An Overview.* https://www.unpri.org/download?ac=4571 (downloaded 30.07.2022).

Rohleder, M., Wilkens, M., & Zink, J. (2022). The effects of mutual fund decarbonization on stock prices and carbon emissions. *Journal of Banking & Finance, 134*, Article 106352. https://doi.org/10.1016/j.jbankfin.2021.106352

Schatzki, T. R. (1996). *Social practices. A Wittgensteinian approach to human activity and the social.* CUP.

Schatzki, T. R., Knorr-Cetina, K., & von Savigny, E. (2001). *The practice turn in contemporary theory.* Routledge.

Scherer, B., & Winston, K. (Eds.). (2012). *The Oxford handbook of quantitative asset management.* Oxford University Press.

Schutz, A. (1967). *The phenomenology of the social world.* Northwestern University Press.

Schutz, A. (1970). *Reflections on the problem of relevance.* Yale University Press.

SFB – Sustainable Finance Beirat. (2021). *Shifting the Trillions. Ein nachhaltiges Finanzsystem für die Große Transformation. 31 Empfehlungen des Sustainable-Finance-Beirats an die Bundesregierung.* Sustainable-Finance-Beirat der Bundesregierung. https://sustainable-finance-beirat.de/wp-content/uploads/2021/02/210224_SFB_-Abschlussbericht-2021.pdf (downloaded 20.05.2022)

Simon, H. A. (1966). Theories of decision-making in economics and behavioural science. In *Surveys of economic theory* (Vol. III, pp. 1–28). The American Economic Association, The Royal Economic Society, Palgrave Macmillan. https://doi.org/10.1007/978-1-349-00210-8_1

Smith, T. (2022). Qualitative analysis. In *Investopedia*. https://www.investopedia.com/terms/q/qualitativeanalysis.asp (downloaded 15.08.2022)

SSF – Swiss Sustainable Finance. (2016). Handbuch nachhaltige Anlagen. https://www.sustainablefinance.ch/upload/cms/user/SSF_Handbuch_Nachhaltige_Anlagen_2016_11_28_einseitig_Web.pdf (downloaded 15.08.2022).

Stiglitz, J. (2019). The revolution of information economics: The past and the future. In K. Basu, D. Rosenblatt, & C. Sepúlveda (Eds.), *The state of economics, the state of the world* (pp. 101–138). MIT Press.

Stroebel, J., & Wurgler, J. (2021). What do you think about climate finance? *Journal of Financial Economics, 142*(2), 487–498. https://doi.org/10.1016/j.jfineco.2021.08.004

Turner, S. P. (1994). *The social theory of practices. Tradition, tacit knowledge and presuppositions*. Polity.

Vescore. (2017). *Warum Quant?*. https://am.vontobel.com/de/insights/why-quant (downloaded 10.04.2022).

Wendt, K. (2021). Theory of change: Defining the research agenda. In K. Wendt (Ed.), *Theories of change. Change leadership tools, models and applications for investing in sustainable development* (pp. 3–12). Springer. https://doi.org/10.1007/978-3-030-52275-9

Chapter 7
Sustainability Across Different Asset Classes: Integration in a Multi-asset Portfolio

Daniel Sailer and Martin Buchner

Institutional investors are increasingly integrating ESG criteria into their decision-making processes; at the same time, regulatory requirements are rising. In the following, we explain how ESG criteria can be taken into account together with regulatory requirements in an asset–liability study and then implemented in the portfolio construction of a multi-asset portfolio.

7.1 Stakeholders and Regulation Set Standards

The results of a 2019 McKinsey survey of more than 500 decision-makers and investment professionals show that pressure from analysts and non-governmental organizations (NGOs), for example, continues to grow to consider ESG criteria in corporate management or investments—i.e., to incorporate environmental, social, and governance issues into strategic and operational decisions. According to the survey, 83% of board-level executives and investment professionals expect ESG programs to contribute more to shareholder value in five years than they do today.

Compared to previous surveys, there has also been an increase in the number of executives and investors who believe that incorporating ESG criteria will improve financial metrics—not least because of rising expectations and scrutiny from investors, consumers, employees, and other stakeholders. Apart from this, institutional investors such as insurance companies and institutions for occupational retirement provisions (IORPs) are confronted with increasing regulatory requirements. This

D. Sailer (✉)
Sustainable Investment Office, Frankfurt, Hesse, Germany
e-mail: daniel.sailer@metzler.com

M. Buchner
Asset Allocation Team, Metzler Asset Management, Frankfurt, Hesse, Germany

K. Wendt, B. Villhauer (eds.), *Sustainable Wealth Management*, Sustainable Finance,
https://doi.org/10.1007/978-3-031-55505-3_7

concerns stricter requirements on the transparency of investments and the use of strategies to monitor and measure sustainability risks.

7.2 Sustainability Criteria in the Asset–Liability Study

Due to the increasing importance of ESG criteria, institutional investors have added ESG exclusion criteria to their investment guidelines in recent years. In addition to companies that are active in so-called "controversial" business areas such as armaments, companies that violate international standards, such as those of the UN Global Compact Initiative, are increasingly being excluded from the investment universe. How do such adjusted investment guidelines affect the expected returns? What recommendations for action can be derived from this?

To answer these questions, sustainability criteria must be integrated into an asset–liability study. With the help of such studies, strategic allocations on the one hand and liabilities on the other, for example for pensions, can be projected simultaneously into the future on the basis of various stochastic scenarios for defined risk factors. The defined risk factors include interest rates, credit spreads, and the expected values for the development of returns on risk assets such as shares.

By integrating ESG criteria into an asset–liability study, statements can be made about the influence of sustainability preferences on the degree to which assets are financed against pension obligations.

7.3 Influence on Return Potential

By including individual ESG exclusion criteria in a model portfolio, we have investigated the influence of sustainability preferences on (potential) portfolio performance for the period 6 April 2010 to 6 April 2020 as part of an asset–liability study.

In principle, we use the expected values for the risk assets for our studies, which are derived from the models and forecasts of our chief economist Edgar Walk. If clients also want sustainability criteria included in the selection and management of their investments, we modify the analyses to include an "ESG impact." The resulting differences between the asset returns, i.e., with and without taking into account the ESG filter, emerge, which include the business areas of animal testing, coal-fired power generation, fracking, and tobacco. The lower historical return in the asset classes High Yield EUR and Investment Grade USD (see Fig. 7.1) is due to the additional exclusion of utilities and oil and gas companies from the bond universe. This effect could be reversed in the future during the transition to a low-carbon economy.

For the model portfolio, we have fully replicated the strategic asset allocation, simulated the development over ten years, and calculated the benchmark returns with or without the controversial companies from the investment universe. The

Share in %; difference in % points, gross return excluding all costs incurred at investor level (e.g. transaction costs).

Benchmark	Benchmark return p. a.	Benchmark return p. a. when applying ESG filter to a model portfolio
Investmentgrade EUR	1,0 %	0,50 %
High Yield EUR	2,40 %	0,25 %
Investmentgrade USD	4,90 %	2,00 %
MSCI World	6,50 %	14,00 %

Source: Metzler

Fig. 7.1 Replication of a sample portfolio over ten years, April 6, 2010 to April 6, 2020

calculation is static, so we have left all assumptions constant in our back-test, for example, on the controversial holdings.

In our analyses, we disregard excess returns—in the example of the MSCI World using the ESG filter—when adjusting the return expectations in accordance with the principle of prudence. Negative return impacts, on the other hand, lead us to adjust the return expectations of the assets in the study by an ESG impact. For example, the exclusion of energy and utility companies through ESG filters leads to a significantly lower return on fixed-income securities, especially in the high-yield universe.

7.4 ESG Integration in a Multi-asset Mandate

Mixed funds or multi-asset funds enjoy a high demand among institutional investors, as these products are characterized by a high degree of customizability coupled with very good diversification properties.

In view of highly valued stock markets and historically low interest rates, however, multi-asset portfolios are expected to yield significantly lower returns than they did a few years ago. In addition, as a result of the zero interest rate policy of leading central banks, the traditional diversification characteristics of government bonds have been reduced, as the scope for further declining yields has been largely exhausted. This means that possible price losses on the stock markets can no longer be compensated to the usual extent.

For investors, this means that they have to act more actively than before in order not to be fully exposed to the trend toward lower returns with more risk. The challenge here is to make effective use of short-term market opportunities without losing sight of the long-term investment objective. In addition to the goal of a return in line with the market, investors are focusing on additional issues. For example, a noticeable trend toward sustainable investment strategies has been evident for several years. This trend presents new opportunities and challenges not only for institutional investors but also for investment managers.

ESG integration—the inclusion of environmental, social, and governance aspects in traditional investment analysis—aims to improve the risk-return profile of funds. In our fundamental multi-asset strategies, we implement sustainability criteria in both mutual funds and special funds. In the case of special funds, client-specific sustainability criteria can be agreed upon, which we take into account in the selection and allocation process.

7.5 Results of the Asset–Liability Study Flow into Portfolio Construction

Before launching a special fund, for example, in the context of assuming pension obligations, we support investors with our special know-how in asset–liability management. The results of the asset–liability study are incorporated into the portfolio construction. The starting point is ESG criteria developed together with the investor. Within the framework of the asset–liability study, the effects of, for example, the exclusion of certain companies from the investment universe on the portfolio performance are analyzed and integrated into the management of the capital investment—as in the case of our multi-asset mandates (see Fig. 7.2). The close cooperation of our experts from the areas of sustainability, economics, portfolio management, and pension management enables us to advise our clients holistically and to smoothly implement their individual and regulatory requirements in their capital investments.

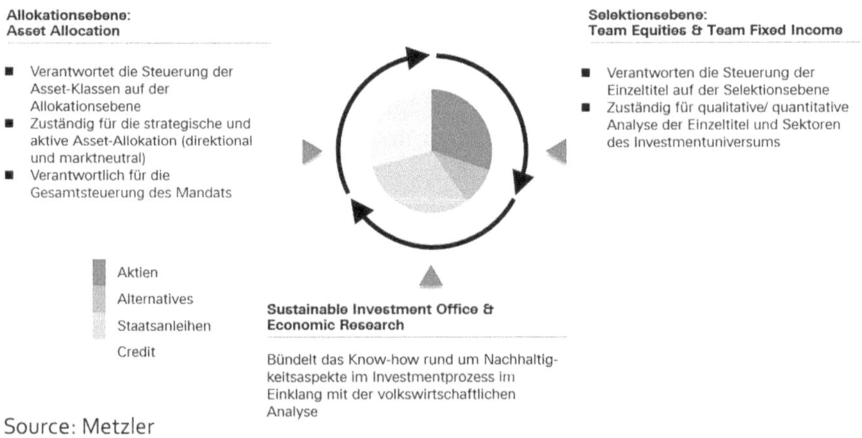

Fig. 7.2 The three dimensions of portfolio construction at Metzler

7.6 Strategic Asset Allocation: The Basis of the Investment Strategy

The basis for long-term investment success is a broadly diversified strategic asset allocation (SAA). At the beginning of the portfolio construction process, we concentrate on deriving the right strategy for our clients. In this context, we always assess asset classes in the context of the overall macroeconomic picture and derive a strategic asset allocation tailored to the client's risk-return profile.

In order to derive a sustainable and ESG-compliant strategic asset allocation, the set of selection criteria must be expanded in such a way that sustainability aspects can already be taken into account when building the portfolio. The fact that both the SAA and the sustainability aspects should be geared to the long term alone gives rise to useful synergies.

7.7 SAA with Consistent ESG Integration Poses a Variety of Challenges

In the case of an SAA with (overly) strict sustainability requirements, it should be noted that an allocation in some asset classes poses challenges for portfolio management due to critical issues in the environmental, social, and governance areas. For example, when including alternative investments such as gold, attention must be paid to the environmental impact of mining and working conditions. Gold serves as an important diversifier in the portfolio, as the safe haven character of this asset class has proven itself, especially in times of crisis and when interest income is lacking. As an alternative to completely foregoing gold investments as a result of ESG controversies, we offer investors the option of investing via an ETC (Exchange-Traded Commodity) that is backed by gold bars procured from 2012 onward and thus fulfills the requirements of the "Responsible Sourcing Program" of the London Bullion Market Association (LBMA). This program is based on the requirements from the OECD Guidelines for Responsible Supply Chains of Minerals from Conflict-Affected and Therefore High-Risk Areas. This includes recommendations to enable companies to procure minerals responsibly, i.e., without contributing to conflict and disregarding human rights.

The SAA can be implemented both through active individual stock selection and through passive products.

Implementation via individual securities enables the inclusion of individual positive and negative lists.

In principle, the integration of sustainability components at the individual stock level is carried out throughout the entire investment process of the stock- and pension-specific lists. Systematic and sector-specific ESG research processes and ESG screenings for a sustainable selection of individual equities, government, and corporate bonds (incl. green bonds) aim to improve long-term risk-adjusted performance. In addition, it is possible to take into account individual positive or negative lists, which the investor draws up together with the special lists of the Metzler Sustainable Investment Office and which are updated regularly. A particular focus can be placed on special topics, such as the exclusion of companies from the weapons, tobacco, or alcohol sectors from the investment universe. The lists are then implemented in the trading system, whereby buy orders for individual securities can be automatically checked for possible active violations of sustainability criteria even before they are sent to trading.

In the case of passive violations of the positive or negative lists, the security in question is sold in a previously defined process.

ETFs can only approximate client ESG requirements.

ETFs (exchange-traded funds) are particularly suitable as a supplement to active stock selection or for building up a passive portfolio that includes sustainability criteria. The great demand in the field of ESG has led to ETF providers introducing a wide range of sustainable products. Here, it is important to always keep an eye on the supply and the development of the market. At Metzler Asset Management, there is also the fact that ETFs have to meet special criteria in order for the portfolio management to be allowed to invest in these instruments. Among other things, the ETFs must be of a certain size and have established a good track record compared to the benchmark.

When selecting sustainable products, the chosen degree of ESG integration must also be taken into account because not every product type fulfills the required ESG criteria and the resulting exclusions equally. Rather, the devil is in the detail: for example, some ETFs exclude the manufacturers of unconventional weapons from the investment universe but not the manufacturers of conventional weapons. The chosen ESG strategy is also highly relevant when it comes to assessing the intensity of ESG integration of individual ETFs. For example, in some strategies, only the weights of the individual stocks are adjusted compared to the benchmark (i.e., not completely excluded from the portfolio); other strategies only invest in companies with the best ESG rating in a sector, which means that, for example, at least the shares of a weapons manufacturer are still represented in the portfolio.

In order to be able to make a custom-fit selection of passive products with ESG integration for the client, the portfolio management must therefore have a good overview of the degree of ESG integration and of the product structure. It should also be noted that ETFs physically replicate their benchmark index, which introduces further imponderables in terms of ESG. In synthetic replication, the ETF acquires an equity portfolio and swaps the performance of its portfolio with the performance of the replicated index using derivative financial instruments (swaps). In addition to the counterparty risk, which the investor also bears, it is difficult in such cases to determine which securities are included in the underlying portfolio of the ETF and whether they meet certain sustainability criteria.

At Metzler Asset Management, we have therefore created a database that portfolio managers can use to compare individual ESG products by region and asset class and monitor their performance. It also classifies the extent to which the ETFs reflect sustainability criteria. The advantages of implementing sustainable capital investment via ETFs are considered to be both the low costs and the broad diversification. However, individual ESG criteria can only be fulfilled approximately via ETF investments, as the investor cannot influence the exclusion of companies from the investment universe of the portfolio.

In addition to the information from the above-mentioned database, Metzler Asset Management has access to ESG key figures for over 100,000 target funds and ETFs, which can be extracted from a review of the fund holding companies' documentation. Together with the experts from the Sustainable Investment Office, the portfolio managers can thus also check ETFs for key figures such as the greenhouse gas intensity of their portfolio values—or the extent to which the companies behind them generate their sales in areas that correspond to the United Nations Sustainable Development Goals (SDGs). This ESG fund data enables supplementary comprehensive ESG reporting.

Conclusion: We consider the strategic asset allocation to be the most efficient solution for a sustainable portfolio structure based on an active selection of individual securities, including sustainability criteria and the selective use of passive products for marginal topics (e.g., emerging market bonds).

7.8 Tactical Asset Allocation: The "Fine Tuning" for Short-Term Market Opportunities

However, focusing exclusively on long-term strategic asset allocation leaves short-term market opportunities untapped. That is why we use our cycle analysis and tactical asset allocation (TAA) to exploit short-term market opportunities in order to increase long-term portfolio returns. In this way, we can also take account of the general market situation over shorter periods of time.

Directional strategies are particularly well suited for portfolio management in market phases with strong trends. These include our cycle analysis and tactical management of equity ratios and duration.

Our market-neutral strategies can also be used to profitably exploit sideways phases. Their use does not influence the equity quota or portfolio duration. Typical examples of market-neutral strategies are the exploitation of interest rate differentials in bonds and currencies and the overweighting or underweighting of countries and sectors in equities.

7.9 Efficient Portfolio Management Not Yet Sustainable

If the risk of the portfolio were to increase due to extreme market events, enormous price movements could override risk-reducing diversification effects in the short term. In this case, we cushion strong loss phases. For this purpose, we have developed a system with which we can recognize extreme market movements without forecasts and thus initiate appropriate risk management.

The aim of risk management is to effectively limit the losses incurred if there is a correction of more than 10% on the international stock markets. However, the equity quota is not fully hedged in order to avoid a possible cash lock and to be able to participate in the subsequent recovery at an early stage. When the situation on the markets calms down again, the hedges are systematically and successively reduced.

Within the framework of the aforementioned decision-making principles, the equity quota and duration in the portfolio are managed efficiently and cost-effectively via liquid equity index and bond futures. Currently, no sustainable futures are used, as the liquidity in individual markets is not yet sufficiently high for this, as is the case with standard futures. We monitor and evaluate the liquidity of the futures on an ongoing basis and will consider ESG-compliant futures management as soon as sufficient liquidity is available in these investment instruments.

7.10 Reporting: Transparent and Comprehensible Reporting for Sustainable Investments

Since 2017, Metzler Asset Management has been working with investors to develop transparent and comprehensible reporting for sustainable capital investments. The result is comprehensive ESG reporting that highlights ESG opportunities and risks and evaluates the capital investment from a sustainable perspective.

On about 15 pages, the following topics are highlighted:

ESG profile of the capital investment, sustainability at a glance
Sales in controversial business areas, violations of international standards and guidelines (see Fig. 7.3)
ESG ratings of individual companies
Climate profile of the investment
Impact measurement of the portfolio with regard to the United Nations Sustainable Development Goals (UN SDGs)
Analyses in the context of regulation and transparency initiatives
Successes of active corporate dialogue and results on the exercise of voting rights
ESG in the country profile (government bonds)

The financial instruments considered include equities, corporate and government bonds, and investment fund units. For comparison, a benchmark (BM) can be defined for strategic asset allocation, or an ESG benchmark can be used.

The evaluation is based on the reporting date and the development of the portfolio—the ESG profile of the respective portfolio is thus viewed over time. Advantage for the client: The changes in the capital investment's ESG profile can be transparently tracked over any reporting period.

Business involvements	Fund	BM	Difference
High proof alcohol	0.0	0.4	-0.4
Nuclear power	0.0	0.7	-0.7
Adult entertainment	0.0	0.0	0.0
Genetic engineering	0.0	0.2	-0.2
Gambling	0.0	0.2	-0.2
Tobaco	0.0	0.5	-0.5
Coal mining	0.0	0.1	-0.1
Coal based power generation	0.0	0.8	-0.8
Controversial weapons	0.0	0.6	-0.6
Conventional weapons	0.0	0.9	-0.9
Business involvement exposure	**0.0**	**3.6**	**-3.6**

Fig. 7.3 Representation of "controversial" business activities in ESG reporting

7.11 Sustainable Multi-asset Portfolios for the Future

Multi-asset portfolios enable investors to reduce market risks and take advantage of return opportunities through their broad diversification. By integrating ESG information, this profile can be further sharpened. Our analysis and experience in portfolio management show that ESG-compliant asset classes have increased resilience to specific risks. Smart risk management systems have also proven their worth in periods of stress on the capital markets. Individual sustainability preferences can be seamlessly integrated into multi-asset strategies. A robust multi-asset portfolio is rounded off by meaningful and transparent ESG reporting.

Chapter 8
Two Sides of the Same Coin: ESG Risk and Opportunity Management in the Investment and Lending Business

B. Tobias Peylo and Christian Nuß

8.1 A Bird's-Eye Perspective

When dealing with a problem, it is often recommended to take a step back and try to perceive the bigger picture, or in other words, gain a bird's-eye perspective, enveloping as many facets of the complex reality as possible. In terms of the bird's-eye perspective, it is reasonable to say that NASA can be granted something like a monopoly on this. It is therefore very fitting that NASA has indeed launched an initiative to work not only on ways of leaving this planet but also on keeping it safe and stable: Its "global climate change" initiative (NASA, 2022) pursues the objective of gathering climate change-related data and information and making it available to the global community.

The introduction to the initiative posted on the NASA website indeed provides a good and compact summary: "Climate change is one of the most complex issues facing us today. It involves many dimensions—science, economics, society, politics, and moral and ethical questions—and is a global problem, felt on local scales, that will be around for thousands of years. [...] Because we are already committed to some level of climate change, responding to climate change involves a two-pronged approach: Reducing emissions of and stabilizing the levels of heat-trapping greenhouse gases in the atmosphere (mitigation) [and] adapting to the climate change already in the pipeline (adaptation)" (ibid).

In fact, in Europe alone, the extreme heat in combination with water scarcity and forest fires not only provides evidence of the truth behind scientists' warnings concerning the consequences of climate change (e.g., Rocha, 2022), but it may well be considered as a mere harbinger of what is to be expected in the future, as mankind has left the stable and beneficial age of the Holocene (the cradle of its existence) and

B. T. Peylo (✉) · C. Nuß
Kempten University of Applied Sciences, Kempten, Germany
e-mail: tobias.peylo@hs-kempten.de

K. Wendt, B. Villhauer (eds.), *Sustainable Wealth Management*, Sustainable Finance,
https://doi.org/10.1007/978-3-031-55505-3_8

enters the yet uncharted realm of the "Anthropocene"—the new, human-dominated geological epoch (Crutzen, 2022).

As Crutzen states, the adverse effects of climate change "have largely been caused by only 25% of the world population. The consequences are, among others, acid precipitation, photochemical 'smog', and climate warming. Hence, according to the latest estimates by the Intergovernmental Panel on Climate Change (IPCC), the Earth will warm by 1.4–5.8 C during this century" (ibid). In this context, even to the eye of the layman, it must become obvious that the colloquial term "environmental protection" is, more than ever, completely misleading: What needs to be protected is also humankind and its survival on this planet, which has been argued to be all but secure (Kemp et al., 2022).

For the scope of this article, let us now leave the biggest version of the big picture and zoom into the economic perspective. With the survival of humankind at stake and a plethora of pressing social and ecological consequences in view, this choice of perspective appears to be neither the most important nor the most urgent. And yet it has a very special significance: First, because most human activities that have caused or intensified climate change result from economic activities and interests. And second, because the greatest resistance to the mitigation measures that are more than urgently needed (according not only to the IPCC but the UNDRR as well; see UNDRR, 2022) also mainly stems from conflicts with economic interests. Indeed, in the context of extreme weather events as a result of climate change, Mami Mizutori (Special Representative of the Secretary-General for Disaster Risk Reduction and Head of UNDRR) states: "By deliberately ignoring risk and failing to integrate it in decision making, the world is effectively bankrolling its own destruction. Critical sectors, from government to development and financial services, must urgently rethink how they perceive and address disaster risk" (ibid).

Also from the economic perspective, the year 2022 may offer a glimpse of what is to come. Here, the economic consequences of climate change are most obvious in the agricultural sector: In France, the European Union's biggest wheat exporter, in 2022 the harvest was significantly reduced by heat, drought, and storms (Durisin, 2022). In the same country, more than half of the nuclear power plants have been unable to produce energy over a long period of time, caused—in addition to an outdated infrastructure—by the excessive heat of the rivers and the resulting problems for the cooling circuits (Kollewe, 2022). Last but not least, the water shortage in many European rivers has led to a temporary standstill of inland waterway transport—which leads not only to costly problems in the supply chain but also to the question as to whether, in the future, this mode will remain a reliable part of the global transport system (e.g., Balser & Ritzer, 2022). In addition to these relatively easy-to-prove consequences, there are a variety of hard-to-measure aspects, ranging from heat-related excess mortality and increased sick leave to infrastructure damage, product damage, increased cooling costs, and many others.

Above, only the damage caused by the chronic consequences of climate change has been taken into consideration. If the acute consequences—and here especially the strongly increased damage caused by extreme weather events (Munich Re, 2022)—are added, the full extent of economic damage quickly becomes apparent.

In total, the reduction in global gross domestic products until the end of the century is estimated to lie between 23% and 45% in the case of warming of between 3° and 5 °C, with crop losses alone ranging between 24% and 60% (BaFin, 2019a, 20).

These figures set into perspective the costs of climate change mitigation. In fact, a recent study by the Potsdam Institute for Climate Impact Research places the economic cost of each ton of CO_2 emissions between 74$ and 140$ in comparison to earlier estimates of around 31$ (Kalkuhl & Wenz, 2022). Consequently, it can be shown that in a comparison between mitigation costs and avoided climate damages, the total costs are lowest if climate change is limited to 2 Celsius (Glanemann et al., 2020). Hence, from a political and overall societal perspective, it makes sense to give climate change mitigation the highest priority in order to avoid both irreparable damage to our planet and livelihoods and economic costs that exceed by far the costs of action.

From the perspective of investors or banks, however, there is an equally pressing postulate: To avoid being impacted by the risks and losses as much as possible and, within the maelstrom of economic change and transformation, to identify those business cases that still are credit-worthy or make for a good investment. The key, here, is to assess and manage ESG risks and opportunities.

8.2 The Machinery of Banking Supervision Sets Into Motion

It is the nature of economic problems in the real economy that they also affect and impact the financial sphere—if sometimes with a time lag. And then, through feedback-loops such as a credit crunch and a lack of financial stability, the damage to the real economy becomes worse. Using an ecological macro model, Dafermos et al. (2018) show that climate change is apt to increase defaults with adverse effects on bank leverage and that it can cause an asset price deflation process. They also show that climate-induced financial instability reinforces the growth-reducing effects of climate change. Given these and other similar findings, it is clear why climate change is high on the agenda of central banks and institutions of banking supervision worldwide.

The consideration of climate change in finance is part of a wider scale of initiatives that include environmental and social aspects in financial decision-making. These are collectively labeled by the terms "Sustainable Finance" or—especially with a focus on climate change—"Green Finance," often without further differentiation. Yet, as has been shown in an earlier chapter of this book, with investment, financing, and risk management these considerations concern very different aspects of the financial sphere and hence different stakeholders, objectives, and financial instruments. They should thus be differentiated accordingly into the following:

- Value-based Green Finance (comprising the implementation of Socially Responsible Investment (SRI) as well as other incarnations of Corporate Social

Responsibility (CSR), corporate sustainability, fairness, and ethical statements in financial instruments and decisions)

- Action-based Green Finance (comprising financial instruments and initiatives aimed at supporting the transformation toward a green economy)
- Risk-based Green Finance (comprising rules and initiatives to secure financial stability and protect against adverse impacts of climate change in investment and credit)

Already commencing with the Action Plan (European Commission, 2018), which can be considered a hallmark and starting point of the new interest in Green Finance, the original SRI-focused Green Finance was enhanced with a two-pronged orientation to foster Sustainable Development: In a "stick and carrot" simile, finance is first intended to act as a leverage to channel money into the green transformation process. Second, the idea is to make investors and bankers aware of the negative impact and adverse consequences of climate change and educate them toward assessing and managing those risks—in their own interests, for the protection of their partners and clients, and, finally, to secure overall financial stability.

Unlike SRI as the main advocate of value-based Green Finance, this risk-based perspective has no arbitrary, morally determined foundation. And unlike the action-based Green Finance, with the Sustainable Development Goals (SDGs) at its core, it is also not the expression of a goal-oriented declaration of intent for transformation. In contrast, it is a collective "startling" of markets in the face of long-discussed, but now actually very real, climate change with its very real threats.

After the Action Plan, the idea and concept of risk-based Green Finance was further detailed and elaborated by an unprecedented series of publications by financial institutions. In Europe, the "Guidance notice on dealing with sustainability risk" by the German Banking Supervision BaFin (2019b) was published near simultaneously with the European Banking Authorities' (EBA) "Action Plan on sustainable finance" (EBA, 2019). The latter was later expanded in detail to produce the "EBA discussion paper on management and supervision of ESG risks for credit institutions and investment firms" (EBA, 2020). Likewise, in 2020, the European Central Bank (ECB) issued a draft "Guide on climate-related and environmental risks," which was published in its final form the following year (ECB, 2021). Finally, probably in preparation for one of the next Basle-installments, the Bank for International Settlement (BIS) has crowned those initiatives with its "Principles for the effective management and supervision of climate-related financial risks" (Basle Committee 2022) after an earlier initiative of a stock-take report. Other central banks and institutions of banking supervision follow suit with their own publications.

In summary, it can be said that a fundamental change is taking place in the financial markets as a result of the activities of the EU, the central banks, and banking supervision. Sustainable activities, which for decades existed as a small niche in the investment process and were disregarded by many, are suddenly being brought into focus through an extensive legislative process. However, they are being fundamentally renewed as this happens. In fact, the methods of sustainable investment/SRI, which have existed as a niche for a long time, even remain in their niche and play no role in the new standards. Instead, there are new, but much further-reaching standards, which are based on other framework conditions and in particular address the risks associated with sustainability and especially climate change. Given the speed, effort, and scope of these initiatives, it is reasonable to expect that this process will change everything that has been discussed so far in terms of financial market-related sustainability management and sustainable finance.

The road ahead is so fast and so demanding that many institutions and associations in the financial sector are already "waving white flags" today and asking for postponement—which, however, will most likely not be granted by the machinery of supervision and legislation that has already been set in motion.

To be fair, it has to be said that the initiatives are so far neither coordinated nor free of contradictions, or at least obvious expressions of different interpretations and priorities. For example, in its "Guidance notice on dealing with sustainability risks" (BaFin, 2019), the German Banking Supervision BaFin (BaFin, 2019) lists in the context of managing ESG and climate risk the SRI methodology of exclusion criteria, positive lists, and best-in-class approaches. As these have been created for the selection of assets in accordance with ethical criteria, it would require some explanation of the way in which they should contribute toward ESG risk management—an explanation that was not offered. Furthermore, the scope of the publications is rather different in both the use of terms (ESG risks vs. sustainability risk) and the consideration of social and reputational aspects, in addition to the focus on climate risks, which is, of course, the lowest common denominator and very much present in all initiatives.

8.3 ESG as the New Keyword for Risk and Opportunity Management

Despite differences in wording and definition, all official documents focus on those risks that have so far been neither recognized nor taken into account in an adequate way by conventional risk management. These risks, which are referred to as "ESG risks" (an abbreviation that comprises Environmental, Social and Governance aspects) or "sustainability risks" by the supervisory authority (BaFin, 2019b; EBA, 2021), have the peculiarity that the name was chosen quite unfortunately. This is because, contrary to what the name suggests, these ESG risks do not result from ESG. Instead, they result from a *lack* of ESG. Here, the deficiency can be on the side of a company if sustainability aspects are not, or not sufficiently, taken into account and this leads to economic or legal disadvantages in the context of the transformation of society and the markets. Or the deficiency can also be on a global level and affect companies in a specific region, e.g., through the effects of climate change—regardless of whether they have made efforts to implement sustainably or not.

Before attending to the resulting risks, banking supervision commences its deliberations with a definition of ESG factors: "ESG factors are environmental, social, or governance matters that may have a positive or negative impact on the financial performance or solvency of an entity, sovereign, or individual" (EBA, 2020, 31). This leads to a differentiation between negative and positive impacts: "While ESG factors can have positive or negative impacts on institutions through their core business activities, this report focuses more on the latter, in line with the prudential approach to risk management. On the negative side, ESG factors may impact institutions' financial performance by materializing through financial risk categories, such as credit, market, operational, liquidity, and funding risks, which are primarily affected by an institution's exposure to its counterparties and invested assets" (EBA, 2020, 32). Furthermore, to distinguish ESG risks from the financial institutions' own operational risks, the indirect effect is emphasized: "From a prudential perspective, ESG risks for institutions can thus be defined as the negative materialization of ESG factors through their counterparties or invested assets" (EBA, 2020, 31).

In the context of the EBA report, ESG risks are therefore the following:

- The risks of any negative financial impact on the bank
- Risks arising from the current or anticipated impact of ESG factors on its counterparties
- Invested assets

Consequently, in the process of ESG risk assessment, it would be too easy to collect and evaluate factors that are related to sustainability. Rather, in order to qualify as an ESG risk, the relevant issues must be characterized by the fact that they lead to economic damage for the company concerned and, moreover, that the damage is so severe as to affect the financial institution that finances/invests in it.

It should be noted that ESG risks do not represent a new risk category in addition to, for example, market or credit risks. Instead, as is highlighted in Fig. 8.1, they are

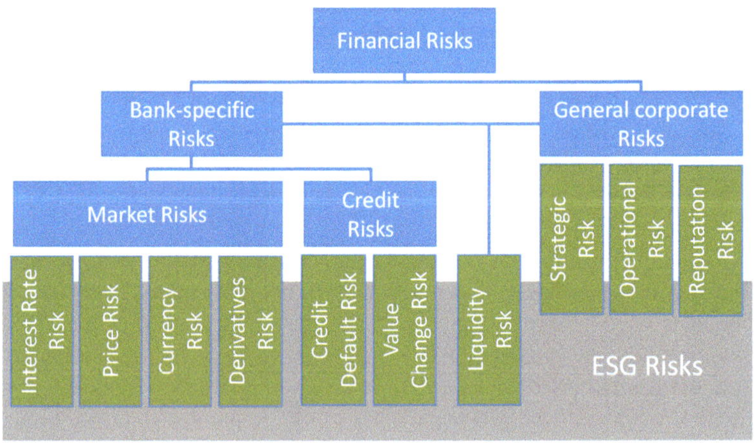

Fig. 8.1 ESG risks as cross risks influencing other financial risks

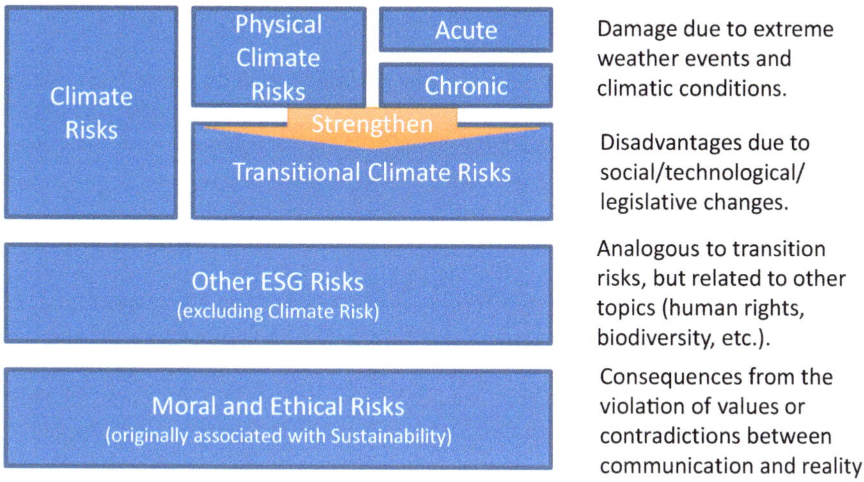

Fig. 8.2 ESG risk overview

to be understood as cross risks that act as drivers of other risks and can cause or intensify them. For example, credit defaults due to floods are still credit risks, but they are caused by ESG factors.

Here, ESG risks themselves can be differentiated into several sub-forms (Fig. 8.2).

8.3.1 The Risk Radar as a Knowledge-Based Approach to ESG-Risk Assessment

There are several approaches to the assessment of ESG risks. Of these, "the exposure method can possibly be described as the most practical method and the most straightforward to implement" (EBA, 2020, 72). In a nutshell, it uses scorings or ratings and "provides institutions and investors with a tool to better understand their individual counterparties and to better understand the ESG performance of their existing portfolios, or potential future portfolios, before making an investment decision" (ibid).

While several tools fitting this approach are already in use, or at least in development, their methods are seldom published, thus preventing an objective discussion. This is in fact a pity, as all tools would certainly benefit from this. Therefore, with the Risk Radar, this "black box" approach was avoided. After thoroughly testing and implementing it at over 90 German savings banks, cooperative banks, and private banks ranging in balance sheet total between approximately one and thirty billion euros, the Risk Radar is now in the process of being implemented and further developed at several central banks. Among those, the National Bank of Georgia is an important development partner and has published both the methodology and the assessment results for discussion (NBG, 2022).

This approach of open discussion was chosen in line with the EBA: "ESG evaluations need to be applied with care. A high level of awareness and a thorough understanding of the rationale and reasoning behind the rating outcomes is of the utmost importance to ensure effective and appropriate application of ESG evaluations" (EBA, 2020, 69).

In contrast to conventional ratings, ESG ratings cannot use the conventional approach of collecting and interpolating past data. Both the consequences of climate change and the impact of transformation are very new developments for which past data cannot offer much in terms of forecast. In addition, even of the relevant information, only a small fraction is available, as it requires so much expertise and effort that only very few companies can generate and provide it. As a consequence, a common feature of some of the current approaches is to assess the information on the sector level and then use this global data as long as no detailed information is at hand. While this is a comprehensible approach, comprehension often stops right there and does not extend to the kind of data that is used or to the way it is combined and weighted. Here, the image comes to mind of a watchmaker throwing all his little gear wheels into a bag and shaking it furiously in the vain hope that a working clockwork will form all by itself.

The data and its interrelationship underlying the ESG rating process are highly complex and characterized by multiple interconnections and mutual influences. Therefore, instead of combining an arbitrary selection of ESG-related indicators, great attention should be paid to this interconnectedness and, in particular, to the weighting and significance of the individual sub-aspects. And because there may well be differences in the assessment even among well-informed experts, disclosure of the methodology and discussion are of particular importance.

The Risk Radar is understood as a knowledge-based scoring system in the context of the exposure method. Influencing factors are defined and weighted in their importance, and they are individually scored between a range of 0 and 4, where

- 0 is used for aspects and developments that are known but rather *theoretical* with very few cases of actual observation.
- 1 is used for risk-related developments that tend to be *perceptible* and can already be proven in individual cases.
- 2 describes *obvious* facts with widely accepted proof and agreement concerning the potential harmful impact.
- 3 is associated with *significant* economic damage and commonly recognized as being very serious.
- 4 is reserved for those aspects whose likelihood of occurrence is certain or whose impact on the company or system is considered to be *existential.*

This scoring system is now applied to all aspects that constitute ESG risks, as disclosed in Fig. 8.3. The resulting score between 0 and 10 for a certain sector or sub-sector can later be modified with individual information to form a counterparty score.

<table>
<tr><th>NACE-Code</th><th colspan="3">Name of Sector or Subsector for which the Assessment is being conducted (e.g. Agriculture, Automotive, etc.)</th><th colspan="3">Scoring</th><th>Reference</th></tr>
<tr><td rowspan="12"></td><td rowspan="2">Physical Climate Risk</td><td colspan="2">Acute</td><td colspan="2">0-4 Weight 50%</td><td rowspan="2">0-4</td><td>1</td></tr>
<tr><td colspan="2">Chronic</td><td colspan="2">0-4 Weight 50%</td><td>2</td></tr>
<tr><td rowspan="5">Transition Climate Risk</td><td colspan="2">GHG-Emission Contribution</td><td colspan="2">0-4 Weight 50%</td><td rowspan="5">0-4</td><td>3</td></tr>
<tr><td rowspan="4">Transitional Intensity</td><td>Probability of regulatory Change</td><td>0-4 Weight 25%</td><td rowspan="4">0-4 Weight 50%</td><td>4</td></tr>
<tr><td>Economic Impact of regulatory Change</td><td>0-4 Weight 25%</td><td>5</td></tr>
<tr><td>Technology Squeeze-out</td><td>0-4 Weight 25%</td><td>6</td></tr>
<tr><td>Customer/ Consumer Behavior</td><td>0-4 Weight 25%</td><td>7</td></tr>
<tr><td rowspan="4">Other ESG Risks</td><td colspan="2">Loss of Biodiversity</td><td colspan="2">+0,5</td><td rowspan="4">0-2</td><td>8</td></tr>
<tr><td colspan="2">Other Environmental Risks</td><td colspan="2">+0,5</td><td>9</td></tr>
<tr><td colspan="2">Possible Human Rights Issues</td><td colspan="2">+0,5</td><td>10</td></tr>
<tr><td colspan="2">Other Social Risks</td><td colspan="2">+0,5</td><td>11</td></tr>
<tr><td colspan="5">ESG-Risk Score at Sector-Level</td><td>0-10</td><td></td></tr>
</table>

Fig. 8.3 The risk radar systematic (NBG, 2022, 12)

Using the reference numbers in the right-hand column, the selected values for the assessment are explained in full, together with the relevant sources as a result of the research and the basis for the assessment. In particular, for the high-risk sectors, these detailed sector assessments are also published (for details and examples, see NBG, 2022) and can be read, discussed, and changed—either in consensus following a discussion or by individual banks using this approach for their own risk assessment.

8.4 The Strategic ESG Matrix

The initiatives of the central banks make it mandatory for investors and banks alike to consider the adverse consequences of the ongoing change in framing conditions—both the natural change that is increasingly influenced by chronic and acute physical climate risk and the transformation being driven by a mix of political influences, technological innovation, and a gradual rethinking by consumers—all in turn influencing economic conditions and processes.

It is important to note, however, that this protection against risk is only one side of the coin. In fact, both investment and credit decisions are subject to the strict specification that all financial decisions should generate value (e.g., Berk & DeMarzo, 2017, 94). Risk management, however, primarily aims at protecting the status quo and is thus often only considered to be a "necessary evil" (Fabozzi & Konishi, 1996, 6) that is more apt to prevent opportunities from being taken than to be a part of generating value. This view, however, does not present the complete picture. Even conventional risk management has an often overlooked side: "In addition to enabling the management of an institution to limit swings […] in earnings and net worth due to factors outside its control, the rigorous economic analysis that accompanies risk management is a key to consistent long-run profitability" (ibid).

This is especially true for ESG risk management, where the understanding of the ongoing processes, their consequences, and their impacts is the only way of distinguishing between business models that will perish (along with the money invested into them) and those that will shape the future—and thus create value. This thought is also present in the EBA's concept: "Such transition to a low-carbon and climate-resilient economy, as mentioned above, can also provide opportunities for the counterparties—and the institutions providing funding to them—if companies contribute to climate mitigation and adaptation" (EBA, 2020, 36).

Therefore, through its thorough analysis of both the framing conditions and the company, with its strategic orientation and positioning, ESG risk management should not be considered as a mere gate that needs to be passed, a threshold that needs to be met, in order to enable a preselection of an investment or credit opportunity. It should instead be actively used to identify new opportunities and new fields of investment. This can be done by carefully balancing the combination of external threat and internal positioning and thus direct the asset- or customer-selection process into a direction that will give the best chances of sustainable profit—with all aspects of this term considered.

It is in this context that the ESG Matrix was developed at Kempten University of Applied Sciences as the main component of a concept for future-oriented guiding of financial decision-making in the investment as well as the credit business. It is based on the view that the situation of the companies within the economy can be very different even when the framing conditions are comparable. In fact, it can be shown that, here as in so many other aspects of business, one company's predicament may be another company's centenary chance.

In the food industry, for example, a fundamental change is taking place. While organic food was for many years a very small niche, customers' behavior has changed to the point where sustainability has to be considered a game changer. As early as 2013, the Federation of German Food & Drink Industries labeled sustainability in the food industry to be an "antidepressant against brand burnout" (BVE & GfK, 2013, 50). This statement was based on the fact that a large part of conventional food brands was found to be losing both loyal customers and casual buyers, while brands focused on organic food and other aspects of sustainability were gaining considerable shares of the market. As sustainability-oriented business cases in the food and drink industry have also been found to generate significantly higher profits than their conventional peers (Bundschuh et al., 2018), the sector can be used as a good example of transformation toward sustainability, strengthening those companies that have positioned themselves accordingly and becoming an existential threat to those that have not.

A similar development is obvious in the automotive sector with the transformation toward electric mobility (formalized in the EU by the sales ban on cars with combustion engines by the year 2035, e.g., Aigner, 2022). Here, again, companies that have positioned themselves accordingly will benefit hugely from this development, while conventional automotive/components companies will have to re-model their business cases or be threatened in their existence.

Naturally, the pressure toward transformation is not equally high in all sectors. With the food and automotive sectors, we have seen examples that are highly affected and—again through a combination of regulation, technical innovation, and consumer behavior—subject to considerable pressure for transformation. In other sectors, this pressure is high as well, but also influenced by other factors working in a contrary direction. For example, there is a strong indication that the initially high transformation pressure in the energy sector has now abated somewhat in the context of the geopolitical crisis and accompanying price rises (Popkostova, 2022). Also, there are many parts of the service sector, for example, in which transformation pressure has seemingly not yet arrived at all.

Pressure for transformation is the first consideration in ESG risk and opportunity management, and very much in focus. The second consideration, however, is equally important and is directed at the company and its positioning. This, of course, is a complex question that cannot be answered easily. Driven by stakeholder demands, larger companies in particular offer a large spectrum of relevant information. In this respect, the CSR guideline and other European initiatives (European Commission, 2022) as well as the recommendations of the Task Force on Climate Related Financial Disclosures (TCFD, 2017) not only supply a large quantity of information but also offer a reasonable degree of standardization. This makes it easier for investors (or CSR rating agencies working for them) to form a coherent picture of the company's strategies and positioning. Banks—especially those working with mid-size and smaller companies—do not have these advantages and volume of relevant information. Instead, they are frequently left to their own devices to form their own opinion, often only scarcely helped by sometimes poorly informed customers.

To enable banks to assess the positioning of financed companies, Kempten University of Applied Sciences has developed a structured assessment scheme based on the reliable and proven "Sustainability Check" (Peylo & Oster, 2019) that has been implemented approx. 400 times in German savings banks and cooperative banks as well as microfinance institutions in six countries on three continents. The basic idea of this check is to consider all possible aspects of the implementation of sustainability in a structured way and rate them in a scoring scheme between 0 (not implemented) and 4 (leading the way). This structured process is oriented along the sustainability landscape, which in Fig. 8.4 is presented in the version for nonfinancial companies. Please note that not all of the fields of action pictured within this

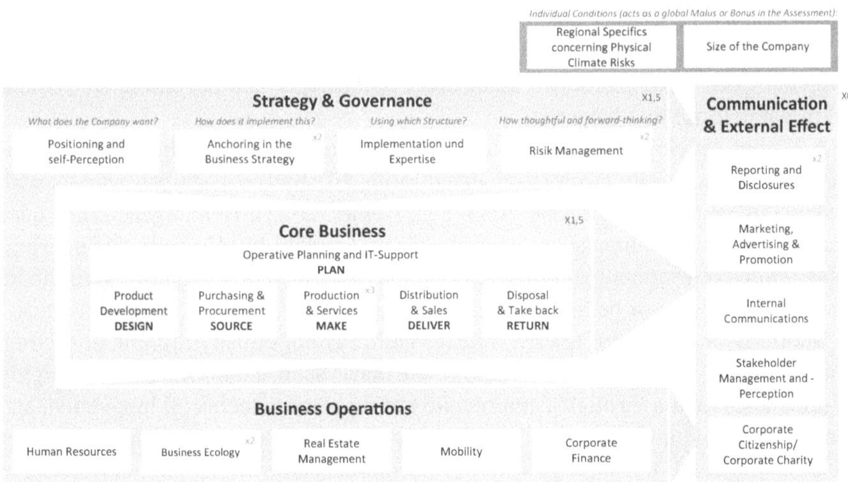

Fig. 8.4 Sustainability landscape for companies

landscape are relevant for all sectors, which is considered within the assessment process.

It is worth mentioning that not all fields of action have the same significance within this structure: Communication, for example, (as impactful as it may seem at first glance) is in the long run of much less importance than the substance formed by strategy and the core business. This is reflected in different weightings between the various fields of action and sometimes also their characteristics (indicated by a small multiplicator in the top right-hand corner in some fields in Fig. 8.4). Within the "core business" field of action, for example, production and services are particularly important and are thus triple weighted in the evaluation.

This, or another equally comprehensive and structured, form of company assessment can be used to reveal how far transformation has already been considered in the company and, accordingly, how well prepared the company is. If a similarly structured approach is used to assess the pressure for transformation (e.g., via the Risk Radar presented above, or in fact any other suitable scoring scheme), a matrix emerges that enables and guides decision-making in the context of ESG opportunities and risks. On the y-axis of the matrix shown in Fig. 8.5, the level of ESG risk in a sector indicates the transformation pressure. On the x-axis, the company's positioning indicates how well it is prepared for this transformation and thus whether it is likely to suffer or benefit.

In a classic 4-field classification, this matrix enables investment or financing decisions to be based on ESG criteria and the inherent risks and opportunities to be identified. The four fields are characterized as follows:

- Where the transformation pressure is low, companies can still survive without adaptation—this is the realm of the *Dinosaurs*, where the business models of the great-grandfathers still persist.

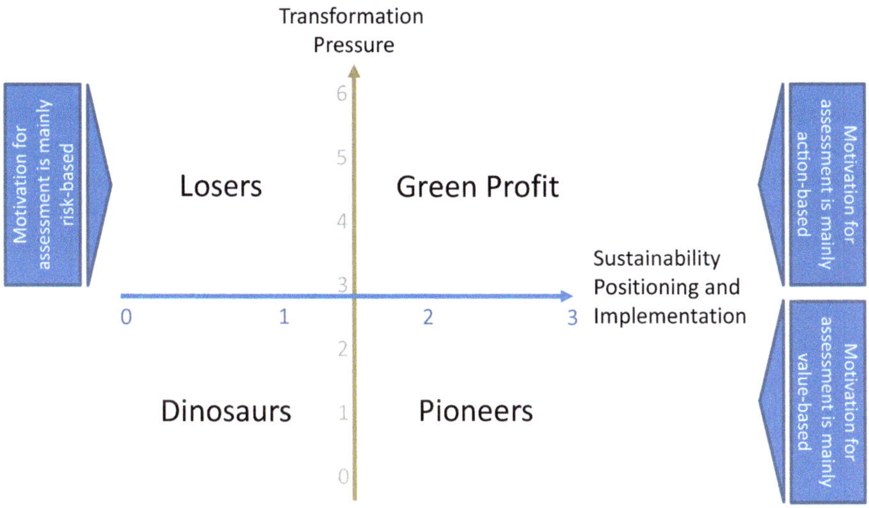

Fig. 8.5 The ESG Matrix

- However, even in these sectors, some *Pioneers* are pushing the borders and changing the landscape. By gradually proving the feasibility of sustainable concepts in innovative ways, they begin to interest consumers, who will later demand these innovations as an industry standard. In this way, sooner or later, the pressure for transformation will also increase in these industries. While these pioneers are not in the focus of transformation and seldom supported, e.g., with subsidy-based development programs, they still make for an interesting investment, especially in the context of SRI or generally value-based motivations.
- Where the transformation pressure is very much felt based on physical climate risks, transformation risk, or both, a Darwinian selection process of the suitability of business models is beginning to take place. Companies that are unwilling or unable to change and to adapt to the new framework conditions will incur losses compared to the status quo and thus, sooner or later, be among the *Losers*. Identifying them and avoiding investment or lending—or at least placing them under strict ancillary conditions—will have to be the new, risk-based motivation in this field.
- Again, in the very same sectors, there are those companies that ride on the high wave of change, supporting adaptation with their solutions and thus, in words attributed to Benjamin Franklin, "doing well while doing good" (McClimaon, 2020). In this field, "*Green Profit*" is generated, which has, in addition to ethical considerations, the great advantage that it generates concepts that help with the colossal task of climate change mitigation and adaptation. The motivation to identify those companies is thus action-based in nature; the future-oriented alignment of this field makes it the most attractive target point for investors and bankers alike.

To sum things up, in the context of the new relevance of ESG, investors and bankers should not only consider the downside—a view that is (for their own good) imposed upon them by central banks and banking supervisors but that only captures one side of the coin. The other side of the coin is not enforced, but it is indeed the more relevant, by offering the business case and the attractive investment and financing opportunities of the future. The ESG Matrix outlined above can provide orientation and guidance in identifying and harnessing these opportunities. However, this depends on stringent and reliable measures for assessing transformation pressure, on the one hand, and a company's positioning, on the other.

8.5 Outlook

Climate change presents humankind with wide-ranging problems, many of which cannot be easily solved. In comparison, the tasks and challenges facing the financial industry are complex but solvable. They require understanding and openness and a willingness to take off blinders and accept new realities. These qualities will be of great importance for the future success of investment and credit businesses alike.

In this chapter, we have approached the topic of ESG, focusing particularly on the impact of climate change from several perspectives: first, from the indispensable risk-based perspective, which imposes a mandate upon investors and banks alike to consider the adverse consequences of climate change and avoid losing a lot of money in the process; second, often neglected perspective is the active search for companies that are willing and able to foster transformation and benefit from it financially.

In particular, for banking, this second perspective may offer a way out of a predicament in the making. As soon as banking supervision enforces the use of ESG ratings, some sectors or subsectors will become seemingly non-investible because their high-risk score precludes engagement. However, this would be very counterproductive in several ways: Banks and investors would run out of alternatives and the competition in the still investible sectors would increase, while certain economic sectors would "run dry" with enormous economic consequences—in fact, none of the high-risk sectors are dispensable from a societal point of view.

Therefore, instead of a binary invest/non-invest mechanism, it will become much more important in the future to allow for differentiated decisions, especially within critical industries. By identifying which companies are both well prepared and even instrumental for the transition, it will not be necessary to decline investment or financing for a whole sector only to avoid taking too high ESG risks. As with our simile of the watchmaker, this identification will not be possible the easy way. However, given some effort, it will be achievable—and well worth the effort, from an economic and social perspective alike.

References

Aigner, J. (2022, June 8). EU Lawmakers Uphold Ban on New Combustion Engine Cars by 2035. *Bloomberg (Europe Edition)*. https://www.bloomberg.com/news/articles/2022-06-08/eu-lawmakers-uphold-ban-on-new-combustion-engine-cars-by-2035#xj4y7vzkg

BaFin. (2019a). *BaFin Perspektiven: Nachhaltigkeit (engl. BaFin Perspectives – Sustainability)*. Bundesaufsichtsamt für Finanzdienstleistungsaufsicht BaFin. https://www.bafin.de/SharedDocs/Downloads/DE/BaFinPerspektiven/2019/bp_19-2_sustainable_finance.html

BaFin. (2019b). *Guidance Notice on dealing with Sustainability Risk*. Bundesaufsichtsamt für Finanzdienstleistungsaufsicht BaFin. https://www.bafin.de/SharedDocs/Downloads/EN/Merkblatt/dl_mb_Nachhaltigkeitsrisiken_en.pdf?__blob=publicationFile&v=5

Balser, M. & Ritzer, U. (2022, Aug 2028). Die Zukunft der Binnenschifffahrt steht infrage (engl. The future of inland navigation is in doubt). *Süddeutsche Zeitung*. https://www.sueddeutsche.de/politik/binnenschiffe-niedrigwasser-zukunft-1.5646179?reduced=true

Berk, J., & DeMarzo, P. (2017). *Corporate finance* (4th ed.). Pearson.

Basel Committee on Banking Supervision. (2022). Principles for the effective management and supervision of climate-related financial risks. Basle: BIS Bank for International Settlement. https://www.bis.org/bcbs/publ/d532.pdf

Bundschuh, C., Dresp, M. & Emunds, P. (2018). *Nachhaltigkeit lohnt sich – Gesellschaft und Unternehmen im Wandel (engl. Sustainability pays off – Society and Business in Transition)*. Landesbank Baden-Württemberg Strategy Research. https://www.lbbw.de/konzern/research/2018/blickpunkte/lb_studie_nachhaltigkeit_wandel_7ax8ein8q_m.pdf

BVE Bundesvereinigung der Deutschen Ernährungsindustrie & GfK Consumer Panels. (2013). *Consumers' Choice '13*. Bundesvereinigung der Deutschen Ernährungsindustrie. https://www.bve-online.de/download/consumers-choice-2013

Crutzen, P. J. (2022). Geology of mankind. *Nature, 415*(23). https://doi.org/10.1038/415023a

Dafermos, Y., Nikolaidi, M., & Galanis, G. (2018). Climate change, financial stability and monetary policy. *Ecological Economics, 152*, 219–234.

Durisin, M. (2022, July 12). French Heat and Drought Shrinks Wheat Harvest in Key EU Exporter. *Bloomberg (Europe Edition)*. https://www.bloomberg.com/news/articles/2022-07-12/french-heat-and-drought-shrinks-wheat-harvest-in-key-eu-exporter#xj4y7vzkg

EBA European Banking Authority. (2019). *Action Plan on Sustainable Finance*. European Banking Authority. https://www.eba.europa.eu/sites/default/documents/files/document_library/EBA%20Action%20plan%20on%20sustainable%20finance.pdf

EBA European Banking Authority. (2020). *EBA Discussion paper on management and supervision of ESG risks for credit institutions and investment firms*. European Banking Authority. https://www.eba.europa.eu/sites/default/documents/files/document_library/Publications/Reports/2021/1015656/EBA%20Report%20on%20ESG%20risks%20management%20and%20supervision.pdf

EBA Eurpean Banking Authority (2021). EBA Report on Management and Supervision of ESG Risks for Credit Institutions and Investment Firms. Paris: EBA. https://www.google.com/url?sa=t&source=web&rct=j&opi=89978449&url=https://www.eba.europa.eu/sites/default/files/document_library/Publications/Reports/2021/1015656/EBA%2520Report%2520on%2520ESG%2520risks%2520management%2520and%2520supervision.pdf&ved=2ahUKEwiIypndvJWGAxWdefEDHVzNAaoQFnoECBoQAQ&usg=AOvVaw0vUYlfR6FMlbEPIcwW8MbN

ECB European Central Bank. (2021). Guide on climate-related and environmental risks. Frankfurt am Main, Germany. European Central Bank. https://www.bankingsupervision.europa.eu/legalframework/publiccons/pdf/climate-related_risks/ssm.202005_draft_guide_on_climate-related_and_environmental_risks.en.pdf

European Commission. (2018). *Action Plan: Financing Sustainable Growth*. European Commission. https://eur-lex.europa.eu/legal-content/EN/TXT/?uri=CELEX:52018DC0097

European Commission. (2022). *Corporate social responsibility (CSR) – EU and national activities in promoting CSR, improving environmental standards in business*. European

Commission. https://ec.europa.eu/info/business-economy-euro/doing-business-eu/corporate-social-responsibility-csr_en

Fabozzi, F. J., & Konishi, A. (1996). *Asset/ liability management* (2nd ed.). McGraw-Hill.

Glanemann, N., Willner, S. N., & Levermann, A. (2020). Paris climate agreement passes the cost-benefit test. *Nature. Communications, 11*(110). https://doi.org/10.1038/s41467-019-13961-1

Kalkuhl, M., & Wenz, L. (2022). The impact of climate conditions on economic production. Evidence from a global panel of regions. *Journal of Environmental Economics and Management, 103*. https://doi.org/10.1016/j.jeem.2020.102360

Kemp, L., Xu, C., Depledge, J., Ebi, K. L., Gibbins, G., Kohler, T. A., Rockström, J., Scheffer, M., Schnellhuber, J., Steffen, W., & Lenton, T. M. (2022). Climate endgame: Exploring catastrophic climate change scenarios. *PNAS, 119*(34). https://doi.org/10.1073/pnas.21081461

Kollewe, J. (2022, Aug 3). EDF cuts output at nuclear power plants as French rivers get too warm. *The Guardian*. https://www.theguardian.com/business/2022/aug/03/edf-to-reduce-nuclear-power-output-as-french-river-temperatures-rise

McClimon, T. J. (2020, April 20). Doing Well And Doing Good. *Forbes*. https://www.forbes.com/sites/timothyjmcclimon/2020/04/20/doing-well-and-doing-good/

Munich Re. (2022). *Data on natural disasters since 1980*. Munich Re. https://www.munichre.com/en/solutions/reinsurance-property-casualty/natcatservice.html

NASA. (2022). *Responding to Climate Change*. National Aeronautics and Space Administration (NASA). https://climate.nasa.gov/solutions/adaptation-mitigation/

NBG National Bank of Georgia. (2022). *Climate-related Risk Radar for Georgian Economic Sectors*. National Bank of Georgia. https://nbg.gov.ge/en/page/climate-risk-radar

Peylo, B. T., & Oster, D. (2019). *Nachhaltigkeitsmanagement in Sparkassen (eng. Sustainability Management in Savings Banks)*. Deutscher Sparkassenverlag.

Popkostova, Y. (2022). *Europe's energy crisis conundrum - Origins, impact and way forward*. European Union Institute for Security Studies EUISS. https://www.iss.europa.eu/content/europes-energy-crisis-conundrum

Rocha, P. A. (2022, Aug 10). Temperatures Rise as Another Heat Wave Blankets Europe. *Bloomberg (Europe Edition)*. https://www.bloomberg.com/news/articles/2022-08-10/temperatures-rise-in-europe-as-another-heat-wave-blankets-region

TCFD Task Force on Climate related Financial Disclosures. (2017). *Recommendations of the Task Force on Climate related Financial Disclosures*. Task Force on Climate related Financial Disclosures. https://www.fsb-tcfd.org/recommendations/

UNDRR United Nations Office for Disaster Risk Reduction. (2022). *Humanity's broken risk perception is reversing global progress in a 'spiral of self-destruction', finds new UN report*. UNDRR.https://www.undrr.org/news/humanitys-broken-risk-perception-reversing-global-progress-spiral-self-destruction-finds-new

Chapter 9
ESG Investing and Firm Efficiency: The Costs and Benefits of SRI Efficiency Screening

Karl Weinmayer

9.1 Introduction

Socially responsible investing has become a mainstream movement over the last 20 years as a steadily rising number of investors have adopted the popular sentiment of "doing well while doing good" (see, e.g., Hamilton et al., 1993) with the goal of maximizing their investor preferences for return, risk, and sustainability. This is underlined by high annual growth rates and roughly USD 12 trillion and EUR 11 trillion of AUM (assets under management) invested in 2018 in the USA and Europe, respectively (European Sustainable Investment Forum, 2018; The Forum for Sustainable and Responsible investment, 2018). The relevance of ESG as a way to assess the environmental, governance, and social behavior of firms has further increased as the EU taxonomy under the sustainable finance disclosure regulation puts strong emphasis on ESG with the aim to provide transparency and standardization to sustainable finance products.[1]

While a number of SRI strategies have been developed over the years to incorporate sustainability-related criteria in the fund management process, the vast majority of assets are still invested based on exclusion (negative screening) as the oldest SRI strategy is already in use since the eighteenth century. This strategy relies on exclusion based on sustainability-related criteria, such as industry, themes, or specific activities. The fastest growing SRI strategy is ESG integration, which relies on the

[1] See Sustainable Finance Disclosures Regulation (European Parliament and the Council of the European Union, 2019).

K. Weinmayer (✉)
Vienna University of Economics and Business, Institute for Finance, Banking and Insurance, Vienna, Austria
e-mail: karl.weinmayer@wu.ac.at

K. Wendt, B. Villhauer (eds.), *Sustainable Wealth Management*, Sustainable Finance,
https://doi.org/10.1007/978-3-031-55505-3_9

use of ESG criteria provided by ESG rating agencies for a large number of firms worldwide relating to the environmental, social, and governance dimensions of firms (European Sustainable Investment Forum, 2018).

The current state of ESG investing faces a number of challenges, the biggest being the lack of standardization of ESG ratings. The consideration of ESG ratings usually happens at the stock selection stage, in which firms are being selected into the portfolio based on negative screening or best-in-class approaches using ESG scores as criteria. The ESG screening intensity is usually rather a function of the size of the asset universe than the direct realization of investor preferences, while best-in-class approaches typically result in a large reduction in the set of available assets introducing potential tradeoffs between diversification and benefits of high screening intensity. Previous studies on SRI funds mostly arrive at the conclusion that no differences compared to conventional funds can be observed.

Furthermore, the fund management process typically follows an ESG-based stock selection followed by a sole focus on financial performance in the asset allocation process, with no joint consideration of financial and ESG criteria in all stages of the portfolio management decision. A few studies propose solutions to this issue by developing multi-criteria portfolio models based on parametric or nonparametric approaches, such as tri-criterion portfolio optimization programs and efficiency analysis.

This study investigates the effects of SRI efficiency-screening intensity on a portfolio's performance under joint consideration of financial and ESG criteria in the analysis of the firms' efficiencies derived from multi-directional efficiency analysis for US and European firms. A number of usual asset allocation strategies are implemented reflecting common SRI fund and ESG index portfolios. The portfolio results indicate a significantly negative screening effect on financial performance for mean-variance strategies for the USA and no significant effect for the EU. A significantly positive relationship can be documented between SRI efficiency-screening intensity and financial as well as ESG performance for naive and value-weighted asset allocation strategies, suggesting a potential application for SRI fund management as well as conventional investors.

The remainder of the paper is structured as follows. Section 9.2 discusses the relevant literature regarding SRI screening and multi-criteria portfolio management. Section 9.3 introduces the research design, while Sect. 9.4 presents the data. Section 9.5 discusses the results of the analysis and Sect. 9.6 provides the conclusion.

9.2 Literature Review

A large number of studies have been conducted in this field broadly related to understanding the relationship between ESG (or more general corporate social responsibility) and financial performance of firms. An excellent overview of this literature is provided by Friede et al. (2015), who show that 90% of prior studies document a non-negative relationship between ESG and financial performance.

This study focuses more specifically on socially responsible portfolio management un- der consideration of financial and sustainability criteria, which can be differentiated into two strands of literature. Several studies investigate the impact of sustainability-based screening as part of the asset selection process. Another strand of literature is dedicated to developing multi-criteria portfolio models, which allow the direct consideration of non-financial sustainability criteria in the asset allocation decision of the portfolio decision-making process. In this context nonparametric frontier analysis, such as data envelopment analysis (DEA) and multi-directional efficiency analysis (MEA), which serves as the basis for this study, will also be discussed. The most relevant studies of these strands of literature will be reviewed in Sects. 9.2.1 and 9.2.2.

9.2.1 Sustainability Screening

Previous studies, which have investigated the impact of social screenings on fund returns, document mixed results with mostly no significant effect. While many earlier studies investigate positive or negative screenings based on industry affiliation (so-called sin sectors), undesirable business practices, or specific sustainability themes, later studies predominantly analyze screening approaches based on social responsibility ratings provided by dedicated rating agencies. ESG integration strategies in particular have become increasingly popular with more financial products using ESG scores for the asset selection and allocation decision as part of the fund management process.

Barnett and Salomon (2006) analyze SRI funds, apply various social screens, and document a curvilinear relationship between social screening intensity and financial returns, as initial diversification losses seem to be offset by selecting higher-quality firms into the portfolio. This is confirmed by Gharghori and Ooi (2016) who argue that this relationship can be explained by the combined effects of stakeholder and modern portfolio theory. Lee et al. (2010) also find a negative and curvilinear relation, but between the fund's screening intensity and its systematic risk, while no effect on unadjusted returns can be confirmed.

Renneboog et al. (2008) investigate SRI funds and find no difference in risk-adjusted re- turns compared to conventional funds, but document lower risk-adjusted returns for funds with a higher number of social and governance screens. They argue that high SRI screening intensity restricts the mean-variance optimization and the ability to pick undervalued stocks. Humphrey and Lee (2011) and Humphrey and Tan (2014) find no difference in returns or risk between screened and unscreened portfolios for negative or positive screening using KLD scores. Capelle-Blancard and Monjon (2014) show that, based on a sample of French SRI funds, industry screening leads to a decrease in financial performance, while other types of screening do not seem to have any significant impact.

Kempf and Osthoff (2007) implement a trading strategy of buying (selling) stocks with high (low) social responsibility rating based on KLD and find positive abnormal returns, which are maximized when a best-in-class approach is used. Halbritter and Dorfleitner (2015) use a similar approach using ESG ratings and find no significant differences in returns between stocks with high and low ESG ratings.

Charles et al. (2016) investigate ESG indices with respect to differences in ESG rating agencies, screening strategies, asset allocation, and investment regions. They find no significant over- or underperformance based on ESG screening strategies, such as exclusion, best-in-class, and integration. Verheyden et al. (2016) explore the relevance of ESG factors for fund managers with no interest in sustainability and compare an unscreened global asset universe with two negative ESG screening strategies excluding the bottom 10% and 25% of firms. They find similar results with almost no evidence of a reduction in returns, but a significant reduction in risk for the ESG screened portfolios. Alessandrini and Jondeau (2020) investigate exclusion strategies based on ESG scores and find improved social responsibility performance at no cost of risk-adjusted performance in the resulting portfolios. Awaysheh et al. (2020) identify best-in-class and worst-in-class firms based on KLD ratings and find no significant relation between operating performance and CSR categories.

Jin (2020) examines the pattern of factor risk-adjusted fund performance with respect to ESG screening intensity by constructing returns-based ESG scores for US equity funds. The study shows that excluding low ESG score funds leads to a reduction in the systematic risk of the portfolio, while specific risks start to increase once the screening intensity reaches higher levels.

9.2.2 Multi-criteria Portfolio Management

While sustainability considerations are relevant in the asset selection decision to make sure that only firms matching the investors' preferences are included in the portfolio, the joint selection based on multiple criteria is not usually the case. Furthermore, the asset allocation decision as the second stage of the fund management process does not necessarily reflect this particular investor preference, if a conventional approach focused on financial performance alone is used. In this case, a negative screening of the worst-in-class firms might lead to acceptable financial performance, but leave sustainability performance potential unrealized, while a strict best-in-class screening will result in an overall strong sustainability-oriented portfolio, but, as shown in Sect. 9.2.1, high screening intensity might have adverse effects on financial performance via diversification considerations.

The second strand of literature relevant for this study explores how a third non-financial dimension affecting investor preferences, such as sustainability, can be incorporated into the asset allocation decision.

Steuer et al. (2005) discuss how the traditional theory of portfolio selection used by standard investors, whose utility function only depends on a portfolio's return, can be extended for application to non-standard investors as a multi-objective stochastic programming problem with the nondominated sets being surfaces instead of frontiers.

Ballestero et al. (2012) investigate the portfolio selection of ethical investors and propose a financial-ethical bi-criteria model by distinguishing between a traditional financial and an ethical goal in the same utility framework. They find that ethical investments lead to risk expo- sure increases. Bilbao-Terol et al. (2012) construct an SRI-attractiveness index for assessing financial products using a goal-programming model to combine financial and ethical investor preferences.

Verheyden et al. (2015) review available MCDA (multi-criteria decision analysis) methods and discuss challenges related to the development of socially responsible investing.

Hirschberger et al. (2013) develop a procedure for computing the tri-criterion nondominated surface using a multiparametric algorithm and demonstrate its application to socially responsible investing.

Gasser et al. (2017) propose a modification of Markowitz' portfolio theory that allows the incorporation of social responsibility as a third criterion. This results in a three-dimensional capital allocation plane illustrating the complete set of feasible optimal portfolios based on two optimal portfolio choices given by the preferences of a "conventional" and "socially responsible" investor. Following a similar direction Alessandrini and Jondeau (2021) construct portfolios by maximizing the portfolio ESG score while imposing constraints related to financial benchmark performance.

Garcia et al. (2019) propose a novel fuzzy multi-objective approach to allow for consideration of return, expected ESG score, and downside risk in the portfolio optimization while imposing real-world constraints, such as budget, floor-ceiling, and cardinality.

Amon et al. (2021a, b) investigate the portfolio-decision-making problem of a socially responsible investor from the perspective of passive management strategies and implement passive ESG-based asset allocation strategies. They demonstrate that these ESG-based strategies dominate traditional passive benchmark strategies, such as naive portfolios and value-weighted indices.

Nonparametric approaches to frontier analysis, such as data envelopment analysis (DEA) and multi-directional efficiency analysis (MEA), are of particular interest for investigating multi-criteria portfolio management as they allow a consideration of several variables of interest. A number of studies demonstrate the application of efficiency analysis for stock selection based on multiple financial variables, such as Chen (2008), who compare portfolios based on DEA stock selection with market returns, and Edirisinghe and Zhang (2008), who investigate a stock selection based on a relative financial strength indicator derived by data envelopment analysis. Pätäri et al. (2010) investigate value portfolios by ranking Finnish non-financial firms based on their DEA efficiency scores and group them into three equally weighted portfolios. Lim et al. (2014) use DEA cross-efficiency evaluation for stock selection in the Korean stock market and demonstrate that the resulting portfolios yield higher risk-adjusted returns compared to benchmark portfolios.

Dia (2009) explore the use of efficiency information beyond stock selection and propose a portfolio selection methodology, in which the weighted sum of the stock's efficiency ratios is optimized.

Chen et al. (2021) develop a three-step SRI optimization approach using a combination of DEA models for evaluating ESG efficiency and the asset screening process. Weinmayer and Rammerstorfer (2023) explore the application of multi-directional efficiency analysis to socially responsible portfolio management by computing relative firm efficiencies using return, risk, and socially responsibility measures as input and output variables. They find significant overall outperformance in strategies, which rely on the firms' multi-dimensional efficiencies in the asset allocation and confirm the usefulness of efficiency analysis for socially responsible portfolio management.

This study contributes to the existing literature in multiple ways. First, the impact of SRI efficiency-screening intensity on a portfolio's financial and sustainability performance is investigated under joint consideration of financial and ESG criteria in the screening process, whereby the stock selection is based on the firms' relative efficiencies derived from multi- directional efficiency analysis. While Weinmayer and Rammerstorfer (2023) also compute MEA efficiency scores using financial and sustainability criteria, the effect of efficiency-based screening intensity for ESG investing is not explored. Second, a comprehensive dataset of US and European firms is used and regional differences are analyzed systematically. Third, MEA efficiency scores are computed based on the cross-section of firms and within sectors for each region following a "best-in-sector" approach to investigate screening-related differences between these two efficiency measurement approaches resulting from the interplay of screening and diversification benefits. Finally, the portfolios are constructed using a number of usual asset allocation strategies such as mean-variance optimization, naive, and value-weighted allocation, reflecting common SRI fund and ESG index portfolios. These strategies are rebalanced quarterly, which also allows the investigation of turnover rates as a proxy for transaction cost for each strategy and efficiency-screening level. This research design allows for a thorough analysis of the effects of screening intensity and diversification on the portfolios' financial and ESG performance under consideration of transaction cost at various levels of firm efficiency.

9.3 Methodology

The approach of using efficiency analysis as a way to compare and improve firms at various levels of their activity is a concept that was first introduced by Koopmans (1951) and Debreu (1951). Based on these studies Farrell (1957) proposes an approach to study the efficiency of operating units based on their production plans, in which one or multiple inputs are used as resources to achieve one or multiple outputs. As a special case of frontier analysis, data envelopment analysis is a non-parametric approach for measuring the relative efficiency of so-called decision-making units (DMU), which can be traced back to Charnes et al. (1978).

In this study, a related approach similar to DEA called multi-directional efficiency analysis (MEA) is used to investigate the relative efficiency of firms. This approach was initially presented by Bogetoft and Hougaard (1999) and further developed by Tone (2001) and Asmild et al. (2003). Unlike DEA, in which the weights used to maximize the ratio of weighted sums of outputs over inputs are estimated using linear programming, multi-directional efficiency analysis allows the estimation of the improvement potential for each factor of the production plan (e.g., for each input and output variable) separately using a system of linear programs.

Based on the set of DMUs under consideration, the maximum improvement potential for each factor is estimated, which results in an ideal production plan and contains the set of optimal factor levels for all input and output variables. Generally, these optimal factor levels are mostly theoretical, as it is usually not possible to realize the ideal production plan due to technological constraints originating from the set of DMUs. However, once the current and ideal production plans are known, the DMU can still move towards the ideal plan along the improvement direction until the technological boundaries do not allow further movement. These boundaries are represented by the efficient frontier based on the set of DMUs and efficient firms are located on the frontier, as they help define it. For these firms, no improvement potential can be realized. Each firm's realizable improvement potential is given by the distance between the current production plan and the efficient frontier in the improvement direction towards the ideal production plan. Firms with larger realizable improvement potential are therefore located further away from the frontier, which implies that these firms are less efficient.

The approach of the multi-directional efficiency analysis is illustrated in Fig. 9.1 for a firm with one input x and one output y in input-output orientation.[2] The figure shows the current and ideal production plans by (x_1, y_1) and (x_1^*, y_1^*), respectively. The realizable and maximum improvement potential between these two points and the efficient frontier are highlighted.[3]

The resulting distance measure obtained by MEA is then transformed to obtain an efficiency measure η, which can be interpreted in a similar way as the traditional Farrell efficiency scores (Farrell, 1957). The score ranges between 0 and 1 with $\eta = 1$ representing fully efficient firms and $\eta < 1$ indicating inefficient firms.

For the application to socially responsible stock selection, an input-output-oriented MEA model with variable returns to scale is implemented, in which, following Weinmayer and Ram- merstorfer (2023), expected stock returns and ESG scores are treated as outputs and volatility of stock returns as input based on quarterly observations. The investigation of the impact of efficiency-screening intensity on the portfolios' financial and sustainability performance follows a three-step process, which is conducted separately for US and European firms. An overview of the research design is shown in Table 9.1.

---

[2] This illustration is motivated by Bogetoft and Hougaard (1999). A similar version of this figure is used in Weinmayer et al. (2023).

[3] For a more formal discussion on multi-directional efficiency analysis, the author refers to, e.g., Weinmayer and Rammerstorfer (2023).

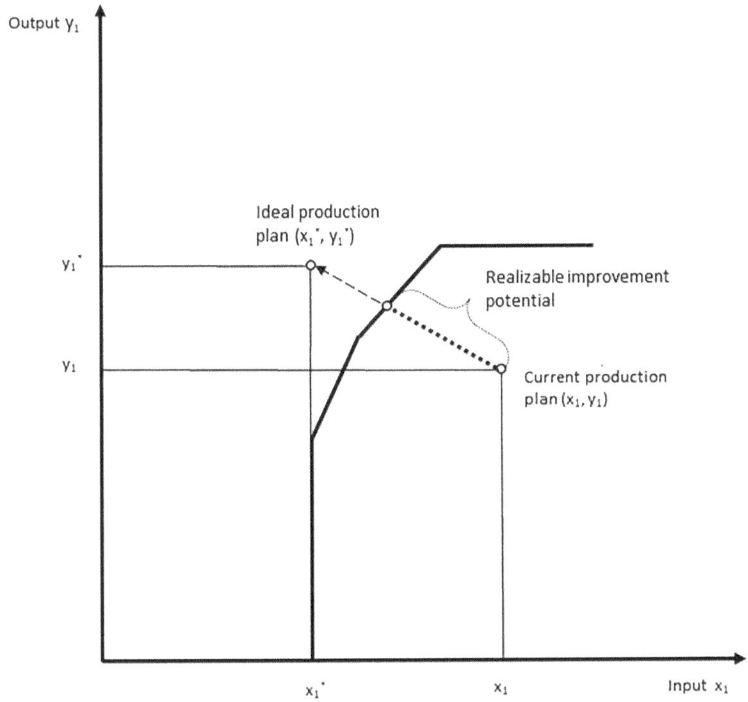

Notes: This figure depicts the estimation of the realizable improvement potential for a DMU with one input x_1 and its ideal reference point x_1^* and one output y_1 and its ideal reference point y_1^* for a MEA model in input-output orientation. The efficient frontier reflecting the technological boundary as a function of the set of DMUs under consideration is represented by the solid line.

Fig. 9.1 Multi-directional efficiency analysis in input-output orientation. Notes: This figure depicts the estimation of the realizable improvement potential for a DMU with one input x_1 and its ideal reference point x_1^* and one output y_1 and its ideal reference point y_1^* for a MEA model in input-output orientation. The efficient frontier reflecting the technological boundary as a function of the set of DMUs under consideration is represented by the solid line

Table 9.1 Overview of research design parameters

Efficiency estimation	Screening level η_S	Asset allocation strategy	Region
Cross-section	$[0, 1] \Rightarrow \{\eta_S \vert 0 \leq \eta_S \leq 1\}$	Mean-variance optimization	USA
Best-in-sector	and $\eta_{S+1} = \eta_S + 0.1$	Naive (1/*N*) Value-weighting (index)	EU

Notes: This table provides an overview of the parameters used to construct the efficiency-based portfolio strategies

First, the firms' relative efficiencies are computed based on two efficiency estimation approaches relating to the identification of the set of DMUs. For the cross-sectional approach the full cross-section of firms is used, while for the "best-in-sector" approach, the efficiency of DMUs is computed within sectors. Potential differences in the final results due to these approaches relate to the efficiency estimation based on the varying homogeneity of DMUs in the sectors and cross-section, as well as the reduced asset universe after the stock selection.

Second, after conducting the efficiency analysis, all firms whose efficiency score exceeds the chosen screening level η_s will be selected into the portfolio. The screening level ranges from $\eta_s = 0$ with no screening applied to $\eta_s = 1$, in which only fully efficient firms are used, representing a best-in-class strategy.

Third, once the stock selection process is completed, common asset allocation strategies, such as mean-variance optimization, naive allocation, and value-weighting, are used to construct the portfolios and strategy-specific differences are investigated.

9.4 Data

The dataset used for this study is composed of public equity firms from the USA and Europe. For each firm the relevant data points required to conduct the efficiency analysis and construct the asset allocation strategies, including stock prices, market capitalization, and ESG scores, are obtained from Thomson Reuters Datastream.[4] The firm-level time series data consists of quarterly observations, as the portfolio strategies follow a quarterly rebalancing schedule. The sample of US firms consists of 411 firms over an observation period of 45 quarters from June 2005 to May 2016. For Europe, the sample is composed of 552 firms over a period of 46 quarters from October 2005 to December 2016. All firms for which complete data is not available are excluded.[5] The total dataset is therefore comprised of 18,495 and 25,392 firm observations for the USA and Europe, respectively.

All firms are classified according to the GICS (Global Industry Classification Standard) as the efficiency analysis is conducted both for the full cross-section and within sectors for each region.[6] The US 3-month Treasury bill rate is used as a risk-free rate.

Descriptive statistics of the dataset are provided in Table 9.2. It can be observed that average ESG scores are notably higher for European than for US firms, a fact which has been documented in previous studies as well (see, e.g., Amon et al.

[4] This study relies on ESG ratings from Thomson Reuters, which have been shown to perform similarly to other ratings in the context of portfolio management (see Amon et al., 2021b). The approach introduced in this paper can be applied using any available rating provider or a combination thereof.

[5] The small differences in sample size and observation period between regions are the result of a procedure aiming to maximize the number of available data points with respect to sample size and length.

[6] According to Golany and Roll (1989), a requirement for the efficiency estimation is that the number of decision-making units is twice as the number of inputs and outputs. For this reason, sector 55 of the GICS is excluded due the small number of firms belonging to this sector in the sample.

Table 9.2 Descriptive statistics

Region	# Firms	# Periods		Market value	ESG score	Return
			Mean	25572.27	65.39	0.11
			SD	44311.38	23.39	0.07
US	411	45	Median	10707.50	69.93	0.10
			Min	516.07	10.72	−0.13
			Max	387052.60	97.02	0.55
			Mean	26141.92	71.07	0.08
			SD	189003.73	22.66	0.10
EU	552	46	Median	5052.04	78.27	0.09
			Min	128.37	3.55	−0.46
			Max	4359100.39	95.96	0.51

Notes: This table provides descriptive statistics of the dataset used for the analysis for both the USA and EU. The mean, median, minimum, and maximum as well as the standard deviation are provided for the full cross-section of firms contained in the sectors 10, 15, 20, 25, 30, 35, 40, 45, 50, and 60 according to the Global Industry Classification Standard (GICS). Market value and ESG scores are reported as average quarterly values, and returns are presented as average annualized values across all firms

(2021b)). The average market value is comparable between regions with a larger range and higher standard deviation for European firms, while higher returns and lower standard deviation of returns can be observed for the USA.

9.5 Results

In this section, the results of the portfolio analysis are discussed. In Figs. 9.2, 9.3, 9.4, 9.5, and 9.6 the out- of-sample portfolio results for each strategy, region, and efficiency estimation approach are presented at increasing levels of efficiency screening.[7]

9.5.1 *Financial Performance*

Figure 9.2 illustrates the out-of-sample results for the Sharpe ratio of all the portfolios. It can be observed that the impact of efficiency-screening intensity depends on the asset allocation strategy as well as the efficiency estimation approach.

For the mean-variance strategy a negative screening effect is observed for both the cross- sectional and "best-in-sector" estimation approaches, which is significant

[7]The significance testing has been conducted based on the log returns of the portfolios using the Sharpe ratio equality test by Wright et al. (2014), T-test for returns, and ESG scores and F-test for variances.

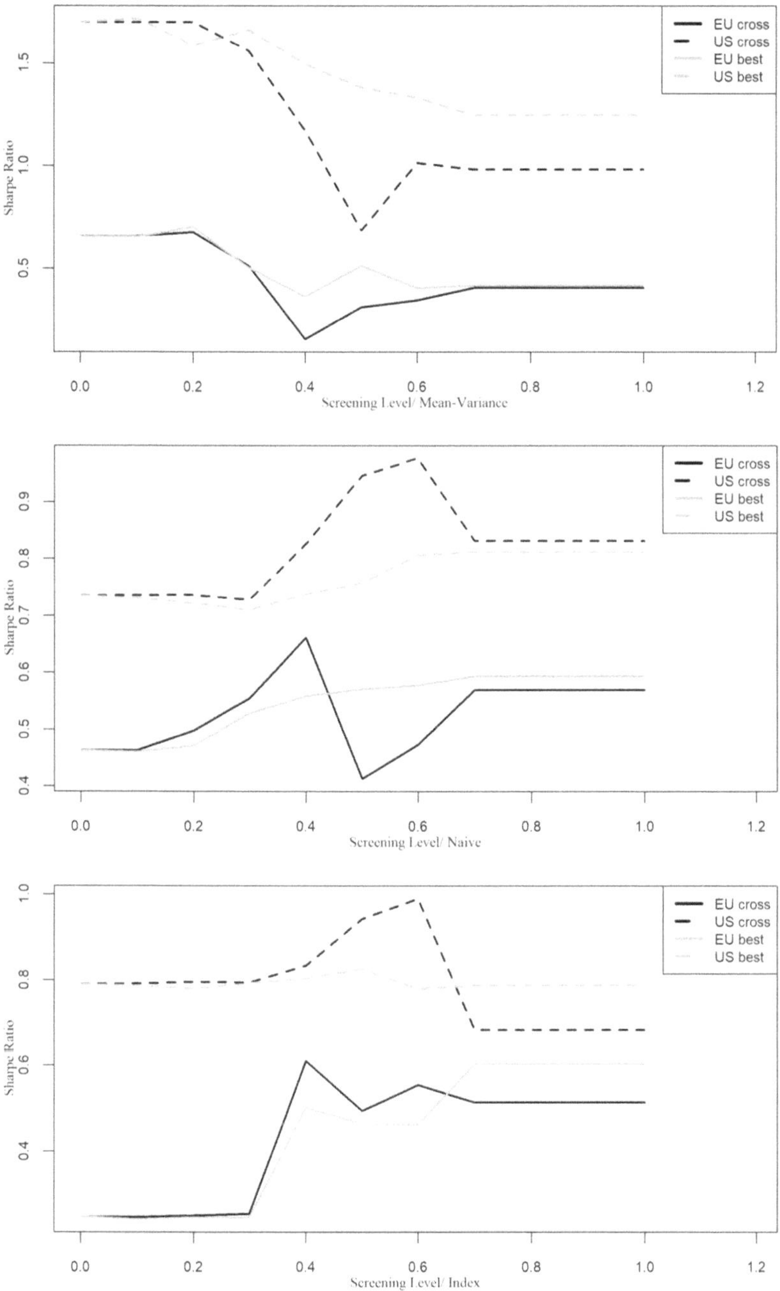

Notes: This set of figures reports the portfolio results regarding the Sharpe Ratio for all efficiency screening levels, efficiency estimation approaches, asset allocation strategies and regions considered. The solid line shows the results of the portfolios for the EU, while the dotted line shows the results for the US. The black line refers to the cross-sectional efficiency estimation approach, while the grey line refers to the "best-in-sector" approach.

Fig. 9.2 Result efficiency screening—Sharpe ratio. Notes: This set of figures reports the portfolio results regarding the Sharpe ratio for all efficiency-screening levels, efficiency estimation approaches, asset allocation strategies, and regions considered. The solid line shows the results of the portfolios for the EU, while the dotted line shows the results for the USA. The black line refers to the cross-sectional efficiency estimation approach, while the gray line refers to the "best-in-sector" approach

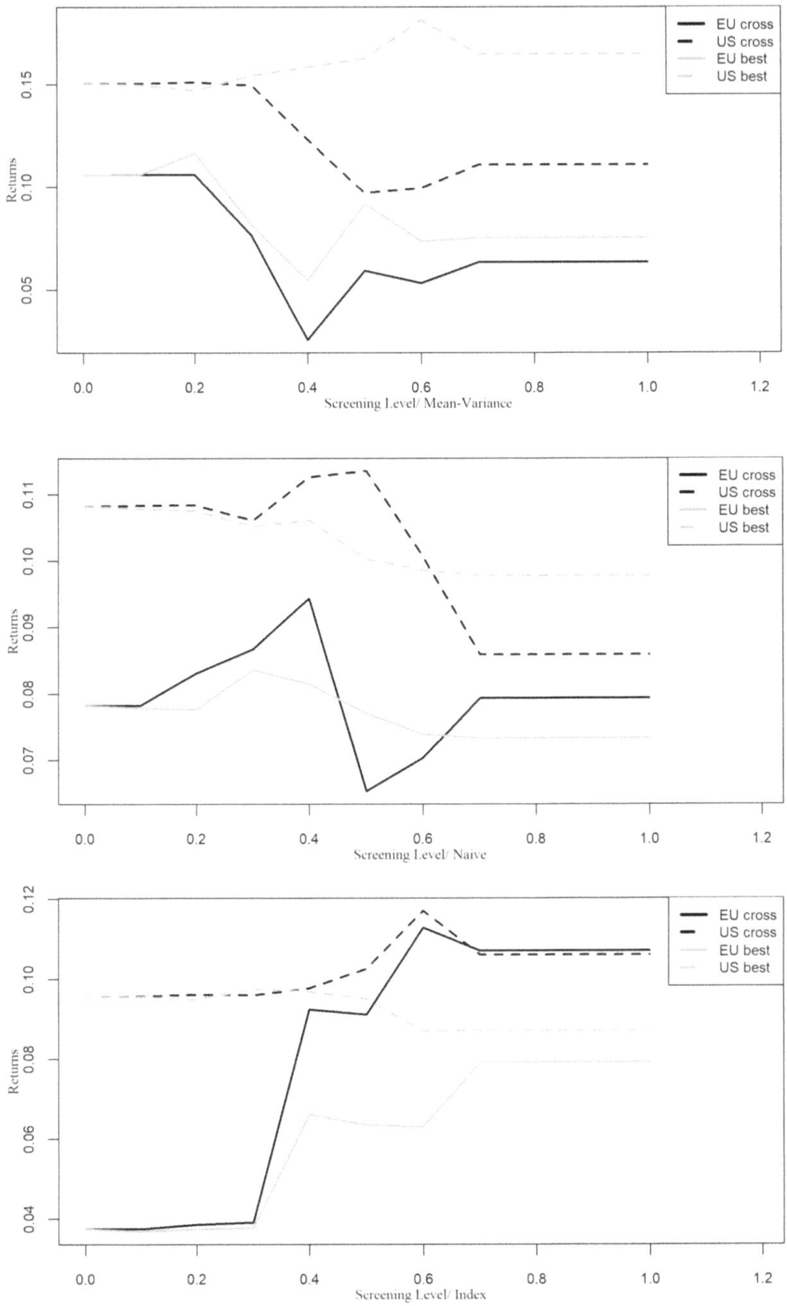

Notes: This set of figures reports the portfolio results regarding the returns for all efficiency screening levels, efficiency estimation approaches, asset allocation strategies and regions considered. The solid line shows the results of the portfolios for the EU, while the dotted line shows the results for the US. The black line refers to the cross-sectional efficiency estimation approach, while the grey line refers to the "best-in-sector" approach.

Fig. 9.3 Result efficiency screening—returns. Notes: This set of figures reports the portfolio results regarding the returns for all efficiency-screening levels, efficiency estimation approaches, asset allocation strategies, and regions considered. The solid line shows the results of the portfolios for the EU, while the dotted line shows the results for the USA. The black line refers to the cross-sectional efficiency estimation approach, while the gray line refers to the "best-in-sector" approach

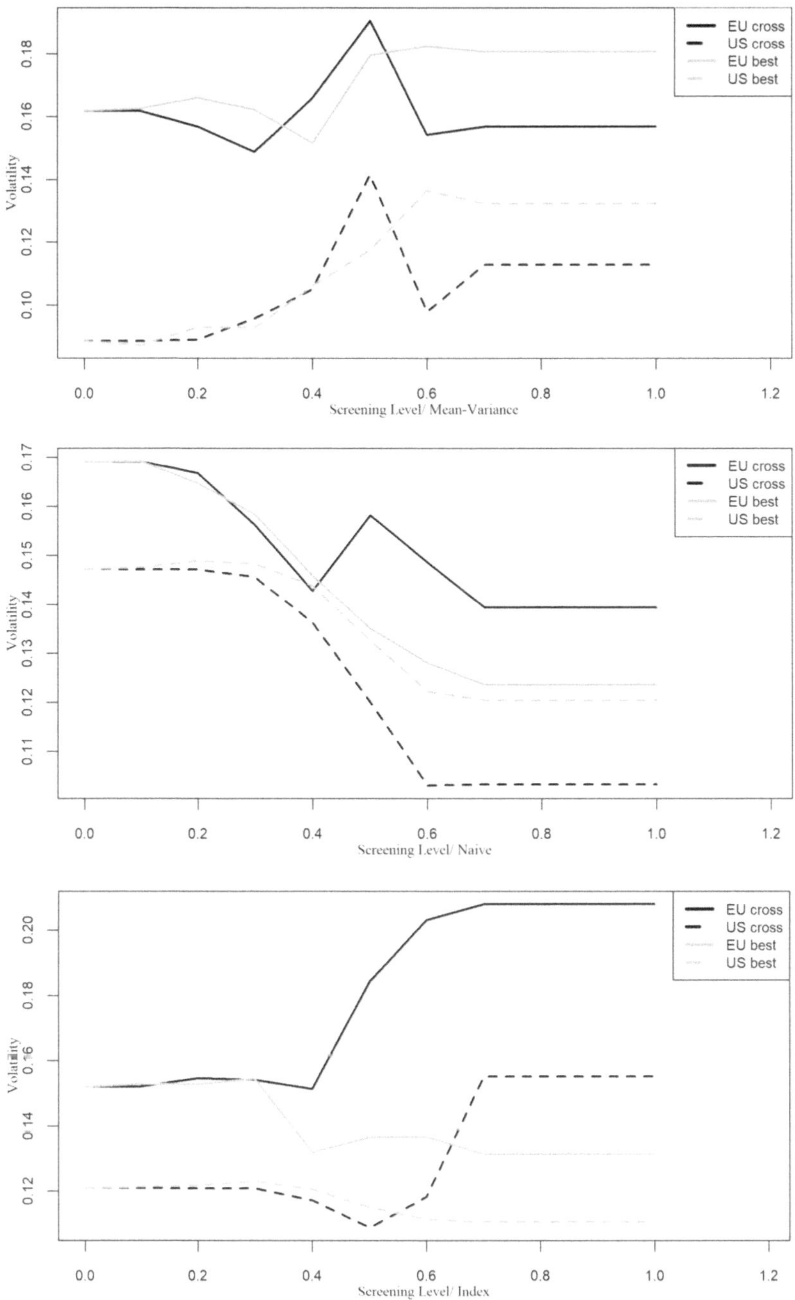

Notes: This set of figures reports the portfolio results regarding the volatility for all efficiency screening levels, efficiency estimation approaches, asset allocation strategies and regions considered. The solid line shows the results of the portfolios for the EU, while the dotted line shows the results for the US. The black line refers to the cross-sectional efficiency estimation approach, while the grey line refers to the "best-in-sector" approach.

Fig. 9.4 Result efficiency screening—volatility. Notes: This set of figures reports the portfolio results regarding the volatility for all efficiency-screening levels, efficiency estimation approaches, asset allocation strategies, and regions considered. The solid line shows the results of the portfolios for the EU, while the dotted line shows the results for the USA. The black line refers to the cross-sectional efficiency estimation approach, while the gray line refers to the "best-in-sector" approach

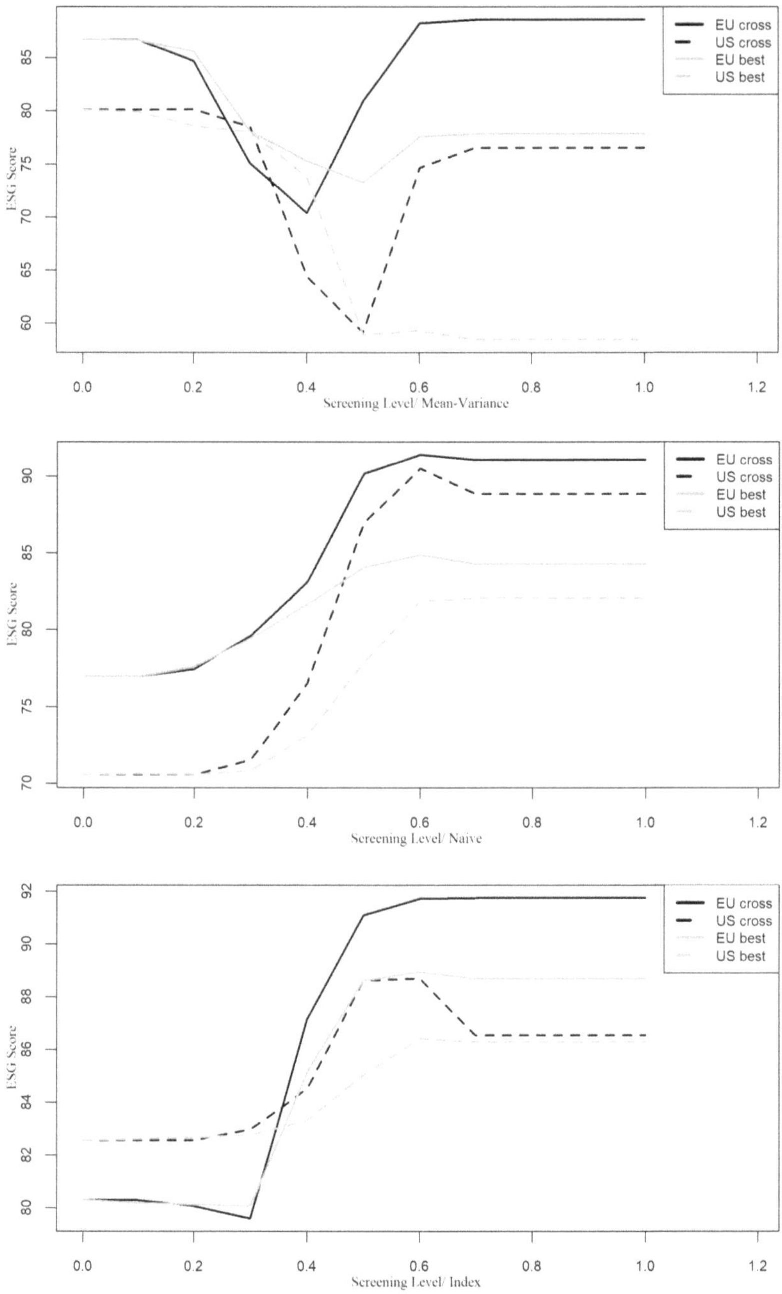

Notes: This set of figures reports the portfolio results regarding the ESG scores for all efficiency screening levels, efficiency estimation approaches, asset allocation strategies and regions considered. The solid line shows the results of the portfolios for the EU, while the dotted line shows the results for the US. The black line refers to the cross-sectional efficiency estimation approach, while the grey line refers to the "best-in-sector" approach.

Fig. 9.5 Result efficiency screening—ESG score. Notes: This set of figures reports the portfolio results regarding the ESG scores for all efficiency-screening levels, efficiency estimation approaches, asset allocation strategies, and regions considered. The solid line shows the results of the portfolios for the EU, while the dotted line shows the results for the USA. The black line refers to the cross-sectional efficiency estimation approach, while the gray line refers to the "best-in-sector" approach

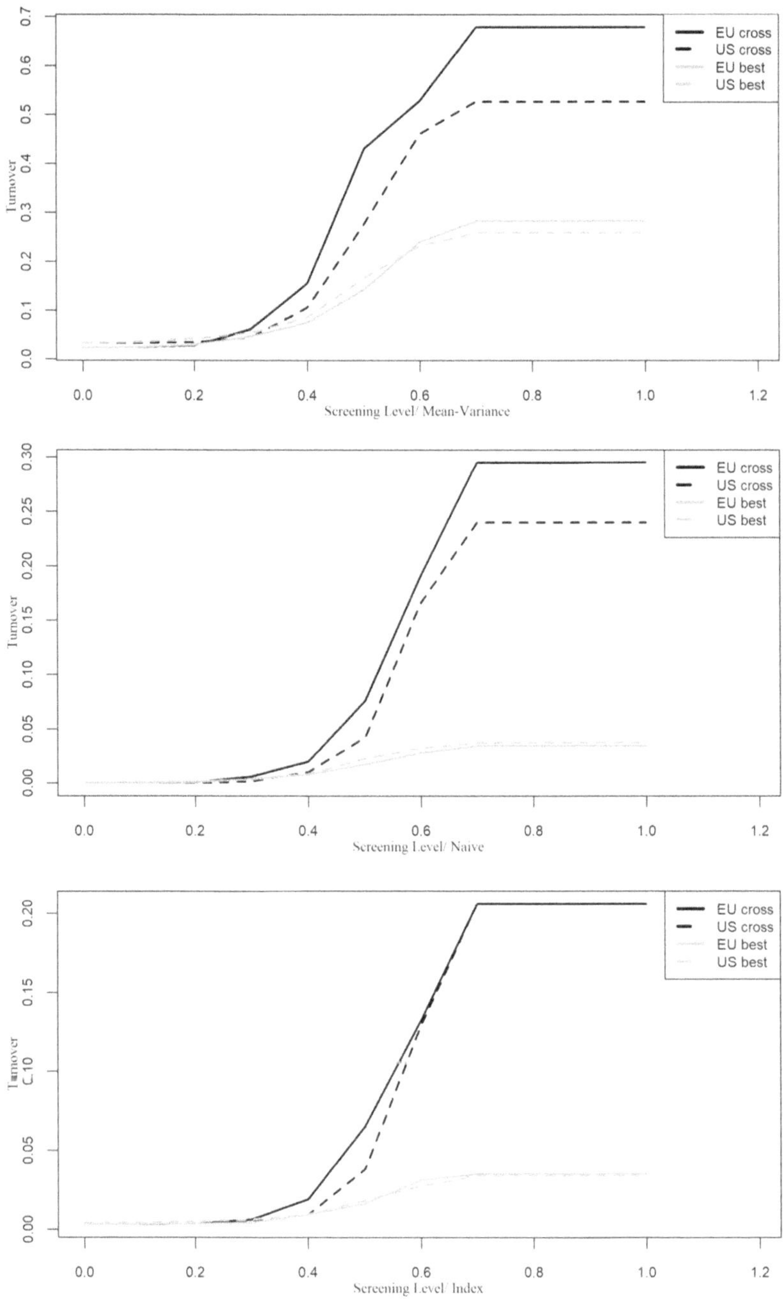

Notes: This set of figures reports the portfolio results regarding the turnover rates for all efficiency screening levels, efficiency estimation approaches, asset allocation strategies and regions considered. The solid line shows the results of the portfolios for the EU, while the dotted line shows the results for the US. The black line refers to the cross-sectional efficiency estimation approach, while the grey line refers to the "best-in-sector" approach.

Fig. 9.6 Result efficiency screening—turnover rates. Notes: This set of figures reports the portfolio results regarding the turnover rates for all efficiency-screening levels, efficiency estimation approaches, asset allocation strategies, and regions considered. The solid line shows the results of the portfolios for the EU, while the dotted line shows the results for the USA. The black line refers to the cross-sectional efficiency estimation approach, while the gray line refers to the "best-in-sector" approach for medium and high screening intensity for the USA. For the EU the effect is insignificant, indicating no screening effect. For the naive strategy significantly positive results can be observed for both regions and estimation approaches.[8] For the index strategy, a significantly positive effect can be shown as well for the USA, but only for medium screening intensity. This also holds for the EU for the "best-in-sector" approach, while it is not significant for the cross-sectional approach.

Regarding the efficiency estimation approaches, a rather linear effect is documented for the "best-in-sector" approach, while the cross-sectional approach shows a significant curvilinear relationship at low to medium intensities. This implies that medium screening intensity leads to a statistically significant improvement in financial performance for the naive and index strategies, while a strict screening would be preferred for the "best-in-sector" approach. The index strategy shows the largest screening gains in terms of financial performance for both efficiency estimation approaches for the EU, while screening gains are overall most consistent for the naive strategy.

The financial performance is further investigated using the portfolio returns and volatilities reported in Figs. 9.3 and 9.4. The screening effect on returns is not consistently positive or negative, while the effect on volatility is positive for the mean-variance and index and negative for the naive strategy. The effect on returns is significantly positive for the naive and index strategies for European portfolios at low and medium screening intensities, respectively. The impact on portfolio volatility is mostly significant for the mean-variance and naive strategies at medium to higher screening intensities for the USA.

9.5.2 ESG Performance

An investigation of the sustainability performance reported in Fig. 9.5 shows a significantly and consistently positive relationship between screening intensity and ESG scores for the naive and index strategies. The index strategy reports the highest ESG scores for the unscreened and strictly screened portfolios,[9] while the naive portfolios show on average the highest improvement along efficiency-screening intensity. For the mean-variance strategy, a significantly negative effect can be observed (except for EU cross, which shows an overall higher ESG score for strict screening intensity), which is most pronounced at medium screening levels.

[8] Apart from the partially negative development shown for EU cross in the naive strategy, which has been tested to be insignificant

[9] The positive relationship between firm size and ESG scores has been previously documented by, e.g., Amon et al. (2021b).

9.5.3 Turnover Rates

The investigation of turnover rates is highly relevant for screening studies, as high screening intensity typically implies increasing turnover rates, which might reduce or even negate a positive screening effect. Figure 9.6 reports the turnover rates for all portfolios, and as expected, a significant increase in turnover is documented for all strategies and efficiency estimation approaches. A notably higher increase can be observed for the cross-sectional approach, reducing the positive screening effect on the portfolios' financial performance, while screening intensity has a much smaller effect on the "best-in-sector" approach. This is somewhat expected as the "best-in-sector" approach estimates firm efficiency based on each sector, which produces an overall more stable stock selection over time, while the cross-sectional approach uses all available firms, which can lead to improved efficiency rankings over all sectors, but also to more frequent changes in the stock selection and therefore higher turnover rates.

The mean-variance strategy reports the highest turnover rates increasing the negative impact of efficiency screening even further, followed by the naive and index strategies. This implies that the combination of SRI efficiency screening and value-weighting produces more stable portfolio weights, even at higher screening intensity compared to a naive or mean-variance strategy.

Overall, it can be concluded that the impact of screening intensity depends on the stock selection approach and asset allocation strategy. The findings of the analysis indicate a negative relationship between screening intensity and portfolio performance for the mean-variance strategy, indicating that diversification losses exceed potential screening benefits due to a reduction in the asset universe caused by the efficiency screening and potentially more concentrated portfolios as a common occurrence of mean-variance optimization.

For the naive and index strategies, significant screening benefits with respect to risk-adjusted financial and ESG performance can be realized at increasing screening intensity for both regions with different implications based on the efficiency estimation approach. Depending on the level of transaction cost, either the cross-sectional approach at medium screening intensity with a positive curvilinear relationship or the "best-in-sector" approach at high intensity is preferred. The results further indicate that the ESG performance is similar between these two alternatives.

In summary, it can be said that socially responsible portfolio management using an SRI efficiency-based stock selection under joint consideration of financial and sustainability criteria is a viable approach, even at high screening intensity depending on the chosen asset allocation strategy and level of transaction costs. The results further indicate that a screening gain in ESG performance can be achieved alongside improved risk-adjusted financial performance, suggesting a potential application for conventional investors as well.

9.6 Conclusion

This study investigates the effect of SRI efficiency-screening intensity on a portfolio's performance under joint consideration of financial and ESG criteria in the analysis of the firms' efficiencies derived from multi-directional efficiency analysis for US and European firms. Two efficiency estimation approaches using the full cross-section and a "best-in-sector" approach as well as a number of usual asset allocation strategies, such as mean-variance optimization, naive allocation, and value-weighting, are implemented, reflecting common SRI fund and ESG index portfolios. Furthermore, the study is conducted for both US and European firms, respectively. The differences between efficiency estimation approach, asset allocation strategy, and region considered are examined systematically regarding the financial and ESG performance of the portfolios.

The results indicate no positive screening effect using the common mean-variance approach, but an improvement in financial and sustainability performance for the naive and value-weighting approaches. Under consideration of transaction cost, the screening intensity matters when the cross-sectional and "best-in-sector" efficiency estimation approaches are compared, suggesting a medium or high screening intensity, respectively.

This implies that socially responsible portfolio management using an SRI efficiency-based stock selection considering financial and non-financial criteria is a viable approach depending on the chosen asset allocation strategy and level of transaction costs. Furthermore, the results indicate that a screening gain in ESG performance can be achieved alongside improved risk- adjusted financial performance, suggesting a potential application for conventional investors as well.

Potential directions for future studies could be the use of multi-criteria asset allocation strategies in the second stage of the SRI portfolio management process alongside the proposed SRI efficiency screening for stock selection as a way to investigate further improvement potential in the financial and/or the sustainability dimension.

References

Alessandrini, F., & Jondeau, E. (2020). Esg investing: From sin stocks to smart beta. *The Journal of Portfolio Management, 46*(3), 75–94.

Alessandrini, F., & Jondeau, E. (2021). Optimal strategies for esg portfolios. *The Journal of Portfolio Management, 47*(6), 114–138.

Amon, J., Rammerstorfer, M., & Weinmayer, K. (2021a). Environmental port- folios—evidence from screening and passive portfolio management. *Sustainability, 13*(22), 12647.

Amon, J., Rammerstorfer, M., & Weinmayer, K. (2021b). Passive esg portfolio management—the benchmark strategy for socially responsible investors. *Sustainability, 13*(16), 9388.

Asmild, M., Hougaard, J. L., Kronborg, D., & Kvist, H. K. (2003). Measuring inefficiency via potential improvements. *Journal of Productivity Analysis, 19*(1), 59–76.

Awaysheh, A., Heron, R. A., Perry, T., & Wilson, J. I. (2020). On the relation between corporate social responsibility and financial performance. *Strategic Management Journal, 41*(6), 965–987.

Ballestero, E., Bravo, M., Pe'rez-Gladish, B., Arenas-Parra, M., & Pla-Santamaria, D. (2012). Socially responsible investment: A multicriteria approach to portfolio selection combining ethical and financial objectives. *European Journal of Operational Research, 216*(2), 487–494.

Barnett, M. L., & Salomon, R. M. (2006). Beyond dichotomy: The curvilinear relationship between social responsibility and financial performance. *Strategic Management Journal, 27*(11), 1101–1122.

Bilbao-Terol, A., Arenas-Parra, M., & Can˜al-Ferna'ndez, V. (2012). Selection of socially responsible portfolios using goal programming and fuzzy technology. *Information Sciences, 189*, 110–125.

Bogetoft, P., & Hougaard, J. L. (1999). Efficiency evaluations based on potential (non- proportional) improvements. *Journal of Productivity Analysis, 12*(3), 233–247.

Capelle-Blancard, G., & Monjon, S. (2014). The performance of socially responsible funds: Does the screening process matter? *European Financial Management, 20*(3), 494–520.

Charles, A., Darne´, O., & Fouilloux, J. (2016). *The impact of screening strategies on the performance of esg indices*. Technical report.

Charnes, A., Cooper, W. W., & Rhodes, E. (1978). Measuring the efficiency of decision making units. *European Journal of Operational Research, 2*(6), 429–444.

Chen, H.-H. (2008). Stock selection using data envelopment analysis. *Industrial Management & Data Systems, 108*, 1255.

Chen, L., Zhang, L., Huang, J., Xiao, H., & Zhou, Z. (2021). Social responsibility portfolio optimization incorporating esg criteria. *Journal of Management Science and Engineering, 6*(1), 75–85.

Debreu, G. (1951). The coefficient of resource utilization. *Econometrica: Journal of the Econometric Society, 19*, 273–292.

Dia, M. (2009). A portfolio selection methodology based on data envelopment analysis. *IN- FOR: Information Systems and Operational Research, 47*(1), 71–79.

Edirisinghe, N. C. P., & Zhang, X. (2008). Portfolio selection under dea-based relative financial strength indicators: Case of us industries. *Journal of the Operational Research Society, 59*(6), 842–856.

European Parliament and the Council of the European Union. (2019). Regulation (eu) 2019/2088 of the european parliament and the council of the european union of 27 november 2019 on sustainability-related disclosures in the financial services sector. *OJ, L 317/1*, 1–16.

European Sustainable Investment Forum. (2018). *European sri study 2018.*

Farrell, M. J. (1957). The measurement of productive efficiency. *Journal of the Royal Statistical Society: Series A (General), 120*(3), 253–281.

Friede, G., Busch, T., & Bassen, A. (2015). Esg and financial performance: aggregated evidence from more than 2000 empirical studies. *Journal of Sustainable Finance & Investment, 5*(4), 210–233.

Garc'ıa, F., Gonza'lez-Bueno, J., Oliver, J., & Riley, N. (2019). Selecting socially responsible portfolios: A fuzzy multicriteria approach. *Sustainability, 11*(9), 2496.

Gasser, S. M., Rammerstorfer, M., & Weinmayer, K. (2017). Markowitz revisited: Social portfolio engineering. *European Journal of Operational Research, 258*(3), 1181–1190.

Gharghori, P., & Ooi, E. (2016). The relationship between screening intensity and performance of socially responsible investment funds. In *Handbook of environmental and sustain- able finance* (pp. 335–357). Elsevier.

Golany, B., & Roll, Y. (1989). An application procedure for dea. *Omega, 17*(3), 237–250.

Halbritter, G., & Dorfleitner, G. (2015). The wages of social responsibility—where are they? a critical review of esg investing. *Review of Financial Economics, 26*, 25–35.

Hamilton, S., Jo, H., & Statman, M. (1993). Doing well while doing good? the investment performance of socially responsible mutual funds. *Financial Analysts Journal, 49*(6), 62–66.

Hirschberger, M., Steuer, R. E., Utz, S., Wimmer, M., & Qi, Y. (2013). Computing the nondominated surface in tri-criterion portfolio selection. *Operations Research, 61*(1), 169–183.

Humphrey, J. E., & Lee, D. D. (2011). Australian socially responsible funds: Performance, risk and screening intensity. *Journal of Business Ethics, 102*(4), 519–535.

Humphrey, J. E., & Tan, D. T. (2014). Does it really hurt to be responsible? *Journal of Business Ethics, 122*(3), 375–386.

Jin, I. (2020). Esg-screening and factor-risk-adjusted performance: The concentration level of screening does matter. *Journal of Sustainable Finance & Investment, 12*, 1–21.

Kempf, A., & Osthoff, P. (2007). The effect of socially responsible investing on portfolio performance. *European Financial Management, 13*(5), 908–922.

Koopmans, T. (1951). Cl,"analysis of production as an efficient combination of activities". In Cap. III of Koopmans, TC (Ed.), *Activity Analysis of Production and Allocation. Cowles Commission Monograph.*

Lee, D. D., Humphrey, J. E., Benson, K. L., & Ahn, J. Y. (2010). Socially responsible investment fund performance: the impact of screening intensity. *Accounting & Finance, 50*(2), 351–370.

Lim, S., Oh, K. W., & Zhu, J. (2014). Use of dea cross-efficiency evaluation in portfolio selection: An application to korean stock market. *European Journal of Operational Research, 236*(1), 361–368.

Pätäri, E. J., Leivo, T. H., & Honkapuro, J. S. (2010). Enhancement of value portfolio performance using data envelopment analysis. *Studies in Economics and Finance, 27*, 223.

Renneboog, L., Ter Horst, J., & Zhang, C. (2008). The price of ethics and stakeholder governance: The performance of socially responsible mutual funds. *Journal of Corporate Finance, 14*(3), 302–322.

Steuer, R. E., Qi, Y., & Hirschberger, M. (2005). Multiple objectives in portfolio selection. *Journal of Financial Decision Making, 1*(1), 5–20.

The Forum for Sustainable and Responsible investment. (2018). *Report on us sustainable, responsible and impact investing trends 2018.*

Tone, K. (2001). A slacks-based measure of efficiency in data envelopment analysis. *European Journal of Operational Research, 130*(3), 498–509.

Verheyden, T., De Moor, L., et al. (2015). Multi-criteria decision analysis: methods to define and evaluate socially responsible investments. *International Journal of Management and Decision Making, 14*(1), 44–65.

Verheyden, T., Eccles, R. G., & Feiner, A. (2016). Esg for all? the impact of esg screening on return, risk, and diversification. *Journal of Applied Corporate Finance, 28*(2), 47–55.

Weinmayer, K., & Rammerstorfer, M. (2023). *Efficiency of socially responsible investments in the context of portfolio management.* Available at SSRN 4039593.

Weinmayer, K., Garaus, M., & Wagner, U. (2023). The impact of corporate sustainability performance on advertising efficiency. *OR Spectrum, 46*, 1–35.

Wright, J. A., Yam, S. C. P., & Yung, S. P. (2014). A test for the equality of multiple sharpe ratios. *Journal of Risk, 16*(4), 3–21.

Chapter 10
SDG Portfolio Construction in Times of the EU Taxonomy

Karen Wendt

10.1 Introduction

Impact investing is still a niche market. Scaling the impact investing market significantly requires actors who invest in it. Institutional investors have increased appetite and strategic interest to invest in positive impact; however, they are often precluded from doing so by Fiduciary Duties and Investment Rules. As JP Morgan notes, impact investing currently is more of a private equity business due to the sheer lot size of transactions, which are just too small to enable institutional investors to participate (Saltuk & Idrissi, 2012).

In their view, the scale of impact investing is hindered by a mismatch between investors' preferences and realistic investment opportunities (ibid).

JP Morgan conducted a survey of leading institutional impact investors and found that absorptive capacity is a critical bottleneck (Saltuk et al., 2011). It is not unusual for mainstream pension funds, insurance companies, institutional investors, and asset managers to consider investing in only those funds that are of significant size (e.g., a minimum of US$500 million according to the Emerging Markets Private Equity Association (EMPEA, 2015)). Furthermore, many investors have minimum commitment sizes (e.g., they want to commit more than US$100 million) and maximum ownership limits (e.g., they cannot represent more than 20% of the fund's interests) according to EMPEA (2015). In comparison, the average size of an impact investing private equity fund is US$7 million, and the average underlying investment is US$2 million (Pitchbook, 2021). This means de-facto institutional investors are precluded from investing in this market.

Currently, institutional investors can either apply a wait-and-see strategy, or create their own small impact investing infrastructure fund through investing in the

K. Wendt (✉)
Eccos Impact GmbH, Cham, Zug, Switzerland
e-mail: karen@sustainablefinance.io

K. Wendt, B. Villhauer (eds.), *Sustainable Wealth Management*, Sustainable Finance,
https://doi.org/10.1007/978-3-031-55505-3_10

primary market. An alternative second-best strategy often chosen is to invest in the secondary market, just including some ESG criteria. Smart beta strategies and Environmental and Social Governance (ESG) approaches work well for passively managed investment funds; a couple of the worst breaches of sustainable or responsible business conduct can be avoided by excluding controversial industries and/or controversial business practices. ESG can be topped up with a best-in-class approach or an integrated ESG rating approach. A further approach is using active ownership through voting at the General Assembly. Active ownership provides the opportunity for huge pension funds to refuse to discharge the board, which makes it a sharp sword. However, this tool so far has been used more by activists like Engine No1, who created a fund and collected funds to refuse to discharge the board of Exxon Mobile and forced them to appoint an ESG Board Member (Engine No1, 2020). The limits of the ESG approach, however, are that all the tools and actions and roles lead finally to the evaluation of the quality of the environmental and social management system of the company and how it deals with environmental, social, and governance issues. It is therefore a risk management tool, and ESG ratings allow for screening and valuing the ESG management system of a company. However, the application of an ESG approach on the secondary market does not create a positive impact. ESG is used more as a risk management tool than as an impact-driven opportunity recognition tool (OECD, 2021). In addition, severe questions came up within the last 2 years. Not only the European Security and Market Authority (ESMA) has raised concerns about the consistency of ESG ratings, but a recent study also showed very low correlations between the ESG ratings of the two biggest ESG rating providers (ESMA, 2022). In a world where investors rely on IFRS standards, they expect the same consistency in ESG ratings; however, there is no standard available that can provide such level of consistency currently. If investors go to traditional rating agencies, which draw on IFRS company reports topped up with some proprietary information, all rating agencies will come up with very similar company ratings, so the correlation between these ratings will be high. However, this is missing in the ESG space, and ESG ratings for companies can vary a lot, although they normally build on the sustainability reports of the companies, which are structured in accordance with the guidance notes of the Global Reporting Initiative (GRI). One example is Tesla shares, which have been rated very high by some ESG rating agencies and low by others. Tesla also has been excluded recently from the Dow Jones Sustainability Index. The EU, with their EU Action Plan and Green New Deal Agenda, is therefore looking to redefine the sustainable finance space with a new approach using a positive selection approach described in the EU Green, social and Brown Taxonomy (EU, 2019). With this new approach, the EU wants to consider both positive impact creation and environmental and social governance management systems.

This paper wants to analyze and investigate whether a positive selection approach in coordination with the EU Taxonomy analysis process can provide an actively selected SDG portfolio from liquid stocks worldwide that also follow a strict ESG compliance methodology beating the MSCI benchmark.

This paper is organized as follows: first, the EU Taxonomy and theories of change are briefly described, then the selection methodology is explained, and thereafter some back-testings are displayed based on the most common methodologies, detailing the fully invested approach. After having illustrated the sustainability quality of the stocks picked by the Positive Selection Mechanism, the paper broaches the issues of whether these stocks are capable of competing from a financial point of view and which portfolio composition approaches are eminently supportive in this respect.

Finally, the author draws a couple of conclusions for further research and portfolio engineering practices.

10.2 The EU Taxonomy

While all ESG initiatives have their merit in awareness raising, it is time to take sustainability to a new level (EUR-LEX, 2020). Since the EU Taxonomy has been published, it has become clear that those filtering approaches based on a passive investment strategy are not compatible with the EU Taxonomy, which formulates a positive list for a green economy with climate-resilient economic growth as well as achieving the SDGs (EU Taxonomy, 2019). Already today, some listed companies apply a theory of change in order to bring it into alignment with the EU Taxonomy or the SDGs (Wendt, 2021). Those companies actively mitigate transition risks. While problem knowledge has been developed over decades (Global Challenges Report, sustainability initiatives, Club of Rome Limits of Growth Reports), it was set for the United Nations SDGs to develop a target knowledge base. This strategy allows institutional investors to pick SDG-aligned companies on the secondary market, which are the ones that push positive impact. By investing in these SDG-aligned companies, the market power of those companies increases.

The EU action plan for financing sustainable growth (in the following action plan) builds on the final report of the EU Commission High-Level Expert Group (HLEG) on sustainable finance and contains a selection of the proposals of the expert committee. The HLEG has created a plan to transform the economy into a sustainable economic system.[1] The ten points proposed essentially include eight of the central HLEG recommendations and additional measures such as the introduction of climate benchmarks, revisiting accounting, and taking sustainability into account in the supervisory regulations for banks and insurance companies, including a "Green Supporting Factor."[2] The centerpiece is a uniform classification system of economic activities, called taxonomy, which should end the fragmentation of the term sustainable or green investments. The taxonomy contains a positive list of

[1] See final report https://ec.europa.eu/info/files/190618-sustainable-finance-teg-report-using-the-taxonomy_en

[2] Green Supporting Factor means that the EU uses incentives to transform the economy with increased green production and investment.

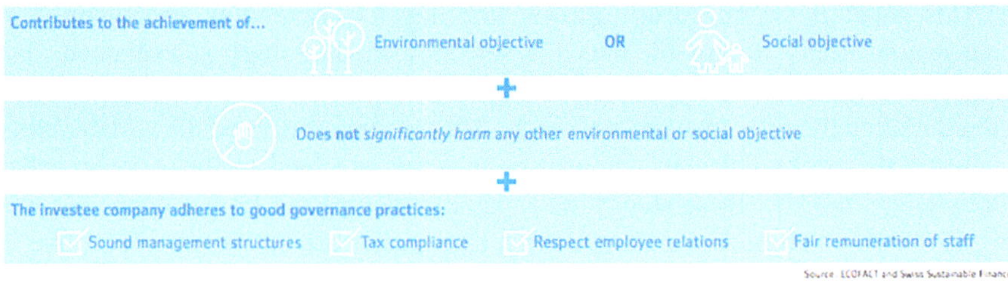

Fig. 10.1 Definition of sustainable Investment according to the EU Action Plan and the Taxonomy

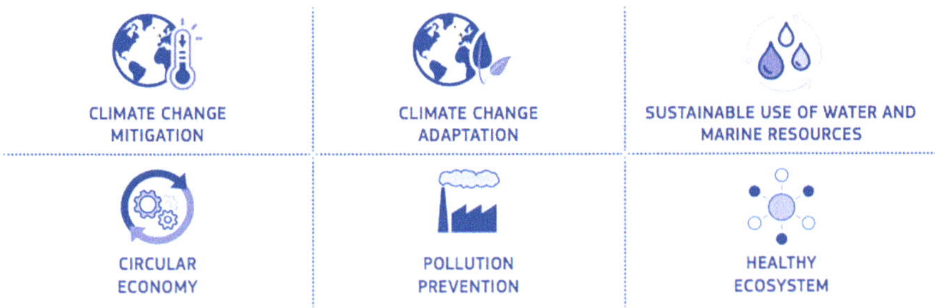

Fig. 10.2 The five objectives of the Green Taxonomy

investments, including a clear description of which investments, companies, projects, and facilities are to be regarded as sustainable in the sense of the EU sustainability definition.

The sustainable investment definition of the EU Action Plan is depicted in Fig. 10.1.

An investment can be defined as sustainable if it contributes to the achievement of an environmental or social objective, does not significantly harm another environmental or social objective (Do no significant harm or DNSH condition), and adheres to good governance practices.[3]

The six objectives of the EU, according to the Green Taxonomy regulation, are the following:

- Climate change mitigation
- Climate adaptation risk
- Sustainable use/protection of water/marine resources (use of water/marine)
- Transition to the circular economy
- Prevention and reduction of pollution (pollution prevention and abatement)
- Protection of healthy ecosystems (Fig. 10.2)

[3]These are enshrined in the so-called OECD MNE guidelines. The guidelines exist for the main industrial sectors and are mandatory for multinational companies.

10.2.1 The SDG Portfolio

In general, the selection methodology has been developed in order to look for innovation and transition opportunities aligned with the SDGs. The Selection methodology starts with an investment universe of zero.

In the positive selection process online stock information from Bloomberg and Morningstar is used as well as from alternative sources.

The portfolio selection is designed for institutional investors that need fund that allows them to invest in an SDG-aligned investment universe alongside EU Taxonomy alignment.

Therefore, a positive portfolio selection methodology has been developed in order to identify liquid shares listed on the stock exchange (secondary market) that address the SDGs with their business model, have at least 70% of their turnover with SDG themes, rate high on innovation, and apply a theory of change.

Also, the stocks are searched in various ESG databases for negative reputations. In such cases, the stock will be likewise refused. Thanks to the strategic selection process, financially successful stocks that align with positive SDG impact can be assembled into an SDG-aligned stock universe. Other embodiments can be added to the selection list like expected returns (using Fama French model and formulas), variance, and correlations between the stocks.

The so-created portfolio forms the basis for mainstream portfolio engineering like equally weighted portfolio (EWP) selection, minimum variance, dynamic weighting, and ESG-optimized strategies.

When turning the positive portfolio selection methodology into a portfolio structure, two general approaches have been applied. While the first approach aims at a constantly fully invested portfolio, the second approach allows hedging strategies using standard stock index future contracts.

The selection algorithm uses Artificial Intelligence, in particular, Machine Learning to find the shares that—based on reported turnover—converge the most with the SDG targets. In a cosine similarity vector space model, the processors detect Sustainable Development Goals associated with the stock. Cosine similarity gives a useful measure of how similar two documents are likely to be in terms of their subject matter.[4]

The SDGs are chosen from a list containing criteria for SDGs 3, 4, 6, 7, 9, 11, 12, and 13. The cosine matching can be performed on a multilevel space.

In the following, the author concentrates on how the SDG selection methodology deals with the EU taxonomy requirements described above in order to deliver decision criteria on whether the selected SDG fund is materially taxonomy compliant.

The fund is focused on investing in liquid shares that fulfill the following SDGs.

---

[4] Singhal (2001).

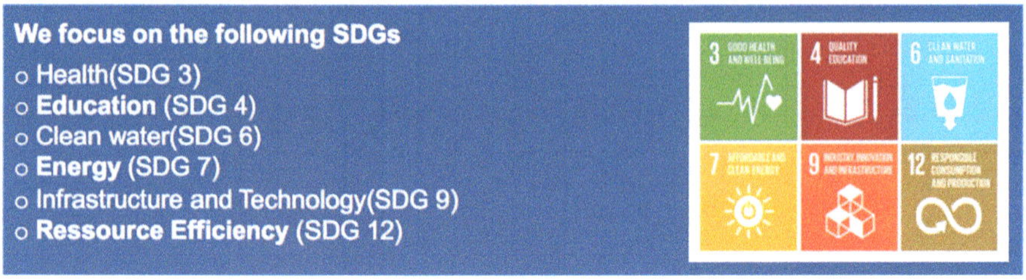

10.2.2 Based on a Theory of Change

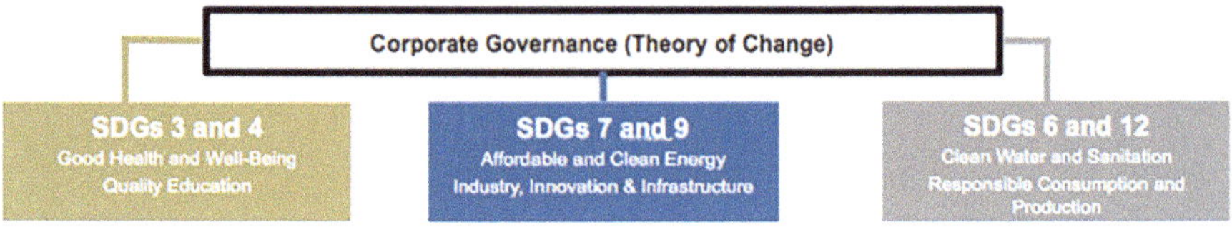

To address the DNSH and uphold a good governance perspective, the theory of change necessitates not only alternative data analysis but also the implementation of policies and strategies. The company must ensure respect for human rights,[5] compliance with ILO[6] standards, the presence of a climate policy or strategy, and the incorporation of relevant certified management systems. Furthermore, the company should maintain ongoing certifications from the ISO organization.

Based on the notion that only SDG-eligible companies aligning with the taxonomy goals in coordination with certified management systems, verified theory of change approach, and demonstrated innovation capacity are eligible for the fund, we conclude that the fund selection is materially compliant with the EU taxonomy.

10.3 Research Application

In the following sections, several portfolio composition approaches are tested, assuming a fully invested portfolio. By this approach, the outcomes can be compared with established market benchmarks and checked against the financial competitiveness of the selected shares.

Arrived at a list of companies delivered by the Positive Selection Methodology, the next step was, of course, to compose a portfolio from this investment universe. To compare the results of our portfolios with the markets' action, established equity

---

[5] UN Framework for Human Righs in Business (Protect, respect, remedy framework developed by Prof. Ruggie).

[6] International Labour Law Organization core Labor Standards.

market indices were used as benchmarks. As the Positive Selection Methodology is applied to companies from developed countries only, the MSCI World Index® is a logical first choice, as this index comprises all developed equity markets but not the emerging ones. However, the weight of US companies in this index is about two-thirds, while in the positive selection SDG universe, only 9 out of 55 companies are US based. This difference is noteworthy because, in the period under examination, the US markets performed significantly better than the rest of the world did. Therefore, the MSCI Europe® is taken into account in addition to the MSCI, reflecting that 60% of our universe is Europe-based.

Fully invested portfolios were constructed for two reasons. First, these portfolios are directly comparable with the established equity market indices. Second, a number of investors are interested in fully invested funds as brickstones for their own active asset allocation and hedging strategies. For such investors who in contrast prefer funds with an active risk management, a feasible dynamic hedging approach can be provided.

Strict company filtering processes as our SDG Positive Selection Methodology result, almost by definition, in rather short lists of stocks. From a portfolio management point of view, this may cause concentration risks. Therefore, several established weighting methods have been applied in order to show that the SDG Positive Selection Methodology generates short lists of stocks that are well diversified as well as unbiased in terms of performance.

For all portfolios, the investment starts on December 31, 2015, ending March 31, 2020. The price data of 2015 are used for some backward-looking optimization approaches. In any simulation, each share has a non-negative, non-zero weight, and the weights add up to 100%, which means that liquidity is not an element of the portfolio. These properties helped to compare the results with those of the market benchmarks.

In order to focus on the effects of the different portfolio construction methods, only one run of the SDG Positive Selection Methodology was performed and the resulting list of companies was frozen. Doing so means the simulation approach does not fully comply with the MiFID 2 requirements for simulations to be used in communication with private clients.[7] However, as public marketing is not the purpose of this paper, the selection was held constant to gain the advantage of avoiding interference between the dynamics of selection and weighting. Accordingly, only those companies were included for which price data existed for the whole examination period and sufficient data for the weighting criteria. Therefore, the challenges of delistings could be avoided, survivorship bias cannot be fully ruled out, and some survivorship bias might have affected results. Yet, this possible bias is unlikely to be

[7] Under the MiFID 2 regulation, the selection would have to be performed as if the investment had really been performed, which, for example, would require a repeated selection with the data then available.

substantial as only five companies had to be skipped and skipped companies were bought at a higher price than the last price before the respective announcement.[8]

10.4 Weighting Methods

In recent years, so-called "smart" approaches have become popular as portfolio management tools. The idea is to employ one or more factors for which empirical significance has been found (for a detailed discussion of this topic, see, e.g., Baltussen, Swinkels, and van Vliet, "Global Factor Premiums", 2019, available at SSRN: https://ssrn.com/abstract=3325720). Popular factors are size, momentum, or value, which in the past tended to produce alpha, i.e., to yield higher returns than the market did. However, if factors work, they do so only if applied not only to a large number of stocks but ideally to the whole market: Any filter is potentially influential on the alpha of a factor. Given the application at hand, the application with the Positive Selection Methodology, which delivers a short list of stocks as an investment universe, smart approaches cannot be expected to be useful, so they have not been employed.

At the beginning, a quite simplistic but common approach of composing a portfolio by equal weighting all shares has been employed as this is the most neutral method of composing a portfolio. Two different rebalancing frequencies were used, quarterly and annually, which also holds true for the following strategies.

Second, straightforwardly the free float market value was used like most market indices do, including the two indices (MSCI World and MSCI Europe) chosen as benchmarks.

Third, ESG scores were used. Following the respective strand of literature, which reports different results for using E, S, and Gas portfolio weighting parameters, the methodology used came back to each of these three scores and to all combinations of them. Special emphasis was put on the "Total ESG" score. To accomplish this, scores of Bloomberg, which are determined by the extent of coverage and transparency a company provides concerning environment, social, and governance issues (ESG), were applied. Given the fact that the Positive Selection Methodology already filtered for a company's performance in this field, the voluntary information scope might offer additional information.

Within the range of possible ESG variables, a carbon dioxide measure was employed. The most encompassing variable, which was the total greenhouse gas emissions, was used.

Best-in-Progress (BiP) approach was not applied for the following reason. The idea of BiP is that if a company with a rather low ESG performance turns its attention toward ESG and starts improving its sustainability performance, the company

[8] The two companies finally failing were Alpiq Holding AG and Alliance Creative Group Inc. The companies bought out were the FinTech Group AG, CA Inc., and Ansaldo STS SpA. The listing of ABN Amro NV started after the beginning of our period.

will more often than not experience a reduction of risks and therefore become more valuable. Therefore, an improving ESG score can be interpreted as a signal for a rising enterprise value and consequently for a higher stock price. However, almost none of the companies in the SDG Positive Selection Method sample showed a significant change in its ESG score over time, providing no starting point for using a BiP measure as a weighting parameter.

The fourth group of simulations drew on Markowitz's types of reasoning. On the one hand, minimum volatility approaches with look-back periods of one quarter, half a year, and full year were used, and, on the other hand, Sharpe ratio maximizations, i.e., maximizing the ratio of return and volatility within the corresponding look-back period, were employed. For this fourth group, minimum and maximum restrictions were imposed. The optimization routines had to assign weights between 0.80% and 4.00% to each stock.

No active FX strategy was applied; the daily returns were transferred from the respective local currency into Euro. There are 11 foreign currencies involved (AUD, CAD, CHF, DKK, GBP, HKD, JPY, KRW, NOK, SEK, USD).

A further important aspect of portfolio optimization is the consideration of transaction costs. It's a well-known feature that quite a lot of dynamic portfolio weighting approaches yield profitable results in terms of costs. However, if realistic transaction costs are taken into account, many approaches lose their cutting edge. Therefore, for a general analysis, we calculated the turnover necessary for each weighting method and presented it by a "round trip" logic, e.g., a turnover of 10% means that, during the period under consideration, the portfolio was modified by selling 10% and buying 10% of other portfolio members.

10.5 Data Description

The SDG Positive Selection Methodology delivered 55 listed companies located in globally developed countries. Two of them had to be skipped because the main decisions of these companies are made in China, notwithstanding that the shares, and in one case the headquarters, too, are located in countries defined as reliable for this approach.[9]

For the shares of the remaining 53 companies, data of daily total gross returns from Jan 1, 2015, until March 31, 2020, was used from a Euro investor's perspective. Every stock is traded at least at one of the big exchanges in New York, London, Paris, Frankfurt, Tokyo, and Sydney.

[9] The two companies skipped are Jinkosolar Holding Co Ltd. and Tencent Holdings Ltd.

10.6 Presentation of Results

Table 10.1 presents the results of selected simulations and of the two chosen benchmarks by the following key indicators, which are all determined before costs and taxes. First, the annualized total return is calculated by transforming the total return of the period to the yearly geometric mean. Second, the annualized volatility is calculated as the standard deviation of daily portfolio returns, annualized by multiplying it with the square root of 260, which is about the number of trade days within a typical year. Third, the Sharpe ratio is calculated as the ratio of the two numbers calculated above, return and volatility, implicitly assuming the risk-free return being zero. Fourth, the maximum drawdown represents the worst performance that could have resulted when buying the portfolio once and selling it again, both at any date within the simulation period. Fifth, the tracking error versus the World (EUR) MSCI is provided., calculated as the standard deviation of the daily return differences. And sixth, an indicator for the potential transaction costs is provided by calculating the average annual turnover caused by the regular portfolio rebalancing.

Let's start by having look at the benchmarks' properties. For both, the annualized return of the period under consideration is about 2.2%. It may be interesting to mention that the conventional MSCI Europe Index performed worse than the MSCI World did, propelled by the US markets. Still, the SRI index could cope with these headwinds as, starting about 2014, the MSCI SRI Europe notoriously beat its conventional index counterpart. Meanwhile, the lower volatility of stocks with above-average ESG ratings is a well-documented empirical fact in the literature of sustainable finance. In line with that, the MSCI SRI Europe reveals a lower volatility compared with the MSCI World index, and accordingly, also its Sharpe Ratio is the better one. Finally, also the Maximum Drawdown is lower for the MSCI SRI Europe. Not surprisingly, this maximum drawdown has been effectuated during the so-called "Corona Crash" between February and March 2020, which will turn out to hold not only for both benchmarks but for all portfolios we present.

Table 10.1 Key results of simulations

Weighting strategy	Rebalancing frequency	Return (%)	Volatility (%)	Sharpe ratio	Maximum drawdown (%)	Track. error	Turnover
MSCI World (EUR)	–	2.21	16.89	0.131	40.05	–	–
MSCI SRI Europe	–	2.22	16.20	0.137	37.67	0.72%	–
Equally	No	1.27	15.33	0.083	34.57	0.56%	0.00%
Equally	Quarterly	1.12	15.55	0.072	35.27	0.59%	17.54%
Equally	Yearly	1.49	15.55	0.096	35.27	0.58%	8.44%
By market value	Yearly	2.19	15.44	0.142	34.56	0.56%	7.93%
By ESG Score	Yearly	1.86	15.56	0.120	34.87	0.58%	8.55%
By G Score	Yearly	2.05	15.72	0.130	35.22	0.57%	9.11%

The first portfolio we simulated from our frozen selection list was the equally weighted one without any rebalancing. The return of this approach was disappointing, falling short of the benchmarks' annualized returns by almost one full percentage point. However, the volatility of this portfolio turned out to be lower than that of both benchmarks. Both results were surprising because equal weighted portfolios by definition allocate higher weights to small caps than the market cap weighted indices do, and therefore, the small cap factor usually lets equal weighted portfolios show higher returns and higher volatilities. Worth noting is also the low tracking error: Despite the relative shortness of the list from which the portfolio is composed of, the tracking error of only 0.56% fortifies the fact that the chosen approach qualifies for concentrated global equity strategies.

In the next step, the equal weights were regularly balanced, one time quarterly and one time yearly, and compared both portfolios with the non-rebalanced one. The rebalancing did not change the results considerably. While, in both cases, the observed volatility rose a bit, the return dropped for the quarterly rebalanced portfolio, resulting in a worse Sharpe Ratio. In contrast, the return of the yearly rebalanced portfolio turned out to be annualized 22 bp higher. These findings harmonize with the stylized facts that in the short term, the momentum effect prevails, while in the longer term, the forces of "return to the mean" are stronger.

Looking at potential transaction costs caused by rebalancing, these costs can be judged as being moderate. Assuming a transaction cost rate of 0.25%, the yearly costs resulting from the quarterly rebalancing are just 9 bp (= 0.09%) of the whole portfolio. When applying yearly rebalancing, this is roughly halved to 4 bp. As an intermediate result, there is some evidence for superiority of less frequent, i.e., for yearly rebalancing.

In the third step, the portfolio was allocated according to the free float market value, using a yearly rebalancing. This weighting scheme led to a significantly higher yearly return, which was on par with those of both benchmarks. Obviously, the larger impact enterprises in the frozen list performed, on average, better than the smaller ones. As the volatility of this portfolio compared with that of the equally weighted portfolios, the market value portfolio emerged with a superior Sharpe Ratio compared to the two benchmarks. Additionally, its Maximum Drawdown was clearly smaller, the turnover is a bit lower, and the tracking error is as low as it gets here.

In a fourth approach, ESG data were employed. Ranking the weights according to the sustainability performance resulted in a portfolio that also had a higher annualized return than the equal weighted ones. However, it fell short of the market value weighted portfolio, not only in terms of return but with any measure observed. Not only the ESG measure was employed, but also its three components, stand-alone and combined. It turned out that the main driver of better returns was the "G," i.e., the measure of good governance. To sum this up, no ESG portfolio showed better results than the market value weighted portfolio. The differences were not huge, not between the results of the different portfolios nor between the most ESG ratings. Obviously, the SDG Positive Selection Methodology did what it was designed for and filtered enterprises with similar sustainability properties so that consequently, ESG weighting schemes cannot unfold huge effects.

Additional specifications were added finally, using alternative ESG data, CO_2-footprint data, Markowitz Optimization, and the Minimum Volatility approach, finding results within a narrow range but not better than those of the market value weighted portfolio.

When interpreting the results in comparison with the MSCI World, one should bear in mind that this global index benefitted, during the period under consideration, from its high share of US stocks (roughly 70%) and especially of the FAANG stocks with a relatively high share. The SDG Positive Selection Portfolios yielded its results without FAANG stocks and with a significantly lower US share. Consequently, the good results of these portfolios are quite remarkable.

While the results of these simulations produce results that are roughly in line with those of the benchmarks, in the future even better results can be expected, for two reasons. First, the period under consideration was affected by the huge outperformance of the so-called FAANG stocks (Facebook, Apple, Amazon, Netflix, Google, and the like). Any portfolio lacking these outperforming heavy weights had difficulties to cope with the results of the indices including them. Second, due to the general shift toward responsible investing and rising regulation, as exemplified by the upcoming initiatives in the EU, stocks that excel with above average ESG scores or with positive impact properties will be increasingly sought after by investors.

10.7 Summary

- The list of stocks picked by the Positive Selection Mechanism proves to be investable in any aspect and to be financially competitive.
- Portfolios composed from the positively picked stocks exhibit less volatility and less severe drawdowns compared with established market benchmarks, independently from the portfolio composition approach chosen.
- However, the tracking error of all our portfolios versus the MSCI World is low enough to qualify them as substitutes for general global equity investments.
- The same portfolios tend to have slightly lower returns than established market benchmarks. This may be due to the lack of Big Tech in the sample under con-

sideration. However, the returns are quite robust against the portfolio composition approach, so investors may realistically expect usual market return patterns.
- These portfolios, which are financially at arm's length, excel with their sustainable impact and are fully compliant with the forthcoming EU regulation.
- For now and in the years ahead, we expect even better results for two reasons. First, the annual application of the Positive Selection Method will enhance the precision of the stocks' list that the portfolio is composed of. Second, stocks with these properties will be significantly more sought after, driven by factors such as EU regulations and the general shift toward sustainable and impact investing.

References

EMPEA. (2015). How private equity models and practitioners can advance impact investing in emerging markets. In K. Wendt (ed) *Responsible investment banking* (pp. 563 ff). Springer Nature 2015. Available at https://link.springer.com/chapter/10.1007/978-3-319-10311-2_38

Engine No. 1. (2020). *Reenergize EXXON*. Available at https://reenergizexom.com/who-is-engine-no-1/

ESMA. (2022). *ESMA to work on ESG disclosures as a new strategic supervisory priority*. Available at https://www.esma.europa.eu/press-news/esma-news/esma-work-esg-disclosures-new-union-strategic-supervisory-priority

EU. (2019). *European Commission: EU taxonomy for sustainable activities*. Available at https://finance.ec.europa.eu/sustainable-finance/tools-and-standards/eu-taxonomy-sustainable-activities_en

EUR-LEX 200: Communication from the Commission to the European Parliament, The Council, The European Economic and Social Committee and the Committee of the Regions. (2020). *A new circular economy action plan for a cleaner and more competitive Europe*. Available at: https://eur-lex.europa.eu/legal-content/EN/TXT/?uri=COM%3A2020%3A98%3AFIN

OECD. (2021). *ESG practice, progress and challenges*. Available at https://www.oecd.org/finance/ESG-Investing-Practices-Progress-Challenges.pdf

Pitchbook. (2021). *Fund market overvies*. Available at https://pitchbook.com/data

Saltuk Y., & Idrissi A. I. (2012). *Global social finance: A Portfolio approach to impact investment*. Available at https://www.jpmorganchase.com/content/dam/jpmc/jpmorgan-chase-and-co/documents/121001_A_Portfolio_Approach_to_Impact_Investment.pdf

Saltuk, Y., et al. (2011). *Insight into the impact investing market*. Available at https://thegiin.org/assets/documents/Insight%20into%20Impact%20Investment%20Market2.pdf

Singhal, A. (2001). Modern information retrieval: A brief overview. *Bulletin of the IEEE Computer Society Technical Committee on Data Engineering, 24*(4), 35–43.

Wendt, K. (2021). Theories of change in light of the EU taxonomy: Foreword. In K. Wendt (Ed.), *Theories of change* (pp. 5–8). Springer Nature.

Chapter 11
The Green Siblings: Exploring the Emerging Structure of Sustainable Finance

B. Tobias Peylo

11.1 The Organic Growth of Sustainable Finance

In conventional finance, the world is often quite simple. Neoclassical economic theory anchors the concept of the "homo economicus", which is applied in rational choice theory as a mandatory compass for all kinds of economic decisions (e.g. Coleman & Coleman, 1992) as well as in investment theory for decisions regarding financial investments (e.g. Spremann, 2005). As a consequence, a decision can only be considered rational if it maximizes material profit. This simplified idea, as well as the implication that it is prudent to consider only money, was at the very heart of the critique brought forward by behavioral finance (Ellsberg, 1961; Allais & Hagen, 1979; Kahneman & Tversky, 1979; Peterson, 2002; Thaler, 1993)—sadly, not to much avail, as the monetary-based rationality concept is still firmly anchored in economic textbooks and practitioners' literature alike (e.g. Berk & DeMarzo, 2017, Fabozzi & Markowitz, 2008 or Haugen, 2001); a perseverance of questionable wisdom, as investors live on the same planet on which they invest and should, purely for reasons of intelligence and self-preservation, be interested in more than financial profit.

A thought quite similar to this—if not motivated by an ecological but rather an ethical or religious perspective—may have prompted John Wesley, a contemporary of Adam Smith, to ask in 1760 in his work "The Use of Money" for boundaries to making profit. This effectively brought negative criteria into existence and can be considered one of the origins of a movement that would much later be termed sustainable investment or socially responsible investment (SRI) and, for a long time, form the essence of sustainable finance (Sparkes, 2006). Together with the application of positive criteria, best-in-class and best-of-class selection and shareholder

B. Tobias Peylo (✉)
Kempten University of Applied Sciences, Kempten, Germany
e-mail: tobias.peylo@hs-kempten.de

K. Wendt, B. Villhauer (eds.), *Sustainable Wealth Management*, Sustainable Finance,
https://doi.org/10.1007/978-3-031-55505-3_11

activism, SRI has, for example, been defined as "an investment philosophy that combines ethical or environmental goals with financial ones" (Sparkes, 1994, 4). Basically, the idea behind SRI is to enhance the investment process with information about the corporate sustainability of the financed companies, reflecting the impact of their strategies, products and production processes on the social and environmental spheres (Statman, 2007). With mostly notional differences, it is also known as sustainable investment, triple bottom line investment or ethical investment (for terminology see Eccles & Viviers, 2011).

The conflict between the rationality of profit-maximization and the wisdom of socially or environmentally motivated self-restraint was discussed in literature for a very long time. Here, the main argument presented by critics was often a vague, non-uniform definition of the concept and its methodology and, most importantly, a possible loss of profit due to a hindrance of perfect diversification (among others, Moses & Krausz, 1995, Troutman, 2001, Kreander et al., 2005, Girard et al., 2007, and Adler & Kritzman, 2008). While the latter argument was empirically rejected by the sheer weight and mass of studies compiled by, e.g., Bauer et al., 2005 or Orlitzky et al., 2003 as well as methodically disproved with the use of portfolio selection theory by Steuer et al., 2008 and Peylo & Schaltegger, 2014, the former has to be given some further thought.

The fact that SRI was not defined top-down in a theoretical, model-supported theory, but rather emerged as an expression of the values of organizations and individuals alike resulted in a rather eclectic mix of methods and applications. For example, the criteria used for investment exclusion (negative criteria) or selection (positive criteria, best-in or best-off-class approaches) are not always coherent or even consistent (Peylo & Villhauer, 2021). Here, unresolved contrasts of priorities often lead to the confusion and, not seldom, disregard of the concept as a whole by many practitioners.

A simple example of the said inconsistencies would be a brewery with organically driven production and several sustainability awards as well as a good SRI-rating. While this could be a picture-perfect investment from the perspective of positive criteria, it conflicts with the exclusion of alcohol as one of the most commonly used exclusion criteria within the concept.

This problem of definitions is caused by the fact that, in contrast to most concepts of conventional finance, the concept of SRI and, with it, the concept of sustainable finance have never been consistently constructed but have simply emerged, organically grown, and been augmented. While the reluctance of practitioners to apply it is probably more explainable by their fear of missing out on profit, the definitional problems have always offered a plausible-sounding excuse. Thus, while SRI has demonstrated some success and in recent years experienced some considerable growth, especially in Europe (Eurosif, 2018), it still has to be considered a very small niche in the world of investment. That is, as long as one uses a substantial definition in contrast to such more lenient ones that nearly define all investments as being sustainable in some way or another.

11.2 The Burden of One-Size-Fits-All

Following the United Nations' Agenda 2030, with the definition of the sustainable development goals (SDG), and the Paris Agreement in 2015, several political initiatives have been undertaken to kick-start and foster transformation toward sustainable development and, in turn, a sustainable economy. Prominently among these, on March 7, 2018, the European Commission released an action plan for financing sustainable growth in response to the recommendations that the High-Level Expert Group (HLEG) on Sustainable Finance had submitted to the Commission on January 31, 2018 (PRI, 2021). This action plan understands the financial sphere as an instrument for transformation toward sustainability, and according to the same logic, both national and international investment plans, such as the European Green Deal (European Commission, 2021), start to channel great sums of money into sustainable investment.

With these new developments of considerable importance, the problem of definition has resurfaced and started to become a burden for sustainable finance. New developments go along with new players, resulting in new objectives, methods, and instruments that are very different from those traditionally associated with SRI. In fact, it can be argued that SRI is no longer the main substance of sustainable finance, at least not in its traditional form. While still in line with many objectives of SRI, the new focus is more on the impact of financial instruments than on the ethics and motivation of the investor.

This can be shown by the example of the mutual fund, which is by far the most important instrument of traditional SRI (Orlitzky et al., 2003; Bauer et al., 2005; Eurosif, 2018). From the investor's perspective, investment via an ethical, responsible or sustainable mutual fund is a suitable instrument to express ethical values and aim for sustainable positioning. These mutual funds, however, are financial instruments from the secondary market—meaning the underlying shares and bonds have long since been issued at the stock exchange, so the issuer has received all securitized funds and the instrument's financing function has ended. Investors may still use these funds to express their dislike of non-sustainable practices by excluding some companies, and to some extent, this exclusion can even be considered to have an indirect impact on the companies (e.g. via reputation, see Oekom research, 2013). But this instrument can neither be used to "channel" money into sustainable companies nor to deny financing to unsustainable ones. For these purposes, both bank loans and instruments such as green bonds are much better suited, causing a shift of focus and considerable growth, especially concerning the latter (Maltais & Nykvist, 2020; Environmental Finance, 2021).

Partly inspired by the action plan, in addition to investors, banks and politicians, a complete new set of new players has now entered the stage of sustainable finance: central banks and institutions of banking supervision. Here, especially European institutions take the lead, with the European Central Bank (ECB) presenting a "Guide on climate-related and environmental risks" (ECB, 2021) and the European Banking Authority (EBA) releasing first a roadmap in the form of the "Action Plan on Sustainable Finance" (EBA, 2019) and then concrete expectations formulated as "EBA Report on Management and Supervision of ESG Risk for Credit Institutions and Investment Firms" (EBA, 2021). But also worldwide, the necessity to act is fairly obvious, prompting thorough regulations in many countries and lately also a recommendation from the Basel Committee on Banking Supervision (2022).

With these new stakeholders, new objectives and a new logic are also being introduced. Here, the basis is the consideration that climate change causes destruction, which will inevitably result in financial losses—either directly to financial institutions or in an indirect way via financed companies—that may be impeded in their ability to repay their loans/obligations (EBA, 2021, 37). However, these "physical climate risks" are not the only source of worry for financial institutions. As (with or without political intervention and subventions) the markets begin to change, some companies will profit while others will perish—again causing financial damage to their investors (EBA, 2021, 40). This is known as "transition risk". In combination, both forms of risks can harm banks and investors and cause considerable financial instability, which is enough to explain the new players' interest in the topic.

All of these developments mentioned above are in one way or another labeled "sustainable finance"—or, with a focus on environmental and here especially climate-related issues, "green finance" (EU HLEG, 2018, 12). However, they are not one topic but form distinct spheres, each with their own stakeholders, objectives and instruments.

As is shown below in Fig. 11.1, these spheres also have interfaces with one another: For example, the supervisory consideration of "stranded assets" as assets losing value due to the transformation of the markets (EBA, 2021, 116) is in line with many exclusion criteria of traditional SRI, as they both concern, e.g., fossil fuels and thus the topic of decarbonization. Also, the interface between traditional SRI and the political initiatives is fairly obvious, e.g. the instrument of green bonds fitting the bill for responsible investment as well as being ideal to channel the money into sustainable transformation. However, this is not the case for many of SRI's negative criteria. When combating climate change, exclusion criteria defined on an

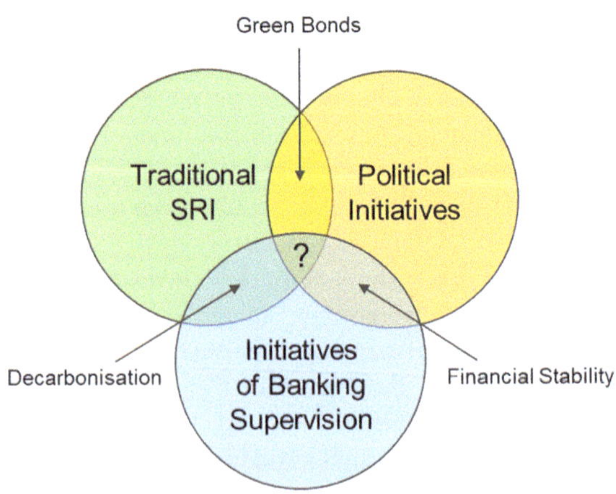

Fig. 11.1 Three thematic spheres in sustainable finance

ethical or religious basis seem poorly suited as decision criteria. In addition, the objective of financial stability can hardly be associated with SRI, even if it concerns both the thematic spheres of politics and banking supervision.

Hence, while there may be fields of complete overlap between all three thematic spheres, judged from the very different priorities, it is quite obvious that this interception would be rather small. As both political initiatives and those from the banking supervision have been accompanied by various calls for a common definition, there have been various efforts to deliver one (a good overview of these calls and efforts can be found in Migliorelli, 2021). Some certainly have their merits, but due to the rather small interception between all three thematic spheres, every definition that tries to focus on their common denominator has to remain rather superficial and "high-level".

As one example among others, Migliorelli's approach to a universal definition for sustainable finance is "finance to support sectors or activities that contribute to the achievement of, or to the improvement in, at least one of the relevant sustainability dimensions". This is a very good definition for capturing the essence of the political initiatives, but it does not cover the initiatives of banking supervision (here, protection via risk-management is the main theme instead of financing) or even SRI (here, investment is the focus, not financing). In fact, it is an important but often neglected fact that investment and financing are not always so closely connected that they can be considered two sides of the same coin. Indeed, as already mentioned in the context of mutual funds, many financial instruments lack a financing characteristic. This is even true for stocks and bonds, because while financing may be the raison d'être for their existence, as soon as they have been issued on the primary market, the financing aspect is done. All further trades happen on the secondary market with no further direct, monetary connection to the issuing company (for a more detailed explanation and the various remaining non-monetary connections, see Spremann & Gantenbein, 2005, 15). Thus, a definition coined for financing does only partly apply to an investment style, which SRI can very much be considered to be (e.g. Beal et al., 2005) and does not apply at all to a new approach towards risk management. Likewise, many examples can be found of definitions failing to cover the essence of sustainable finance as a whole because they are only focusing on distinctive parts.

This lack of clarity and definition is by no means a mere academic problem, as the one-size-fits-all approach to sustainable finance is not only becoming slightly chaotic, but can even be considered as hindering the progress of implementation on the part of the practitioners. The confusion created can be highlighted by the example of the "Guidance Notice on Dealing with Sustainability Risks" of the German Banking Supervision BaFin (BaFin, 2019), slightly preceding the matching EBA publication. Here, under the heading "Risk Management", the SRI methodology of exclusion criteria, positive lists and best-in-class approaches is named in the context of managing ESG and climate risk. For experts and newcomers alike, it is less than obvious how these instruments created for the selection of assets in good conscience would generate a reliable protection effect in the portfolio, and no explanation is offered to this effect. An educated guess would be that they are named here because they belong to the family of sustainable finance, as do ESG- or climate-risk management, and, as an additional bonus, they are available as a best practice approach—which is more than can currently be said about a methodology for the management of ESG risk or climate risk. As a consequence, however, there is a considerable risk that this situation with vague, high-level definitions and transplanted methodologies without a catchy and understandable application benefit fosters rejection instead of acceptance on the part of many practitioners.

11.3 Naming the Children

It is in this situation that we recommend saying farewell to the objective of finding— formulated as an homage to Tolkien's masterly picture of absolute subsumption—the one ringing definition "to find them all and to bind them all" (together). Instead, it should be acknowledged that the mother of sustainable finance may have given birth not to one but to three children, who, like all siblings, certainly have some distinctive family similarities but are quite different nevertheless.

To get to know these siblings, it may be a good start to bring some order into the family history in the form of a viable anchoring theory. While conventional finance derives its descent from the homo economicus as a forefather, the lineage of sustainable finance is more clouded. There have been some approaches to anchoring a suitable image of humanity. Godbout (2000) sees the positive counterproposal in the homo donator, who receives the world as gift and, out of obligation, preserves it. Faber et al. (2002) propose the homo politicus, as a responsible, social being. With other, more or less suited replacements for the emblem of unconscionable profit maximization available (for an overview see O'Boyle, 2007), we are drawn toward the homo reciprocans (Gintis & Orr, 2001), as a human being who "is motivated by improving its environment through positive reciprocity (rewarding other individuals) or negative reciprocity (punishing other individuals), even in situations without foreseeable benefit for themselves". This ancestry ties neatly into stakeholder theory (Freeman, 1984), which, for corporate sustainability, can also be considered to be the theoretical basis and the major driving force (Schaltegger et al., 2003; Hörisch et al., 2014).

As a matter of fact, in all expressions and materializations of sustainable finance, there is a driving group of distinctive stakeholders behind things, trying to influence the financial markets and modify them to better suit their objectives. With SRI, it's the investors who, on the one hand, want to express their ethical ideas or religious beliefs in their way of investing, but some of whom, on the other hand, also want a transformation of financial markets toward a more ethical and sustainability-oriented concept. This transformation in the form that enables climate and sustainability objectives to be reached also influences political actors as well as equally minded pressure groups and NGOs, whereas central banks and institutions of banking supervision pursue the objective of financial stability and modify the rules and regulatory requirements accordingly.

Thus, all forms of sustainable finance are initiated, brought forward, and built upon by distinctive stakeholder groups. Their efforts to pursue their objectives and the measures they use can fittingly be described with the model of socio-economic rationality within the context of stakeholder theory (Schaltegger et al., 2003, 36 f.). They interact within the spheres of the market, the regulatory system, sociocultural partnerships, and the political arena. The only adaptation required for using this proven model is that, in this case, these stakeholders are not limited to a single entity or company, but encompass all the companies and institutions forming the financial markets as a system.

Based on stakeholder theory as a fundament and the three thematic spheres discussed in the previous section, the small interception between all three thematic spheres, and hence the common denominator of sustainable finance where all its forms converge (one could say the family name of the three siblings), could be defined as *the consideration of non-financial, sustainability-related aspects in financial decision-making*. While this is rather elevated and abstract, it is allowed to be so, as the details are embedded in the differentiation into the following three forms (Fig. 11.2):

- Value-based sustainable finance
- Action-based sustainable finance
- Risk-based sustainable finance

As the oldest sibling of the three, *value-based sustainable finance* comprises the traditional field of SRI, which has already been defined as "an investment philosophy that combines ethical or environmental goals with financial ones" (Sparkes, 1994, 4). Consequently, the stakeholders of the financial market institutions are the SRI investors (private or institutional).

As a way of classifying these investors, Beal et al. (2005) have proposed differentiating between three basic types of SRI-investor: First, the small group of

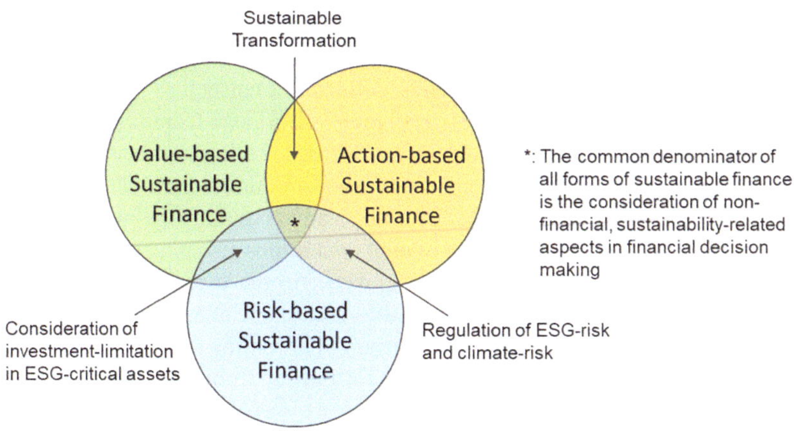

Fig. 11.2 The three forms of sustainable finance

conventional investors choosing SRI in the hope of extraordinary profit (termed "rational investors"). Second, the prevailing group of individuals or organizations for whom sustainability either plays an integral, yet not dominant role, or who at least feel compelled to give that appearance ("consumption investors"). For them, investing with a clear conscience (for private investors) or intact reputation (for institutional investors) is the prevailing motive. Third, those investors driven by internal motives based on ethics, morality, responsibility and ideals who feel an intrinsic need to express these motives in their way of investing and who are also interested in being part of a transformation toward sustainability ("investing investors"). Of these, the consumption investors and the investing investors are the main force behind the concept, and they can be identified as primary stakeholders.

These primary stakeholders, however, are not the only ones promoting the concept, its significance and its impact. There are other stakeholders in the second row, which in the following will be labeled as "enforcing stakeholders". While they do not necessarily take part in SRI investments themselves, for their own motives, they put the market participants under pressure to implement SRI. These can be critical customers, the general public and, most importantly, NGOs. For institutional investors, SRI-rating agencies also play an important role, as the engagement in SRI plays a substantial role in their assessments of corporate sustainability (e.g. ISS, 2021).

The motives of the primary stakeholders differ. Consumption investors see SRI as a form of lifestyle, "investing with good conscience" or "not being on the side of the bad" on the part of the private investors. Institutional investors in that category see themselves driven by their stakeholders and want to preserve or improve their reputation. Investing investors, however, are intrinsically motivated and live by their ideas of morals and ethics. Some also want to be part of a sustainable transformation. The chance of this transformation actually happening, however, was previously limited, especially due to the limitations of mutual funds, mandates and ETFs as the primary financial instruments of SRI (let alone savings products without standardization or supervision and thus sometimes of disputable SRI quality).

Concerning this chance of transformation, *action-based, sustainable finance* makes a huge difference. It comprises the political initiatives in the context of the SDGs and the Paris Agreement and can be defined in a nutshell as "*reorienting capital flows towards a more sustainable economy*" (European Commission, 2018, 2). Consequently, its primary stakeholders are different bodies and institutions in the political realm, in Europe primarily the European Commission. There are many enforcing stakeholders, with NGOs taking the lead in building up the pressure in the public opinion, although science and related institutions also play an important part in providing both data and analyses/prognoses. As these activities and the large sums of money invested naturally draw the interest of investors, rational/conventional investors can also be added to the group of enforcing stakeholders.

As has already been discussed, the motivation and objectives of this form of sustainable finance are to enable a transformation toward a more sustainable society and especially economy—with climate change mitigation and adaption being the most important factors due to their expected threat (for a documented expectation for that stakeholder group of decision makers, e.g. in the form of the global risk landscape, see World Economic Forum, 2021). Much more distinctively than within value-based sustainable finance, these objectives have a high demand concerning the impact of instruments. Green bonds and social bonds are an adequate means to an end, as is the traditional instrument of subventions. Another very important instrument here is the credit/loan market from banks and its instrumentalization toward transformation with adequate measures (as already begun with the action plan, European Commission, 2018). Here, especially financing activities that conform with the taxonomy (Technical Expert Group on Sustainable Finance, 2020) will become a supporting pillar.

The credit/loan market is also in the *focus of risk-based sustainable finance*, however for different reasons. Here, the prevailing question is the security of the loan portfolio and its protection against adverse consequences from ESG risks and climate risks. It can thus be defined as the "transparency on risks related to ESG factors that may impact the financial system, and the mitigation of such risks through the appropriate governance of financial and corporate actors" (EBA, 2020, 21).

Risk-driven sustainable finance comprises all initiatives and activities on the part of central banks and institutions of banking supervision, both of which naturally are the primary stakeholders. In this context, the enforcing stakeholders are shareholders, financial rating institutionsand market partners. All of those stakeholders have a distinct interest in financial stability as a whole and especially that of the financial companies, which constitutes the primary objective in this concept. Consequently, the financial instruments considered are all those making up the balance sheet of financial institutions and thus needing to be protected from adverse effects, be they loans or own investments.

As can be seen from Fig. 11.3 below, the attribution of stakeholders, objectives and instruments is not without overlaps. This is congruent to the overlap between the spheres illustrated in Figs. 11.1 and 11.2 and thus only natural: While, for example, an investing investor as a stakeholder may be primarily anchored in SRI with a focus on investment, due to her/his motivation to contribute to a transformation, she/he is also drawn to action-based sustainable finance. The same is true for the green bond as a financial instrument, which is very much at home in both forms.

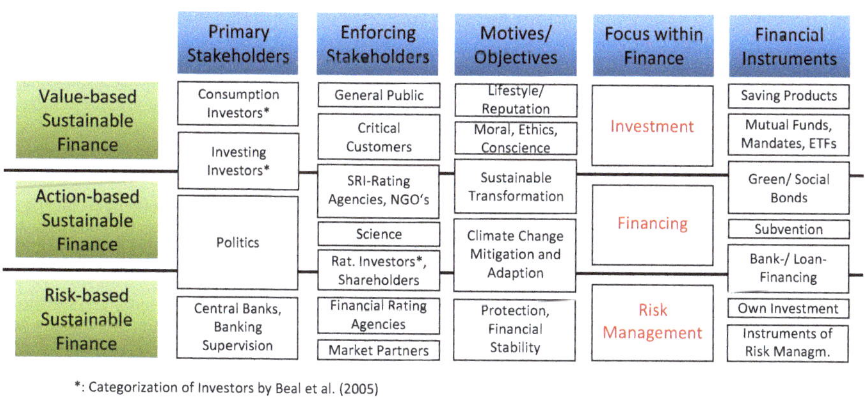

Fig. 11.3 Summary and complete overview of the three forms of sustainable finance

Finally, it should be said that, while the term sustainable finance has been used in the explanation as well as in the figures, the very same classification could be used for the environmental focus, namely value-based, action-based and risk-based green finance.

11.4 Application Benefits

So why is this differentiation of sustainable finance into the three forms needed?

The first benefit is that the previous one-size-fits-all approach toward sustainable finance (with the lingering question as to what this size, or rather definition, actually is) is replaced by the acknowledgement that, emerging from developments rather than planned on a drawing board, there is not one form of sustainable finance but three. These three all have in common that they consider non-financial aspects, however, in a very different way and for very different reasons. And, naturally, they are not free of contradictions and conflicting goals. To understand and accept this creates some clarity, which can be very helpful, especially for practitioners, to get a better understanding of this topic and its implementation.

The second benefit concerns exactly that implementation, as here the foundation in the concept of stakeholder theory enables a sensible prioritization. In stakeholder theory, a company is advised to always fulfill the most important demands of its most important stakeholders. Using the stakeholder listing in Fig. 11.2, it is clear that the priority of the stakeholders for financial institutions is arranged from bottom to top. Thus, the implementation of risk-based green finance can be classified as a "must", and the implementation of action-based sustainable finance could be labeled as a pronounced "should". In addition to the continuing high significance of the stakeholders, this necessity is highlighted by the transformation and the accompanying shift in business opportunities and models. This leaves value-driven sustainable finance as a question of individual morality and conscience. So, from a project manager's perspective, it could be labeled as "can"—however, with a recommendation never to underestimate the possibly harmful consequences of a total neglect. It can, however, be safely stated that the pressure and urgency to consider this form are far below the other two.

The third advantage of the concept is that, within the implementation process, it is possible to focus and not have to look at everything at once. For example, when implementing the requirements of the banking supervision, no ethically based exclusion criteria are necessary; however, it is also clear that implementing a climate risk concept does not give a company more moral integrity or make it more socially responsible. This separation greatly simplifies not only the practitioner's task of planning and pursuing the implementation, but also the formulation of the requirements on the part of the primary stakeholders, as they now are not tasked with explaining sustainable finance as a whole but only their respective parts of it.

In combination, it is argued that a clear differentiation of sustainable finance into three distinct forms based upon its stakeholders, their objectives and the suitable financial instruments can be useful to bring structure into the important and rapidly developing sphere of sustainable finance.

References

Adler, T., & Kritzman, M. (2008). The cost of socially responsible investing. *The Journal of Portfolio Management, 35*(1), 52–56. https://doi.org/10.3905/JPM.2008.35.1.52

Allais, M. & Hagen, G.M. (Eds.). (1979). Expected utility hypotheses and the Allais Paradox. Contemporary discussions of the decisions under uncertainty with Allais' rejoinder. Springer.

BaFin Bundesaufsichtsamt für Finanzdiensteistungsaufsicht (2019). Guidance Notice on dealing with Sustainability Risk. Frankfurt am Main: Bundesaufsichtsamt für Finanzdiensteistungsaufsicht BaFin. https://www.bafin.de/SharedDocs/Downloads/EN/Merkblatt/dl_mb_Nachhaltigkeitsrisiken_en.pdf?__blob=publicationFile&v=5

Basel Committee on Banking Supervision. (2022). *Principles for the effective management and supervision of climate-related financial risks*. BIS Bank for International Settlement. https://www.bis.org/bcbs/publ/d532.pdf

Bauer, R., Koedijk, K., & Otten, R. (2005). International evidence on ethical mutual fund performance and investment style. *Journal of Banking & Finance, 26*(29), 1751–1767. https://doi.org/10.1016/j.jbankfin.2004.06.035

Beal, D. J., Goyen, M., & Phillips, P. (2005). Why do we invest ethically? *The Journal of Investing, 14*(3), 66–77. https://doi.org/10.3905/joi.2005.580551

Berk, J., & DeMarzo, P. (2017). *Corporate finance* (4th ed.). Pearson.

Coleman, J. S., & Coleman, J. S. (Eds.). (1992). *Rational choice theory – Advocacy and critique*. SAGE Publications.

EBA European Banking Authority. (2019). *Action plan on sustainable finance*. European Banking Authority. https://www.eba.europa.eu/sites/default/documents/files/document_library/EBA%20Action%20plan%20on%20sustainable%20finance.pdf

EBA European Banking Authority. (2020). *EBA Discussion paper on management and supervision of ESG risks for credit institutions and investment firms*. European Banking Authority. https://www.eba.europa.eu/sites/default/documents/files/document_library/Publications/Reports/2021/1015656/EBA%20Report%20on%20ESG%20risks%20management%20and%20supervision.pdf

EBA European Banking Authority. (2021). *EBA report on management and supervision of ESG risk for credit institutions and investment firms*. European Banking Authority. https://www.eba.europa.eu/sites/default/documents/files/document_library/Publications/Reports/2021/1015656/EBA%20Report%20on%20ESG%20risks%20management%20and%20supervision.pdf

ECB European Central Bank. (2021). *Guide on climate-related and environmental risks*. European Central Bank. https://www.bankingsupervision.europa.eu/legalframework/publiccons/pdf/climate-related_risks/ssm.202005_draft_guide_on_climate-related_and_environmental_risks.en.pdf

Eccles, N. S., & Viviers, S. (2011). The origins and meanings of names describing investment practices that integrate a consideration of ESG issues in the academic literature. *Journal of Business Ethics, 104*(3), 389–402. https://doi.org/10.1007/s10551-011-0917-7

Ellsberg, D. (1961). Risk, ambiguity, and the savage axioms. *The Quarterly Journal of Economics, 75*(4), 643–669. https://doi.org/10.2307/1884324

Environmental Finance. (2021, September 25). *The Sustainable Bond Market beyond 2020*. Environmental Finance. https://www.environmental-finance.com/content/the-green-bond-hub/the-sustainable-bond-market-beyond-2020-green-bonds-strike-back.html

EU HLEG European High Level Expert Group on Sustainable Finance. (2018). *Financing a Sustainable European Economy*. European Commission. https://ec.europa.eu/info/sites/default/files/180131-sustainable-finance-final-report_en.pdf

European Commission. (2018). *Action plan: Financing sustainable growth*. European Commission. https://eur-lex.europa.eu/legal-content/EN/TXT/?uri=CELEX:52018DC0097

European Commission. (2021). *A European Green Deal – Striving to be the first climate-neutral continent*. European Commission. https.//ec.europa.eu/info/strategy/priorities-2019-2024/european-green-deal_en.

Eurosif. (2018). *European SRI Study 2018*. Eurosif. https://www.eurosif.org/wp-content/uploads/2021/10/European-SRI-2018-Study.pdf

Faber, M., Petersen, T., & Schiller, J. (2002). Homo oeconomicus and homo politicus in Ecological Economics. *Ecological Economics, 40*(3), 323–333. https://doi.org/10.1016/S0921-8009(01)00279-8

Fabozzi, F. J., & Markowitz, H. M. (Eds.). (2008). *The theory and practice of investment management*. Wiley.

Freeman, E. (1984). *Strategic management – A stakeholder approach*. Pitman.

Gintis, H., & Orr, H. A. (2001). Why do we cooperate? *Boston Review, Michigan State University Press Online*. http://bostonreview.mit.edu/bostonreview/BR23.1/Gintis.html

Girard, E., Rahman, H., & Stone, B. (2007). Socially responsible investments: Goody-two-shoes or bad to the bone? *The Journal of Investing, 16*(1), 96–11. https://doi.org/10.3905/joi.2007.681827

Godbout, J. T. (2000). Homo donator versus homo oeconomicus. In A. Vandevelde (Ed.), *Gifts and interests* (pp. 38–46). Peteers.

Haugen, R. A. (2001). *Modern investment theory* (5th ed.). Prentice Hall.

Hörisch, J., Freeman, R. E., & Schaltegger, S. (2014). Applying stakeholder theory in sustainability management: Links, similarities, dissimilarities, and a conceptual framework. *Organization & Environment, 27*(4), 328–346. https://doi.org/10.1177/1086026614535786

ISS Institutional Shareholder Services. (2021, September 26). *ESG Corporate Rating*. Institutional Shareholder Services. https://www.issgovernance.com/esg/ratings/corporate-rating/

Kahneman, D., & Tversky, A. (1979). Prospect theory: An analysis of decision under risk. *Econometrica, 47*(2), 263–292. https://doi.org/10.2307/1914185

Kreander, N., Gray, R., Power, D., & Sinclair, C. (2005). Evaluating the performance of ethical and non-ethical funds. A matched pair analysis. *Journal of Business Finance & Accounting, 32*(7–8), 1465–1493. https://doi.org/10.1111/j.0306-686X.2005.00636.x

Maltais, A. & Nykvist, B. (2020). Understanding the role of green bonds in advancing sustainability. *Journal of Sustainable Finance & Investment, Published online*. 14 Feb 2020. https://doi.org/10.1080/20430795.2020.1724864

Migliorelli, M. (2021). What do we mean by sustainable finance? Assessing existing frameworks and policy risks. *Sustainability, 13*, 975. https://doi.org/10.3390/su13020975

Moses, L. P., & Krausz, J. (1995). *Corporate responsibility and financial performance: The paradox of social cost*. Quorum.

O'Boyle, E. J. (2007). Requiem for homo economicus. *Journal of Markets & Morality, 10*(2), 321–337. https://www.marketsandmorality.com/index.php/mandm/article/view/235

Oekom Research. (2013). *Der Einfluss nachhaltiger Kapitalanlagen auf Unternehmen (the influence of sustainable investment on companies)*. Oekom Research.

Orlitzky, M., Schmidt, F. L., & Rynes, S. L. (2003). Corporate social and financial performance: A meta-analysis. *Organization Studies, 24*(3), 403–441. https://doi.org/10.1177/0170840603024003910

Peterson, R. L. (2002). Buy on the rumor: Anticipatory affect and investor behavior. *Journal of Behavioral Finance, 3*(4), 218–226. https://doi.org/10.1002/9781119219149.ch10

Peylo, B. T., & Schaltegger, S. (2014). An equation with many variables: Unhiding the relationship between sustainability and investment performance. *Journal of Sustainable Finance & Investment, 4*(2), 110–126. https://doi.org/10.1080/20430795.2013.837808

Peylo, B. T., & Villhauer, B. (2021). Clustering of negative criteria. A pragmatic approach for the implementation of SRI. In K. Wendt (Ed.), *Theories of change – Change leadership tools, models and applications for investing in sustainable development* (pp. 109–121). Springer Nature.

PRI Principles for Responsible Investment. (2021, September 25). *Explaining the EU action plan for financing sustainable growth*. Principles for Responsible Investment. https://www.unpri.org/sustainable-financial-system/explaining-the-eu-action-plan-for-financing-sustainable-growth/3000.article

Schaltegger, S., Burritt, R., & Petersen, H. (2003). *An Introduction to corporate environmental management: Striving for sustainability*. Greenleaf Publishers.

Sparkes, R. (1994). *The ethical investor*. HarperCollins.

Sparkes, R. (2006). A historical perspective on the growth of socially responsible investment. In R. Sullivan & C. Mackenzie (Eds.), *Responsible investment* (pp. 39–54). Greenleaf Publishing.

Spremann, K. (2005). *Modern Finance*. Oldenbourg.

Spremann, K., & Gantenbein, P. (2005). *Kapitalmärkte (Capital Markets)*. Lucis & Lucius.

Statman, M. (2007). Socially responsible investments. *Journal of Investment Consulting, 8*(2), 17–37. https://doi.org/10.2139/ssrn.995271

Steuer, R. E., Qi, Y., & Hirschberger, M. (2008). Portfolio selection in the presence of multiple criteria. In C. Zopounidis, M. Doumpos, & P. M. Pardalos (Eds.), *Handbook of financial engineering* (pp. 3–24). Springer US.

Technical Expert Group on Sustainable Finance. (2020). *Taxonomy – Final report of the Technical Expert Group on Sustainable Finance*. European Commission. https://ec.europa.eu/info/sites/info/files/business_economy_euro/banking_and_finance/documents/200309-sustainable-finance-teg-final-report-taxonomy_en.pdf

Thaler, R. H. (1993). *Advances in behavioral finance*. Russell Sage Foundation.

Troutman, M. L. (2001). Risk control techniques for social investing. *The Journal of Investing, 10*(4), 51–57. https://doi.org/10.3905/joi.2001.319486

World Economic Forum. (2021, September 26). *The Global Risk Landscape 2021*. World Economic Forum. https://www.weforum.org/reports/the-global-risks-report-2021

Chapter 12
Custom ESG Indexing: How Direct ESG Indexing Can Solve Many Responsible Investing Problems

Dirk Soehnholz

12.1 Broad Responsible Investment Criticism

Criticism of so-called responsible investing is rising for several reasons:

- Strictly responsible investors use many exclusions, but we seem to need gas, nuclear energy, heavy weapons, genetically manipulated and fertilized crops, etc. still for some time.
- The many fans of diversified index tracking funds argue heavily against exclusions because they claim that the resulting tracking errors increase their risks.
- Tilting investments toward better Environmental, Social and Governance (ESG)-rated issuers is criticized, too, because ESG ratings differ often quite considerably.
- Others criticize that with investments in secondary markets, nothing will change in the real economy anyhow.

There are other arguments against responsible investing as well.[1] I try to address many of them and show solutions for investors who really want to invest in a responsible way.

Since the definition of what is considered responsible can vary significantly, customized portfolios seem to be required. I will show simple ways to customize responsible portfolios with mutual funds and with direct investments. These solutions can be delivered by wealth managers or used by self-directed investors.

[1] Compare Soehnholz (2020b).

D. Soehnholz (✉)
Leipzig University, Eicklingen, Germany
e-mail: dirk@soehnholzesg.com

K. Wendt, B. Villhauer (eds.), *Sustainable Wealth Management*, Sustainable Finance,
https://doi.org/10.1007/978-3-031-55505-3_12

12.2 Solutions for ESG Investing Problems

12.2.1 No Standard Definition of Sustainable Investing

Unfortunately, there is no standard definition for responsible or sustainable investments.[2] Regulators try to provide some guidelines with efforts such as the European Taxonomy for Sustainable Investments,[3] but responsible investment regulation is complex and slow. The reason for the difficulties in defining such investments becomes obvious if one looks at the different dimensions of defining responsible investment policies. The dimensions are mainly exclusions, positive criteria, and ESG criteria, as well as voting and engagement policies.

12.2.1.1 Exclusions Can Be Defined in Many Ways

Exclusions of unwanted exposures are the oldest and most frequently used approach to sustainable investments. Initially, it is necessary to decide how an exclusion is defined. If an investor wants to exclude alcohol from its portfolio, it is obvious that she does not want to have any producers of alcoholic beverages in her portfolio. But what about a soft drink- company that sells some alcoholic beverages from a third-party producer? Or what about a food retailer or an airline that generates some revenues from sales of alcoholic beverages? I include a railway operator in a portfolio that rents space to alcohol selling duty free shops. Should I exclude that company? Also, a pure stock-listed producer of soft drinks may have a majority or minority alcoholic beverage company as a shareholder, as a supplier, or as a client.

I decided to exclude all producers and sellers of alcoholic beverages from my portfolios.[4] And I use several other production and trading exclusions. Few other investors seem to use many strict exclusion categories, though.[5] Even one of the strictest currently available indices that is used for many responsible ETFs, the Socially Responsible Index (SRI) series by MSCI, uses only a relatively small number of exclusion categories and allows for some activities within the "excluded" categories. ETFs based on these indices include "good" ESG-rated companies for many market segments, which may be undesirable for responsible investors, such as fossil fuels, fast-food, airlines, traditional car manufacturers, cement companies, luxury goods suppliers, and tourism companies.

In summary: Responsible investment products differ regarding the definitions and the number of exclusions they use.

---

[2] In this chapter, I use the terms sustainable or responsible investing interchangeably, but I consider responsible investing to be the broader term since sustainable investing focuses on ecological issues only, typically.

[3] See European Commission (2022).

[4] See Soehnholz (2022b, pp. 113–124).

[5] See e.g. Forum Nachhaltige Geldanlagen (2022b).

12.2.1.2 Positive Criteria: Limitations of Labels, Norms, and Themes

Exclusions are negative selection criteria. Responsible investors often also use positive selection criteria. The public fund database of the Forum Nachhaltige Geldanlagen,[6] for example, allows fund selectors to use these labels: Eurosif, ISR, Greenfin, CIES, Luxflag, Nordic Swan, Austrian Ecolabel. Out of the 286 equity funds in the database,[7] 245 claim to have a Eurosif transparency logo, 133 an FNG label, 52 a French, 37 an Austrian, 22 a Luxembourg, and 2 a Nordic label.

Labels aggregate different sustainability information with varying criteria into "with label" or "without label" groups. Label providers who make money with their labels have an incentive to label many funds, which may mean that the criteria for receiving labels may be rather low. "Without label" funds may not have applied for a label for various reasons, one may be costs for the labeling process.

Also, labels can typically only be applied to mutual funds. Therefore, only part of an investor's portfolio can be "labeled". Private investments, as well as investments in stocks and bonds, directly typically are not covered by labels.

Norms, themes, and impact selection criteria, e.g., from the FNG fund profile database, are also of the "yes" or "no" type.[8] But they can be applied to all kinds of portfolios, and they do not necessarily require payments to service providers.

275 of the 287 funds claim to follow sustainability norms. Following "norms" as such is therefore not helpful fund selection criterium. For fund selection, the required norm to follow—e.g., Islamic investing—should be specified in order to be useful. One hundred and twenty-six equity funds indicate to use a thematic and 64 an impact approach. These two approaches will be discussed further below.

12.2.1.3 ESG Criteria

No Standard ESG Definition

ESG investments use environmental, social and governance criteria for security selection and/or weightings of securities. Most investors use ESG data from service providers. These service providers, e.g., ESG rating agencies, aggregate many different so-called "non-financial" information into ESG ratings. Since methods and data used for such ratings vary, so do ESG ratings by different rating providers for the same issuer.

But the differences in ESG ratings are no excuse to neglect ESG-information altogether. Academic evidence shows,[9] that ESG is often relevant for investment risk and can have effects on returns as well. Investors who manage money for others therefore have a trustee obligation to consider ESG information. Thus, investors

[6] Compare Forum Nachhaltige Geldanlagen (2022a).

[7] As of June 24th, 2022.

[8] Specific norm/theme fulfilled (yes) or not fulfilled (no).

[9] Compare Atz et al. (2021).

should carefully select the ESG data provider with an approach they like and potentially use one or more additional such data providers.

Detailed ESG data can be cumbersome to collect and analyze, and good and detailed ESG data can be costly. Rating agencies demand especially high prices when their information is being made public. Therefore, asset managers may use detailed data for themselves but publish only limited information for potential investors.

Limitations of Aggregated ESG Scores

Since exchange traded funds (ETFs) must be transparent, it is rather easy to analyze their approaches to ESG investing. The reference indices for most sustainable ETFs usually work with aggregated ESG scores. Good corporate management can thus compensate for a poor environmental score. For strict, responsible investors, minimum standards are required for E, S, and G scores separately. One could argue that within these three categories, additional minimum requirements have to be fixed, e.g., for air and water quality separately.

Unfortunately, the more criteria with minimum requirements are used, the smaller becomes the pool of eligible securities. Example: 50% of the investable universe may have an ESG score above 50 on a scale from 0 to 100. But the number of eligible investments drops significantly, if a minimum score of 50 is required for E, S, and G at the same time. This also means that a portfolio that uses a minimum ESG score of 50% is generally less "responsible" than a portfolio that requires a minimum score of 50% for E, S, and G respectively.

Best-in-Universe (BiU) Is Better Than Best-in-Class (BiC)

It is important whether a so-called BiU or BiC process is used. Assume that only the 25% of the best companies in a global investment universe in terms of an ESG score may be included in a portfolio (Best-in-Universe or BiU approach). This would probably result in oil companies, for example, not being included in a portfolio. However, since many investors do not want to have too large deviations from broad indices (so-called tracking error), they want to have securities from all major industries and countries in their portfolios. Therefore, they select the best ESG-rated securities from and by the required classes (countries, industries) for their portfolio (Best-in-Class or BiC approach).

ESG Scores: Minimum, Weight or Progress?

Minimum scoring means that, for example, the worst 25% according to ESG scores or separate E, S, and G criteria are not permitted for a portfolio. Some "responsible" products do not apply minimum scores, but instead reduce the weight of companies with low scores compared to those with high scores, while retaining them in the portfolio. Others use a so-called "progress" approach and only select or overweight companies with the best recent improvement in ESG-scores. This means, that companies with rather low—but improving—ESG scores are preferred over companies with rather high but stable ESG scores. To be consequent, such investors should sell their holdings once those companies have improved to reinvest the sales proceeds in bad ESG securities again. This is not a responsible investment strategy, in my opinion.

ESG Measurement Frequency: More Often May Be Better
In the past, ESG data providers mostly compiled their ratings based on questionnaires for the respective companies, which were updated once a year. Now, most rating data providers seem to use all kinds of internal and external public information about issuers to generate their ratings. This can be done for rather large number of issuers if machine learning or artificial intelligence is used. An early example of such a rating provider is S-Ray (now ESG Book[10]). I use Clarity.[11] Clarity currently analyzes more than 30,000 listed companies, 300,000 mutual funds, and almost 200 countries, as well as other issuers of securities. Both providers are now also offering to rate private companies.

Ratings can be updated with every new piece of information, but then typically, transparency suffers because the number of information used for ratings vastly increases. And the stability of ratings can be an indicator of stable processes: If ratings change often and significantly, the rating aggregation method is not very robust.

Of the 287 equity funds in the FNG fund profile database, 245 use some ESG data (ESG-Integration) and 137 use a Best-in-Class or Best-of-Class approach. Unfortunately, with this database, Best-in-Universe cannot be selected separately and the same is true for minimum ESG-Rating thresholds. And since only 137 of the 245 use a "Best-of" approach, the other 108 funds probably use rather lax ESG selection criteria.

12.2.1.4 Impact and the Question of Liquid or Illiquid Investing

Since ESG ratings usually only indicate the respective risks for the companies, one needs additional criteria to select companies with good products or services. In determining "impact", one can use the Sustainable Development Goals of the United Nations (SDG) as guidelines.[12] These goals have been developed for a general improvement of the world and not with financial investments in mind, e.g., SDG Goal number two is "zero hunger". It should be kept in mind, though, that listed companies primarily pursue their own profit targets in the interests of their shareholders and not non-commercial positive impact. Also, for several SDGs, there are no or only very few investable, for-profit companies available.

Some financial service providers use the SDGs quite freely. In so-called impact indices, companies like Danone can be found "only" because Danone produces food. Also, traditional production or energy companies are sometimes included in such portfolios simply because they have a small share of turnover in the sense of the SDG objectives. I think that only net sales in terms of the SDG targets should be counted. A portfolio is considered more responsible the more net sales, aggregated in terms of alignment with the SDG goals, the companies in the portfolio generate.

---

[10] https://www.arabesque.com/de/arabesque-s-ray/

[11] https://clarity.ai/

[12] See United Nations (2022).

These net sales can be up to 100% for a pure portfolio of renewable energy producers, for example, and 0% for a company with 50% fossil fuel and 50% renewable energy sales. Very few listed companies generate more than 50% of their sales in SDG segments.

Unfortunately, the sales or revenues are not ideal to measure SDG alignment. In theory, renewable energy can be generated, for example, by violating human rights in the process of extracting raw materials. But by using strict ESG requirements alongside SDG criteria, this criticism can be mitigated.

Impact investors typically require additionality. This means that investment targets should show that the financing is used to create additional positive impact. Investments in already listed securities of public companies do not provide additional capital, though. But one could argue that buying securities of such public issuers can be positive,[13] if they are directed towards growing companies ("growth investments").

Instead of revenues, one could also try to measure SDG-aligned capital expenditures, which are more oriented towards the future. Unfortunately, measurement of capital expenditures, e.g., in the case of intellectual or other intangible capital, is much less objective than revenues.

Rating providers such as Clarity offer SDG ratings, too. I consider specific SDG ratings not to be helpful yet since they seem to mostly use data points that are already considered for ESG ratings.[14]

Some people argue that impact can only be created with additional private investments and not with secondary public market investments. But there is a huge overhang of private equity and debt capital. This means, that private equity or debt "impact" investments just may crowd out other potential investors. In other words: The capital of a private equity or debt type impact fund may be additional capital for an investment target if there are no other potential investors for that investment. Also, investor capital may be additional capital for a private equity or private debt type investment fund if the fund has not reached its fundraising target yet.

Angel investments and investments via impact fintechs provide more likely additional capital, since they typically only provide relatively small investment amounts to potential impact targets, which are only targeted by relatively few investors. Also, with small investment amounts per target even private investors with limited capital may be able to diversify their investments somewhat. On the other hand, such small investors may not provide enough professional due diligence upfront or ongoing support after the investments.

To create a positive impact with liquid investments, many market participants advocate for voting and engagement.

---

[13] See arguments regarding signaling further below.

[14] Companies from industries with high potential revenue alignment with SDGs such as healthcare seem to receive high ratings. Therefore, SDG ratings may not provide much additional information compared with SDG-related (net) sales.

12.2.1.5 Voting, Engagement, or Signaling?

Limited Effect of Shareholder Voting

Other than with bonds, direct investments in stocks usually come with the right to vote at annual and extraordinary shareholder meetings. Exercising voting rights in person requires the time to prepare for their travel to the companies' headquarters and is easy for concentrated portfolios of companies with headquarters in the vicinity of the investor. Fortunately, voting rights can be exercised via service providers so that physical presence is not necessary. Still, exercising voting rights globally becomes more complicated the more companies and languages are involved.

Voting is limited to the topics on the agendas of a shareholder meetings, and many responsible investment topics do not reach that status. And some proposals such as linking variable compensation of the top management to sustainability sound good but may even be counterproductive, since they can lead to a rising pay gap between top executives and other employees within a company.[15] Other proposals are vague or need a long time to lead to real sustainability improvements.

Also, monitoring all potential proposals for all investments is cumbersome. Statistics show that even the largest asset managers only participate in relatively few shareholder votes and often vote with the top management and not necessarily for more sustainable proposals.[16]

Active Engagement Is Basically Good

Shareholder engagement goes beyond voting and is intended to exert an active influence regarding responsible corporate activities. Investors who target companies that are relatively poor in terms of responsibility criteria can potentially achieve the largest ESG improvements. But successful engagement requires significant know-how and time and will typically only lead to selective improvements in the future. Therefore, it seems to be more responsible, to select investment targets that are already strongly intrinsically motived to become more responsible.

Signaling May Lead Others to Follow

It is more responsible to invest only in the already best ESG or SDG-aligned companies and convince other investors to do the same. With successful communication using traditional media or social networks, even limited investment amounts may be able to induce sustainable action. If one can convince others to invest in a similar way, the prices of the selected securities may rise more than the ones of less responsible securities. Thus, financing via equity or credit may become cheaper for the most sustainable companies. Higher security-prices for more responsible companies may reduce future investment returns. But rising demand for sustainable and shrinking demand for non-sustainable investing may have a positive influence on investor returns and the sustainability risk and therefore the overall risk of such investments should be lower, too.

---

[15] Compare Cohen et al. (2022).

[16] See e.g. Soehnholz (2020a).

Signaling has its limits, though. Fund providers may not want to disclose their underlying securities and less so actively promote them. Fortunately, many products officially follow indices for which full disclosure of components is easily accessible. Also, all public investment funds must disclose their top holdings. Current and potential future investors, as well as media, therefore can see which securities are deemed to be especially responsible, discuss them and promote them, if they like what they discover.

12.2.1.6 The DVFA Policies for Responsible Investing Tool (DVFA PRISC) as Anti-greenwashing Tool

The discussion above shows that the definition of responsible investing lies in the eye of the beholder. Therefore, any investors should start with a clear responsible investment policy. This policy should detail the use of negative and positive responsible investment criteria. Voting and engagement should be addressed as well as requirements for ESG ratings.

The Sustainable Investing Commission of the German Association of Financial Analysts and Asset Managers (DVFA) has developed a tool for the holistic development and measurement of responsible investment policies of investors and investment portfolios.[17] In doing so, the DVFA deliberately does not want to prescribe any levels of responsibility but rather to give investors and providers of financial investments the opportunity to determine these themselves.

The tool is made available free of charge to interested parties as a changeable calculation model. In addition, investors are provided with documentation as modifiable texts to document bespoke sustainable investment policies. The tool comprises eight assessment dimensions, each with three characteristics, and enables their aggregation to form a comprehensive, responsible investment policy assessment. The dimensions are:

- Exclusions (avoiding "bad" investments, exclusions, or negative screening)
- Impact/SDG-Score ("good" investments or positive screening)
- ESG score definition (aggregated versus differentiated ESG score)
- ESG score application (best-in-universe versus best-in-class)
- ESG score cut-off (ESG minimum requirements)
- ESG-Score measurement frequency (Incidents)
- Exercising voting rights (Voting)
- Active attempts to exert influence (Engagement)

In the standard version of the tool, these categories are equally weighted. Users of the tool can change the weightings, add categories, and make other changes. An

[17] See DVFA (2022). I am a member of that commission and initiator of that tool. I am also the author of the tools' documentation. I used some sentences/paragraphs of that documentation for this article.

additional category could be the carbon footprint, for example, which has not been added by the DVFA because such information is part of the ESG ratings. Investors may also want to add labels and/or norms as separate dimensions.

The tool can help identify so called greenwashing. Greenwashing means that investments are portrayed as greener or more sustainable than they really are. And greenwashing accusations are increasingly prominent. Greenwashing accusations can cause significant reputational risks and costs. And greenwashing allegations can reduce the willingness of investors to try to invest in a responsible way.

Unfortunately, there is still no database including all mutual funds and all criteria of the tool. The Fund Profile database of the Forum Nachhaltige Geldanlagen, which has been mentioned above can help somewhat, though.[18]

12.2.1.7 Poor Real Economy?

ESG critics argue that we need, e.g., fossil fuels for many years to come. That is true, but many fossil fuel companies have and will continue to produce huge profits as can be seen in the current energy crisis. Therefore, they have a lot of money available to mitigate climate risks. In addition, if they need more funds, they could reduce their costs or increase product prices to account for the external effects that they are causing. They may also decide to lower the dividends for their shareholders. Given these, often abundant, internal financing abilities, additional external equity or loans therefore may not be very important for them.

And sure, CO2-filter investments by fossil fuel companies often make sense to improve air quality. But should investors buy stocks of a company that has neglected such investments in the past? Maybe so if the shareholders, who often received high dividends in the past, and the management are new and truly committed. But maybe politics and regulation should make sure that traditional energy companies invest their own capital in CO2-filters.

Instead of such an investment, investors can opt to dedicate their (limited) capital to wind and solar energy production. They can invest in a traditional energy provider wanting to improve or, alternatively, invest in a renewable's specialist that has proven its commitment and abilities since quite some time.

Private capital invested in poor ESG companies or companies in shunned industries initially may provide attractive returns for investors. But it also may end up as stranded investment.

[18] I mentioned some of the limitations of that database at the end of the Sect. 12.2.1.3. The number of funds in the database is limited, the data is directly supplied by the product providers and not necessarily updated regularly, best-in-universe and segregated E, S, and G ratings cannot be easily identified, etc.

12.2.2 *Increasing Number of Sustainable Products Available*

12.2.2.1 Different (Sustainable) Investment Philosophies

Unfortunately, investment philosophy is rarely discussed. Yet it is worth discussing. I distinguish between three different philosophies: *discretionary investors* (also called active investors) who use forecasts but very few formal rules, *quantitative (rule-based) investors* based on forecasts, and *rule-based forecast-free investors* (e.g. ETFs).[19] A rule-based forecast-free investment philosophy typically provides the most transparent portfolio construction approaches and portfolios and therefore is especially suitable for responsible investors who need transparency to evaluate investments according to their individual responsibility criteria.

Different philosophies can also be defined with respect to sustainable investments. For example, those who want to make the world a better place with their investments can be called *impact investors*. They primarily use private equity and debt investments because, unlike listed investments, these can bring additional capital to issuers. However, in doing so, they run high illiquidity risks.

Nowadays, the majority at least of institutional investors tend to take a sustainability-light approach and mix a small proportion of sustainability investments into their financial assets. I call this group the *satellite sustainability investors*. More and more private investors shift from investing *non-responsible* to this group over time.

I myself belong to the very small group of *pure sustainability investors*. I try to make all my investments as sustainable as possible but keep the investments highly liquid.

For discretionary, quant, and impact investors, ETFs are not attractive long-term holdings since they usually do not fit their philosophy. For the large sustainability-light group, on the other hand, sustainable ETFs may be especially attractive. For pure sustainability investors, most currently available ETFs have major disadvantages, though.

12.2.2.2 Problematic Actively Managed Sustainable Mutual Funds and ETFs

The number of so called "responsible" products is increasing rapidly. But this does not mean that it is easy for investors to find suitable investments. I tried to illustrate that above by using the fund profile database of the Forum Nachhaltige Geldanlagen. If investors have several demanding responsibility criteria, they may not find enough suitable investment products.

[19] See Soehnholz (2013).

There are several reasons for this. As a general rule, actively managed funds try to outperform their benchmarks. This is easier if they deviate from those benchmarks. But deviation from benchmarks also risks delivering underperformance to benchmarks. Statistically, actively managed funds underperform their benchmarks. Therefore, because they are rather risk averse, many actively managed funds try to stick closely to their benchmarks. And the most often used benchmarks are rather diversified indices.

Also, the fund industry is dominated by large asset managers. These asset managers offer mainly very large mutual funds, and these funds must be diversified to accommodate all their investments.

In addition, active fund managers try to stick to their investment strategies. This makes sense from a fund selector standpoint, too. But by trying to stick to traditional investment strategies, traditional investment selection and weighting criteria prevail. Responsibility selection and weighting criteria are typically only used as more or less unimportant add-on criteria.

Responsible investment funds can use traditional or responsible benchmarks. Responsible benchmarks typically try to have fewer tracking errors than traditional benchmarks. Therefore, even if funds use responsible benchmarks, those benchmarks typically incorporate only few hard exclusions. The benchmarks also use Best-in-Class and aggregated ESG ratings and mostly rather low minimum requirements for such ratings. Obviously, this approach also is a risk from a greenwashing perspective.

Investors looking for consequent responsible portfolios may have to look elsewhere, therefore. A solution may be rather small or new responsible investment funds from truly committed managers.

When I started my own company in 2015, I initially only wanted to use ETFs for my portfolios. But even the strictest responsible ETFs included many components that I did not like. Also, I could not find mutual funds which were fully aligned with my values. Therefore, I started to create my own model portfolios based directly on stocks.

Since I was very skeptical regarding traditional investment selection criteria I decided to (almost) only use responsibility criteria for investment selection. Thus, my portfolios could be much more sustainable than other portfolios. Since model portfolios can include many components without high additional costs, I still had to decide on the number of market segments, countries, and stocks I wanted to use.

12.2.2.3 The Diversification Myth: ESG as Antipode to ETFs?

Diversification across countries and industries certainly makes sense. But statistically, additional diversification typically brings little benefit. To generate a risk-return profile that is similar to an investment in all public equities, one doesn't need to invest in Russia or China or in all major industries. Everybody can verify this with the Portfoliovisualizer tool.[20] With that free tool, one can test a concentrated portfolio of a few even arbitrarily selected stocks with the "backtest portfolio" function and compare the results with broad indices.

In contrast, if one starts with the most responsible investment possible, e.g., a solar power investment for an orphanage in central Africa, further diversification will reduce average responsibility. Thus, concentrated portfolios can be much more responsible than broadly diversified portfolios. The picture below illustrates these relations in a simplified manner.

Additional portfolio diversification reduces sustainability with little – if any - performance benefits (conceptual illustration)

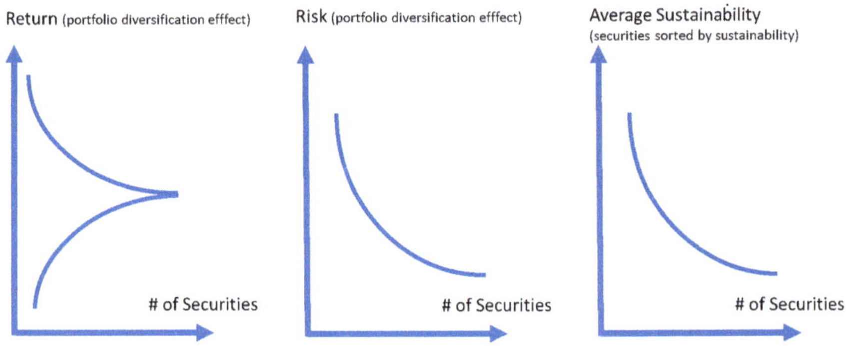

Source: Soehnholz ESG GmbH 2022

Many investors are afraid of concentration. I am not. My most concentrated equity portfolio includes only my five best ESG stocks worldwide. And my Global Equities ESG Portfolio consists of only the best 30 ESG stocks according to my responsibility criteria. I use many hard exclusions and high minimum ESG requirements but no traditional financial information to build these portfolios. Stocks from Brazil, China, Russian and many other countries and industries are explicitly excluded. Usually there are almost no high-tech nor mega-cap companies in my portfolios. Nevertheless, since their start in early 2017, both portfolios had similar or better returns than highly diversified global stock ETFs. The volatility for the 5-stock portfolio was rather high, but the risk for the 30-stock portfolio was very similar to diversified ETFs.[21]

Even concentrated SDG-aligned portfolios can be attractive. I only include very few market segments such as healthcare and renewables but also the 30-stock Global ESG SDG portfolio that I started in 2017 performs very similar to a traditional world equity ETF.

[20] Compare Silicon Cloud (2022).

[21] See Soehnholz ESG GmbH (2022).

12.2.3 *Early Stages of Custom ESG Indexing*[22]

12.2.3.1 Direct Indexing on the Rise

Charles Schwab, Blackrock, JP Morgan, Morgan Stanley, Goldman Sachs, Vanguard, Morningstar, Franklin Templeton, and First Trust have all recently acquired companies with direct indexing capabilities. And faster growth for the already large direct indexing market than for exchange traded funds is predicted.[23]

Direct indexing means investing directly in the underlying securities of an index. For US-based investors, direct indexing can reduce a portion of the relatively high capital gains tax by buying and selling selected index components. But direct indexing is very attractive for customized responsible investment portfolios, too.

ETFs can be cheap because they efficiently standardize investments. But standardized products often make too many investment compromises for responsible investors. And responsibility criteria often vary by client. Custom ESG (direct) indexing can solve that problem. Based on a starting index or portfolio, investors can deselect investments according to their own responsibility criteria and/or underweight or overweight certain allocations.

12.2.3.2 Stock-Unpicking Is Not the Same as Active Portfolio Management

Direct indexing ideally starts with transparent rules-based indices or portfolios and not with often opaque actively created investment portfolios. The next steps typically are deletions from these starting indices/portfolios.

Active portfolio management typically leads to underperformance in comparison to the respective benchmarks. It is unclear, though, if simple stock-unpicking from indices is good or bad for investment performance. Stock-unpicking reduces diversification but mathematically diversification benefits decrease fast after about 15 stocks, anyhow. And deselecting stocks for social and/or ecological reasons should reduce future social and ecological risks of an investment portfolio.

Whereas values-based deselection seems to be rather easy even for laypersons, the direct ESG-indexing case for over- and underweighting of stocks is not very strong. Liking or disliking a stock for ecological or social reasons is often easy to argue, but it requires much more knowhow to decide on the best weight of companies in a portfolio. This argument also applies to the theoretical option of adding securities to direct indexing starting indices/portfolios.

[22] This chapter is based on Soehnholz (2022a).

[23] Cerulli Assoicates (2021).

12.2.3.3 Benefits of Custom ESG Self-Indexing

For direct indexing, it is very important to start with a good index or base portfolio. With several million indices available, index selection can be very complex. A very diversified index may not be the best place to start direct indexing. Simply put, using more securities for the same investment universe means less rigid—e.g., ESG—selection criteria for the index components. And it is much easier for investors to judge index components if there are only few of them: A S&P Global 100 index can be easier analyzed regarding an individual responsibility fit than an MSCI world index with more than 1800 components. On the other hand, investors may not want to use only mega-caps in their portfolios as can be found in the S&P Global 100 or other concentrated indices. Also, investors with strict responsibility criteria may only find very few convincing stocks in such concentrated mega-cap indices.

Self-indexing may be an alternative. Self-indexing differs from active portfolio management since it typically consists of a set of rules that should be transparent so that third parties can replicate the (self-)index. My own global equity (self-)index consists of about 600 out of almost 30,000 stocks with ESG information.[24] With my best-in-universe approach, I only select the top E, S, and G-rated investments independently of predefined investment industries or classes. I neither use minimum or maximum allocations to industries or countries nor traditional financial stock selection criteria.

Even if investors like best-in-class approaches, they may want a different execution. Best-in-class ESG ETFs typically use aggregated ESG ratings for stock selection and/or weightings. Thus, a good corporate governance score can compensate for bad social or ecological ratings. With self-indexing, one can use high minimum requirements for E, S, and G separately, instead.

Also, by owning securities directly and not through an ETF, investors can use their voting rights as they like. They do not have to rely on the often not very responsible voting services of an ETF provider.[25] An additional advantage of self-indexing is that there are no index licensing fees, which can be high compared to overall investment costs.

12.2.3.4 Direct Bond and Multi-asset Indexing and Risk Management

Today, investors can choose from many responsible equity and bond indices, but very few for other asset classes such as real estate or infrastructure. This makes responsible direct indexing for real estate investment trusts and stocks, as well as for infrastructure equities, especially attractive. This is also true for thematic equity indices, which rarely use demanding responsibility criteria, if any.

[24] Soehnholz (2022b, pp. 113–124).

[25] See e.g. Soehnholz (2020a).

Bond direct indexing is more difficult than stock indexing considering the many rather illiquid bond markets and rather high minimum investment requirements for many single bonds. Instead of using direct bond indexing, investors can combine direct equity indices with responsible bond ETFs. But so-called responsible bond ETFs have basically the same responsibility-shortcomings as their equity siblings. Therefore, I use an ETF on multinational development bank bonds to avoid unsustainable corporate and government bond issuers. As an alternative to bond allocations, simple and transparent trend following can easily be applied to direct indexing equity portfolios to reduce risks.[26]

Direct indexing providers could provide simple-to-understand back-testing, risk measurement, scenario analysis, and simulation tools. Thus, interested investors can benchmark their individually generated direct indexing portfolios.

12.2.3.5 Fractional Shares as Bottleneck for Mass-Marketing

A few US companies already offer direct indexing services for portfolios, starting at $100,000. In other countries and even in the U.S.A., for international investments, providers of direct indexing services often require minimum investments of one million US dollars or even more. With almost free trading available through neo-brokers and the use of so-called fractional shares, lower minimum hurdles are certainly possible. But even in the US, fractional trading so far is mostly limited to US large caps. And if fractional trading is offered, it is often based on blockchain/token applications, which are considered risky or unsustainable by many responsible investors.

For investors who have sufficient funds to invest, direct indexing is easy to implement through wealth or asset management mandates or bespoke investment funds. Also, since structured products can be created fast and often rather efficiently, they may be especially interesting for direct index implementations.

The good news is that affordable direct indexing software is now available. Allindex, a Swiss fintech founded in 2018 with clients and representatives in Europe, the US, and Asia, is one such provider.[27] The business-to-business (B2B) software allows B2B partners and their clients an instant and bespoke index creation based on market and/or proprietary data, including ESG information from different ESG data suppliers. The services can be offered under private labels.

Some investors may be overwhelmed with the task of creating their own direct ESG portfolios. Hence, Allindex targets wealth managers, which can provide their investors with their own starting portfolios and guidance. For example, investors could use my rules-based universe of 600 out of almost 30.000 ESG-rated stocks, including 100 SDG-aligned stocks, as basis to create individual portfolios.

---

[26] Soehnholz (2016).

[27] I work part-time as ESG and SDG consultant to ALLINDEX (www.allindex.com).

12.2.3.6 ETF Marketing May Be the Biggest Enemy of Direct Indexing

ETFs are very successfully marketed as especially smart investments with the arguments that they are passive, low cost, and heavily diversified. Standard direct indexing, as it is offered today by the major US providers, is also passive and highly diversified albeit more expensive, even though it is typically cheaper than active investing. But the more focused an investment is, the easier it is to understand and the more it can be aligned with the values of a responsible investor. Therefore, custom ESG indexing is also passive in nature and not very expensive but will typically not be heavily diversified.

Whereas the additional cost of direct ESG indexing can be seen as low for customization, low-diversification criticism may be more difficult to overcome, especially since regulators and investor-advocates often heavily favor high diversification. Therefore, product providers and client advisors alike often avoid concentrated portfolios because they can be made liable for wrong selection decisions.

12.3 Summary and Outlook: Core-Satellite Responsible Investing Approach?

Criticism of so-called responsible investing has been rising. I started by outlining different dimensions and characteristics of responsible investments. I also described a free tool to develop a bespoke responsible investment policy. There are now many standard active and passive so-called responsible mutual funds available. By using another free fund selection tool, I show that strict responsibility criteria are only used by few actively managed funds. In addition, I describe several conceptual limits of responsible passive funds. In summary, since responsible investments can vary pretty much by investors, most standard funds may not be ideal for investors.

Much of the legitimate criticism of responsible investing can be avoided with bespoke portfolios. I outlined simple ways to customize responsible portfolios with direct investments, not limited to equity investments. There are many arguments for rather concentrated direct rule-based ESG investments. These (self-indexed) solutions could be efficiently delivered by wealth managers or used by self-directed investors. (Over-)diversification focus of mutual fund providers and investment advisors may be the biggest limitation for the growth of direct or custom ESG indexing. Most of the arguments apply to private and institutional investors alike, although institutional investors will probably diversify more than private investors.

References

Atz, U., Liu, Z. Z., Bruno, C., & Van Holt, T. (2021, August 31). Does sustainability generate better financial performance? Review, meta-analysis, and propositions. Working Paper. https://doi.org/10.2139/ssrn.3708495

Cerulli Associates. (2021). Direct indexing growth projected to outpace ETFs, mutual funds, and separate accounts over next five years, according to Cerulli, Press Release, August 16.

Cohen, S., Kadach, I., Ormazabal, G. and Reichelstein, S. J. (2022, April 25). Executive compensation tied to ESG performance: International evidence. IESE Business School Working Paper. https://papers.ssrn.com/sol3/papers.cfm?abstract_id=4094283

Deutsche Vereinigung für Finanzanalyse und Asset Management (DVFA 2022). DVFA Policy for Responsible Investment Scoring (DVFA PRISC). https://www.dvfa.de/der-berufsverband/kommissionen/sustainable-investing/prisc-tool-webanwendung.html

European Commission. (2022). EU taxonomy for sustainable activities. https://ec.europa.eu/info/business-economy-euro/banking-and-finance/sustainable-finance/eu-taxonomy-sustainable-activities_en

Forum Nachhaltige Geldanlagen. (2022a). FNG-Sustainability profiles. https://www.forum-ng.org/en/fng-sustainability-profiles

Forum Nachhaltige Geldanlagen. (2022b). Marktbericht 2022 – Deutschland. Nachhaltige Geldanlagen und verantwortliche Investments in Deutschland. https://fng-marktbericht.org/deutschland

Silicon Cloud Technologies. (2022). Portfolio Visualizer. https://www.portfoliovisualizer.com/

Soehnholz, D. (2013). Systematisierung und Diversifikation von Investmentphilosophien, in Absolut Report Nr. 6, 64–69.

Soehnholz, D. (2016, September 10). Einfaches Risikomanagement kann gut funktionieren. https://prof-soehnholz.com/einfaches-risikomanagement-kann-erstaunlich-gut-funktionieren/

Soehnholz, D. (2020a). Divestments bewirken mehr als Stimmrechtsausübungen oder Engagement. In C. Döpfner, K. Gabriel, R. Ostmann, K. Schaefers, S. Utz, & G. Vögele (Eds.), *Nachhaltige Finanzen*. Springer Gabler. https://doi.org/10.1007/978-3-658-31214-5_9

Soehnholz, D. (2020b, February 23). ESG Investing: > 20 false arguments. ESG Investing: > 20 false arguments – Responsible Investments (Blog) (prof-soehnholz.com).

Soehnholz, D. (2022a, March 4). Custom ESG indexing can challenge popularity of ETFs. Asia Financial News. Custom ESG Indexing Can Challenge Popularity Of ETFs – Asia Financial News.

Soehnholz, D. (2022b, January 31). Das Soehnholz ESG und SDG Portfoliobuch. https://soehnholzesg.com/de/wp-content/uploads/Das-Soehnholz-ESG-und-SDG-Portfoliobuch.pdf

Soehnholz ESG GmbH. (2022). Homepage. https://soehnholzesg.com/de/#/

United Nations. (2022). Do you know all 17 SDGs? https://sdgs.un.org/goals

Chapter 13
Customized Portfolios Using Machine Learning: Interview with Stefan Klauser

Karen Wendt and Stefan Klauser

13.1 Interview with K. Wendt, Sustainable Finance, 31.1.2023

Q1: Stefan, how do you imagine the future of asset management 10 years from now and what will be the role of AISOT in that transition?

Future asset management will be real time and hyper-personalized. Meaning, investors decide at any point in time about markets, sustainability criteria, themes, titles, risk-reward ratios, and other factors they want to have in their investment universe.

While it is possible today to personalize portfolios, it is not yet possible to have personalized portfolios that adjust to market developments in real time. Typically, the scope, speed, and scale of how data is analyzed are not sufficient in today's products. This kind of challenge requires next-generation data processing infrastructure and algorithms. Unfortunately, these things tend to be very expensive as talent in this area is extremely scarce. Moreover, today's financial institutions mostly attempt siloed approaches to implement AI in asset management while lacking digital maturity and access to skills to run complex AI deployments. Considering that any AI application consumes excessive amounts of energy due to high levels of computing power needed, siloed AI operations are highly inefficient when it comes to energy but also data usage. This is why AISOT develops an AI platform for asset management that allows not only real-time personaliza-

K. Wendt
Eccos Impact GmbH, Cham, Zug, Switzerland
e-mail: karen@sustainablefinance.io

S. Klauser (✉)
Aisot Technologies AG, Zurich, Switzerland
e-mail: stefan@aisot.ch

K. Wendt, B. Villhauer (eds.), *Sustainable Wealth Management*, Sustainable Finance,
https://doi.org/10.1007/978-3-031-55505-3_13

tion and optimization of portfolios but also to share data, AI models, and computing power securely and efficiently.

Q2: With low margins and increasing competition transforming the opportunity set for asset managers/owners, you believe successful AI integration in the investment decision process is key. What solutions are you offering to the market and why should asset managers care?

Indeed, margins are getting smaller for active managers. With this comes the pressure to increase efficiency and to automate labor-intense tasks in asset management.

Two researchers at MIT, S.P. Kothari and Robert C. Pozen, recently described it as follows: "To remain competitive, it is imperative that asset managers arm themselves with ML to guide their portfolio construction and trading decisions. However, in a competitive market, the benefits from ML are likely to be copied and commoditized (…)." Kothari and Pozen come to the conclusion that customization and personalization are the only ways asset managers can stay ahead of the competition in the future.

And that's exactly what AISOT does: supporting asset managers with efficiently finding well performing while fully personalized strategies and portfolios.

Q3: Is the goal to beat the market through active asset management? If yes, how? Many have tried, and many have failed.

Passive index investing is fine and offers low-cost solutions for investors that are OK with being left with a standard product they cannot influence. However, the cost for active asset management products, including personalized portfolios, does not necessarily have to be very high.

Through automated data harvesting, processing, and forecasting, one can generate personalized portfolios at a relatively low price point. And they even perform well. It is not only about beating the market though, it is about offering clients an investment portfolio that reflects their individual needs and preferences at a fair price and great risk return ratios. Our portfolios and strategies are indeed performing well so far, but outperformance is not the only relevant aspect here.

Q4: What is the difference between your tools and what I can get today to "predict the market," like sentiment and momentum analysis.

Sentiments and market signals are an essential part of an AI-based portfolio tool. But they are only one step. They do not take into account a number of elements, such as the composition of a portfolio and what this means in terms of covariances and associated risks but also time-related aspects. How long does the effect of a certain sentiment last? When is a good time to rebalance? And usually sentiments and momentum are based on one source of information, such as news or recent performance, and thus hardly give a complete view of the situation.

At AISOT, in contrast, we integrate hundreds and thousands of data features and millions of data points to build our portfolios. We feed them into our AI forecasting and risk optimization engine and additionally take covariance effects into account. This allows us to deliver more meaningful signals and strategies for clearly defined time horizons.

Q5: You want to democratize asset management. So what does that mean?

The integration of advanced, real-time ML solutions into day-to-day operations is a standard that only the largest financial institutions can afford. And even large organizations struggle with it. According to VentureBeat and Deloitte, only one in ten ML models make it into production. This number is in stark contrast with more than 90% of tech executives who believe that ML is at the center of the current technological revolution.

ML models can be compared to living organisms. Once developed and deployed, they are challenging to maintain. Financial institutions often attempt siloed approaches to implement ML models while lacking digital maturity and access to skills to run complex ML deployments.

By offering an independent third-party platform to apply ML to financial challenges, we broaden access to this technology and help to maintain a broad space of asset management companies that cater to specific needs of their clientele in a professional and cost-efficient manner.

Q6: How does your platform help with it?

At AISOT, asset and wealth managers can define the investment universe and personal inputs of their clients and derive the necessary insights in an interactive process. They can also choose data components to be integrated and connect their own data resources and return views. Finally, they can access the analytics, forecasts, and portfolios generated directly on the platform, download data files, and/or connect through APIs. Like this, clients can access next-generation AI tools at a fraction of the costs as compared to building their own AI resources while not giving away their unique differentiating elements.

Q7: To what extent is active asset management a solution to environmental, social problems, and governance issues?

Actively managed portfolios can react to changing environments in real time. If there is growing concern about the sustainability of a company and/or a respective change in ESG score, one can do justice to this without any delays. A modern asset management tool needs to integrate different ESG scores and allow clients to optimize portfolios on this basis. If then, in turn, companies that do not score well in any ESG dimension are more often excluded from client portfolios, this will put great pressure on companies to improve their sustainability efforts.

And the performance of a portfolio is no excuse to keep unsustainable titles in a portfolio. Sustainable companies perform well, and by applying AI to the selection and optimization process, we get the maximum out of it without sacrificing vulnerable groups and/or the environment.

Q8: What exactly are you doing in the sphere of ESG and impact investing?

We are working on offering ESG metrics in our equity portfolio optimization tool and allow clients to train our models on specific ESG settings in order to maximize risk return ratios. Going forward, we also want to offer AI-optimized, ESG-related actively managed investment products in collaboration with a bank or asset manager. This way, we can further lower the entry barrier for groups of investors with smaller pockets. And last but not least, by allowing to access shared computation power and data pools, we make sure that energy consumption within the industry can be kept at more sustainable levels and is used as efficiently as possible.

Part III
Developments in China

Chapter 14
Internet Finance, Private Firm Financing, and Investment: Evidence from China

Na Shen and Lei Xu

14.1 Introduction

Private firms often face financing gaps, especially those in transition economies (Le et al., 2006). For example, Allen et al. (2005), Poncet et al. (2010), and Fu et al. (2015) show that Chinese private firms are credit constrained, while state-owned firms and foreign-owned firms are not. When private firms have limited access to formal financing (Yiu et al., 2013), they may switch to informal financing (Lu et al., 2015). A recent study shows that the usage of informal financing is more popular in smaller and younger firms (Allen et al., 2019).

More recently, the scope of informal finance has expanded into the broader universe of shadow banking (Tsai, 2015a). Shadow banking refers to all financial instruments that fulfil functions of credit intermediation typically performed by banks (such as liquidity, maturity, and credit risk transformation) but reduce the burden of, or bypass, banking regulation (Ehlers et al., 2018). Globally the scale of shadow banking assets exceeds global GDP (Tsai, 2015b). In China, shadow banking has expanded significantly since the 2009 fiscal stimulus (Chen et al., 2020), and the scale of shadow banking in China ranges from an estimated 26–69% of the country's GDP as of late 2012 (Tsai, 2015a).

Among shadow banking, internet finance has received particular attention. Internet finance includes the internetization of finance, mobile and third-party payments, digital currency, using big data for credit scoring and network loans, peer-to-peer (P2P) network loans, and crowdfunding (Xie et al., 2015). As society is moving toward digitalization, internet finance is developing fast. As such, the Chinese

N. Shen
Department of Business Administration, Hong Kong Shue Yan University, Hong Kong, China

L. Xu (✉)
UniSA Business, University of South Australia, Adelaide, SA, Australia
e-mail: Lei.Xu@unisa.edu.au

K. Wendt, B. Villhauer (eds.), *Sustainable Wealth Management*, Sustainable Finance,
https://doi.org/10.1007/978-3-031-55505-3_14

government set out a series of policies and regulatory rules to encourage the innovation of internet finance and support its healthy development (Xie et al., 2016).

Based on this prior discussion, a natural question arises: will the development of shadow banking, particularly, internet finance, help in private firms' financing and investment? There is scarce literature investigating such relationship to guide us in answering this question. One exception is Tsai (2017) who argue that shadow banking can be productive in providing finance to small and medium enterprises (SMEs) in China, though no empirical analysis is provided. Therefore, this study attempts to fill the research gap by investigating private firms' financing and investment via internet finance with empirical evidence.

China is chosen as the research context due to the following reasons. First, Chinese private firms face significant barriers in accessing credit from banks (Wu & Xu, 2020). Chinese private firms' financing is also consistently a hot topic in academic research and in practice. Second, internet finance has, historically, developed quickly in China. To back this assertation, Peking University publishes an internet finance development index, starting from 2014, which highlights the internet finance development. Third, there are large institutional variations across regions in China (Shen et al., 2020). Such variation also exists concerning internet finance development. Therefore, this study can use regional internet finance development as the research perspective to answer the research question on the relationship between internet finance development and private firms' financing.

Based on the unique dataset surveying private firms in all provinces in China and the unique research perspective of regional internet finance development, this study aims to give an overview of Chinese private firms' financing and investment via internet finance. This study initially conducts a descriptive study on Chinese private firms' financing behavior. The variations among different financing channels (including internet finance) and in different geographical regions will be identified. Further, this study will investigate the relationship between private firms' financing and regional internet finance development. Specifically, in regions with more developed internet finance, do private firms borrow more through internet finance? Do they pay higher or lower interest rates for internet finance? In addition, this study will investigate whether private firms use funds borrowed from internet finance for new investments, that is, does internet finance help in private firms' investment? All these questions are interesting and important to both academics and practitioners.

The paper is structured as follows. The second section gives a general introduction and descriptive analysis about private firms' financing behavior via internet finance. The third section discusses the hypothesis development based on the literature. The fourth section introduces the research method while, the fifth section presents the regression results. The last section discusses and concludes.

14.2 Internet Finance in China

14.2.1 Literature

Elliott et al. (2015) define shadow banks as "financial firms that perform similar functions and assume similar risks to banks." Most shadow banking tools originated from North America and Europe. Nevertheless, they have gone through significant development and innovations in China.

Shen and Huang (2016) treat "internet finance" (IF) as the same concept as "digital finance" and "fintech," but "internet finance" a more often used term in China. They further argue that such digital tools, although boosting the development of shadow banking, are not exclusive to traditional banking. Digital finance cannot be viewed as a subset of shadow banking. Indeed, according to the Guidelines for Promoting the Healthy Development of Internet Finance (State Council, 2015), China's Ministry of Finance defines IF as a new financial business model in which traditional financial institutions and internet enterprises use the internet and other telecommunication technology to realize financing, payment, investment, and information intermediary services.

Despite rapid development, the share of internet finance relative to total financial transactions is still small in China (Xu, 2017). However, internet finance has gradually diversified the financing channels for private firms and SMEs (Zheng, 2018). China has a different financial system from the USA and Europe's, which is attributable to different financing environments for firms. Elliott and Yan, (2013) claim that, although the bond market and insurance industry in China are experiencing rapid growth, their absolute volumes remain small. As such, the banking industry still plays a dominant role in the debt financing market, which is utterly different to that of western developed countries. As for stock markets, Elliott and Yan, (2013) argue that Chinese regulators are essentially imposing informal quotas through tight controls on initial public offerings (IPOs). These quotas and controls have made large-scale equity financing almost inaccessible to most of China's private firms. As a result, indirect financing is still the major debt-financing channel available to Chinese firms. Therefore, internet finance has become more essential for private firms urging for capital.

Despite the importance of internet finance to private firms, the literature on this field is quite limited. Moreover, researchers realize data from internet finance is not perfectly accurate (Xu, 2017). Therefore, this study will contribute by filling research gaps and providing an accurate analysis based on datasets from national survey.

14.2.2 Private Firm's Financing Via Internet Finance: Descriptive Analysis

To better understand the reality of private firm's financing and investment via internet finance, this study refers to data from a survey on Chinese private firms, which was jointly conducted by (i) the United Front Work Department of the Central Committee of the Communist Party of China, (ii) the All-China Federation of Industry and Commerce, (iii) the State Administration for Industry and Commerce of the People's Republic of China, and (iv) the Private Economy Research Institute of China. The purpose of the survey is for the government to understand the thoughts, opinions, and requests by private business founders (entrepreneurs) and to identify problems that private firms may encounter in their growing stages. The survey applies multistage, stratified sampling to select a sample that is representative of the regions and industries in China. Table 14.1 presents the sample distribution by regions in 2013 and 2015. The survey is conducted every 2 years and serves as a reliable data source (e.g., Zhou, 2013).

This study uses two datasets from the survey, in 2013 and 2015. For the 2013 data, the sample size is 6144 firms, while for the 2015 data the sample size is 8114 firms. Data from 2013 and 2015 is chosen because China's internet finance industry developed explosively from 2012 to 2015 (Xu, 2017). In particular, 2013 is sometimes referred to as "the Year of Internet Finance" (Xu, 2017). To better compare internet finance and other financing channels, we describe private firms' borrowing from all channels including commercial banks, small financial institutions, private loans, and internet finance. As China is a country with large variation among regions, this study will describe the financing behavior within all 31 provinces.

Tables 14.2, 14.3, 14.4, and 14.5 present the basic findings. Tables 14.2 and 14.4 present the average debt amounts from different financing channels for firms in each province in 2013 and 2015, respectively. Tables 14.3 and 14.5 present the average interest rate from different financing channels for firms in each province in 2013 and 2015, respectively.

Table 14.2 shows that internet financing has emerged as a new financing channel in China, though formal financing, through commercial banks, is still dominant in most regions in 2013, except Hainan and Qinghai.[1] Interestingly, average bank loan sizes are much bigger in less-developed regions. For example, in Beijing and Shanghai private firms' average bank debt liabilities are less than 20 million RMB. However, the average bank debts liabilities are over 90 million (RMB) in Ningxia and Xinjiang. In Henan, bank debt liabilities are even larger at over 470 million RMB. Small financial institution debt follows bank loans as the second source of funding for private firms. In regions such as Hainan and Qinghai, small financial institutions play more important roles than banks in providing loans to private firms.

[1] Hainan Development Bank set the first bank failure record in modern China and results in the underdevelopment of regional banking sector. The network of banks may impose a lending constraint to the scattered borrowers in Qinghai.

Table 14.1 Sample distribution by region in 2013 and 2015

Region	No. of firms in 2013	Percentage	No. of firms in 2015	Percentage
1. Beijing	326	5.3	333	4.1
2. Tianjin	126	2.1	153	1.9
3. Hebei	174	2.8	238	2.9
4. Shanxi	162	2.6	246	3.0
5. Inner Mongolia	114	1.9	129	1.6
6. Liaoning	192	3.1	396	4.9
7. Jilin	195	3.2	267	3.3
8. Heilongjiang	145	2.4	191	2.4
9. Shanghai	345	5.6	377	4.6
10. Jiangsu	435	7.1	513	6.3
11. Zhejiang	465	7.6	542	6.7
12. Anhui	201	3.3	229	2.8
13. Fujian	172	2.8	316	3.9
14. Jiangxi	174	2.8	240	3.0
15. Shandong	410	6.7	417	5.1
16. Henan	171	2.8	221	2.7
17. Hubei	301	4.9	403	5.0
18. Hunan	146	2.4	182	2.2
19. Guangdong	473	7.7	639	7.9
20. Guangxi	164	2.7	186	2.3
21. Hainan	92	1.5	127	1.6
22. Chongqing	210	3.4	260	3.2
23. Sichuan	222	3.6	335	4.1
24. Guizhou	141	2.3	252	3.1
25. Yunnan	136	2.2	224	2.8
26. Xizang	26	0.4	32	0.4
27. Shaanxi	144	2.3	249	3.1
28. Gansu	92	1.5	140	1.7
29. Qinghai	33	0.5	92	1.1
30. Ningxia	132	2.1	80	1.0
31. Xinjiang	25	0.4	105	1.3
Total	6144	100	8114	100

Private loans are an important supplement to bank and small financial institution loans. Interestingly, private loans surpass small financial institution loans in Beijing. In Chongqing, private loans provide similar support to private firms as loans provided by small financial institutions. Although occurring much later than the previous three funding sources, internet financing quickly catches the level of funding provided by private loans in Shanxi, Jiangsu, and Shanghai.

Table 14.3 reports the average interest cost of debt in 2013. Bank loans tend to be cheaper than other sources of funding, followed by small financial institution and private loans. Internet financing appears to be the most expensive debt source for

Table 14.2 Average debt amount by region (year 2013)

Region	From commercial bank	From small financial institutions	From private loans	From internet finance
1. Beijing	1992.53	48.80	74.78	0.00
2. Tianjin	4410.01	1516.38	9.71	0.48
3. Hebei	2500.73	304.50	36.72	0.00
4. Shanxi	296.97	164.94	74.51	66.09
5. Inner Mongolia	3812.25	663.53	213.61	0.00
6. Liaoning	821.64	114.58	9.53	0.58
7. Jilin	545.63	23.58	23.01	0.07
8. Heilongjiang	210.93	19.48	14.72	0.00
9. Shanghai	1515.72	66.03	9.62	4.44
10. Jiangsu	1370.34	266.35	25.06	17.49
11. Zhejiang	3303.53	573.38	41.32	0.24
12. Anhui	1654.39	456.64	122.64	0.00
13. Fujian	6490.69	108.52	64.66	0.33
14. Jiangxi	1603.59	261.85	15.22	0.00
15. Shandong	6504.19	434.20	190.79	3.35
16. Henan	47,233.54	1062.33	107.82	0.00
17. Hubei	2560.47	295.43	83.38	1.89
18. Hunan	958.95	78.51	20.12	4.11
19. Guangdong	881.39	180.93	51.84	5.66
20. Guangxi	2203.37	228.21	14.56	0.00
21. Hainan	146.05	170.61	18.67	0.24
22. Chongqing	1914.88	173.82	172.54	0.00
23. Sichuan	1075.60	381.62	67.38	7.81
24. Guizhou	1678.74	436.55	142.18	0.00
25. Yunnan	694.65	415.78	87.98	0.00
26. Xizang	210.37	107.86	10.00	0.00
27. Shaanxi	1298.44	355.02	50.00	0.00
28. Gansu	3942.59	308.49	65.28	0.00
29. Qinghai	1951.20	3415.00	116.00	0.00
30. Ningxia	9103.66	127.25	53.93	0.00
31. Xinjiang	9636.70	273.08	56.84	0.00
Total	3598.67	334.16	67.78	4.44

All numbers are in 10K RMB

private firms. The cost of internet financing can be as low as 9% in Fujian or as high as 48% in Shanxi, with an average of 20.8% across all regions. In comparison, the reported costs of bank loans, small financial institution loans, and private loans are 8.02%, 8.87%, and 12.88%, respectively. These results are consistent with Allen and Gu (2021) in that interest rates for nonaffiliated loans are on average twice as high as official bank loan rates.

Table 14.3 Average debt interest by region (year 2013)

Region	From commercial bank	From small financial institutions	From private loans	From internet finance
1. Beijing	8.82	9.04	11.45	NA
2. Tianjin	8.64	7.42	9.25	31.00
3. Hebei	9.28	6.94	23.40	NA
4. Shanxi	7.90	9.27	9.77	48.00
5. Inner Mongolia	6.13	5.43	6.05	NA
6. Liaoning	9.24	8.91	14.00	NA
7. Jilin	10.97	15.26	13.32	20.00
8. Heilongjiang	10.42	9.85	13.50	NA
9. Shanghai	7.12	7.85	8.43	19.05
10. Jiangsu	7.42	9.63	13.19	24.75
11. Zhejiang	7.70	7.07	10.04	24.00
12. Anhui	11.17	11.95	12.71	NA
13. Fujian	7.94	9.25	14.62	9.00
14. Jiangxi	7.40	8.73	13.59	NA
15. Shandong	8.09	7.40	11.93	21.36
16. Henan	7.01	7.21	12.11	NA
17. Hubei	7.51	10.25	7.96	NA
18. Hunan	6.88	7.26	11.59	NA
19. Guangdong	8.24	7.69	12.68	15.45
20. Guangxi	8.35	9.46	17.44	NA
21. Hainan	8.96	12.95	22.50	13.00
22. Chongqing	7.99	14.37	16.45	9.00
23. Sichuan	10.78	9.79	10.46	15.00
24. Guizhou	8.10	8.18	15.00	NA
25. Yunnan	8.05	8.42	16.45	NA
26. Xizang	4.67	3.26	12.00	NA
27. Shaanxi	7.48	11.71	7.00	NA
28. Gansu	7.65	9.19	9.61	NA
29. Qinghai	6.35	6.85	2.00	NA
30. Ningxia	6.27	7.83	12.25	NA
31. Xinjiang	6.05	6.68	28.67	NA
Total	8.02	8.87	12.88	20.80

Table 14.4 reports private firms' borrowing behavior in 2015. Compared to the 2013 data in Table 14.2, both bank and small financial institution loans grow in excess of 30%. For instance, from 2013 to 2015, average bank loan sizes grow from 36 to 50 million RMB. Small financial institution loans grow relatively slower than bank loans from an average of 3.3 to 4.6 million RMB. Of particular interest, bank loans grew sharply in Shandong from 65 to 699 million RMB. However, private loans and internet financing seem to get sharply smaller in loan sizes on average. The highly active regions of private loans and internet financing observed in 2013

Table 14.4 Average debt amount by region (year 2015)

Region	From commercial bank	From small financial institutions	From private loans	From internet finance
1. Beijing	2436.59	80.73	86.13	0.02
2. Tianjin	3141.23	50.72	4.90	0.00
3. Hebei	1637.53	366.08	65.44	3.57
4. Shanxi	1573.21	39.47	58.45	0.00
5. Inner Mongolia	360.88	12.09	2.45	0.00
6. Liaoning	954.28	294.22	106.29	0.36
7. Jilin	248.11	19.54	68.24	0.05
8. Heilongjiang	100.15	17.88	13.52	0.18
9. Shanghai	1203.12	73.73	18.74	0.00
10. Jiangsu	1551.81	213.31	30.15	0.44
11. Zhejiang	3443.53	838.99	29.81	2.25
12. Anhui	1276.40	86.55	47.63	0.64
13. Fujian	1779.88	94.54	30.49	0.53
14. Jiangxi	518.97	2938.79	4.42	0.66
15. Shandong	69,856.08	3940.12	14.22	0.00
16. Henan	1504.47	98.44	24.12	0.00
17. Hubei	732.90	44.00	28.49	2.83
18. Hunan	526.51	52.58	19.33	0.28
19. Guangdong	1139.10	132.58	42.63	0.24
20. Guangxi	2056.61	683.27	7.55	0.00
21. Hainan	181.26	9.35	13.96	0.08
22. Chongqing	2388.57	991.56	17.75	0.08
23. Sichuan	1262.55	46.93	113.46	1.12
24. Guizhou	319.51	26.82	15.20	0.28
25. Yunnan	4509.71	52.66	219.12	0.01
26. Xizang	1686.96	210.50	55.00	0.00
27. Shaanxi	2294.18	158.81	76.34	0.09
28. Gansu	2832.31	41.03	29.21	0.00
29. Qinghai	3542.88	94.76	57.14	0.00
30. Ningxia	4380.62	9.75	0.09	0.00
31. Xinjiang	427.81	67.21	52.09	0.00
Total	5005.97	456.97	45.66	0.64

All numbers are in 10K RMB

to supplement formal loans are not demonstrated in 2015. This change may be related to the policies of China Banking Regulatory Commission (CBRC), of People's Bank of China (PBC), and of other regulatory policies since 2014 on SME loans to support economic growth in the country,[2] which subsequently increased the

[2] Such as "Guidelines to Promote Financial Services for Small and Micro Enterprises" in 2013. In addition, the China Banking Regulatory Commission adjusted the calculation of the loan-to-

Table 14.5 Average debt interest by region (year 2015)

Region	From commercial bank	From small financial institutions	From private loans	From internet finance
1. Beijing	7.55	13.57	9.14	16.50
2. Tianjin	6.74	8.88	12.5	NA
3. Hebei	6.94	9.71	17.41	15.40
4. Shanxi	9.23	13.45	11.72	NA
5. Inner Mongolia	6.05	7.52	8.49	NA
6. Liaoning	7.44	13.12	12.82	NA
7. Jilin	10.55	7.86	10.71	6.50
8. Heilongjiang	7.38	3.77	10.29	NA
9. Shanghai	6.93	6.12	11.58	NA
10. Jiangsu	6.46	7.53	8.51	17.00
11. Zhejiang	6.49	7.57	9.59	12.35
12. Anhui	6.77	10.22	12.45	10.53
13. Fujian	7.22	11.89	13.93	7.50
14. Jiangxi	8.19	11.86	12.44	8.00
15. Shandong	7.13	6.64	9.25	NA
16. Henan	7.35	9.44	10.01	NA
17. Hubei	7.64	8.23	11.24	14.17
18. Hunan	7.96	7.23	10.54	8.77
19. Guangdong	5.82	6.18	13.61	10.5
20. Guangxi	7.09	6.65	10.98	NA
21. Hainan	6.55	9.00	10.69	9.00
22. Chongqing	7.62	6.28	10.5	20.00
23. Sichuan	6.53	7.94	8.97	12.00
24. Guizhou	6.42	7.37	13.11	18.50
25. Yunnan	6.12	6.15	7.98	NA
26. Xizang	3.41	5.17	12.00	NA
27. Shaanxi	7.83	8.39	10.46	6.60
28. Gansu	7.41	8.00	8.05	NA
29. Qinghai	6.89	9.45	15.00	NA
30. Ningxia	5.45	5.96	NA	NA
31. Xinjiang	7.27	11.56	14.78	NA
Total	7.05	8.47	11.29	12.08

loan supply to SMEs and concurrently decreased the supply of funds away from internet financing.

Table 14.5 reports the private firms' funding costs in 2015. Following the PBC's lowering of benchmark lending rates in November 2014, February 2015, and October 2015, Chinese banks, which have either direct or indirect dominant state

deposit ratio of commercial banks, released the credit supply, and issued "returning loans" for small and microenterprises.

ownership, lowered their loan interest rates. Such changes are observed from the average bank loan cost decreasing from 8.02% in 2013 to 7.05% in 2015. Similarly, small financial institutions also lowered their loan interest rates from an average of 8.87% in 2013 to 8.47% in 2015. In line with banks and small financial institutions, private loans and internet finance also lowered their rates from 12.88% and 20.80% in 2013 to 11.29% and 12.08% in 2015, respectively. We observe the sudden crackdown of high lending rates by internet lenders. In 2013, the average internet interest rate can be as high as 48% in Shanxi. However the highest for 2015 is only 20% in Chongqing. China's Supreme Court ordered that lending rates above 36% would not be protected by the courts in the country.[3] This regulation might be the primary reason to explain the decrease of internet finance interest rate, though other possible reasons also account.

14.3 Hypotheses

14.3.1 Private Firms' Financing Choice Via Internet Finance

Chinese private firms face financial constraints due to many reasons such as the loan interest rate cap set by People's Bank of China[4] and significant credit rate spread between state-owned enterprises (SOEs) and private firms (Poncet et al., 2010). Poncet et al. (2010) argue that different types of firms face different extents of credit constraints. Specifically, Chinese private firms face the most stringent credit constraints, while SOEs and foreign-owned firms face less stringent constraints. Similarly, Gao et al. (2019) find that banks prefer to lend to inefficient SOEs over more productive private firms.

In China, internet finance focuses on the "de-banking" process for the credit demands of individuals and SMEs which shifts the financing resources from state-owned sectors to private sectors (Xie et al., 2016). Tsai (2017) argues that regulated and well-managed nonbanking financial institutions could provide an enduring foundation for commercialized financial intermediation serving SMEs. Wang et al. (2019) claim that the shadow banking sector in China channels funds to capital-deprived and high-productivity private firms. Ji (2017) claims that internet finance is of great significance for financing of SMEs in China.

Section 14.2 highlights private firms' financing behavior in different regions and shows a large variation among regions. This finding is consistent with the Internet Finance Development Index (IFDI), developed by the Institute of Internet Finance, Peking University, to measure the evolution of China's internet finance (Guo et al.,

[3] See China News 6 August 2015 "24% and 36%, Supreme Courts draws the red line for private lending rates" http://www.chinanews.com/cj/2015/08-06/7451642.shtml (in Chinese).

[4] Elliott and Yan (2013) held the idea that although China's central government is committed to interest rate marketization and gradually loosening the control these years, commercial banks do not have the culture and ability to lend successfully to small private firms.

2016). They find that internet finance development has a positive correlation to local economic development, internet availability, and the maturity of the local traditional banking industry. The disparity of internet finance development among regions is displayed when comparing coastal cities which exhibit a higher volume but a lower growth rate of internet finance in comparison to inland cities.

Based on the above arguments, the literature suggests that internet finance may help in solving private firms' financing constraints. We posit a positive relationship between private firms' financing from internet finance and internet finance development in the region where the private firm is located. Therefore, we propose the first hypothesis:

H1: There is a positive relationship between regional internet finance development and private firm's debt from internet finance across China.

14.3.2 Private Firms' Financing Cost Via Internet Finance

Internet finance also constitutes a dual-track interest rate liberalization, which introduces a market credit track alongside the preexisting controlled credit track (Wang et al., 2019). In China, incremental liberalization of interest rates on loans has occurred since the late 1990s, with the upper limit on lending rates being removed in 2013 (Tsai, 2017). The model by Wang et al. (2019) shows that dual-track interest rate liberalization rather than full interest rate liberalization achieves Pareto improvement.

The development of internet finance has reduced the financing cost of SMEs to some extent (Zheng, 2018). However, the risks accumulate with the development of internet finance. Take Shanghai Lujiazui International Financial Asset Trading Co., Ltd., the leader in P2P lending, as an example. It was reported to have a $250 million RMB bad debt in March 2015, which led to distrust on online platforms from investors. Moreover, as internet finance is new to the market, the Chinese legal system on the protection and regulation of internet financial operations are quite deficient (Zheng, 2018).

Regarding interest rates, as players in internet finance are driven by business profits, they seek risk-adjusted returns. Private firms, as we discussed before, are riskier than SOEs and foreign-owned firms. With the development of internet finance, the risks also accumulate. Therefore, if regional internet finance is well developed, private firms are prone to borrowing through internet finance. In the meantime, they have to pay higher interest rates to compensate for their higher risks than other borrowers. Therefore, we propose the second hypothesis:

H2: There is a positive relationship between regional internet finance development and private firm's debt interest rates from internet finance across China.

14.3.3 Private Firms' Investment Via Internet Finance

There are a lot of research investigating how firms catch growth opportunity via external or internal financing (e.g., Rahaman, 2011). After Chinese private firms borrow via internet finance, do they use the fund to finance new investment to catch growth opportunities? Unfortunately, no current study answers this question.

Gu (2020) explains that the intention of "Interim Management Guideline for Internet Loans by Commercial Banks" is to support SMEs and suggests that regulators hope that internet loans can be used to boost the real economy. However, as most lending firms in the shadow banking system are not financial firms, a concern is whether they can properly monitor borrowers (Jiang & Kim, 2020).

Private firms usually exhibit lower investment sensitivity to growth opportunities than publicly listed firms (Mortal & Reisel, 2013). Carbo-Valverde et al. (2008) find that increased bank loan funding will not be associated with increased capital expenditures for constrained firms. When the desired amount of loans exceeds the supplied amount of loans at constrained firms, loans will not predict/cause investment at constrained firms. For private firms, if they have to borrow via expensive internet finance, they should be regarded as financially constrained. Therefore, the loans will not be used for new investment to catch growth opportunity.

Tang et al. (2019) finds P2P platforms complement banks by providing small loans. Given the high financing cost of internet finance, a firm will only resort to it when funds from other sources are not available. Therefore, the use of internet finance is a signal of tighter financial constraints and weaker financial status, which should be associated with reduced investment. Thus, we propose the third hypothesis as follows:

H3: Private firms' debt from internet finance will not increase the firm's new investment in China.

14.4 Method

14.4.1 Variables and Measurement

14.4.1.1 Dependent Variables

There are three dependent variables in the three models testing the hypotheses. The first dependent variable relates to hypothesis 1 and is *internet debt dummy* which is created based on whether a firm has internet debt. In the survey, a question is about the amount of internet debt. If a firm fills in "0," i.e. no debt, the internet debt dummy is coded as "0." If a firm fills in any number larger than zero, internet debt dummy is coded as "1." The second dependent variable, *internet debt interest rate*, relates to hypothesis 2 and uses the interest rate for internet debt. In the survey, a question relates to the annual interest rate from internet debt. The survey answer is as a percentage, and we recoded it by multiplying by 100. The third dependent variable, namely, *new investment*, measures firms' new investment and relates to the third hypothesis. Again, a question in the survey relates to new investment and is recorded in 10K RMB.

14.4.1.2 Independent Variables

Index is the internet finance development index. It is published by the Institute of Internet Finance (IDF), Peking University. To construct this index, six areas are chosen including internet payment, internet currency funds, internet credit, internet insurance, internet investment, and wealth management. According to the breadth and width indicator of each area, IDF composed one transaction development index and drafted the overall index reflecting the overall development of digital finance. The data used to construct the index is obtained from Ant Financial Services Group, internet finance institutions, and third parties. The index is published every month beginning in January 2014. Based on the relative ratio of different regions and attributes to the national development, IDF computed the region and attribute indexes. This study uses the regional index reflecting internet finance development for each province. As our firm data is from 2013 and 2015, we chose regional index in December 2013 and December 2015, respectively. This independent variable is used in H1 and H2.

The independent variable used in H3 is *internet debt*. In the survey, one question is about the amount of internet debt, and it is recorded in 10K RMB.

14.4.1.3 Control Variables

Firm age is the number of years since the establishment of the firm. Literature has documented that young firms face greater difficulty in securing commercial bank debt than more established firms (Robb, 2002). Therefore, firm age is a necessary control variable.

Firm size is measured as the logarithm of the number of employees. Literature has documented that small firms have less access to formal sources of external finance (Beck & Demirguc-Kunt, 2006). Therefore, firm size needs to be controlled.

Debt ratio is the debt percentage in firms' working capital. Debt from other channels such as national banks, small financial institutions, and private lending is also used.

As regional GDP is highly correlated with the internet finance development index, to avoid a possible multicollinearity issue, regional GDP will not be included.

14.4.2 Analysis Method

We use two approaches to test the models. We apply logistic regression to estimate the probability of a firm to borrow via internet finance (H1). In addition, we employ the ordinary least squares (OLS) regression to test the relationship between the debt interest rate from internet finance and the regional internet finance development index (H2) as well as the relationship between new investment and internet finance (H3).

14.5 Regression Results

Table 14.6 presents the descriptive statistics of each variable in the regression using 2013 data, while Table 14.7 presents the descriptive statistics of each variable in the regression using 2015 data.

Tables 14.6 and 14.7 indicate that borrowing from internet finance is not popular. Consistent with previous tables, the amount of borrowing from national banks is the largest. The second largest amount of borrowing is from small financial institutions, followed by private lending.

The two tables also reveal some dynamics. The internet finance development index is higher in 2015 than in 2013, showing a rapid development in internet finance across the country. Debt amount from national banks and small financial

Table 14.6 Descriptive statistics for 2013 data

	Observations	Mean	Std. deviation	Minimum	Maximum
Dependent variable					
Internet debt dummy	4385	0.01	0.08	0.00	1.00
Internet debt interest rate (in percentage)	41	20.80	24.56	0.00	100.00
New investment (10K RMB)	5380	958.51	15,473.61	0.00	1,000,000.00
Independent variables					
Internet finance development index	6144	113.99	58.97	55.25	243.56
Internet debt (10K RMB)	4385	4.44	149.739	0.00	7600.00
Controls					
Firm age	5908	9.55	6.26	0.00	40.00
Firm size	5969	3.97	1.69	0.00	10.65
Debt ratio (in percentage)	5113	23.89	41.47	0.00	100.00
Debt from national banks (10K RMB)	5115	3598.67	86,334.89	0.00	6,096,900.00
Debt from small financial institutions (10K RMB)	4641	334.16	2824.17	0.00	129,090.00
Private lending (10K RMB)	4518	67.78	835.95	0.00	43,356.00

Table 14.7 Descriptive statistics for 2015 data

	Observations	Mean	Std. deviation	Minimum	Maximum
Dependent variable					
Internet debt dummy	5932	0.01	0.07	0.00	1.00
Internet debt interest rate (in percentage)	45	12.08	20.06	0.05	100.00
New investment (10K RMB)	6808	1691.30	50,255.67	0.00	4,000,000.00
Independent variables					
Internet finance development index	8114	411.23	172.91	221.97	796.35
Internet debt (10K RMB)	5932	0.64	18.51	0.00	999.00
Controls					
Firm age	7668	8.88	6.88	0.00	42.00
Firm size	7638	3.23	1.85	0.00	11.00
Debt ratio (in percentage)	6532	18.32	23.41	0.00	100.00
Debt from national banks (10K RMB)	6768	5005.97	243,675.82	0.00	20,000,000.00
Debt from small financial institutions (10K RMB)	6116	456.97	12,085.58	0.00	500,000.00
Private lending (10K RMB)	6083	45.66	648.83	0.00	30,000.00

institutions is higher in 2015 than in 2013. On the contrary, debt amount from private lending and internet finance is higher in 2013 than in 2015.

Table 14.8 presents the regression results for H1 and H2. Columns (1) and (2) use the internet debt dummy as the dependent variable, and, as indicated, a logistic regression is applied. Columns (3) and (4) use the internet debt interest rate as the dependent variable, and a linear regression model is applied.

Column (1) demonstrates that internet finance development index is significantly and positively related to internet debt by private firms in 2013 ($b = 0.007, p \leq 0.1$). Column (2) demonstrates that internet finance development index is significantly and positively related to internet debt by private firms in 2015 ($b = 0.003, p \leq 0.1$). Therefore, H1 is supported. The results indicate that, in any region, if internet finance is developed, private firms in that region are more likely to borrow via internet finance.

In regard to the control variables, the debt ratio is significantly and positively related to internet debt by private firms in both 2013 and 2015. Firm age is significantly and negatively related to internet debt for the 2013 data which indicates that young firms are more likely to borrow via internet finance. Young firms, due to lack of credibility, are often rejected by traditional financial institutions. Therefore, internet finance provides a promising channel for them. The result confirms that internet finance helps private firms source finance, especially for young firms.

Column (3) demonstrates that the *internet finance development index* is not significantly related to the *internet debt interest rate* for private firms in 2013. However, in contrast to the 2013 results, Column (4) demonstrates that the *internet finance*

Table 14.8 Regression results for H1 and H2

	1	2	3	4
DV in the model	Internet debt dummy in 2013	Internet debt dummy in 2015	Internet debt interest rate in 2013	Internet debt interest rate in 2015
IV: Internet finance development index	0.007* (0.004)	0.003* (0.002)	0.038 (0.071)	0.067* (0.027)
Controls:				
Firm age	−0.113** (0.057)	−0.030 (0.039)	1.216 (0.653)	0.252 (0.340)
Firm size	0.128 (0.195)	0.218 (0.145)	−1.707 (2.41)	−1.323 (2.077)
Debt ratio	0.026*** (0.009)	0.029*** (0.008)	−0.079 ()0.153	0.091 (0.153)
Debt from national banks	0.000 (0.000)	0.000 (0.000)	1.181 (0.825)	0.211 (0.730)
Debt from small financial institutions	0.000 (0.000)	0.000 (0.000)	0.259 (0.307)	0.865 (0.505)
Private lending	0.000 (0.001)	0.000 (0.000)	−0.114 (0.105)	0.009 (0.524)
Model fit: R^2	0.07	0.08	0.45	0.92
Observations	3642	4747	41	45

*significant at 0.1; **significant at 0.05; ***significant at 0.01

development index is significantly and positively related to the *internet debt interest rate* for private firms in 2015 ($b = 0.067$, $p \leq 0.1$). The results partially support H2. If internet finance is well developed, private firms are more likely to borrow via internet finance; however, they have to pay high interest rates. A plausible rationale for the positive relation of the index to internet debt interest rates may be that if internet finance is developed, all firms, not only private firms, are more likely to borrow via internet finance. Faced with the competition from other privileged firms in financing, private firms have to pay higher interest rates to compensate for the higher risks.

Table 14.9 presents the regression results for H3. The results show that internet finance is not significantly related to private firms' new investment in 2013 and 2015. As such, internet finance does not facilitate new investments by private firms. In contrast is the result showing a significantly and positive relation between debt from small financial institutions and firms' new investments ($b = 0.377$, $p \leq 0.01$ in 2013 and $b = 0.482$, $p \leq 0.01$ in 2015). A mixed result is obtained when looking at debt from national banks and firms' new investments. We find no significance in 2013, while a significant and positive relationship is found in 2015 ($b = 0.200$, $p \leq 0.01$). *Firm size* is significantly and positively related to firms' new investment, while *debt ratio* is significantly and negatively related to firms' new investments which is consistent with the literature.

To further check the relationship between internet finance and new investment, a t-test is conducted. The sample is divided into two groups: those borrowed via

Table 14.9 Regression results for H3

	1	2
DV in the model	New investment in 2013	New investment in 2015
IV: Internet debt	−2.584 (10.473)	−0.715 (30.208)
Controls:		
Firm age	−25.363 (55.201)	−11.443 (28.601)
Firm size	1562.81*** (211.882)	389.890*** (110.289)
Debt ratio	−26.254* (14.216)	−16.290** (7.886)
Debt from national banks	0.003 (0.003)	0.200*** (0.001)
Debt from small financial institutions	0.377*** (0.143)	0.482*** (0.012)
Private lending	0.104 (0.354)	−0.351 (0.261)
Model fit: R^2	0.021	0.966
Observations	3521	4430

*significant at 0.1; **significant at 0.05; ***significant at 0.01

Table 14.10 T-test for H3

	New investment in 2013 (mean)	*t* value	New investment in 2015	*t* value
Borrow from internet finance	153.16	3.227***	143.87	1.971**
Not borrow from internet finance	1051.36		1653.60	

Mean number in 10K RMB
*significant at 0.1; **significant at 0.05; ***significant at 0.01

internet finance and those without borrowing. We compare the two groups' new investment in 2013 and 2015, respectively. Table 14.10 shows the results. Private firms borrowing from internet finance make significantly less new investment than firms that do not borrow from internet finance in 2013 and 2015. The results support H3. Firms borrowing from expensive internet finance are financially constrained firms, and the money borrowed is not used for new investment purposes.

We also conducted robustness checks. For H1, we use *internet debt* as an alternative dependent variable. For H3, we use *internet debt dummy* as an alternative independent variable. The results are consistent. We also chose an instrumental variable to address any possible reverse causality issues. The chosen variable is the Digital Financial Inclusion Index of China (DFIIC). This index is designed by the Institute of Digital Finance, Peking University (Guo et al., 2019). It is closely related to Internet Finance Development Index but is uncorrelated with private firm's internet debt and interest rate from internet debt. Results from the 2SLS model still support H1 and H2. The robustness check results are not shown in the paper but available upon request.

14.6 Discussions and Conclusion

In this study, we use data from two national surveys on private firms in China. Data from 2013 and 2015 reveal the trend and dynamics in private firms' borrowing from different channels and in different regions. Descriptive analysis shows private firms' borrowing from national banks is the largest. Borrowing from small financial institutions is the second largest, private lending the third, and internet finance the smallest. Interest rates for private firms' borrowing rank from highest to lowest as internet finance, private lending, small financial institutions, and national banks. Regression results find a positive relationship between the regional internet finance development index and private firms' debt from internet finance. However, regional internet finance development cannot guarantee low interest rates for private firms' borrowing from internet finance as lenders require higher returns to compensate for higher risks. Moreover, internet finance does not help private firms for new investments. We find no significant relationship between a private firm's internet debt and their new investments.

The study makes contributions to literature in several ways. First, thanks to the unique dataset, this study reveals the big picture of private firms' financing behavior in China. The variations among different financing channels, in different regions, and in different years are identified. The results are valuable for financial sector, researchers, and policymakers. It also contributes to the broader literature of Fintech (e.g., Lu et al., 2020).

Second, the study is the first to investigate the relationship between private firms' debt from internet finance and regional internet finance development. Though the internet can lessen the impact of geographic boundaries, internet finance is closely related to local financial development (Guo et al., 2016). Studying regional internet finance development reveals the real picture as there are large variations in regions in China.

Third, besides the amount private firms borrow from internet finance and their borrowing cost, this study further investigates how they use funds from internet finance. We find that private firms do not use funds borrowed from internet finance to make new investments in China. To the best of our knowledge, this study is the first to discuss the usage of internet finance by private firms in China. This study also extends literature on private firms' investment (e.g., Tang et al., 2019) by adding internet finance perspective.

As the second hypothesis is partially supported, future research may further investigate internet finance in regard to interest rates. Another future research direction may be qualitative studies, for example, analyzing why firms choose internet finance and how they use it. This qualitative approach may achieve a better understanding on the motivation, preference, and trend of the use of internet finance. Further research may also extend the current study to compare private firms' financing and investment in different countries with different internet finance development. A caveat is that such data is not easy to acquire as different countries have different criteria on the definition and measurement of internet finance.

In summary, this study describes the financing behavior for private firms in China. It investigates several interesting relationships in internet finance. Internet finance is developing quickly; however, the literature is limited. This research provides an initial empirical evidence, promoting a deeper understanding of internet finance and contributing to both the academic and practitioner's knowledge. Based on the findings, policymakers may consider policies to promote the development of internet finance which benefits private firms' financing and investment.

References

Allen, F., & Gu, X. (2021). Shadow banking in China compared to other countries. *The Manchester School, 89*, 407–419. https://doi.org/10.1111/manc.12331

Allen, F., Qian, J., & Qian, M. (2005). Law, finance, and economic growth in China. *Journal of Financial Economics, 77*(1), 57–116.

Allen, F., Qian, M., & Xie, J. (2019). Understanding informal financing. *Journal of Financial Intermediation, 39*, 19–33.

Beck, T., & Demirguc-Kunt, A. (2006). Small and medium-size enterprises: Access to finance as a growth constraint. *Journal of Banking & Finance, 30*(11), 2931–2943.

Carbo-Valverde, S., Rodriguez-Fernandez, F., & Udell, G. (2008). *Bank lending, financing constraints and SME investment* (Working Paper, No. 2008-04). Federal Reserve Bank of Chicago, Chicago, IL.

Chen, Z., He, Z., & Liu, C. (2020). The financing of local government in China: Stimulus loan wanes and shadow banking waxes. *Journal of Financial Economics, 137*, 42–71.

Ehlers, T., Kong, S., & Zhu, F. (2018). *Mapping shadow banking in China: Structure and dynamics* (BIS Working Papers No. 701).

Elliott, D. J., & Yan, K. (2013). *The Chinese financial system: An introduction and overview*. Brookings Institution.

Elliott, D., Kroeber, A., & Qiao, Y. (2015). Shadow banking in China: A primer. *Economic Studies at Brookings, 3*, 1–7.

Fu, Y., Lee, S., Xu, L., & Zurgruegg, R. (2015). The effectiveness of capital regulation on behavior in China. *International Review of Finance, 15*(3), 321–345.

Gao, H., Ru, H., Townsend, R., & Yang, X. (2019). *Rise of bank competition: Evidence from banking deregulation in China* (NBER Working Paper No. 25795). National Bureau of Economic Research.

Gu, L. (2020). *Support SMEs and micro enterprises, and let internet finance help real economy*. http://xw.sinoins.com/2020-05/15/content_343664.htm

Guo, F., Kong, S., & Wang, J. (2016). General patterns and regional disparity of internet finance development in China: Evidence from the Peking University Internet Finance Development Index. *China Economic Journal, 9*(3), 253–271.

Guo, F., Wang, J., et al. (2019). *The Peking University Digital Financial Inclusion Index of China*. Institute of Digital Finance, Peking University.

Ji, X. (2017). Analysis on financing problems of SME in Internet finance mode. In *2nd International Conference on Advanced Education and Management Engineering (AEME 2017)*.

Jiang, F., & Kim, K. (2020). Corporate governance in China: A survey. *Review of Finance, 24*(4), 733–772.

Le, N. T. B., Venkatesh, S., & Nguyen, T. V. (2006). Getting bank financing: A study of Vietnamese private firms. *Asia Pacific Journal of Management, 23*, 209–227.

Lu, Y., Guo, H., Kao, E. H., & Fung, H. G. (2015). Shadow banking and firm financing in China. *International Review of Economics & Finance, 36*, 40–53.

Lu, H., Wang, B., Wu, Q., & Ye, J. (2020). Fintech and the future of financial service: A literature review and research agenda. *China Accounting and Finance Review, 22*(3), 107–136.
Mortal, S., & Reisel, N. (2013). Capital allocation by public and private firms. *Journal of Financial and Quantitative Analysis, 48*(1), 77–103.
Poncet, S., Steingress, W., & Vandenbussche, H. (2010). Financial constraints in China: Firm-level evidence. *China Economic Review, 21*(3), 411–422.
Rahaman, M. (2011). Access to financing and firm growth. *Journal of Banking & Finance, 35*(3), 709–723.
Robb, A. M. (2002). Small business financing: Differences between young and old firms. *Journal of Entrepreneurial Finance and Business Ventures, 7*(2), 45–64.
Shen, Y., & Huang, Y. (2016). Introduction to the special issue: Internet finance in China. *China Economic Journal, 9*(3), 221–224.
Shen, N., Au, K., & Li, W. (2020). Strategic alignment of intangible assets: The role of corporate social responsibility. *Asia Pacific Journal of Management, 37*, 1119–1139.
State Council (2015). The Guideline on Promoting the Healthy Development of Internet Finance. issued and effective on 18 July, http://english.www.gov.cn/state_council/ministries/2015/07/18/content_281475149456440.htm
Tang, J., Tang, Z., Zhu, R., & Li, X. (2019). Entrepreneurs' resource background, innovation, philanthropy and the exit of external investment in private ventures in China. *Asia Pacific Journal of Management, 38*, 467–489. https://doi.org/10.1007/s10490-019-09674-0
Tsai, K. S. (2015a). *The rise of shadow banking in China: The political economy of modern Chinese state capitalism* (HKUST Thought Leadership Briefs No. 10).
Tsai, K. S. (2015b). *Financing small and medium enterprises in China: Recent trends and prospects beyond shadow banking* (HKUST IEMS Working Paper No. 2015-24).
Tsai, K. S. (2017). When shadow banking can be productive: Financing small and medium enterprises in China. *The Journal of Development Studies, 53*(12), 2005–2028.
Wang, H., Wang, H., Wang, L., & Zhou, H. (2019). *Shadow banking: China's dual-track interest rate liberalization* (Working Paper).
Wu, L., & Xu, L. (2020). Venture capital certification of small and medium-sized enterprises towards banks: Evidence from China. *Accounting & Finance, 60*(2), 1601–1633.
Xie, P., Zou, C., & Liu, H. (2015). *Internet finance in China: Introduction and practical approaches*. Routledge.
Xie, P., Zou, C., & Liu, H. (2016). The fundamentals of internet finance and its policy implications in China. *China Economic Journal, 9*(3), 240–252.
Xu, J. (2017). China's internet finance: A critical review. *China & World Economy, 25*(4), 78–92.
Yiu, D. W., Su, J., & Xu, Y. (2013). Alternative financing and private firm performance. *Asia Pacific Journal of Management, 30*, 829–852.
Zheng, A. (2018). Influence of Internet finance on SME financing—A case study of P2P model. In *4th International Conference on Social Science and Management (ICSSM 2018)*.
Zhou, W. (2013). Political connections and entrepreneurial investment: Evidence from China's transition economy. *Journal of Business Venturing, 28*(2), 299–315.

Chapter 15
Corporate Tax Reform and Firm Share Price: Evidence from China

Guodong Yuan, Ron McIver, and Lei Xu

15.1 Introduction

Historical events often have significant and long-lasting impacts on firm operations. Since joining the World Trade Organization (WTO) in 2001, China has profoundly escalated its economic power to become the second largest economy and the world's "powerhouse". Given its successful control over COVID-19, China is now taking a lead in fast recovery and will soon overtake the USA as the largest economy.

Despite the principle of national treatment in the WTO agreement, China adopted, in the early years of its membership, "super-national treatment" to foreign investors in its domestic market. For example, foreign firms in China could enjoy years of tax-free treatment followed by very generous tax concessions thereafter. In the meantime, domestic firms, including the banks, had to pay an average of 33% income tax (Xu & Lin, 2007). The favourable tax treatments for foreign firms in effect served the purpose of attracting more foreign direct investments (FDIs), which subsequently played important roles in driving China's modernization, technological upgrades, expansion into international markets, and so on.

As part of its continuous reforms, after nearly two decades of favourable tax treatment towards foreign firms, China decided to follow the rule of national treatment in the WTO. On 16 March 2007, China announced its Enterprise Income Tax Law (2008) effective on 1 January 2008, applying the same corporate income tax rates to all firms in the country. The Law also lowered the corporate tax rate from 33% to 25%. For the first time in modern China, taxation bias towards domestic firms was removed, allowing the tax regime to become more transparent, stable, and predictable (Zhang et al., 2007; Chang & Huang, 2017). In other words, domestic and foreign firms could compete equally in the largest emerging market after this

G. Yuan · R. McIver · L. Xu (✉)
UniSA Business, University of South Australia, Adelaide, SA, Australia
e-mail: lei.xu@unisa.edu.au

K. Wendt, B. Villhauer (eds.), *Sustainable Wealth Management*, Sustainable Finance,
https://doi.org/10.1007/978-3-031-55505-3_15

tax reform. The Law became the most important corporate tax reform in modern China.

The Law may have induced significant responses from the stock market. Academic literature based on developed markets suggests that investors often pay close attention to a firm's tax management behaviour (Desai & Dharmapala, 2009; Yuan et al., 2018), and firm announcements over tax issues commonly trigger volatilities in share prices (Desai & Hines Jr., 2002; Seida & Wempe, 2003). Court rulings over firm taxation disputes may also lead to noticeable market responses (Dhaliwal & Erickson, 1998). However, these event studies on taxation issues mostly argue with firm-level observations without evidence from an exogenous shock or that of market level (Hanlon & Slemrod, 2009). Given the features of legal regimes in developed markets, significant tax reforms are rare. As a result, the Law provides a scarce natural experiment to examine the impact of an exogenous shock by the tax regulator on firm values.

In this study, we examine the impact of the Law on firm share price through a sample of listed firms on the Shanghai and Shenzhen Stock Exchanges. We adopt an event study method suitable for share price valuation following a regulatory shock (Schäfer et al., 2012). In our measurements, we apply a 5-day event time window to calculate firms' abnormal return (*AR*), standardized abnormal return (*SAR*), cumulative abnormal return (*CAR*), total standardized abnormal return (*TSAR*), cumulative total standardized abnormal return (*CTSAR*), and cumulative average standardized abnormal return (*CATSAR*). Our findings suggest that corporate tax reform has significant impact on firm values. In addition, firm ownership structure, tax aggressiveness, and stock exchange differences can effectively moderate such an impact in China's institutional context. This study can contribute meaningful academic discussion on taxation reforms in emerging markets.

The rest of this chapter is structured as follows. Section 15.2 reviews the literature. Section 15.3 describes our data and methodology. Section 15.4 analyses the results, and Sect. 15.5 concludes the chapter.

15.2 Literature Review

Stock market investors often efficiently respond to incidents involving their invested firms. Event study has been widely applied as the research methodology on firm share price in relation to certain market events, such as firm disclosures and news reports (Ball & Brown, 1968; Fama et al., 1969). The efficient market hypothesis suggests that public information can be fast embodied in firm share prices on the stock exchange (Malkiel & Fama, 1970). Event studies normally need to identify an impactful incident either internal or external towards the firm, such as its earnings announcement, and select a short time window in their measurements of share price changes or alternative indicators such as the bid-ask spread and trade volume (Voeller & Müller, 2011).

However, only a few studies have explored share price response to regulatory changes. The imposition of the Sarbanes-Oxley Act (2002) and the Statement of Financial Accounting Standards (SFAS) No. 123 (2004) in the USA and International Financial Reporting Standards (IFRS) in the EU provides rare event study opportunities in the developed countries with market-level evidence (Espahbodi et al., 2002; Li et al., 2008a, b; Armstrong et al., 2010). Most event studies present firm-level evidence on market responses to firm disclosures or specific news involving the firm (Reese Jr, 1998; Blouin et al., 2003; Cloyd et al., 2003; Voeller & Müller, 2011).

Similarly, there are event studies applied to taxation incidents. Amoako-Adu et al. (1992) explore the capital gains tax reduction in Canada. Lang and Shackelford (2000) and Liang et al. (2002) examine the share price changes around the Tax Relief Act (1997). Dhaliwal and Erickson (1998) follow the court rulings on depreciation of intangible assets. Frischmann et al. (2008) apply event study on FASB Fin 48, an interpretation of FASB Statement No. 109, supposedly to lower accounting differences over corporate income tax. Hanlon and Heitzman (2010) find that firm share price would be lower when investors expect increases in corporate tax burdens. However, there can be share price increase when investors expect improvements in firm disclosures. The OECD (2020) argues that the COVID-19 event would lead to significantly lower corporate tax revenues than economic productivity declines. In comparison, event studies present more evidence on firm-level incidents. For example, news on tax aggressiveness would lower firm's share prices, especially those in sectors serving consumers (Hanlon & Slemrod, 2009).

Compared to the literature on developed markets, studies on taxation events are scarce. Lowering the stamp duty on trading firm shares may have no impact on share prices (Wang, 2002; Song & Zhang, 2005). However, opposite evidence may also exist in the short term in this developing market. To the best of our knowledge, there has not been adequate study on the tax reform in 2008.

15.3 Data and Methodology

15.3.1 Event and Measurement Window

We adopt the official announcement of the Law on 16 March 2017 as the event day and 5 days as the measurement window, including 2 days, respectively, before and after the event. Since there are no standardized time windows for event studies (Seiler, 2004), we also capture share prices 130 trading days before and after the event date.

15.3.2 Data

We derive stock market data, firm financials, and ownership structure information from the CSMAR database. Our sample covers all listed firms on the Shanghai and Shenzhen Stock Exchanges. Given the features of significant state ownership and illiquidity of shares before the full circulation reform in China's stock market (Li et al., 2008a, b; Xu et al., 2016; Cui et al., 2021), our initial sample covers 758 state-controlled firms and 1370 private ones. Excluding financial institutions, firms of special treatment (ST) or particular treatment (PT), those with missing data, or with insufficient observations, we have 1013 effective sample firms (see Table 15.1).

15.3.3 Normal and Abnormal Returns

We apply the market model in the measurement of firm normal returns, without estimation during the event time. The market model Eq. (15.1) is developed as follows:

$$R_{it} = a_i + \beta_i \times R_{mt} + \varepsilon_{it} \tag{13.1}$$

In Eq. (15.1), R_{it} is the normal (expected) return on the stock i on day t with consideration of cash dividends as reinvestments. R_{mt} is the market return on day t, calculated through the weighted average circulation market value. The coefficients

Table 15.1 Sample firms

	Number	Percent of original sample
Sample firms on the Shanghai and Shenzhen stock exchanges	2128	100.00
By type of stock		
A	1956	91.91
B	22	1.03
AB	84	3.95
AH	66	3.10
By ownership characteristics		
State controlled	758	35.59
Non-state controlled	1370	64.41
Less:		
Firms marked as ST and PT	167	7.85
Financial corporations	38	1.79
Firms with incomplete data	699	32.88
Firms without enough observations within the event and estimation window	*211*	*9.92*
Final sample firms	*1013*	*47.60*

a_i and β_i are estimated by running an OLS over the estimation period. ε_{it} is the error term.

We apply AR, average abnormal return (AAR), CAR, and average cumulative abnormal return (ACAR) in our measurements of abnormal returns, which are defined as the following equations:

$$\text{AR}_{it} = r_{it} - \left(a_i + \beta_i \times R_{mt}\right) \tag{13.2}$$

$$\text{AAR}_i = \frac{1}{N}\sum_{i=1}^{N}\text{AR}_i \tag{13.3}$$

$$\text{CAR}_i = \sum_{j=1}^{t}\text{AR}_{T_1+j,i} \tag{13.4}$$

$$\text{ACAR} = \frac{1}{N}\sum_{i=1}^{N}\text{CAR}_{i(t_1,t_2)} \tag{13.5}$$

We further use the standardized abnormal return (SAR) to correct the weakness of AR in cross-sectional t-tests in its ignorance of variances from events (Patell, 1976). SAR is calculated as in Eq. (15.6):

$$\text{SAR}_{it} = \frac{\text{AR}_{it}}{\sqrt{s^2\text{AR}_{it}}} \tag{13.6}$$

$\sqrt{s^2\text{AR}_{it}}$ is the square root of the variance of the AR for stock i at time t, which is also the standard deviation of the AR.

Following Seiler (2004), $s^2\text{AR}_{it}$ can be measured by Eq. (15.7):

$$s^2_{\text{AR}_{it}} = \left[\frac{\sum_{t=t1}^{t2}\left(\text{AR}_{it(\text{est.period})} - \overline{\text{AR}}_{i(\text{est.period})}\right)^2}{D_i - 2}\right] \times \left[1 + \frac{1}{D_i} + \frac{\left(R_{mt(\text{event.window})} - \overline{R_{m(\text{est.period})}}\right)^2}{\sum_{t=t1}^{t2}\left(R_{mt(\text{est.period})} - \overline{R_{m(\text{est.period}}}\right)^2}\right] \tag{13.7}$$

where $\overline{\text{AR}}_{i(\text{est.period})}$ is the mean of AR. D_i is number of observed returns for stock i over the estimation period. $R_{m(\text{est.period})}$ is the mean return on the market at time t

over the estimation period. $t1$ and $t2$ are, respectively, the first and last day of the estimation period.

We also calculate the TSAR to test the average effects of the event on the stock market.

$$\text{TSAR}_i = \sum_{i=1}^{n} \text{SAR}_{i,t} \tag{13.8}$$

Based on the SAR, the average standardized abnormal return (ASAR), CTSAR, and CATSAR can be achieved as in Eqs. (15.9)–(15.11):

$$\text{ASAR}_t = \frac{1}{N}\sum_{i=1}^{N} \text{SAR}_{i,t} \tag{13.9}$$

$$\text{CTSAR}_{(T1,T2),i} = \sum_{t=T1}^{T2} \text{TSAR}_{t,i} \tag{13.10}$$

$$\text{CATSAR} = \frac{1}{N}\sum_{i=1}^{N} \text{CTSAR}_i \tag{13.11}$$

15.3.4 Statistical Test

To test the market efficiency in terms of the significance of TSAR and CTSAR at the fixed level of significance, we apply *Z*-statistics in both parametric and non-parametric tests.

The parametric test model Eq. (15.12) is developed as follows:

$$Z-\text{statistic}_t = \frac{\text{TSAR}_t}{\sqrt{\sum_{j=1}^{N} \frac{D_i - 2}{D_i - 4}}} \tag{13.12}$$

We further adopt Eq. (15.13) to measure the level of significance of the results, through statistical test Z_t, the cumulative TSAR *Z*-statistic for each day in the event window, for CTSAR.

$$Z_t = \left[\frac{1}{\sqrt{N}}\right]\left[\frac{\left[\sum_{T1}^{T2} \text{SAR}_{it}\right]}{\sqrt{(T_2 - T_1 + 1)\left[\frac{D_i - 2}{D_i - 4}\right]}}\right] \tag{13.13}$$

We also do a non-parametric test to avoid specific assumptions on the distribution of returns in our parametric test. For such a purpose, we adopt the sign test as in Eq. (15.14), which is based on the ratio of positive cumulative abnormal returns p_0^+ in the event window. Under the null hypothesis, p_0^+ shall not be significantly different from the same ratio over the estimation window p_{EW}^+ (Cowan, 1992).

$$t_{sign} = \frac{p_0^+ - p_{est}^+}{\sqrt{\frac{p_{EW}^+\left(1 - p_{EW}^+\right)}{N}}} \tag{13.14}$$

Then the non-parametric generalized sign test Z_{sign} can be expressed by Eq. (15.15):

$$Z_{sign} = \frac{\left[\left(\frac{N^+}{N}\right) - 0.5\right] \times N^{\frac{1}{2}}}{0.5} \tag{13.15}$$

where N^+ is the abnormal return with a positive sign. *N* denotes the total number of samples. The expected proportion of positive abnormal returns is set as 0.5.

15.4 Results Analysis

15.4.1 Event Window Test Results

Table 15.2 reports our measurement results on abnormal returns as indicated by *AAR*, *CAR*, *ACAR*, *TSAR*, *ASAR*, *CTSAR*, and *CATSAR* under the market model. Within the 5-day event window, *AAR* and *ASAR* show mostly equal abnormal returns. *AAR* is positive on days (−2), (−1), and (2) but negative on days (0) and (1), with the highest value of 0.0119 on day (2) and the lowest value of −0.0045 on day (1). Similarly, *ASAR* has the highest value of 5.5241 on day (2) and the lowest value of −1.4473 on day (1). Both *AAR* and *ASAR* suggest that the Law has an impact on firm share prices.

Table 15.2 Abnormal returns with the full sample ($N = 1013$)

Days	AAR	CAR	ACAR	TSAR	ASAR	CTSAR	CATSAR
−2	0.0045	4.5189	0.0045	1505.9360	1.4866	1505.9360	1.4866
−1	0.0024	6.9163	0.0068	1056.6130	1.0431	2562.5480	2.5297
0	−0.0028	4.1287	0.0041	−815.8983	−0.8054	1746.6500	1.7242
1	−0.0045	−0.3874	−0.0004	−1466.1120	−1.4473	280.5378	0.2769
2	0.0119	11.6670	0.0115	5595.8850	5.5241	5876.4220	5.8010

In addition, *ACAR* and *CATSAR* demonstrate a pattern of volatility as increase-decrease-increase. *ACAR* has a value of 0.0045 on day (−2), which increases to 0.0068 on day (−1), drops to −0.0004 on day (1), and rebounds on day (2). *CATSAR* shows a similar pattern. Given the features of semi-efficient and inefficient markets, *ACAR* and *CATSAR* suggest that the Law may have been leaked to the market before its official announcement.

Table 15.3 reports our significance test results. *Z*-statistics results for both *TSAR* and *CTSAR* are significantly different from zero. The null hypothesis of indifference between positive and negative returns is rejected in non-parametric tests.

From the above analysis, we can tell that the Law has significant and positive impact on firm share prices. The announcement of the Law brings market-level responses to the tax reform. Volatility in day (−1) suggests that leakage of the information may have caused changes in abnormal returns. In addition, the unstable *CAAR* after the event date suggests that China's stock market does not capture impactful information in a timely way. In other words, the market is semi-efficient (Maitra & Dey, 2012).

15.4.2 Moderators Towards the Event Impact

We further examine moderation factors towards the event impact. Given the noticeable features of the listed firms in China, we do such tests from the perspectives of firm-level tax aggressiveness, measured as the permanent book-tax difference (PBTD), ownership structure, and regulatory differences between the Shanghai and Shenzhen Stock Exchanges.

Literature suggests that tax aggressiveness and firm share prices are related. Firms with higher CASH ETR, or which are less tax aggressive, often have more positive share price movements in response to news on tax aggressiveness (Desai & Dharmapala, 2009; Hanlon & Slemrod, 2009; Rego & Wilson, 2009). As a result, we categorize sample firms into high and low groups by the median PBTD.

Following Frank et al. (2008), Rego and Wilson (2009), and Khurana and Moser (2009), *PBTD* can be measured by Eq. (15.16):

Table 15.3 Significance test results ($N = 1013$)

Days	Z-statistics TSAR	*p*-Value TSAR	Z-statistics CTSAR	*p*-Value CTSAR	Z_{sign} (non-parametric) AR
−2	46.9442	0.0000***	46.9442	0.0000	−5.4355*
−1	32.9376	0.0000***	56.4849	0.0000	−3.6132*
0	−25.4338	0.0000***	31.4355	0.0000	−10.2112*
1	−45.7028	0.0000***	4.3726	0.0000	−10.1484*
2	174.4393	0.0000***	81.9226	0.0000	10.0227*

Note: ***, **, and *, respectively, indicate significant levels at 0.001, 0.01, and 0.05. When the absolute value of Z_{sign} is more than 1.96, test score is statistically significant at 0.05

$$\text{PBTD}_{it} = \frac{\left(\text{BI}_{it} - \dfrac{\text{CTE}_{it}}{\text{STR}} - \dfrac{\text{DTE}_{it}}{\text{STR}}\right)}{\text{Assets}_{it-1}} \tag{13.16}$$

where BI_{it} is the firm's pre-tax book income. CTE_{it} is an estimate of taxable income derived from the current tax expense. DTE_{it} is deferred tax expense. STR is the statutory corporate tax rate. $\text{Assets}_{i,t-1}$ is the beginning period total assets.

Table 15.4 reports the moderating effects of PBTD. *P*-values of *TSAR* and *CTSAR* are significant for both categories during the time window, suggesting that firms in both PBTD groups show significant changes in share prices. In comparison, *ASAR* shows different patterns in the two groups. In the group of more tax aggressiveness, *ASAR* starts with 0.5973 on day (−2), increases to 0.8553 on day (−1), decreases to −1.8516 on day (1), and then increases again on day (2) to 4.0612. However, *the ASAR* of less tax-aggressive firms keeps declining before the event date and increases afterwards. In comparison, *CATSAR* movements are in the same direction in both groups as that of the whole sample. In short, both groups of firms show negative responses before the announcement date towards the possible information leakage. However, less tax-aggressive firms demonstrate stronger positive responses after the event date, suggesting that investors interpret the Law as a more positive signal towards their invested firms.

Considering the differences in corporate culture, business philosophy, and the diversified types of investors in the stock market, we measure ownership structure from two dimensions: the types of shares and state or private ownership. In other words, the Law may have different impacts on the domestic A shares and foreign B, AB, and AH shares, as well as the state-controlled and private firms.

Table 15.5 reports our comparison results by grouping sample firms into domestic only A-share firms and those of B, AB, or AH shares. Except the *p*-value of *TSAR* of A-share on day (1), the other *p*-values of *TSAR* and *CTSAR* are significant at the 5% level. *The ASAR* and *CATAR* of B, AB, or AH shares have more positive values than A shares, suggesting that non-A-share firms react more positively in share prices to the Law than the A-share firms. In other words, investors may expect stronger impact by the Law on the non-A-share firms.

Ownership structure often affects the quality of firm governance (La Porta et al., 2000; Xu et al., 2016). Given China's institutional background, state-controlled firms tend to have weaker governance or efficiency than private ones (He et al., 2019; Li et al., 2020). As a possible result, however, regulatory improvements may lead to noticeable improvements among state-controlled firms of ex ante weak governance (Jimenez-Angueira, 2008; Dong et al., 2021).

Table 15.6 reports our measurement results by categorizing firms into state-controlled and private ones. *P*-values of *TSAR* and *CTSAR* in both groups are significant on every event day, indicating similar share price movements by these two types of firms. Interestingly, *AAR*, *ATSAR*, and *CATSAR* have higher values in the group of private firms than those of state-controlled ones, suggesting that the Law has more impact on private firms. These results may also be related to the lower

Table 15.4 Moderation effect by the level of tax aggressiveness (PBTD)

	AAR	TSAR	ASAR	CTSAR	CATSAR	Z-statistics TSAR	*p*-Value TSAR	Z-statistics CTSAR	*p*-Value CTSAR
Firms of higher tax-aggressive level: above median PBTD (≥0.013927) (#obs:504)									
−2	0.0018	301.0565	0.5973	301.0565	0.5973	13.3049	0.0000	13.3049	0.0000
−1	0.0015	431.0487	0.8553	732.1052	1.4526	19.0498	0.0000	22.8783	0.0000
0	−0.0014	−163.8439	−0.3251	568.2614	1.1275	−7.2409	0.0000	14.4995	0.0000
1	−0.0060	−933.1901	−1.8516	−364.9287	−0.7241	−41.2416	0.0000	−8.0639	0.0000
2	0.0080	2046.823	4.0612	1681.8950	3.3371	90.4577	0.0000	33.2414	0.0000
Firms of lower tax aggressive level: below median PBTD (<0.013927) (#obs:509)									
−2	0.0071	1204.879	2.3671	1204.8790	2.3671	52.9865	0.0000	52.9865	0.0000
−1	0.0032	625.5639	1.2290	1830.4430	3.5962	27.5102	0.0000	56.9197	0.0000
0	−0.0040	−652.0544	−1.2810	1178.3890	2.3151	−28.6751	0.0000	29.9192	0.0000
1	−0.0029	−532.9221	−1.0470	645.4665	1.2681	−23.4361	0.0000	14.1927	0.0000
2	0.0157	3549.061	6.9726	4194.5280	8.2407	156.0755	0.0000	82.4934	0.0000

Table 15.5 Types of shares

	AAR	TSAR	ASAR	CTSAR	CATSAR	*Z*-statistics TSAR	*p*-Value TSAR	*Z*-statistics CTSAR	*p*-Value CTSAR
Category 1: A share (#obs:918)									
−2	0.0046	1413.724	1.5400	1413.724	1.5400	46.2939	0.0000	46.2939	0.0000
−1	0.0022	880.9572	0.9596	2294.681	2.4997	28.8479	0.0000	53.1332	0.0000
0	−0.0035	−937.4725	−1.0212	1357.209	1.4784	−30.6985	0.0000	25.6593	0.0000
1	−0.0046	−1386.959	−1.5108	−29.75012	−0.0324	−45.4174	0.6262	−0.4871	0.0000
2	0.0124	5243.014	5.7113	5213.264	5.6789	171.6880	0.0000	76.3455	0.0000
Category 2: B, AB, and AH shares (#obs:95)									
−2	0.0027	92.21174	0.9706	92.21174	0.9706	9.3865	0.0000	9.3865	0.0000
−1	0.0041	175.6555	1.3490	267.8672	2.8197	17.8805	0.0000	19.2807	0.0000
0	0.0046	121.5741	1.2797	389.4413	4.0994	12.3754	0.0000	22.8876	0.0000
1	−0.0034	−79.15345	−0.8332	310.2879	3.2662	−8.0573	0.0000	15.7926	0.0000
2	0.0071	352.8703	3.7144	663.1582	6.9806	35.9198	0.0000	30.1891	0.0000

Table 15.6 State vs. private ownership

	AAR	TSAR	ASAR	CTSAR	CATSAR	*Z*-statistics TSAR	*p*-Value TSAR	*Z*-statistics CTSAR	*p*-Value CTSAR
Category 1: State controlled (#obs:467)									
−2	0.0040	617.0333	1.3213	617.0333	1.3213	28.3289	0.0000	28.3289	0.0000
−1	0.0020	447.1211	0.9574	1064.154	2.2787	20.5280	0.0000	34.5471	0.0000
0	−0.0028	−464.607	−0.9949	599.5474	1.2838	−21.3308	0.0000	15.8922	0.0000
1	−0.0059	−997.3774	−2.1357	−397.83	−0.8519	−45.7911	0.0000	−9.1325	0.0000
2	0.0105	2369.82	5.0746	1971.99	4.2227	108.8021	0.0000	40.4894	0.0000
Category 2: Private (#obs:546)									
−2	0.0049	888.9023	1.6280	888.9023	1.6280	37.7431	0.0000	37.7431	0.0000
−1	0.0026	609.4916	1.1163	1498.394	2.7443	25.8793	0.0000	44.9878	0.0000
0	−0.0027	−351.2914	−0.6434	1147.103	2.1009	−14.9160	0.0000	28.1207	0.0000
1	−0.0032	−468.7348	−0.8585	678.3677	1.2424	−19.9027	0.0000	14.4019	0.0000
2	0.0131	3226.065	5.9085	3904.433	7.1510	136.9800	0.0000	74.1407	0.0000

sensitivity to taxation by state-controlled firms or state-owned enterprises (SOEs). In other words, state-controlled firms often have more political connections and subsequent favourable tax treatments from the government (He et al., 2019; Li et al., 2020). The state-controlled firms also tend to reward society through actively taking social responsibilities rather than making profits (Dong et al., 2021; Cui et al., 2021).

In addition to tax aggressiveness and ownership structure, we also examine the impact of the regulation on the two stock exchanges, since Shanghai and Shenzhen Stock Exchanges tend to demonstrate a variety of features of firm sizes, maturity, degree of openness, and regulatory differences (Dong & Xu, 2016).

Table 15.7 reports our comparison between the firms on Shanghai and Shenzhen Stock Exchanges. Our results on *AAR*, *ASAR*, and *CATSAR* suggest that the Law has similar impacts on firms of the two stock exchanges. In addition, information leakage has similar impacts on the two stock exchanges. The *ASAR* and *CATSAR* differences suggest that firms on the Shenzhen Stock Exchange may be more responsive to the Law than their counterparts on the Shanghai Stock Exchange, indicating an efficiency difference between the two markets.

15.4.3 Further Tests

Given that the above moderators identified towards the Law's impact on firm share prices, we further develop a test of the direct links between firm characteristics and their response to the Law. Table 15.8 presents the results of the regression using *AR* in the event window.

The estimated coefficient (–0.0590) on *PBTD* is negative and significant on the second day after the announcement, suggesting the more tax aggressiveness of the firms corresponding to more negative market responses. The estimated coefficient on *State* is 0.00820, significant at the 5% level of significance. It suggests that the market reacted positively and significantly before the announcement. However, there is no significant result on the event day and after the event day. In comparison, we did not find any significant result on *State*× *PBTD* in the time window. Our results show that on day (–1), the estimated coefficient of *Foreign* is 0.0214, significant at the 5% level, suggesting that the market reacted significantly before the announcement was released. In addition, the coefficient on *Foreign*× *PBTD* is significant (0.444) on the event day, suggesting the proportion of investors and tradable B, AB, and AH shares are indeed moderate or affect the relationship between the tax aggressiveness and the corresponding market reaction. The dummy variable *Stktype* differentiates Shenzhen (1) from Shanghai (0) Stock Exchange. The estimated coefficient of *Stktype* is 0.00840 and significant at the level of 0.001 on day (1), suggesting that the market reaction to the announcement is 0.48% higher on the Shenzhen market. Regarding tax aggressiveness links, we find the interaction *Stktype*× *PBTD* is negatively significant (a coefficient of –0.0809) only on day (–2), confirming information leakage before the announcement in the Shenzhen market, which

Table 15.7 Shanghai vs. Shenzhen

	AAR	TSAR	ASAR	CTSAR	CATSAR	Z-statistics TSAR	p-Value TSAR	Z-statistics CTSAR	p-Value CTSAR
Category 1: Shanghai stock exchange (#obs:628)									
−2	0.0052	941.8848	1.4998	941.8848	1.4998	37.2905	0.0000	37.2905	0.0000
−1	0.0031	864.644	1.3768	1806.529	2.8766	34.2324	0.0000	50.5744	0.0000
0	−0.0026	−495.0026	−0.7882	1311.526	2.0884	−19.5978	0.0000	29.9790	0.0000
1	−0.0079	−1693.253	−2.6963	−381.7264	−0.6078	−67.0382	0.0000	−7.5565	0.0000
2	0.0128	3854.865	6.1383	3473.138	5.5305	152.6194	0.0000	61.4947	0.0000
Category 2: Shenzhen stock exchange (#obs:385)									
−2	0.0033	564.0508	1.4651	564.0508	1.4651	28.5212	0.0000	28.5212	0.0000
−1	0.0012	191.9686	0.4986	756.0194	1.9637	9.7069	0.0000	27.0314	0.0000
0	−0.0030	−320.8957	−0.8335	435.1237	1.1302	−16.2261	0.0000	12.7029	0.0000
1	0.0011	227.1405	0.5900	662.2642	1.7202	11.4854	0.0000	16.7437	0.0000
2	0.0105	1741.02	4.5221	2403.284	6.2423	88.0347	0.0000	54.3463	0.0000

Table 15.8 AR as a dependent variable for event window ($N = 1013$)

Variables	Day (−2)	Day (−1)	Day (0)	Day (1)	Day (2)
PBTD	0.00573	0.00912	0.00349	−0.0166	−0.0590**
	(0.21)	(0.42)	(0.13)	(−0.63)	(−2.72)
State	−0.00748	0.00820*	−0.00779	0.000782	−0.00621
	(−1.44)	(1.97)	(−1.49)	(0.15)	(−1.48)
Foreign	−0.00898	0.0214*	−0.000723	0.0113	0.000952
	(−0.81)	(2.42)	(−0.07)	(1.04)	(0.11)
Stktype	−0.000238	−0.000709	−0.00252	0.00840***	−0.00200
	(−0.10)	(−0.38)	(−1.07)	(3.66)	(−1.05)
Statex P_BTD	−0.0321	−0.0499	0.0812	−0.0162	−0.0188
	(−0.51)	(−0.99)	(1.29)	(−0.26)	(−0.37)
Foreignx P_BTD	−0.0623	−0.158	0.444*	−0.136	−0.169
	(−0.32)	(−1.03)	(2.29)	(−0.72)	(−1.09)
Stktypex P_BTD	−0.0809*	−0.0295	0.0418	0.0304	−0.00205
	(−2.36)	(−1.07)	(1.21)	(0.90)	(−0.07)
ROE	−0.000427	0.000298	−0.000528	−0.0000400	−0.00122*
	(−0.62)	(0.54)	(−0.77)	(−0.06)	(−2.21)
Salesgr	−0.000235	0.000482	−0.0000512	0.000132	−0.000423
	(−0.59)	(1.52)	(−0.13)	(0.34)	(−1.32)
Leverage	−0.00812	−0.00755	−0.00282	−0.00146	0.00253
	(−1.32)	(−1.53)	(−0.45)	(−0.24)	(0.51)
PP&E	−0.00581	−0.00505	0.00196	0.00380	−0.00485
	(−1.51)	(−1.64)	(0.51)	(1.01)	(−1.56)
INTA	0.00825	0.00512	0.000374	0.00125	0.0284**
	(0.64)	(0.50)	(0.03)	(0.10)	(2.72)
TA	−0.00284	−0.00306	0.00870	−0.00146	−0.0124**
	(−0.49)	(−0.66)	(1.50)	(−0.26)	(−2.65)
Constant	0.0138***	0.00505	−0.000362	−0.00879*	0.0153***
	(3.55)	(1.63)	(−0.09)	(−2.32)	(4.88)

Note: *State* represents the proportion of shares held by the state; *Foreign* represents the proportion of shares held by foreign investors; and *Stktype* is a dummy variable to indicate stock exchange differences. Based on previous studies and consistent with Wang (2002), to isolate other confounding factors, a set of control variables expected to be associated with abnormal returns includes $ROE_{i,t}$, return on equity, measured as net income scaled by common equity; *Salesgr*, sales growth, measured as net sales divided by lagged net sales; *leverage*, measured as long-term debt scaled by lagged assets; *PP&E*, the property, plant, and equipment scaled by lagged assets; *INTA*, measured as intangible assets scaled by lagged asset; and *Ln*(*TA*), natural log of total assets. *t* statistics in parentheses: $^{*}p < 0.05$, $^{**}p < 0.01$, $^{***}p < 0.001$

Table 15.9 Robustness test results during event window (N = 1013)

Variables	Day (−2)	Day (−1)	Day (0)	Day (+1)	Day (+2)
PBTD	−0.278	3.846	1.206	−4.958	−21.80*
	(−0.03)	(0.49)	(0.15)	(−0.51)	(−2.35)
State	−2.518	3.339*	−2.527	−0.301	−2.086
	(−1.42)	(2.19)	(−1.62)	(−0.16)	(−1.16)
Foreign	−2.483	7.391*	0.475	4.161	0.633
	(−0.65)	(2.28)	(0.14)	(1.04)	(0.17)
Stktype	0.596	−0.454	−0.701	3.053***	−1.476
	(0.74)	(−0.66)	(−1.00)	(3.60)	(−1.82)
State× P_BTD	−3.765	−18.17	15.18	−1.774	−9.724
	(−0.17)	(−0.99)	(0.81)	(−0.08)	(−0.45)
Foreign× P_BTD	−26.35	−54.31	115.9*	−19.71	−72.24
	(−0.40)	(−0.96)	(2.00)	(−0.28)	(−1.09)
Stktype× P_BTD	−27.89*	−10.10	14.37	9.762	0.529
	(−2.36)	(−1.00)	(1.40)	(0.79)	(0.04)
ROE	−0.121	0.0559	−0.102	0.0148	−0.436
	(−0.51)	(0.28)	(−0.50)	(0.06)	(−1.85)
Salesgr	−0.128	0.138	−0.0157	0.0570	−0.171
	(−0.94)	(1.19)	(−0.13)	(0.40)	(−1.25)
Leverage	−3.684	−3.517	−0.852	0.443	0.360
	(−1.74)	(−1.94)	(−0.46)	(0.20)	(0.17)
PP&E	−1.340	−1.379	0.749	1.479	−1.760
	(−1.01)	(−1.22)	(0.65)	(1.06)	(−1.33)
INTA	1.518	0.716	0.960	4.132	12.24**
	(0.34)	(0.19)	(0.25)	(0.88)	(2.75)
TA	−0.820	−0.888	2.343	−0.211	−6.695***
	(−0.41)	(−0.52)	(1.35)	(−0.10)	(−3.35)
Constant	4.724***	2.300*	−0.140	−3.663**	7.159***
	(3.53)	(2.02)	(−0.12)	(−2.61)	(5.35)

Note: t statistics in parentheses; $^{*}p < 0.05$, $^{**}p < 0.01$, $^{***}p < 0.001$

moderates a significant but negative relation between tax aggressiveness and abnormal returns.

15.4.4 Robustness

For robustness purposes, we replace AR with SAR. Table 15.9 reports our robustness results, which are consistent with our previous findings.

15.5 Conclusion

The Law provides a rare opportunity for us to examine the impact of regulatory change in corporate taxation on firm share prices. We may conclude our findings in two aspects. First, the overall market demonstrates a noticeable response to the Law. However, information leakage before the official announcement weakens the stock market responses. Coupled with a less timely response towards the official announcement, China's markets seem less efficient than their counterparts in developed countries. Investors do not perceive the impact of the Law in a timely way. Second, firm features, including tax aggressiveness, ownership structure, and stock exchange features may also moderate the Law's impact. Less tax-aggressive firms demonstrate more positive share price movements, suggesting that investors have better confidence in these firms. Compared to A-share firms, non-A-share firms show stronger positive responses to the Law. In comparison, there is no significant difference between state-owned and private firms. The two stock exchanges demonstrate different efficiencies in response to the taxation change.

References

Amoako-Adu, B., et al. (1992). Capital gains tax and equity values: Empirical test of stock price reaction to the introduction and reduction of capital gains tax exemption. *Journal of Banking & Finance, 16*(2), 275–287.

Armstrong, C. S., et al. (2010). Market reaction to the adoption of IFRS in Europe. *The Accounting Review, 85*(1), 31–61.

Ball, R., & Brown, P. (1968). An empirical evaluation of accounting income numbers. *Journal of Accounting Research, 6*(2), 159–178.

Blouin, J. L., et al. (2003). Capital gains taxes and equity trading: Empirical evidence. *Journal of Accounting Research, 41*(4), 611–651.

Chang, M., & Huang, D. (2017). The effect of tax reforms on the association between tax avoidance and ownership structure. *Accounting and Finance Research, 6*(2), 206–229.

Cloyd, C. B., et al. (2003). Firm valuation effects of the expatriation of US corporations to tax-haven countries. *Journal of the American Taxation Association, 25*(1), 87–109.

Cowan, A. R. (1992). Nonparametric event study tests. *Review of Quantitative Finance and Accounting, 2*(4), 343–358.

Cui, X., Xu, L., Zhang, H., & Zhang, Y. (2021). Executive compensation and firm performance: Evidence from cross-listed AH-share firms. *International Journal of Finance & Economics, 26*(1), 88–102.

Desai, M. A., & Dharmapala, D. (2009). Corporate tax avoidance and firm value. *The Review of Economics and Statistics, 91*(3), 537–546.

Desai, M. A., & Hines, J. R., Jr. (2002). *Expectations and expatriations: Tracing the causes and consequences of corporate inversions*. National Bureau of Economic Research.

Dhaliwal, D. S., & Erickson, M. (1998). Wealth effects of tax-related court rulings. *The Journal of the American Taxation Association, 20*, 21–48.

Dong, S., & Xu, L. (2016). The impact of explicit CSR regulation: Evidence from China's mining firms. *Journal of Applied Accounting Research, 17*(2), 237–258.

Dong, S., Xu, L., & McIver, R. (2021). China's financial sector sustainability and "green finance" disclosures. *Sustainability Accounting, Management and Policy Journal, 12*(2), 353–384.

Espahbodi, H., et al. (2002). Stock price reaction and value relevance of recognition versus disclosure: The case of stock-based compensation. *Journal of Accounting and Economics, 33*(3), 343–373.

Fama, E. F., et al. (1969). The adjustment of stock prices to new information. *International Economic Review, 10*(1), 1–21.

Frank, M., Lynch, L., & Rego, S. (2008). *Does aggressive financial reporting accompany aggressive tax reporting (and vice versa)?* (Working Paper). University of Virginia and University of Iowa.

Frischmann, P. J., et al. (2008). Economic consequences of increasing the conformity in accounting for uncertain tax benefits. *Journal of Accounting and Economics, 46*(2–3), 261–278.

Hanlon, M., & Heitzman, S. (2010). A review of tax research. *Journal of Accounting and Economics, 50*(2), 127–178.

Hanlon, M., & Slemrod, J. (2009). What does tax aggressiveness signal? Evidence from stock price reactions to news about tax shelter involvement. *Journal of Public Economics, 93*(1–2), 126–141.

He, Y., Xu, L., & McIver, R. (2019). How does political connection affect firm financial distress and resolution in China? *Applied Economics, 51*(26), 2770–2792.

Jimenez-Angueira, C. E. (2008). *Tax aggressiveness, tax environment changes, and corporate governance*. University of Florida.

Khurana, I. K., & Moser, W. J. (2009). *Shareholder investment horizons and tax aggressiveness*. Available at SSRN 1517913.

La Porta, R., et al. (2000). Investor protection and corporate governance. *Journal of Financial Economics, 58*(1), 3–27.

Lang, M. H., & Shackelford, D. A. (2000). Capitalization of capital gains taxes: Evidence from stock price reactions to the 1997 rate reduction. *Journal of Public Economics, 76*(1), 69–85.

Li, H., et al. (2008a). Market reaction to events surrounding the Sarbanes-Oxley Act of 2002 and earnings management. *Journal of Law and Economics, 51*(1), 111–134.

Li, K., Wang, T., Cheung, Y., & Jiang, P. (2008b). Privatization and risk sharing: Evidence from the split share structure reform in China. *Review of Financial Studies, 24*(7), 2499–2525.

Li, B., Pan, A., Xu, L., Liu, X., & Qin, S. (2020). Imprinting and peer effects in acquiring state ownership: Evidence from private firms in China. *Pacific-Basin Finance Journal, 61*, 101337.

Liang, J.-W., et al. (2002). The effect of the expected holding period on the market reaction to a decline in the capital gains tax rate. *Journal of the American Taxation Association, 24*(S-1), 49–64.

Maitra, D., & Dey, K. (2012). Dividend announcement and market response in Indian stock market: An event-study analysis. *Global Business Review, 13*(2), 269–283.

Malkiel, B. G., & Fama, E. F. (1970). Efficient capital markets: A review of theory and empirical work. *The Journal of Finance, 25*(2), 383–417.

OECD. (2020). *Revenue statistics in Asian and Pacific economies 2020*. Retrieved 16 February 2021, from https://www.oecd-ilibrary.org/taxation/revenue-statistics-in-asian-and-pacific-economies-2020_d47d0ae3-en

Patell, J. M. (1976). Corporate forecasts of earnings per share and stock price behavior: Empirical test. *Journal of Accounting Research, 14*(2), 246–276.

Reese, W. A., Jr. (1998). Capital gains taxation and stock market activity: Evidence from IPOs. *The Journal of Finance, 53*(5), 1799–1819.

Rego, S., & Wilson, R. (2009). *Executive compensation, tax reporting aggressiveness, and future firm performance* (Working Paper). University of Iowa.

Schäfer, A., et al. (2012). *How have markets reacted to financial sector reforms? An event-study analysis* (Center for Economic Policy Research Discussion Paper 9502), 1–38.

Seida, J., & Wempe, W. (2003). *Investors' and managers' reactions to corporate inversion transactions*. Available at SSRN 359820.

Seiler, M. J. (2004). *Performing financial studies: A methodological cookbook*. Prentice Hall.

Song, F. M., & Zhang, J. (2005). Securities transaction tax and market volatility. *The Economic Journal, 115*(506), 1103–1120.
Voeller, D., & Müller, J. (2011). *Investors' reaction to a reform of corporate income taxation* (Working Paper).
Wang, Y. (2002). The sensitivity analysis of the changes of China's corporate income tax rate for listed companies. *Economy Research, 009*, 74–80.
Xu, L., & Lin, C. T. (2007). Can Chinese banks compete after access to WTO? *Journal of Asian Economics, 18*(6), 883–903.
Xu, L., McIver, R. P., Shan, Y. G., & Wang, X. (2016). Governance and performance in China's real estate sector. *Managerial Finance, 42*(6), 585–603.
Yuan, G., McIver, R. P., Xu, L., & Kang, S. H. (2018). Corporate income tax avoidance in China: Using regulatory change to encourage corporate tax sustainability. In *Sustainable financial innovation* (pp. 284–306). CRC Press.
Zhang, L., Kadet, J., & Ye, B. (2007). China enacts unified enterprise income tax law. *Tax Management International Journal, 36*(6), 275–278.

Chapter 16
Over-Investment, Internal Control, and Government Intervention: Evidence from China's State-Owned Enterprises

Guodong Yuan, Ron McIver, and Lei Xu

16.1 Introduction

While enterprise investment behavior affects own business performance, it also plays a key role in the sustainability and strength of a country's economic development (Modigliani & Miller, 1958, p. 261; Goel & Thakor, 2005, p. 2255). In China, industries and regions have, to varying degrees, experienced an "overheated investment" phenomenon. This has led to problems such as energy and resource shortages, excess production capacity, distortion of economic structure, and duplication of construction. Additionally, state-owned enterprises (SOEs) are more likely to invest in projects with nonoptimal returns. So, how to restrain "overheated investment," especially of SOEs, has become an urgent issue in the context of China's economic development. In this context, China has initiated efforts to form the legal system around enterprise internal control by issuing a series of guiding documents on their establishment (Yuan et al., 2018, p. 284). China's 2008 implementation of its Basic Internal Control Norms for Enterprises is a good example, where one of the goals of enterprise internal control is improving the efficiency of corporate operations.

Over-investment is a key factor that affects corporate operations, leading to significant discussion on how to restrain enterprise over-investment behaviors (Aggarwal & Samwick, 2006, p. 489). Empirical studies have concluded that internal control, as an important governance mechanism, has an inhibitory effect on inefficient investment (Li et al., 2011, p. 81). However, its effects are constrained by the external environment. As a transition economy, China's unique institutional environment should be considered when studying internal control's governance effects (Yuan et al., 2012, p. 144). Under current institutional structures,

G. Yuan · R. McIver · L. Xu (✉)
UniSA Business, University of South Australia, Adelaide, SA, Australia
e-mail: lei.xu@unisa.edu.au

K. Wendt, B. Villhauer (eds.), *Sustainable Wealth Management*, Sustainable Finance,
https://doi.org/10.1007/978-3-031-55505-3_16

government intervention is a significant factor affecting both the efficiency of corporate investment and the role of internal governance mechanisms. However, the degree of government intervention varies among China's diverse forms of enterprise. It is more difficult for the government to intervene in private enterprises because these have privatized property rights protected by law under China's current market-oriented economic system. In contrast, SOEs are more directly controlled or influenced by the government (Yuan et al., 2021, p. 171), and so its consideration adds significance to this study's examination of the governance effect of SOE internal control on over-investment.

In this chapter, we use listed SOEs from 2010 to 2012 as a sample to test this effect. Our literature review investigates the reasons for SOE over-investment, finding agency problems and government intervention are key reasons. Although internal control can resolve agency problems, government intervention partially moderates its governance effect on over-investment. Therefore, this study examines empirically whether government intervention leads to the fact that internal control cannot play its role in the governance of over-investment in state-owned enterprises.

This study can contribute to meaningful academic discussion on the reform of state-owned enterprises in an emerging market. Since government intervention may affect the performance of internal control, can the government reduce the intervention by decentralizing control power to improve the governance effect of internal control? The policy suggestion of this study is to further accelerate the separation of government functions from enterprise management and reduce the government's intervention on state-owned enterprises and, at the same time, encourage state-owned enterprises to improve their internal governance mechanism and internal control, thus contributing to the reform of state-owned enterprises in China.

The rest of this chapter is structured as follows. Section 16.2 reviews the literature and develops hypotheses. Section 16.3 describes our data and methodology. Section 16.4 analyses the results, and Sect. 16.5 concludes the chapter.

16.2 Literature and Hypotheses

16.2.1 Internal Control and Investment Efficiency

A significant component of the existing research on the corporate investment efficiency–internal control relationship is based on principal agent and information asymmetry theories (Kim et al., 2011, p. 1157). By affecting corporate investment decisions, internal control may alter levels of investment efficiency. However, conclusions about the effectiveness of internal control on levels of corporate investment differ. Most researchers believe that internal control can improve the efficiency of corporate investment, and a correlation between internal control and corporate over-investment can be identified (Yuan, 2013; Hu & Gan, 2017).

Effective internal control will improve the quality of accounting information, alleviate information asymmetry and related issues (Ashbaugh-Skaife e al., 2007, p. 166), inhibit insider trading, and improve the fairness of investment (Brochet, 2010, p. 419). Biddle (2009, p. 122) also proposes that an efficient internal control system can reduce the agency problem, improving investment efficiency. Li et al. (2011, p. 81) find improvement of internal control disclosure can reduce the degree of information asymmetry, inhibiting excessive investment; in contrast, defective internal control can cause inefficient investment. Cheng et al. (2013, p. 18) find investment efficiency improved significantly after the defective internal control system was rectified. Fang and Jin (2013, p. 63) find internal control can effectively inhibit inefficient investment.

However, there are still differing opinions about the effects of internal control. Beneish et al. (2008, p. 665) find that disclosure of information on internal control deficiencies does not affect the company's share price, because this disclosure does not send an obviously bad signal to the market. Some researchers argue that the establishment of an internal control mechanisms increases the economic burden on small and medium-sized enterprises; the cost of information disclosure within the company damages company value in the short term, impairs trust between shareholders and management, and so negatively impacts on company's investment decisions (Liu & Zhang, 2017, p. 1075; Gao, 2010, p. 1). There are also strands of literature that recognize the governance effect of internal control on investment inefficiency but do not support that it can solve agency problems (Fang & Jin, 2013, p. 63).

Another segment of the literature examines the governance effect of internal control on investment inefficiency in diverse forms of enterprises. Yuan (2013) finds the correlation between the quality of internal control and investment inefficiency is greater for state-controlled listed companies, as these SOEs have more serious investment inefficiency issues than non-SOEs. Sun and Cheng (2013, p. 65) find the impact of the quality of internal control on investment efficiency of central government-controlled SOEs is more larger than that of local government-controlled SOEs.

Outcomes involving investment inefficiency can be divided into underinvestment and over-investment (Fazzari et al., 1988, p. 141). The previous analysis supports the potential for internal control to constrain enterprise over-investment behavior by reducing agency problems and information asymmetries. Thus, internal control, as an internal governance mechanism, can also constrain China's SOEs' over-investment behavior. Based on this, we propose the following hypothesis:

Hypothesis 1: Excluding the influence of other factors, the quality of internal control is negatively related to the level of SOE over-investment.

16.2.2 Internal Control and Investment Efficiency in the Context of Government Intervention

From the perspective of the company's external environment, enterprise development is affected by a country's legal environment, religious culture, government intervention, and credit system. Government, therefore, has a certain degree of influence on corporate behavior (Roe, 2006). In China 70% of its listed companies have state holdings. The government plays the role of both shareholder and controller in many SOEs. Some local governments even directly participate in the daily management of enterprises. Based on this special institutional background, government intervention is the most important external environmental factor affecting Chinese enterprise investment behavior.

There are two opinions regarding government intervention in enterprise business activities. One view, the "helping hand," believes government intervention assists enterprises to make more optimal choices in the competitive market environment and reduces the excesses associated with the profit-seeking nature of their business activities. Another point of view, the "grabbing hand," believes government forces enterprises to make inefficient investments to pursue social goals, such as increasing the employment rate, increasing fiscal revenue, and development of the local economy (Shleifer & Vishny, 1998). In China, the government mostly plays the role of the "grabbing hand."

In comparison to those in developed countries, the Chinese government has a stronger motive to intervene in the investment activities of enterprises (Cheng et al., 2008, p. 3). There are three major motivations. The first is the government's social goals. Local governments require enterprises to participate in various investment projects to stimulate local economy development to achieve their social and political goals, such as increasing employment and fiscal revenue. The second is government officials' promotion. The key performance indicators (KPIs) for promotion of local government officials are GDP and fiscal revenue. To meet these goals, local government officials usually seek to increase investment inputs to stimulate the local economy. The third is power and rent seeking of government officials (Shleifer, 1997, p. 365). Driven by this motivation, government officials interfere with companies requiring investment in projects from which they can benefit in pursuit of the maximization of personal utility, regardless of economic viability (Chen et al., 2011, p. 259).

In theory, internal control can constrain over-investment by solving agency problems and reducing information asymmetry. However, the institutional background of Chinese listed companies is quite unique. For SOEs, the issue of over-investment is not only caused by agency problems and information asymmetry but also government intervention. All these interventions can result in more serious level over-investment in the enterprises in which such intervention occurs. Therefore, internal control may not fully constrain over-investment. The more serious the government intervention in SOEs, the more serious the level of over-investment, and the weaker the governance effect of internal control on over-investment.

The degree of government intervention also varies among regions and areas where disparities in social and economic development exist. In areas with low fiscal deficits or unemployment rates, government intervention is normally less, and thus the investment objective of the company is simply to maximize economic return. However, in areas with more government intervention, the government has a stronger motivation to perform its social functions through the investment activities of the companies they control. The government imposes its goals of public utility management into business decision-making, resulting in multiple investment objectives for the company rather than a single goal of maximizing the net present value of the investment project, which easily leads to over-investment (Chen et al., 2011, p. 259). In regions with a low degree of marketization and large fiscal deficits, senior executives of SOEs are often directly appointed by the government or are government officials, which provides opportunities for the government to easily participate in and influence enterprise investment decisions (Chen & Huang, 2007, p. 7). Thus, even if the enterprise has established a sound internal control system, it may not be sufficient to constrain over-investment behavior.

In areas with greater government intervention, internal control has a weaker inhibitory effect on over-investment. Based on this, we propose the following hypothesis:

Hypothesis 2: Excluding the influence of other factors, the negative relationship between the quality of internal control and level of SOE over-investment is greater in areas with weak government intervention than areas with strong government intervention.

16.3 Sample and Research Design

16.3.1 Sample Selection

The choice of 2010–2012 as the sample period reflects requirements for China's companies to adopt the Basic Internal Control Norms for Enterprises to improve enterprise internal control. An original sample of state-controlled listed companies was derived from the current Shanghai (SHSE) and Shenzhen (SZSE) stock exchanges for the 2010–2012 period. Financial service companies were excluded from the companies listed in the original sample, due to differences in their reporting basis and the characteristics of their financial reporting data. Similarly, special treatment (ST) and particular transfer (PT) listed companies were excluded from the sample as they usually have poor or no profits, so their income tax expense behavior is unlikely to be consistent with that of profitable companies. The resultant panel data sample set is comprised of matched company observations for the 3 years within the sample period. Firm-year observations with missing or insufficient data and abnormal values were deleted from the unbalanced panel sample. As companies were classified by ownership structure, based on being state controlled or non-state controlled, some companies were excluded from the sample due to the identity of the ultimate controller not being able to be determined. The data panel for this study is comprised of the remaining 1237 observations. To avoid the influence of extreme values, we "Winsorized" the sample data.

16.3.2 Data Collection

Annual company financial report, shareholder information, internal control information, and financial reporting information for the years 2010–2012 were collected from the CSMAR database. Some data on the quality of internal control was collected manually by viewing the company's annual report, internal control self-assessment report, and internal control assurance report. Data on government intervention was collected manually from the China Market Index Database (CMD). An audit of the collected data was undertaken.

16.3.3 Research Design

16.3.3.1 Model

Following Richardson (2006, p.159), we use a linear regression model to examine the impact of internal control on enterprise over-investment. The model is as follows:

$$Over\_Invst_{i,t} = \beta_0 + \beta_1 IC_{i,t} + \sum Control_{i,t} + \sum Year + Industry + \mu_{i,t} \tag{14.1}$$

The dependent variable Over_Invst$_{i,t}$ represents the over-investment level in company *i* at time *t*. The explanatory variable $IC_{i,t}$ represents the level of internal control. Control$_{i,t}$ contains a group of standard control variables. *Year* and *Industry* control for year and industry effects.

16.3.3.2 Dependent Variable (Over_Invst): Measurement of Enterprise Over-Investment

Richardson (2006, p. 159) uses the regression residuals from a regression model estimating the normal level of capital investment of enterprises as proxy variables for measuring underinvestment or over-investment. This model has been widely applied in the research on investment efficiency (Xin et al., 2007, p. 110; Li & Wang, 2010; Tang et al., 2010, p. 33). Following Richardson (2006, p. 159), the following model has been constructed:

$$\begin{aligned}\text{Invst}_{i,t} = &\alpha_0 + \alpha_1\text{Invst}_{i,t-1} + \alpha_2\text{Grow}_{i,t-1} + \alpha_3\text{Rio}_{i,t-1} + \alpha_4\text{Cash}_{i,t-1} + \alpha_5\text{Ret}_{i,t-1} \\ &+ \alpha_6\text{Age}_{i,t-1} + \alpha_7\text{Size}_{i,t-1} + \sum Year + \sum Industry + \varepsilon_{i,t}\end{aligned} \tag{14.2}$$

$\text{Invst}_{i,t}$ is the ratio of the amount of capital investment for the company in year t divided by total assets at the end of year $t-1$. The amount of capital investment is calculated as the sum of cash paid for purchases of fixed assets, intangible assets, and other long-term assets, cash paid for purchase and disposal of subsidiaries and other business units, cash paid for equity investment and debt investment expenditure, and cash paid for other investment-related activities. $\text{Invst}_{i,t-1}$ is the ratio for year $t-1$. $\text{Grow}_{i,t-1}$ is the company's growth opportunity measured using Tobin's q at the end of year t-1 as a proxy. $\text{Rio}_{i,t-1}$ is the debt ratio. $\text{Cash}_{i,t-1}$ is calculated as the sum of cash and short-term investments divided by total assets. $\text{Ret}_{i,t-1}$ is the annual rate of return on the firm's shares. $\text{Age}_{i,t-1}$ is the time since the company was listed on the SHSE or SZSE. $\text{Size}_{i,t-1}$ is calculated as the natural logarithm of the company's total assets at the end of year $t-1$.

The residual ε is the difference between the actual level of investment and the estimated or optimal expected level of investment. If ε is greater than 0, it indicates that the company has over-invested, and its value is the estimated enterprise over-investment denoted as $\text{Over\_invst}_{i,t}$ in Eq. (16.1). The larger $\text{Over\_invest}_{i,t}$, the more serious the enterprise's over-investment behavior.

16.3.3.3 Independent Variable (IC): Measurement of Internal Control and Measurement of Government Intervention (GI)

The Basic Internal Control Norms for Enterprises introduced five components for the internal control framework. These are control environment, risk assessment, control activities, information and communication, and monitoring. These components are effective criteria that can be used to measure internal control. We base our measure of internal control (IC) on the above five components and refer to the Dibo Internal Control and Risk Management database (DIB database) to manually select the indicators and score each indicator. The weighted score calculated for each company is used to measure the quality of its internal control.

Regarding government intervention, this study uses a government intervention (GI) index to measure the level of government intervention. Based on the marketization index released by Fan et al. (2011) and the data from the China Market Index Database (CMD), we identify the subindex named "the relation between the government and the market" from the marketization index and use it as a basis for distinguishing the strength of government intervention in each region. We compare the sub-index value of each region with the median of the index for the entire market. If the difference is less than 0, we define the region as being in the group with strong government intervention; and if the difference is greater than 0, we define the region as being in the group with weak government intervention.

16.3.3.4 Control Variables

Based on the previous analysis, we identify that the principal agent problem is one of the main factors leading to over-investment. Therefore, the management expense ratio and the amount of capital used by major shareholders are selected as the two major control variables to represent principal agent problems which are controlled for to exclude their impacts on other explanatory variables (Love, 2003, p. 765; Myers & Majluf, 1984, p. 187). Following Richardson (2006, p. 159), this study uses the following control variables:

Managmt—the management expense ratio—calculated as administrative expenses as a percentage of primary business revenue as reported in the accounts.
Major_Occupied—capital occupied by major shareholders—calculated as net accounts receivable as a percentage of total assets at the end of the period.
Cashflow-F—net cash flow from financing activities—calculated as net cash flows from financing activities as a percentage of total assets at the beginning of the period.
FCF—free cash flow—calculated as the percentage of net cash flows from the operating activities deducted by depreciation and expected new investment and then divided by the total asset.
Grow—the company's growth opportunity—measured with Tobin's q as a proxy.
Size—the company's size—calculated as the natural logarithm of the company's total assets.

Major_Occupied captures the effects of tunneling by major shareholders through other accounts receivable (Li et al., 2004), reflecting their ability to exercise control rights over the firm. Since the theory of "free cash flow" was introduced by Jensen (1986, p. 323), free cash flow has been widely used as a controlled variable in the empirical research on the correlation between factors and over-investment (Vogt, 1994, p. 3), thus being the basis for our use of this variable. The use of Grow reflects that the more investment opportunities a company faces, the higher its level of over-investment may be. Finally, most of the literature has adopted the company's size as a control variable. For example, when a company is small, it may have a stronger incentive to expand through more investments.

16.4 Results and Discussion

16.4.1 Descriptive Statistics

Table 16.1 presents the descriptive statistics for the major variables by the group.

For the total observations (1237), the maximum value for over-investment is 0.298, and the minimum value is close to 0, indicating large differences in the degree of over-investment among state-controlled enterprises. The maximum value

Table 16.1 Descriptive statistics for the major variables by group

Government intervention (GI)	Variable	*N*	Min	Max	Mean	p25	Median	p75	sd
High level	Over_Invst	387	0.000	0.298	0.045	0.009	0.025	0.058	0.054
	IC	387	38.007	69.581	62.821	61.148	63.055	64.913	3.375
	Managmt	387	0.006	0.630	0.090	0.044	0.072	0.102	0.081
	Major_ Occupied	387	0.000	0.931	0.231	0.007	0.025	0.520	0.286
	Cashflow_*F*	387	−0.177	1.396	0.074	−0.009	0.032	0.110	0.165
	FCF	387	−0.840	0.361	−0.025	−0.078	−0.024	0.037	0.104
	Grow	387	−0.881	43.607	0.657	0.027	0.164	0.341	3.192
	Size	387	19.032	24.661	21.988	21.325	22.015	22.711	1.086
Low level	Over_Invst	850	0.000	0.274	0.043	0.010	0.026	0.060	0.047
	IC	850	47.841	78.007	64.002	62.401	64.032	65.769	3.097
	Managmt	850	0.003	0.307	0.072	0.038	0.061	0.096	0.048
	Major_ Occupied	850	0.000	0.920	0.189	0.005	0.018	0.412	0.267
	Cashflow_*F*	850	−0.314	3.384	0.084	−0.013	0.041	0.132	0.200
	FCF	850	−0.348	0.423	−0.042	−0.090	−0.044	0.005	0.088
	Grow	850	−0.725	38.120	0.342	0.048	0.163	0.330	1.818
	Size	850	19.895	28.405	22.596	21.699	22.407	23.306	1.329
Total	Over_Invst	1237	0.000	0.298	0.044	0.010	0.026	0.060	0.049
	IC	1237	38.007	78.007	63.633	61.865	63.800	65.516	3.232
	Managmt	1237	0.003	0.630	0.078	0.039	0.064	0.097	0.061
	Major_ Occupied	1237	0.000	0.931	0.202	0.006	0.019	0.456	0.274
	Cashflow_*F*	1237	−0.314	3.384	0.080	−0.012	0.037	0.124	0.190
	FCF	1237	−0.840	0.423	−0.037	−0.088	−0.039	0.011	0.093
	Grow	1237	−0.881	43.607	0.441	0.045	0.164	0.332	2.340
	Size	1237	19.032	28.405	22.405	21.564	22.276	23.081	1.288

of internal control quality is 78.007, and the mean value is 63.633, indicating that the overall level of the internal control quality of listed SOEs is not high. The maximum value for the management expense ratio is 0.630, but the minimum value is only 0.003, again indicating significant variation. The maximum value for funds occupied by major shareholders is about 0.931, with a minimum value is close to 0, indicating that for some companies the funds are occupied by their major shareholders, while for some companies the funds are retained by the management to maintain business operations. The maximum value for a company's growth opportunities is 43.607, but the minimum value is −0.881 showing a negative growth rate, indicating the development opportunities vary among companies.

Of the total 1237 observations, 387 are classified into the high level of government intervention group, and 850 observations are classified into the group with low levels of government intervention.

The mean value for the over-investment for the group with high levels of government intervention is 0.045, which is higher than that of the group with low levels of government intervention, at 0.043. The mean value for internal control quality for the group with low levels of government intervention (64.002) is higher than that for the group with high levels of government intervention (62.821).

16.4.2 Hypothesis Testing

This study uses OLS regression models. The results from estimation of the regression models are summarized in Table 16.2. Results for the group with a high level of government intervention are given in the second column (Group (1)), those for the group with a low level of government intervention in the third column (Group (2)), and results for the full sample in the final column (Group (3)).

Two correlation measures (Spearman and Pearson) were calculated to identify relationships between the independent variables. As no correlation coefficient between the independent variables is greater than 0.8, and the calculated variance inflation factors (VIFs) are low (smaller than 10), it can be concluded that serious multicollinearity problems are unlikely to be present in the regression model

Table 16.2 Regression results for the dependent variable Over_Invst

	Group (1)	Group (2)	Group (3)
Variables	High level of government intervention	Low level of government intervention	Whole sample
IC	−0.0008 (−0.95)	−0.0003** (−0.44)	−0.0005* (−1.16)
Managmt	−0.1027** (−2.21)	0.0247 (0.66)	−0.0123 (−0.46)
Major_ Occupied	−0.0280 (−1.52)	−0.0194* (−1.86)	−0.0216** (−2.38)
Cashflow_F	0.0716*** (3.32)	0.0595*** (4.09)	0.0628*** (5.10)
FCF	0.0087 (0.28)	0.0204 (0.98)	0.0148 (0.89)
Grow	0.0053** (2.03)	0.0018 (0.83)	0.0039** (2.06)
Size	−0.0029 (−1.04)	−0.0004 (−0.27)	−0.0010 (−0.87)
Year	Control	Control	Control
Industry	Control	Control	Control
Constant	0.1489* (1.89)	0.0534 (1.30)	0.0877** (2.44)
Observations (*N*)	387	850	1237
Adjusted R^2	0.1561	0.0960	0.1130
F	.	6.160	8.630

Robust *t*-statistics in parentheses
*** $p < 0.01$, ** $p < 0.05$, * $p < 0.1$

specified in Eq. (16.2). The adjusted-R^2 and the F-statistics for the models suggest that the independent variables provide statistically significant information about the dependent variable, enterprise over-investment, as captured in the chosen measure (Over_Invst).

The regression results for Group (3) in Table 16.2 report the effect of internal control on the over-investment behavior for the whole sample of SOEs. The significant t-statistic (at the 10% level) for IC suggests a significant negative relationship between the quality of internal control and SOE over-investment. Accordingly, Hypothesis 1 is supported. This result is consistent with existing theories that agency problems prevail in state-controlled enterprises, and internal control can take a governance role in restraining enterprise over-investment. Regression results for the control variables suggest that over-investment is significantly and positively correlated with cash flows from financing activities and the company's growth opportunities, respectively, indicating that the more cash and investment opportunities the company can obtain, the more likely it is to overinvest.

The regression results for Group (1) and Group (2) from Table 16.2 report the effect of internal control on the over-investment behavior of SOEs from two perspectives: the group with a high level of government intervention and the group with a low level of government intervention. There is a significant t-statistic (at 5% level) with a negative sign for IC for the group with the low level of government intervention. The t-statistic (at the 5% level) for this group is also significant at a lower significance level than that of the whole sample. However, even though it is negative, the t-statistic for the group with a high level of government intervention is not statistically significant. These results suggest that internal control has a statistically significant inhibitory effect on state-controlled enterprises in the group with low government intervention, as compared to that on the group with a high level of government intervention. Accordingly, Hypothesis 2 is partially supported.

16.4.3 Robustness Test

We perform a quantile regression as the alternative regression modeling strategy. We divide our sample into three groups in each given year: (1) companies whose over-investments are in the first quantile (low Over_invst group), (2) companies whose over-investments are in the second, third, and fourth quantiles (medium Over_invst group), and (3) companies whose over-investments are in fifth quantile (high Over_invst group). The quantile regressions are run for these three groups.

We also adopt an alternative measure of the quality of internal control. We use the internal control quality index (ICQ) from DIB to proxy for the effectiveness of corporate internal control systems. In summary, our main findings are robust to alternative regression methods and use of alternative measures.

16.5 Conclusions

This study examines the relationship between internal control and the over-investment of state-controlled enterprises listed on the Shanghai and Shenzhen stock exchanges from 2010 to 2012, in the context of government intervention. We conclude that the two major reasons causing the over-investment of SOEs are government intervention and agency problems which have combined effects on over-investment. Internal control can play a governance role in constraining over-investment in SOEs due to the existence of agency problems. We also conclude that the governance effect of internal control on the over-investment of SOEs is moderated by government intervention, which is one of the external environmental factors. In regions where government intervention in state-controlled enterprises is greater, the local governments intervene in enterprise investment decisions to achieve their political or personal promotion goals, thus leading to more serious over-investment behavior. Under this situation, internal control, as an internal enterprise governance mechanism, cannot properly perform its governance role in constraining over-investment.

Existing research has often examined the relationship between internal control and investment efficiency. Much of this previous research did not address the moderating effect of the external environment on the relationship. It is in this context that this study extends the research on the economic consequences of internal control. We find empirical support for the claim that government intervention in SOEs—as an external environmental factor—will weaken the governance effect of internal control, especially in the context of transition economies like that of China. This leads to the final implication of the study: to suggest that future policy initiatives to facilitate decentralization and separation of the government's economic functions and improve the internal control system of the state-controlled enterprises are warranted.

References

Aggarwal, R. K., & Samwick, A. A. (2006). Empire-builders and shirkers: Investment, firm performance, and managerial incentives. *Journal of Corporate Finance, 12*(3), 489–515.

Ashbaugh-Skaife, H., Collins, D. W., & Kinney, W. R., Jr. (2007). The discovery and reporting of internal control deficiencies prior to SOX-mandated audits. *Journal of Accounting and Economics, 44*(1–2), 166–192.

Beneish, M. D., Billings, M. B., & Hodder, L. D. (2008). Internal control weaknesses and information uncertainty. *The Accounting Review, 83*(3), 665–703.

Biddle, G. C., Hilary, G., & Verdi, R. S. (2009). How does financial reporting quality relate to investment efficiency? *Journal of Accounting and Economics, 48*(2–3), 112–131.

Brochet, F. (2010). Information content of insider trades before and after the Sarbanes-Oxley Act. *The Accounting Review, 85*(2), 419–446.

Chen, X., & Huang, J. (2007). Government intervention, diversification and firm performance. *Management World, 1*(92), 7.

Chen, S., Sun, Z., Tang, S., & Wu, D. (2011). Government intervention and investment efficiency: Evidence from China. *Journal of Corporate Finance, 17*(2), 259–271.
Cheng, Z., Xia, X., & Yu, M. (2008). Government intervention, the pyramid structure and the investment of local state-owned listed companies. *Management World, 9*, 3–10.
Cheng, M., Dhaliwal, D., & Zhang, Y. (2013). Does investment efficiency improve after the disclosure of material weaknesses in internal control over financial reporting? *Journal of Accounting and Economics, 56*(1), 1–18.
Fan, G., Wang, X., & Zhu, H. (2011). *The marketization index of China: The process of regional marketization report 2011*. Press of Economic Science. (in Chinese).
Fang, H., & Jin, Y. (2013). Corporate governance, internal control and inefficient investment: Theoretical analysis and empirical evidence. *Accounting Research, 7*(1), 63–69.
Fazzari, S. M., Hubbard, R. G., & Petersen, B. C. (1988). Financing constraints on corporate investment. *Brookings Papers on Economic Activity*, 141–195.
Gao, P. (2010). Disclosure quality, cost of capital, and investor welfare. *The Accounting Review, 85*(1), 1–29.
Goel, A. M., & Thakor, A. V. (2005). Green with envy: Implications for corporate investment distortions. *The Journal of Business, 78*(6), 2255–2288.
Hu, M., & Gan, S. (2017). Life cycle stage effects, CEO power and internal control quality: Evidence from listed family firms in China. *China Journal of Accounting Studies, 5*(2), 211–233.
Jensen, M. C. (1986). Agency costs of free cash flow, corporate finance, and takeovers. *The American Economic Review, 76*(2), 323–329.
Kim, J. B., Song, B. Y., & Zhang, L. (2011). Internal control weakness and bank loan contracting: Evidence from SOX Section 404 disclosures. *The Accounting Review, 86*(4), 1157–1188.
Li, Q., & Wang, T. (2010). *Financial reporting quality and corporate investment efficiency: Chinese experience*. Nankai Business Review International (Vol. 1, p. 197).
Li, Z., Sun, Z., & Wang, Z. (2004). Tunneling and ownership structure of a firm: Evidence from controlling Shareholder's embezzlement of listed company's funds in China. *Accounting Research, 12*, 3–14.
Li, W., Lin, B., & Song, L. (2011). The role played by the internal control in companies' investment: Is it a promotion of efficiency or a repression thereof? *Management World, 2*, 81–99 and 188.
Liu, X., & Zhang, C. (2017). Corporate governance, social responsibility information disclosure, and enterprise value in China. *Journal of Cleaner Production, 142*, 1075–1084.
Love, I. (2003). Financial development and financing constraints: International evidence from the structural investment model. *The Review of Financial Studies, 16*(3), 765–791.
Modigliani, F., & Miller, M. H. (1958). The cost of capital, corporation finance and the theory of investment. *The American Economic Review, 48*(3), 261–297.
Myers, S. C., & Majluf, N. S. (1984). Corporate financing and investment decisions when firms have information that investors do not have. *Journal of Financial Economics, 13*(2), 187–221.
Richardson, S. (2006). Over-investment of free cash flow. *Review of Accounting Studies, 11*(2), 159–189.
Roe, M. J. (2006). *Political determinants of corporate governance: Political context, corporate impact*. Oxford University Press.
Shleifer, A. (1997). Government in transition. *European Economic Review, 41*(3–5), 385–410.
Shleifer, A., & Vishny, R. W. (1998). *The grabbing hand: Government pathologies and their cures*. Harvard University Press.
Sun, H., & Cheng, K. (2013). Government level internal control and investment efficiency: Evidence from state-owned listed companies. *Accounting and Economic Research, 27*(03), 65–74.
Tang, X., Zhou, X., & Ma, R. (2010). Government intervention, GDP growth and local state-owned enterprises over-investment. *Journal of Finance, 8*, 33–48.
Vogt, S. C. (1994). The cash flow/investment relationship: Evidence from US manufacturing firms. *Financial Management*, 3–20.

Xin, Q., Lin, B., & Wang, Y. (2007). Government control, executive compensation and capital investment. *Economic Research Journal, 8*(4), 110–122.
Yuan, X. (2013). *Internal control, property right and corporate investment efficiency*. Communication of Finance and Accounting.
Yuan, G., McIver, R. P., & Burrow, M. (2012). Corporate income tax aggressiveness in China: Regulatory environment and ownership impact. *Journal of Business Management, 5*, 144–161.
Yuan, G., McIver, R. P., Xu, L., & Kang, S. H. (2018). Corporate income tax avoidance in China: Using regulatory change to encourage corporate tax sustainability. In *Sustainable financial innovations* (pp. 284–306). CRC Press.
Yuan, G., McIver, R. P., & Xu, L. (2021). Tax reform, tax aggressiveness and corporate value: Evidence from China's Enterprise income tax law reform. In *Green and social economy finance* (pp. 171–191). CRC Press.

Chapter 17
Exploring Financial Institution Environmental Disclosures: Evidence from China

Shidi Dong, Ron McIver, and Lei Xu

17.1 Introduction

Damage to the environment and climate change pose the greatest current challenges for humankind (Szombatfalvy, 2010). The United Nations General Assembly's September 2015 adoption of the 17 Sustainable Development Goals (SDGs) at the New York Sustainable Development Summit seeks to attend to these problems while fostering sustainable development globally. Both the SDGs and the December 2015 "Paris Agreement" on climate change have clarified that pursuit of sustainable development and redress of climate change require make changes that "ensure sustainable consumption and production patterns" (UN, 2015, Goal 12).

The financial services industry has a lower direct environmental impact than traditional polluting industries (e.g., oil and gas, manufacturing, chemical, paper, and pulp). However, its indirect impact on the natural environment and sustainable development is considered significant. This reflects the financial services sector's access to financial capital and primary capital market intermediary functions (Weber, 2014), with environmental sensitivity to its lending and investing activities potentially being comparable to the direct impacts of polluting industries (Branco & Rodrigues, 2006). Thus, the financial services industry has a key role to play in achieving the SDGs, via its investment, credit, asset management, and insurance underwriting roles. This will be through channeling capital toward more environmentally sustainable technologies and businesses, contributing to the creation of a low-carbon, climate-resilient, green economy. In doing so, the financial services

S. Dong (✉)
School of Management, Shenyang University of Technology, Shenyang, China
e-mail: dongshidi@sut.edu.cn

R. McIver · L. Xu (✉)
UniSA Business, University of South Australia, Adelaide, SA, Australia
e-mail: ronald.mciver@unisa.edu.au; lei.xu@unisa.edu.au

K. Wendt, B. Villhauer (eds.), *Sustainable Wealth Management*, Sustainable Finance,
https://doi.org/10.1007/978-3-031-55505-3_17

industry would be able to act as a catalyst, influencing the environmental and social behaviors of clients and other industry sectors (Thompson & Cowton, 2004; Cuesta-González et al. 2006). However, where financial institutions evidence poor environmental practices, widespread negative external effects will ultimately impact on society and the wider economy (Bose et al., 2018).

The Financial Stability Board's (FSB's) December 2015 establishment of the Task Force on Climate-related Financial Disclosures (TCFD)[1] represents an international initiative to mitigate impacts on the environment and promote climate-related accounting disclosure within the financial sector and in the nonfinancial sectors accounting for the largest proportion of GHG emissions and energy and water usage (TCFD, 2017). The TCFD was tasked with design of a set of recommendations for voluntary, consistent, climate-related disclosures for organizations across sectors, including those in the financial sector, as adoption in this sector may promote "early assessment of climate-related risks and opportunities" (TCFD, 2017, p. 15). Additionally, financial institutions are encouraged to disclose their exposures to climate risks and their management to facilitate market discipline, encourage firms to manage what they are measuring, and provide systemic-level data to facilitate authorities' assessments of the materiality of climate change risks to the financial sector and the channels through which this is most likely to be transmitted (TCFD, 2016a). However, while the TCFD's latest results identify increases in the average level of disclosure in the banking and insurance industries by 13% and 12%, respectively, over 2018–2020, the percentage of banks disclosing relevant information is lower than the average across all companies reviewed (TCFD, 2021).

Environmental information disclosure by financial institutions is receiving more interest as their indirect impact on the environment is significant. However, relative to traditional polluting industries, financial institutions have received little attention in the important environmental literature strand within social accounting (Thompson & Cowton, 2004). Previous studies on environmental reporting usually exclude the financial services industry from the sample, arguing that it has a low environmental impact compared to environmentally sensitive industries and a different operating and reporting structure (Pucheta-Martínez & López-Zamora, 2018; Arena & Michelon, 2018).

Most prior studies in the corporate social responsibility (CSR) sphere that investigate financial sector CSR or sustainability disclosures primarily focus on banks, rather than the financial sector more generally (Dong et al., 2021), with a few providing very limited insights into financial institutions' environmental disclosures. Scholtens (2009) identifies that most international banks have explicit environmental policies, as well as supply chain policies that explicitly account for environmental and social issues. Most banks are found to have qualitative environmental goals, with their lending policies requiring the performance some type of environmental risk analysis. Weber et al. (2014) analyze the global financial sector's sustainability

[1] TCFD's work focuses on voluntary climate-related financial disclosures pertaining to the physical and nonphysical impacts faced by both financial and nonfinancial companies and recommends that such disclosures are made in financial fillings (TCFD, 2016a).

performance, identifying that its CSR reporting underperforms that of most other sectors. However, the introduction of environmental regulations, relatively long history of environmental management, and increasing regard of environmental risks in the sector suggest a medium-level performance on the environment. Vilar and Simão (2015) identify a predominance of environmental themes in the information disclosed in international banks' websites, and around 63% of the websites analyzed have detailed information on environmental management. Pathak and Tewari (2017) analyze the top 60 banks' sustainability reporting and find banks' sustainability reporting focuses on the immediate and elementary needs of the business ecosystem, such as energy, wind, and water. Empirical studies on the financial industry's environmental disclosures remain inconclusive, even with growing demands for reporting of climate and environmental information by the financial sector (e.g., TCFD) and growing recognition of the sector's important role in achieving a low-carbon economy (Alberici & Querci, 2016; Bose et al., 2018).

This study aims to fill gaps in the prior literature by studying the financial industry's environmental disclosures, which evidence the industry's commitment to environmental sustainability and the transition to a low-carbon economy. Previous comparative studies have shown significant international differences in the level of CSR or environmental disclosures under different institutional environments (Pucheta-Martínez & Gallego-Álvarez, 2018). Therefore, we study the Chinese financial sector as it provides a unique set of contexts. First, post the global financial crisis, China's financial institutions are among the world's largest, playing an important intermediary role globally as well as in the Chinese economy (Shan & Xu, 2012). Second, in China listed financial firms were among the first mandated to issue CSR reports along with annual report information by the stock exchange (SSE, 2008). Third, the finance sector is an integral component in the Chinese government's "green finance" agenda, which it initiated in 2012. As part of the agenda, the China Banking Regulatory Commission (CBRC) (now China Banking and Insurance Regulatory Commission (CBIRC)) released the "Green Credit Guidelines" in 2012, requiring banks to fully disclose their green credit strategies and policies, development of green credit, and credit provision associated with major environmental and social risks. Further, seven departments in China, including the People's Bank of China, Ministry of Finance, and Ministry of Environmental Protection, jointly issued the 2016 "Guiding Opinions on Establishing a Green Finance System," strengthening environmental information disclosure requirements and specifically supporting improved environmental information disclosures for borrowing enterprises, bond issuers, and investment institutions (MEP, 2016). Additionally, working with the FSB, some leading Chinese financial institutions, mostly banks, participated in the "Climate and Environmental Information Disclosure Pilot," established at the ninth UK–China Economic and Financial Dialogue by the Chinese and UK governments on December 15, 2017 (GFI, 2018). Lastly, in July 2021, "Guidelines for Financial Institutions Environmental Information Disclosure" were released by the People's Bank of China and the China Financial Standardization Technical Committee. This is the first official document in China providing guidance on the form and content of financial institutions' environmental information disclosures, covering commercial banks, asset managers, insurance, trust, securities, and other financial institutions.

Empirical investigation on the Chinese financial sector's commitment to environmental sustainability through its environmental information disclosures is limited. In some international studies on CSR reporting, China's financial intermediaries are found to be "poor disclosers" on environmental policy (Jain et al., 2015; Alberici & Querci, 2016). Therefore, given the "green finance" context in which it operates, the intent of this research is to provide preliminary evidence on China's financial sector's 2016–2020 environmental disclosures. The financial sector examined in this study includes banks, securities firms, and insurance companies, in accord with the "Revision on Guidelines for the Industry Classification of Listed firms" issued by the China Securities Regulatory Commission (CSRC) in 2012. Specifically, two questions are answered: (1) What is the extent of Chinese financial institutions' disclosures of environmental information over 2016–2020? (2) To what extent is the content and quality of environmental information disclosed by Chinese financial institutions in accordance with the "Guidelines for Financial Institutions Environmental Information Disclosure"?

To address these questions, this study collects secondary data on environmental information from the CSMAR electronic database, the most widely used electronic database for China-based economic and financial research. Content analysis based on the "Guidelines for Financial Institutions Environmental Information Disclosure" is then applied to the environmental disclosures of 285 listed financial institutions. Our results identify that China's financial institutions have not paid sufficient attention to the reporting of environmental information, compared to other categories of CSR. Environmental disclosure is still not a primary focus for China's financial institutions, even at a time when recognition of the financial sector's role in contributing to a green and low-carbon economy has grown among international bodies, governments, and stock exchanges. However, awareness by financial institutions of their role in environmental sustainability is improving over time. Banks are at the forefront in terms of environmental disclosure. For the sampled institutions information on the direct environmental impact of their own business activities is the most common aspect of disclosure, followed by the environmental impacts of their investment and financing activities and, lastly, qualitative indicators. This study provides several contributions. First, it adds to an existing and emerging literature on the environmental performance of the financial sector in general. Second, it addresses a scarcity of literature on financial institutions' environmental reporting practices in the Chinese context. Third, it addresses a gap created by a shortage of investigations into environmental disclosures by financial institutions belonging to different subsectors within the financial services sector.

The rest of this chapter is organized as follows. Section 17.2 provides a comprehensive literature review on financial institutions' CSR reporting practices, with a focus on their environmental disclosures. Section 17.3 provides discussion of the theoretical framework. Section 17.4 describes the research methods, and Sect. 17.5

presents results and discussion. Section 17.6 provides conclusions, research limitations, and possible directions for future research.

17.2 Literature Review

17.2.1 CSR Reporting in the Financial Sector

Studies specifically examining environmental reporting practices in the banking or broader financial sectors are limited. However, a range of studies examining the banking or financial sector's CSR reporting practices have been conducted in different countries, providing some insights. The KPMG survey (2015, 2017) has examined the status of environmental information disclosures within the financial sector's CSR reporting, finding that while 71% of companies in the financial service sector report CSR information, only 36% acknowledge climate risk in their financial reports. Moreover, the survey identifies that the sector has a low rate of reporting on carbon emissions, implying that financial firms are focused on the direct carbon impacts of their own operations, which are small relative to those of other industries. Therefore, financial services firms still need to consider and acknowledge the carbon impact of the businesses they fund or invest in and their exposures to carbon-related risks in their loan and investment portfolios. Cuesta-González et al. (2006) analyze both internal and external dimensions of social performance by some representative Spanish banks. They identify that these banks are more likely to offer information on internal dimensions of social performance, such as corporate governance and stakeholder management, but are only beginning to integrate ethical or environmental issues into their decision-making and project finance evaluations. Branco and Rodrigues (2006) examine the CSR disclosure by Portuguese banks and find that, when compared to human resource, product and consumer, and community involvement disclosures, bank reporting of environmental information is limited. Branco and Rodrigues (2006) conclude that relative to lesser-known banks, and consistent with legitimacy theory, environmental disclosures are used as a distinguishing feature by higher visibility banks as part of their legitimation strategies. Day and Woodward (2009) examine the UK financial sector's CSR reporting, finding that 59% of financial companies—banks, insurance providers, building societies, and other—disclose environmental information on indirect impacts. Environmental issues including "materials consumption" and "waste management" are the most reported areas by UK financial institutions, while "property design and management" is the lowest. However, the sector has not responded well to issues on the public agenda, such as global warming, pollution, and depletion of natural resources. Using corporate governance and agency theory perspectives, Jizi et al. (2014) examine the US banks' CSR disclosure quality, identifying that only 12% of their annual reports disclose information related to environmental projects and initiatives, a much lower frequency than other categories, such as community involvement, employees, and product and customer services.

In Scholtens' (2009) study, ten environmental indicators are assessed to examine the CSR performance of international banks. These include indicators on environmental policy, supply chain management, environmental management targets, transparency of environmental performance, exclusion of specific sectors, and guidelines on environmental risk management. Scholtens (2009) identifies that almost all international banks have environmental and supply chain policies that explicitly account for environmental and social issues. Most banks are found to have qualitative environmental goals and policies requiring performance of some type of environmental risk analysis with lending. Chih et al. (2010) conclude the financial industry's environmental dimension is comprised of three criteria: environmental performance (e.g., eco-efficiency), environmental reporting, and industry specific. Weber et al. (2014) analyze the global financial industry's sustainability performance, finding it underperforms most of the other sectors with regard to CSR reporting. However, it displays a medium level of performance on the environment given the introduction of environmental regulations, a relatively long history of environmental management, and increasing awareness of environmental risks in the sector. Vilar and Simão (2015) find that environmental themes predominate in the information disclosed on international banks' websites, and around 63% of websites analyzed have detailed information on environmental management. Pathak and Tewari (2017) analyze the sustainability reporting of the top 60 banks finding their sustainability reporting focuses on immediate and elementary business ecosystem needs, such as energy, agriculture, wind, and water.

17.2.2 Environmental Disclosures by Financial Institutions

Environmental information disclosure in the financial services industry has not been explored extensively. However, several international comparative studies have shed light on this sector's environmental reporting practices in general, with a few studies also having investigated influencing factors from different theoretical perspectives, including sociopolitical theories, corporate governance, and the varieties of capitalism (Alberici & Querci, 2016).

Tarna (2001) examines 12 environmental reports from the financial sector, including banks and insurers from different countries. Basing itself on the VfU reporting initiative, the study considers several aspects of environmental issues, including general information, environmental management, operating ecology, product ecology, financial aspects related to the environment, and stakeholder management. Tarna (2001) identifies that environmental reporting in financial institutions is still rare, but the industry's environmental awareness is growing. However, reporting on environmental aspects related to financial performance and product ecology need improvement. Kolk et al.'s (2001) study of the Fortune Global 250's environmental reporting highlights sectoral differences, identifying the financial industry's low reporting frequencies, compared to nonfinancial industries, given its low direct environmental impact. The study also finds more than 70% of the financial industry's environmental reports come from banks. Darus et al. (2013) and Yusoff and Darus (2014) study the environmental disclosures of financial institutions in Malaysia, showing that, overall, the Malaysian institutions' environmental information disclosures are minimal, general, and of a qualitative nature. The key areas focused on are the conservation of the environment, environmental education, environmental audit and independent verification of environmental information, climate change mitigation and adaptation, and the prevention of polluting activities.

Carè (2017) uses a multiple case study approach to analyze the level and quality of "environmental risk" disclosures made by Euro area banks. Carè (2017) finds a lack of consistency in type, quantity, and quality of environmental disclosures and concludes that reputation or perceived potential reputational risk is the core driver of banks' corporate environmental reporting. Zabawa (2018) examines the scope, diversity, and methodology (specifically use of the Global Reporting Initiative (GRI) standards) of pro-environmental information reporting in the five largest banks in Poland at the end of 2016. The study identifies a large degree of differentiation within the environmental information disclosures presented by these banks. Ryszawska and Zabawa (2018) review the CSR reporting standards employed by the world's five largest banks (four of which are China's), together with detailed note-taking on the pro-environmental activities included in their reports. They find that the banks studied can be regarded as environmentally responsible entities. The banks' reports and disclosures are produced in accordance with internationally recognized standards. A critique of the standards used for reporting environmental information is that it leads to production of a set of indicators but not necessarily a change in corporate values. However, Ryszawska and Zabawa (2018) argue that the weaknesses of such reporting does not suggest a lessening of support for the benefits derived from following GRI guidelines.

17.2.3 Factors Influencing Financial Sector Environmental Disclosures

A limited set of extant studies examine the factors that influence financial sector environmental disclosures. Alberici and Querci (2016) investigate the quality of 129 financial intermediaries' voluntary disclosures on environmental policy based on GRI data. They report a high degree of heterogeneity in the quality of the selected financial intermediaries' environmental disclosures and that over 50% of financial institutions provided no information on half of the environmental items identified by the GRI. Using the lenses of legitimacy, stakeholder, and institutional theory, Alberici and Querci (2016) identify that the quality of financial intermediaries' environmental disclosures is associated with firm size, firm operating profitability, national economic wealth, and national environmental performance but is not influenced by stock market price or business area. Addressing different institutional environments, Gallego-Álvarez and Pucheta-Martínez (2019) analyze bank environmental reporting in both coordinated market economies (CMEs) and liberal market economies (LMEs) and examine the moderating role of gender diversity and board membership. The study identifies that environmental disclosure is low on average, and banks should take more steps to increase the reporting of environmental issues. Moreover, banks operating in CME countries are involved in more environmental matters than banks domiciled in LME countries as CMEs are more stakeholder orientated. Therefore, banks reporting environmental information in CMEs may avoid external pressures from stakeholders.

In the context of Turkey and focusing on one specific dimension of environmental disclosures, Kılıç and Kuzey (2019) investigate the influence of corporate characteristics on banks' voluntary climate change disclosures. They identify that a significant number of banks have not incorporated climate change-related issues into their lending policies or corporate strategies. Bank size, ownership diffusion, and listing status have had a strong positive impact upon the extent of banks' climate change-related disclosures. Profitability and age show only a weak positive influence, while foreign ownership exerts a negative impact. Focusing on environmental, social, and governance (ESG) disclosures, Brogi and Lagasio (2019) identify a significant and positive association between disclosures and company profitability, while the association between ESG score and ROA is greater in the bank than in the industrial sample. Hossain et al. (2018) and Bose et al. (2018) look at Bangladesh's "green banking disclosures." Both studies identify that "green banking disclosures" are used by banks to gain legitimacy from the regulator—the central bank. Based on institutional and corporate governance theory, Bose et al. (2018) conclude that imitation within the banking industry has, over time, led to the adoption of "green banking" reporting practices as a routine process in the developing country context of Bangladesh. The study identifies that institutional factors, such as regulatory guidance and institutional investor pressure, and corporate governance elements, such as board size, can positively influence the level of "green banking" disclosures. Hossain et al. (2018) find that "green banking" disclosures lack consistency. As an impression management tool, "green banking" reporting is used by banks to enhance corporate reputation and to gain legitimacy from the regulator and society.

17.2.4 Relevant Studies in the Chinese Context

It is difficult to draw a picture for China's financial institutions' engagement in environmental sustainability from previous studies. A range of studies investigate China's financial sector's sustainability reporting but have not focused on how the sector engages with environmental matters. With respect to the Chinese financial sector's sustainability reporting practices, some prior studies provide evidence. Sun et al. (2015), in the context of institutional theory, identify that early adoption and the spread of CSR reporting within China's banking subsector are influenced by the local community in which the bank operates. Jain et al. (2015) identify that Chinese banks' CSR reporting scores significantly exceed those of Japanese and Indian banks and that environmental reporting has increased over the 2005–2011 period. Weber (2017) identifies that Chinese banks' sustainability performance increased significantly between 2009 and 2013, and China's "green credit" policy has driven its banks' increased corporate sustainability performance. Dong et al. (2021) conclude that adoption of sustainability reporting has become institutionalized in China's financial sector over 2007–2016, consistent with general regulatory pressures, but that this is mainly in the banking subsector.

The above review suggests gaps in the literature examining nonpolluting industries' environmental practices in both the developed and developing country contexts. China provides an interesting and worthy institutional context for study given the Chinese government's relatively recent issue of its "green finance" policies. Therefore, this study aims to understand how China's financial sector engages with environmental matters through its public reporting and in doing so to address the gap identified. This is done against the background of the Chinese government's advocacy of green finance policies, including the "Green Credit Guidelines" issued by the China Banking Regulatory Commission (CBRC) in 2012 and the "Guiding Opinions on Establishing a Green Finance System" issued in 2016.

17.3 Theoretical Framework

Although many studies examine motivations underlying firms' environmental disclosures, much of the extant empirical evidence has focused on industrial sectors. Sociopolitical theories, including legitimacy theory, institutional theory, and stakeholder theory, dominate in providing explanations as to why firms make environmental disclosures, or CSR disclosures in general, in the prior social accounting literature. As argued by Chen and Roberts (2010), these theoretical perspectives are complementary and overlap, rather than compete, and analyze issues of concern from differing levels of specificity. These complementary perspectives embrace the vision of firms as porous organizations exposed to external pressures (Alberici & Querci, 2016). Therefore, from these sociopolitical perspectives, firms can gain general legitimacy in the eyes of "society," conform to institutionalized norms or rules, or meet stakeholder expectations, through their disclosures of environmental information. However, despite these theoretical perspectives dominating the environmental reporting literature dealing with heavy polluting firms, these perspectives have received less attention and application in the analysis of industries which have significant indirect impacts on the environment.

Among the sociopolitical theories identified, institutional theory is an appropriate choice for investigating specific corporate structures, systems, programs, or practices that are commonly implemented by similar organizations in their normal business operations (Chen & Roberts, 2010). Institutional theory complements legitimacy theory, by explicitly asserting that companies incorporate institutionalized management practices to become homogenous to gain legitimacy and maintain survival prospects. This occurs via three isomorphic processes: coercive, mimetic, and normative. Using this institutional perspective, the organization's adoption, diffusion, or adaption of management practices over time can be viewed as organizational responses to changes in the wider institutional setting. A tradition of high "power distance" in Chinese culture, consistent with the centralization of power and authority in the Chinese government, supports use of the institutional perspective to view economic, social, and organizational change in China and will lead to a better understanding of Chinese firm behavior and characteristics (Yang et al., 2015). Institutional theory has been applied in explaining Chinese financial companies' CSR and polluting industries environmental reporting practices (Sun et al., 2015; Weber, 2017; Dong et al., 2021).

Financial institutions, as economic entities, cannot detach themselves from the social context in which they exist and operate and through which they are formed and influenced. The Chinese institutional context provides a strong set of institutional pressures that may be expected to influence the financial industry's environmental reporting. As a market-based institutional arrangement, green finance policy has recently played an important role in the promotion of environmental protection and the building of an ecological society in China (Green Finance Task Force, 2015). The concept of "green finance" is different from but overlaps with the sustainable development or CSR concepts promoted by the Chinese government over the last decade (G20 Green Finance Study Group, 2016). It provides a new policy-driven space for financial industry development, requiring all financial flows to be "greened" to respond to environmental risks, primarily through promotion of green credit, green securities, and green insurance in commercial financial institutions (DRC and IISD, 2015). In 2016, seven departments in China, including the People's Bank of China, Ministry of Finance, and Ministry of Environmental Protection, jointly issued the "Guiding Opinions on Establishing a Green Finance System" (the "Guiding Opinions"). The "Guiding Opinions" emphasize that eco-friendliness be embodied in green credit, green securities, green funds, and environmental insurance and requires financial institutions to incorporate environmental factors into decision-making processes, adopt environmental risk management tools, and provide environmental disclosures (MEP, 2016). In responding to the TCFD's climate-related disclosure recommendations and the country's target for carbon neutrality, the "Guidelines for Financial Institutions Environmental Information Disclosure" (the "Guidelines") were released in 2021. The "Guidelines" provide a mandate on and structure for financial institutions' environmental information disclosures. All these policies have led to coercive institutional isomorphism caused by political influence and the need to maintain legitimacy. In responding to institutional pressures, a financial institution may use environmental reporting to attract support within its institutional context; in turn, environmental disclosure practices are influenced by the context in which each financial institution operates. Therefore, to survive, each financial institution needs to respond to these coercive pressures, with environmental disclosure being part of the reporting processes needed to create and maintain this support.

17.4 Method

17.4.1 Sample Selection

Our sample includes financial institutions listed on the Shanghai stock (SSE) and Shenzhen stock (SZSE) exchanges during the consecutive 5 years from 2016 to 2020. As one of the major mainland stock exchanges, the SSE includes main board shares, while the SZSE includes the small and medium enterprise (SME) board and ChiNext as well as the main board. The selection of financial institutions from both stock exchanges enables additional comparisons to be made on differences in financial institutions' reporting behavior. Second, the year 2016 is the year when the "Guidelines for Establishing the Green Financial System" were issued. The selection of the 2016–2020 study period provides a more recent period for examination than in previous studies. It also aligns with a period where increased promotion of environmental disclosures practices for the financial sector occurred both nationally and internationally, including the TCFD, and so provides a unique set of institutional arrangements for investigation. Our sample includes a total of 57 listed financial institutions covering the three main subsectors, banking, securities, and insurance, providing 285 firm-year observations over the study period. Table 17.1 summarizes the distributions by subsector and exchange of the financial institution in the study's sample.

17.4.2 Data Sources

The study involves manual data collection from financial institutions' annual and sustainability reports and use of secondary data collected from the CSMAR electronic database. "CSMAR," short for "China Stock Market & Accounting Research,"

Table 17.1 Financial institutions included in the sample by subsector and listing exchange

Type of institutions	No
Banks	23
Securities	28
Insurance	6
Total	57
SSE listed	42
SZSE listed	15
Total	57

is the most widely used electronic database for China-based economic and financial research. The database has been developed by GTA Information Technology Co. Ltd., a leading financial data services provider in China. CSMAR has been widely used in previous empirical studies for the collection of financial and nonfinancial data. In 2015, CSMAR released a new sub-database, the "China Listed Firm's Corporate Social Responsibility Research Database" (CSSR). Therefore, this study utilizes financial institutions' environmental disclosures derived from the CSSR database. CSSR contains nine categories of general and detailed sustainability and CSR information collected from China's listed firm's annual, sustainability, and environmental reports, including environmental sustainability information. After initial data collection, content analysis is applied to manually sort the environmental disclosures based on different information content as shown in Table 17.2.

17.4.3 Content Analysis and Measurement

Given its common and accepted use as a research methodology for analyzing sustainability or CSR disclosures in previous studies, we use content analysis to quantify financial institutions' environmental disclosures. Content analysis involves codifying qualitative and quantitative information into predefined categories to derive patterns in the presentation and reporting of information (Guthrie et al., 2004). The core requirement in performing content analysis is the development of a classification scheme with well-defined disclosure categories and decision rules (Hackston & Milne, 1996). In this study, an information scheme for analyzing the content of environmental disclosures is developed for financial institutions. The information scheme is developed based on the following considerations and procedures. Cuesta-González et al. (2006) and Yin (2018)[2] argue that financial institutions' environmental impacts differ from those of high polluting industries, having two major parts: those from their own business activities and those associated with their investment and financing activities. Therefore, an information scheme for analyzing financial institutions' environmental disclosures should include both parts. The July 2021 release of the "Guidelines" by the People's Bank of China and China Financial Standardization Technical Committee was the concluding result of the "Climate and Environmental Information Disclosure Pilot" established at the ninth UK–China Economic and Financial Dialogue by the Chinese and UK governments on December 15, 2017 (GFI, 2018). The "Guidelines" are based on the TCFD's recommendations on climate-related financial disclosures, combined with the actual country and institution situations, with the final information scheme as developed being shown in Table 17.2. In total, 28 indicators across 7 categories have been developed for measuring financial institutions' environmental disclosures. The first five categories are about environment-related qualitative information and

[2] In Chinese.

Table 17.2 Recommended environmental dimension disclosed by financial institutions

1. *Environment-related governance structure*	1. The existence of green finance committee at the board level
	2. The environment-related strategic objectives set up by the committee
	3. The board's analysis and judgment of environmental risks and opportunities
	4. The board's management, supervision, and discussion of environment-related issues
	5. The green finance-related positions set up at senior management level and main responsibilities and reporting routes
	6. The implementation and results of green finance-related work at the department
2. *Environment-related strategies and policies*	7. The development of internal management system related to environment
	8. Report on new policies and initiatives implemented during the year
	9. The implementation of national and local environmental policies, regulations, and standards
	10. Compliance with international climate and environment conventions, frameworks, initiatives, etc.
3. *Environment-related product and service innovation*	11. Green finance innovative products and services
	12. Environmental and social benefits of green product and service innovation
4. *Environmental risk management and process*	13. Processes for identifying and assessing environment-related risks
	14. Processes for managing and controlling environment-related risks
5. *Environment-related opportunities and risk*	15. Identify short-, medium-, and long-term environment-related risks and opportunities
	16. The impact of environmental risks on the business and strategy of financial institutions
	17. Measures taken by financial institutions to deal with environmental impacts and their effects
6. *Environmental impacts of investment and financing activities of financial institutions*	18. Summarize the overall investment and financing situation and its impact on the environment
	19. Changes in industry investment and financing structure compared with previous years and its impact on the environment
	20. Customer investment and financing and its impact on the environment
	21. Green investment assets managed on behalf of clients and their changes
	22. The implementation effect of green investment and financing policies
	23. Green investment and financing cases
	24. Green supply chain and its impact on the environment

(continued)

Table 17.2 (continued)

7. *Environmental impact of financial institution's own business activities*	25. Greenhouse gas emissions and natural resource consumption directly generated by operating (scope 1)
	26. Indirect greenhouse gas emissions and indirect natural resource consumption from purchased products and service (scope 2)
	27. Resources and energy consumption saved or replaced by online business, paperless office, building energy-saving transformation, and encouraging employees to choose public transportation
	28. Information on training activities or public welfare activities held to promote environmental awareness among staff and the general public, including number of activities, number of participants, and social impact

indicators. For each financial institution, we code "1" if an environmental item is disclosed and "0" otherwise. The score for environmental disclosure for each financial institution is calculated as the ratio of indicators disclosed to the total indicators that should be disclosed (Yusoff & Darus, 2014).

17.5 Results and Discussions

As required by the SSE and SZSE, listed financial firms are mandated to disclose CSR information. Based on the secondary data collected from CSRR, most financial institutions in the sample disclosed CSR information over the whole 2016–2020 period. This was in at least a subset of categories, including the protection of the interests of shareholders, creditors, customers, and employees, work safety, public relations and welfare, CSR system construction and improvement, and environmental sustainability. However, when compared to mainstream CSR categories, such as the protection of the various stakeholders' interests, a smaller proportion of the sample financial institutions disclosed information in the category of environmental sustainability over 2016–2020. As shown in Fig. 17.1, only 58.9% (168/285) of firm-year observations identify financial institution disclosure of information on environmental sustainability even though mandated by stock exchanges. The results show that, overall, financial institutions have not addressed enough attention to the reporting of environmental information. Also, compared to other CSR categories, environmental disclosure is still not a primary focus for financial institutions even at a time when international bodies, governments, and stock exchanges have recognized the financial sector's role in contributing to creating a green and low-carbon economy. Our analysis indicates external coercive pressures may not be strong enough and that financial institutions lack sufficient endogenous motivation to provide environmental information disclosures.

Examining environmental disclosures by China's financial institutions over time shows that the number of financial institutions making environmental disclosures is

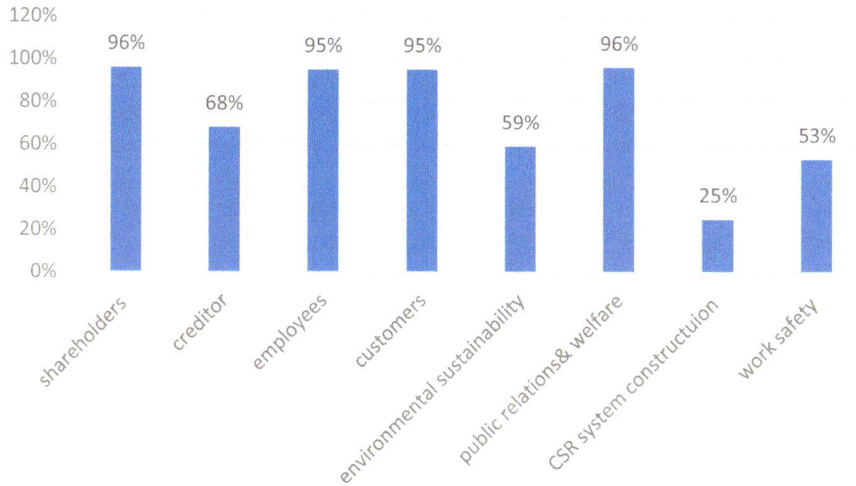

Fig. 17.1 Number of financial institutions disclosing CSR information by category

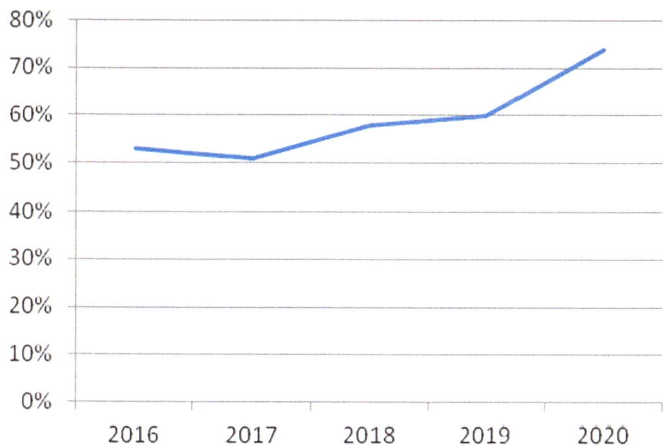

Fig. 17.2 Percentage of financial institutions disclosing environmental information by year

growing, increasing from 53% of the total sample in 2016 to 74% in 2020 (Fig. 17.2). The result indicates financial institutions' awareness of their role in environmental sustainability is deepening even though it is still not a primary focus, requiring that more and more financial institutions start disclosing environmental information.

According to the information scheme used for content analysis, total environmental disclosures are grouped into 7 main categories covering 28 indicators. Table 17.3 presents the Chinese financial institutions' disclosures of environmental information as measured by the number of indicators (from Table 17.2) reported by year. Therefore, for each financial institution, the minimum possible score is 0 and the maximum possible 28. However, as shown in Table 17.3, the performance of the sample financial institutions in terms of indicators reported is low. Over the 2016–2020 sample period, the mean score of 1.72 suggests disclosure of environmental information is still generally marginal as it is less than 6.15% of the maximum possible score. Considering next the environmental score as measured by the number of disclosed indicators by individual year, the mean score increases slightly from 2016 to 2020. However, it is still less than 7.5% of the possible maximum score in each year. Our analysis indicates that, while sample financial institutions have started to pay attention to their environmental behavior, the overall levels of environmental disclosures by sample institutions under current "green finance" institutional arrangements are inadequate.

A summary of environmental score over 2016–2020 by subsector is presented in Fig. 17.3. Banks have the highest mean score (2.64), followed by insurance institutions (2.17), with securities being the lowest (0.86). This suggests that banks are at the forefront in terms of financial institution environmental disclosure, consistent with some previous findings (e.g., Dong et al., 2021). The financial sector per se shows a certain degree of diversity, and in the Chinese context the financial sector is bank dominated. Therefore, the banks' essential role in the Chinese financial system gives them much more visibility than other financial institutions (Alberici & Querci, 2016). The higher level of environmental information disclosure of the sample banks may derive from the relatively advanced status of green financial supervision in the banking industry. Following the issue of the "Green Credit Guidelines" in 2012 and reinforced by the "Green Finance Policy" in 2016, banks have engaged in environmental sustainability more actively than other financial institution subsectors. As concluded by Dong et al. (2021), the banking subsector's engagement in sustainability reporting has been institutionalized, as the practice has been adopted both over time and consistent with general regulatory pressures.

Table 17.4 presents a simple summary of financial institutions' environmental disclosures by information category. Scores for "environmental impact of financial institution's own business activities," as measured by the number of indicators reported, have the highest mean score (1.11), while the "qualitative indicators" category, which includes environment-related governance structure, environmental risk management and process, environmental-related strategies and policies, environment-related product and service innovation, and environment-related opportunities and risk, receives the lowest score (0.25). The score for "environmental impacts of investment and financing activities" is 0.45. This suggests that the

Table 17.3 Mean scores for environmental disclosure indicators over the study period

Year	Minimum	Maximum	Mean	Std. dev.
2016	0	7	1.54	1.89
2017	0	6	1.54	1.79
2018	0	6	1.72	1.84
2019	0	6	1.78	1.82
2020	0	6	2.02	1.77
2016–2020	0	7	1.72	1.82

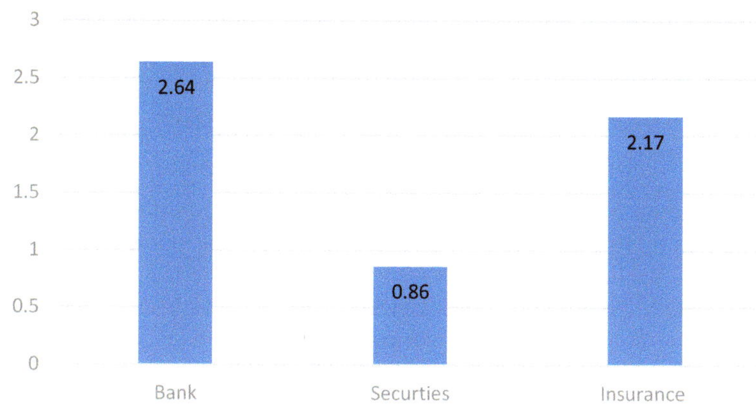

Fig. 17.3 Mean score of environmental disclosures by subsector

Table 17.4 Mean scores for key areas of environmental disclosures by category

	Min	Max	Mean	Std. dev.
Qualitative indicators	0	3	0.25	0.50
Environmental impacts of investment and financing activities of financial institutions	0	3	0.45	0.72
Environmental impact of financial institution's own business activities	0	4	1.11	1.23

sample institutions are not managing their environmental issues comprehensively. Most financial institutions (51.5%) disclose information on the direct environmental impact of their own business activities due to the availability of such data. However, the overall environmental impact of financial institutions is not fully reflected in their disclosure.

17.6 Conclusion

Against the background of the TCFD's promotion of climate-related disclosures for financial and nonfinancial companies, this study examined the environmental disclosures of financial institutions in China over the 2016–2020 period and presented preliminary evidence on the state of environmental disclosures by these financial institutions. A motivation is that examination of financial sector environmental reporting in previous studies is limited compared to that focusing on traditionally polluting industries. The Chinese financial sector provides a unique institutional context for study due to its recent exposure to institutional pressures, such as the 2012 "Green Credit Guidelines," the 2016 "Guiding Opinions on Establishing a Green Finance System," the "Climate and Environmental Information Disclosure

Pilot" in 2017, and the recently released "Guidelines for Financial Institutions Environmental Information Disclosure."

Our analysis of environmental disclosures reveals that disclosure of environmental information is still marginal within the Chinese financial sector, although increasing over the study period. Compared to other categories of CSR, environmental information is still not a primary focus of financial institutions. However, their awareness of their role in environmental sustainability is deepening due to the institutional pressures to which the sector is exposed. In addition, our investigation identifies that sampled financial institutions are not managing their environmental issues comprehensively, with only 51.5% of these institutions disclosing information on the direct environmental impact of their own business activities, followed by lesser reporting of the environmental impacts of their investment and financing activities and limited reporting of qualitative indicators. Of the 28 environmental indicators considered, the "top three" most frequently disclosed include *indicator 26* "Indirect greenhouse gas emissions and indirect natural resource consumption from purchased products and service (scope 2)"; *indicator 25* "Greenhouse gas emissions and natural resource consumption directly generated by operating (scope 1)"; and *indicator 27* "Resources and energy consumption saved or replaced by online business." Overall, this study fills gaps in studies on CSR reporting and environmental reports, providing preliminary evidence and a better understanding of the environmental disclosure within China's financial sector in the context of green finance and China's transition into a green economy.

This study provides preliminary evidence on the financial sector's environmental reporting practices in the Chinese context. Future studies could provide more comprehensive or empirical investigation in different institutional contexts. The implications of this study are that as a capital intermediary, lender, money manager, and risk evaluator, the financial sector needs to improve its awareness of its role in environmental sustainability and manage environmental issues in a more systematic way. Furthermore, an increased level of environmental information disclosure for financial institutions should be promoted by industrial policy and regulatory means.

References

Alberici, A., & Querci, F. (2016). The quality of disclosures on environmental policy: The profile of financial intermediaries. *Corporate Social Responsibility and Environmental Management, 23*, 283–296.

Arena, C., & Michelon, G. (2018). A matter of control or identity? Family firms' environmental reporting decisions along the corporate life cycle. *Business Strategy and the Environment, 27*, 1596–1608.

Bose, S., Khan, H. Z., Rashid, A., et al. (2018). What drives green banking disclosure? An institutional and corporate governance perspective. *Asia Pacific Journal of Management, 35*(2), 501–527.

Branco, M. C., & Rodrigues, L. L. (2006). Communication of corporate social responsibility by Portuguese banks: A legitimacy theory perspective. *Corporate Communications: An International Journal, 11*(3), 232–248.

Brogi, M., & Lagasio, V. (2019). Environmental, social, and governance and company profitability: Are financial intermediaries different? *Corporate Social Responsibility and Environmental Management, 26*, 576–587.

Carè, R. (2017). Exploring environmental disclosure in banks. Evidence from the Euro area. *ACRN Oxford Journal of Finance and Risk Perspectives, 6*(2), 18–40.

Chen, J. C., & Roberts, R. W. (2010). Toward a more coherent understanding of the organization – Society relationship: A theoretical consideration for social and environmental accounting research. *Journal of Business Ethics, 97*, 651–665.

Chih, H.-L., Chih, H.-H., & Chen, T.-Y. (2010). On the determinants of corporate social responsibility, international evidence on the financial industry. *Journal of Business Ethics, 93*, 115–135.

Cuesta-González, M., Munõz-Torres, M., & Fernández-Izquierdo, M. Á. (2006). Analysis of social performance in the Spanish financial industry through public data. A proposal. *Journal of Business Ethics, 69*(3), 289–304.

Darus, F., Yusoff, H., Azhari, N. K., & Mohd. (2013). Environmental disclosure of Islamic financial institutions (IFIs): Preliminary evidence from Malaysia. *Journal of Energy Technologies and Policy, 3*(11), 433–439.

Day, R., & Woodward, T. (2009). CSR reporting and the UK financial services sector. *Journal of Applied Accounting Research, 10*(3), 159–175.

Dong, S., Xu, L., & McIver, R. (2021). China's financial sector sustainability and "green finance" disclosures. *Sustainability Accounting, Management and Policy Journal, 12*(2), 353–384.

DRC and IISD. (2015). *Greening China's financial system*. Retrieved: www.iisd.org/pdf/2014/greening_china_financial_system_en.pdf

Gallego-Álvarez, I., & Pucheta-Martínez, M. C. (2019). Environmental strategy in the global banking industry within the varieties of capitalism approach: The moderating role of gender diversity and board members with specific skills. *Business Strategy and the Environment, 29*(2), 1–14.

Green Finance Initiative (GFI). (2018). *UK-China Climate and Environmental Information Disclosure Pilot Action Plan*. Retrieved: https://www.ukchinagreen.org/publication/uk-china-climate-and-environmental-information-disclosure-pilot-action-plan/?nowprocket=1

G20 Green Finance Study Group (GFSG). (2016). *G20 green finance synthesis report*.

Green Finance Task Force. (2015). *Establishing China's green financial system*. Retrieved: http://www.unepfi.org/fileadmin/communications/EstablishingChinasGreenFinancialSystem.pdf

Guthrie, R. P., Yongvanich, K., & Ricceri, F. (2004). Using content analysis as a research method to inquire into intellectual capital reporting. *Journal of Intellectual Capital, 5*(2), 282–293.

Hackston, D., & Milne, M. J. (1996). Some determinants of social and environmental disclosures in New Zealand companies. *Accounting, Auditing & Accountability Journal, 9*(1), 77–108.

Hossain, D. M., Bir, A., Momen, A., et al. (2018). Disclosure of green banking issues in the annual reports: A study on Bangladeshi banks. *Middle East Journal of Business, 11*(1), 19–30.

Jain, A., Keneley, M., & Thomson, D. (2015). Voluntary CSR disclosure works! Evidence from Asia-Pacific banks. *Social Responsibility Journal, 11*(1), 2–18.

Jizi, M. I., Salama, A., Dixon, R., et al. (2014). Corporate governance and corporate social responsibility disclosure: Evidence from the US banking sector. *Journal of Business Ethics, 125*, 601–615.

Kılıç, M., & Kuzey, C. (2019). Determinants of climate change disclosures in the Turkish banking industry. *International Journal of Bank Marketing, 37*(3), 901–926.

Kolk, A., Walhain, S., & Van de Wateringen, S. (2001). Environmental reporting by the fortune global 250: Exploring the influence of nationality and sector. *Business Strategy and the Environment, 10*, 15–28.

KPMG. (2015, 2017). *The KPMG survey of corporate responsibility reporting*. Retrieved: https://home.kpmg.com/xx/en/home/insights/2017/10/the-kpmg-survey-of-corporate responsibility-reporting-2017.html

Ministry of Environmental Protection of the People's Republic of China (MEP). (2016). *The guiding opinions on establishing a green finance system*. Retrieved from: http://www.mep.gov.cn/gkml/hbb/gwy/201611/t20161124_368163.htm

Pathak, T., & Tewari, R. (2017). Theoretical grounding for sustainability reporting: A comparison between Indian and European banks. *ACRN Oxford Journal of Finance and Risk Perspectives, 6*(3), 107–120.

Pucheta-Martínez, M. C., & Gallego-Álvarez, I. (2018). Environmental reporting policy and corporate structures: An international analysis. *Corporate Social Responsibility and Environmental Management, 25*, 788–798.

Pucheta-Martínez, M. C., & López-Zamora, B. (2018). Engagement of directors representing institutional investors on environmental disclosure. *Corporate Social Responsibility and Environmental Management, 25*, 1108–1120.

Ryszawska, B., & Zabawa, J. (2018). The environmental responsibility of the world's largest banks. *Economics and Business, 32*, 51–64.

Scholtens, B. (2009). Corporate social responsibility in the international banking industry. *Journal of Business Ethics, 86*, 159–175.

Shan, G., & Xu, L. (2012). Do internal governance mechanisms impact on firm performance? Empirical evidence from the financial industry in China. *Journal of Asia-Pacific Business, 13*, 114–142.

Shanghai Stock Exchange (SSE). (2008). *Notice on strengthening social responsibility of listed companies*. Retrieved: http://english.sse.com.cn/aboutsse/news/newsrelease/c/3993550.shtml

Sun, J. X., Wang, F., & Wang, F. G. (2015). Community institutions and initial diffusion of corporate social responsibility practices in China's banking industry. *Management and Organization Review, 11*, 441–468.

Szombatfalvy, L. (2010). *The greatest challenges of our time* (pp. 18–20). Ekerlids.

Tarna, K. (2001). Reporting on the environment: Current practice in the financial services sector. In J. J. Bouma, M. Jeucken, & L. Klinkers (Eds.), *Sustainable banking: The greening of finance*. Taylor & Francis Group. http://ebookcentral.proquest.com/lib/unisa/detail.action?docID=1741729

TCFD. (2016a). *Phase I Report of the Task Force on Climate-Related Financial Disclosures*. https://assets.bbhub.io/company/sites/60/2020/10/Phase_I_Report_v15.pdf

TCFD. (2016b). *Recommendations of the Task Force on Climate-related Financial Disclosures*. https://assets.bbhub.io/company/sites/60/2020/10/16_1221_TCFD_Report_Letter.pdf

TCFD. (2017). *Final Report: Recommendations of the Task Force on Climate-related Financial Disclosures*. https://assets.bbhub.io/company/sites/60/2021/10/FINAL-2017-TCFD-Report.pdf

TCFD. (2021). *Status Report: Task Force on Climate-related Financial Disclosures*. https://assets.bbhub.io/company/sites/60/2021/07/2021-TCFD-Status_Report.pdf

Thompson, P., & Cowton, C. (2004). Bringing the environment into bank lending: Implications for environmental reporting. *The British Accounting Review, 36*(2), 197–218.

United Nations. (2015). *Transforming our world: The 2030 Agenda for Sustainable Development*. Retrieved: http://www.un.org/ga/search/view_doc.asp?symbol=A/RES/70/1&Lang=E

Vilar, V. H., & Simão, J. (2015). CSR disclosure on the web: Major themes in the banking sector. *International Journal of Social Economics, 42*(3), 296–318.

Weber, O. (2014). The financial sector's impact on sustainable development. *Journal of Sustainable Finance & Investment, 4*(1), 1–8.

Weber, O. (2017). Corporate sustainability and financial performance of Chinese banks. *Sustainability Accounting, Management and Policy Journal, 8*(3), 358–385.

Weber, O., Diaz, M., & Schwegler, R. (2014). Corporate social responsibility of the financial industry – Strengths, weaknesses and the impact on sustainable development. *Sustainable Development, 22*, 321–335.

Yang, H. H., Craig, R., & Farley, A. (2015). A review of Chinese and English language studies on corporate environmental reporting in China. *Critical Perspectives on Accounting, 28*, 30–48.

Yin, H. (2018). Financial institutions environmental information disclosure: Connotation, significance, current situation and implementation suggestions. *China's Banking Industry, 3*, 50–74. (In Chinese).

Yusoff, H., & Darus, F. (2014). Mitigation of climate change and prevention of pollution activities: Environmental disclosure practice in Islamic financial institutions. *Procedia – Social and Behavioral Sciences, 145*, 195–203.

Zabawa, J. (2018). *Reporting of environmental information in the largest banks in Poland. Scope, measurement, formal and legal condition* (Research Papers of Wrocław University of Economics, Nr 520). Prace Naukowe Uniwersytetu Ekonomicznego we Wrocław.

Part IV
Sustainable FinTech

Chapter 18
Towards Its Digital and Sustainable Economy: A Review of Recent Fintech Policies and Developments in China

Lei Xu

18.1 Introduction

This chapter reviews the recent Fintech policies and developments in China to support its transformation towards its digital and sustainable economy. Given China's leading position in Fintech investments and market growth, a review of its recent Fintech policies and developments seems necessary to boost research in related areas. This review covers key aspects in Fintech, which include crypto currency, peer-to-peer (P2P) lending, supply chain finance (SCF), payment platforms, and banking enhancement.

Recent scientific and technological breakthroughs have greatly promoted Fintech development based on advances in big data, cloud computing, artificial intelligence, and block chain. The Financial Stability Board (FSB) defines Fintech as "technologically enabled innovation in financial services that could result in new business models, applications, processes or products with an associated material effect on financial markets and institutions and the provision of financial services" (FSB website). Further promoted by its Big Data Development Plan 2016–2020, China has noticeably integrated information technology (IT) and financial services. According to China Academy of Information and Communications Technology (2020), well-diversified applications of Fintech, such as that in supply chain finance, have fundamentally changed traditional firm operations, provided new opportunities for business growth, and enhanced efficiency in allocating financial resources.

China, the largest bank-based economy, has also become the forefront leader and the largest market in Fintech (Wharton, 2019). In accordance with the country's 14th Five-Year Plan, the People's Bank of China (PBC) recently introduced the Fintech Development Plan (2022–2025) (PBC, 2021a) to further promote Fintech

---

L. Xu (✉)
UniSA Business, University of South Australia, Adelaide, SA, Australia
e-mail: lei.xu@unisa.edu.au

K. Wendt, B. Villhauer (eds.), *Sustainable Wealth Management*, Sustainable Finance,
https://doi.org/10.1007/978-3-031-55505-3_18

development with clear principles of being digital driven, smart for the people, green and low carbon, fair, and inclusive, to achieve leapfrog enhancement of its Fintech level and core competitiveness. In comparison to the Fintech Development Plan (2019–2021) (PBC, 2019), which is the country's first dedicated Fintech strategy by finance regulators, the new plan has also updated Fintech principles from integrity and innovation, safety and controllability, inclusive to people's livelihood, openness, and win-win based. The Fintech Development Plan (2022–2025) better focuses on digital transformation of China's real economy, green finance, and financial inclusion.

18.2 China Bans Crypto Currency

18.2.1 Crypto Currency and Anti-corruption

The ongoing corruption scandals may be a hard problem to resolve in the largest emerging market. One the one hand, government officials often control key resources for firms, especially the private ones, to compete and to grow in the marketplace (Xu et al., 2011; He et al., 2019, 2021; Li et al., 2020a). Firms have to rely on political connections, which may be developed through bribery, to access rents, government resources, and protection (Jiang & Nie, 2014; Liu, 2014; Pan & Tian, 2020). On the other, government officials often show endemic corruption, involving financing of bribes, for personal advancement in the government bureaucracies (Kahana & Liu, 2010).

China's anti-corruption has been going on for decades, which may meaningfully reduce rent-seeking and improve firm productivity and efficiency of its economy (He, 2000; Kong et al., 2020). Despite the effectively and widely imposed anti-money laundering rules, real-name bank accounts, real-name real estate registration, regular reporting by carders to their supervisory agencies on personal assets, cash transaction limitations, and so on by various regulators within the country, corruption and the aggravation of bribery have experienced structural changes in modern China (Ko & Weng, 2012).

Crypto currency, such as Bitcoin, may effectively provide additional means for capital flight by converting RMB into US dollar (Ju et al., 2015). Crypto currency, such as Bitcoin, has been so technically advanced and disruptive for its global operation and decentralised P2P system that it can serve various illegal purposes (European Central Bank, 2012). Although China prohibited, on 5 December 2013, financial institutions and payment firms to transact in Bitcoin, the capital flight could still escalate without Chinese regulator's detection (Ju et al., 2015). The Central Commission for Discipline Inspection (CCDI) announced that crypto currency-related activities, such as production and trading, often involve corrupted officials (CCDI, 2022).

It can be ironic that most of the crypto currency trading could have taken place in China and US markets, and the Shanghai-based BTC China was once the largest bitcoin exchange in the world (Yermack, 2014). Back to early 2017, around 90% of Bitcoin transactions took place in China, signalling further alerts to its regulators.

The regulators have eventually banned crypto currency in China. PBC and other regulators jointly issued warnings to crypto currency traders and stopped initial coin offering (ICO) on 4 September 2017 (PBC, 2017). In 2018, PBC illegalised crypto currency and its trading platforms (Xinhua, 2018). However, in the meantime, Hong Kong and Japan officially allowed more crypto currency trading activities. In 2021, PBC further tightened the ban on crypto currency within the country (PBC, 2020b).

18.2.2 Crypto Currency and Exchange Control

Given China's state ownership of the banking system (Allen et al., 2005; Xu & Lin, 2007; Shan & Xu, 2012a; Fu et al., 2015), the state-owned commercial banks (SOCBs) are often required by the PBC and State Administration of Foreign Exchange (SAFE) to help maintain the exchange control measures as well as the RMB exchange rate. However, it can be hard for the PBC and SAFE to monitor crypto currency transactions. Since none of the SOCBs or joint stock commercial banks (JSCBs), which control over 80% of market share within the country, is involved in the crypto currency business, the regulators may find it impossible to crack down the money laundering practices or capital flight through the established means.

Therefore, crypto currency may impose severe threats on the exchange control regime of the country. The disruptive blockchain technology, when applied on crypto currencies, can bring direct challenge to existing capital control across borders. The existing exchange control rules legally allow capital flows across the border through either qualified foreign financial institutions (QFIIs) or qualified domestic institutional investors (QDIIs). All other capital flows across the border are subject to SAFE approval on case-by-case basis. Figure 18.1 illustrates the tangible threat by crypto currency to China's exchange control regime.

Since RMB is not a free currency in the world, PBC and SAFE's delicate balance between effective exchange control and gradual internationalisation of RMB may also be seriously challenged by crypto currency. Despite China's total ban on crypto currency activities in recent years, a growing number of the impactful global banks, such as those on the Wall Street, have widely expanded into crypto currency transactions. Arguably, EI Salvador has made Bitcoin its legal tender since 2021. The diversified legislation on crypto currency may also further challenge China's exchange control regime as well as its full introduction of digital RMB in the foreseeable future.

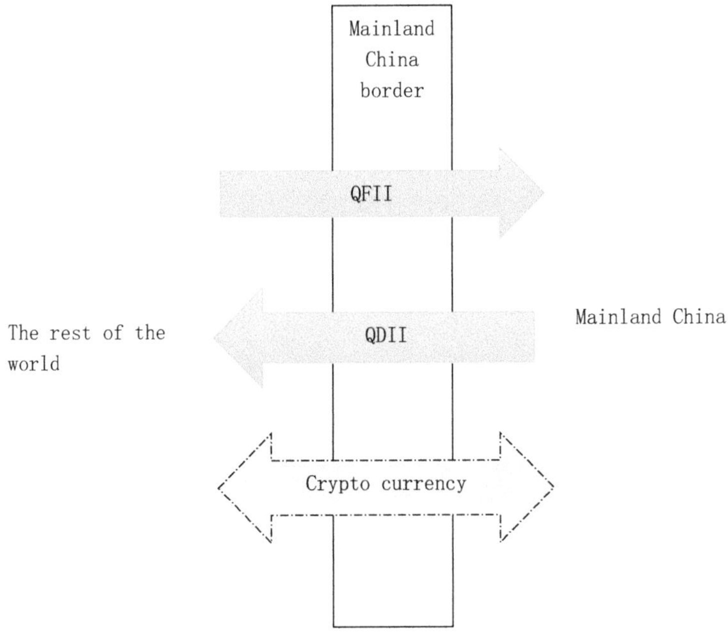

Fig. 18.1 Crypto currency and its challenge to exchange control

18.2.3 Crypto Currency and Environmental Concerns

In addition, crypto currency can also impose environmental concerns on the regulators. The production of crypto currency consumes more energy than that of gold mining (Wang et al., 2022). For example, the energy consumption on production of Bitcoin increased from 4.8 Twh in 2017 to 73.12 Twh in 2019 (Zade et al., 2019). To make things worse, the trading and confirmation of crypto currency can further cause crypto damage to the environment (Krause & Tolaymat, 2018; Huynh et al., 2022). Crypto currency, therefore, is subject to significant concerns on environmental issues, which may further challenge the meaning or existence of this Fintech product (Corbet et al., 2021).

Such a situation can be more demanding in China's context. On the one hand, China has severe environmental issues and subsequently imposed strict rules on environmental protection (Dong & Xu, 2016; Li et al., 2020b; Wu & Xu, 2022). On the other, crypto currency, which has been wildly growing due to under-regulation, would impose higher demands on energy consumption in the largest green gas emission country in the world. Electricity, however, is mostly thermos generated in China (Xu et al., 2021). As a result, the total ban of crypto currency seems a must towards the policymakers.

18.3 P2P and Related Issues

18.3.1 Shadow Banking and P2P Lending

Since the Fiscal Stimulus Plan in 2008, shadow banking has been growing so fast that such alternative financing activities have threatened the stability of China's financial system (Li et al., 2014; Li & Lin, 2016; Allen & Gu, 2021). Chinese banks, although less efficient than their western counterparts, have traditionally controlled over 90% of financial resources within the country (Xu & Lin, 2007; Shan & Xu, 2012a, b). On the one hand, the dominant SOCBs have historically incurred huge amount of non-performing loans (NPLs) and are often conduits of government policies, which may incur further financial losses (Xu & Lin, 2007; Shan & Xu, 2012b; Xu et al., 2015). On the other, the PBC creates the largest interest rate gap, between deposits and loans, for the banking sector through its interest rate regimes (Xu & Lin, 2007, 2008; Wu & Xu, 2022). In other words, Chinese banks may enjoy larger net interest margins (NIMs) than that the market could entail.

The fast development of Fintech and the contractionary monetary policies jointly push various shadow banking practices to expand (Chen et al., 2018; Luo et al., 2022). P2P lending platforms allow the lenders and borrowers to get around the banks, which have traditionally escalated borrowers' thresholds and supressed depositors' returns. Chinese firms, especially the small- and medium-sized enterprises (SMEs) and those of private ownership, are often significantly disadvantaged to access bank loans in the largest bank-based economy (He et al., 2019; Wu & Xu, 2020; Li et al., 2022). When banks actively commit to wealth management products (WMPs) (Chen et al., 2018; Allen et al., 2019; Arora & Zhang, 2019), state-owned enterprises (SOEs) borrow from the banks and re-lend to private firms at much higher rates (Yao et al., 2019); P2P lending platforms, therefore, became an outstanding form of shadow banking practice by the unsatisfied bank depositors and borrowers as well as arbitrage players in the money market (Lu et al., 2015; Allen & Gu, 2021).

18.3.2 P2P Lending Advantages

The lack of regulation also induced over 10,000 P2P lending platforms that have been launched within a time window of 13 years. From the first P2P lending platform, PaiPaiDai, in June 2007, to the peak number of around 5000 platforms in 2015, and to zero in November 2021 (Wei, 2020). The initial implicit support by Chinese authorities, coupled with high mobile phone penetration and related technology, had driven explosive growth of P2P lending platforms between 2014 and 2017 (Sutton & Taylor, 2020).

Compared to conventional banks, P2P lending platforms have been advantaged in the following aspects. First, financial institutions, especially the banks, are most heavily regulated within the country. Their capital adequacy ratios (CARs) are pushed higher and higher following China's implementation of Basel I and Basel III (Xu & Lin, 2007; Fu et al., 2015; Xu et al., 2015). In addition to the global banking regulations, the China Banking Regulatory Commission (CBRC) and its successor China Banking and Insurance Regulatory Commission (CBIRC) strictly prohibit bank funds from flowing into the problematic A-share markets (Xu & Lin, 2007; Wu & Xu, 2020). Furthermore, the PBC also mandates compulsory reserve deposit ratios, where Chinese banks are often required to maintain a loan to deposit ratio less than 75%, to assure the safety and liquidity of the banking system. However, due to the lack of regulation, P2P lending platforms can be started by various entities without attending the regulatory costs imposed on the banks. As a result, P2P lending platforms may directly compete with the banks with apparent advantages. Second, P2P lending platforms can target the SMEs, private firms, or individuals which are conventionally biased by the banks. P2P lenders adopt alternative means, such as the business owners' or individual borrowers' residence, cars, spending behaviour, and other personal information for credit rationing purpose, different from that adopted by the conventional banks (Lin et al., 2017). P2P lending platforms, therefore, can fill a large gap in the lending market. Third, both the P2P lenders and borrowers may benefit from the market rates. Different from the banks, whose deposits and lending rates are mostly the same as regulated by the PBC across the country, P2P lending platforms may bring 12–15% annual rate of return to investors and require 25–30% annualised costs to borrowers (Wei, 2020).

18.3.3 P2P Lending Platforms Threaten the Bank-Based Financial System

When P2P lending platforms achieved around 3 trillion RMB annual volumes in 2015, they imposed direct threat to the Chinese banks (Xinhua, 2020). The legal system in China, mostly following the Glass-Steagall Act (1933), requires its banks to focus on deposits and loans, and most banks rely on interest incomes for profitability purpose. In the meantime, the PBC through its interest rate regime imposes a healthy profit margin for the banks. The profitability then would allow the government to use the banks as conduits for various policies, such as the social harmony loans, and to absorb the NPLs from their lending practice to SOEs. However, P2P lending platforms can lead to a noticeable drain of core deposits away from the banks. When depositors find that they can easily make more than three times investment returns through P2P platforms than that from their bank accounts, they withdraw their bank deposits. Subsequently banks' profitability and capability to absorb potential losses are weakened. Furthermore, the borrowers are less constrained by their loan purposes on P2P platforms than those borrowing from banks. In other words, the borrowers on P2P may commit to highly speculative activities, such as the reported speculation of agricultural products, commodities, real estate, shares, and so on. The borrowers' expectation of high profits can also induce the P2P lending rates to go higher. The Supreme Court has to mandate reasonable range of private lending rates in the country (The Supreme People's Court, 2015, 2020).

These practices by participants of P2P lending platforms can also effectively challenge the policymakers. For example, many SOEs take advantage of their better access to cheaper bank loans, re-lend through P2P platforms at higher interest rates, and behave as non-bank financial institutions. This phenomenon can significantly reduce the effectiveness of government policies and change the purpose of bank loans in practice, adding more risks to the banks and diversifying the SOEs from their core businesses. In addition, the firewall between banking and stock markets can be easily circumvented. If we link the Fintech applications between crypto currency and P2P lending platforms, then China's legal regime over its financial system could be further challenged.

Due to the lack of regulation, P2P lending platforms have incurred other unexpected issues. For example, Panzi scheme can be implemented through P2P lending platforms. Ezubo is one of impactful cases of Panzi scheme (The Wall Street Journal, 2017). In addition, when P2P lending platforms collapse, group protests by millions of victims have also been witnessed, suggesting various social issues as consequences. The lack of regulation can also lead the P2P lending platforms to focus more on short-term benefits than effective risk control. Dozens of P2P lending platforms encountered various problems on monthly basis between 2014 and 2019, with a peak of 200 in August 2018 (Sutton & Taylor, 2020). The intensive exposure of challenging issues by P2P lending platforms in 2015 and 2016 forced CBRC to consider tightening its regulation on these platforms (Wei, 2020).

18.3.4 Closing Down of P2P Lending Platforms

CBRC, the Ministry of Industry and Information Technology, the Ministry of Public Security, and the State Information Office jointly issued the No. 1 Document regulating P2P lending platforms in 2016 (CBRC, 2016a). This document confined P2P lending platforms to providing information between lenders and borrowers. In the meantime, this document prevented fund raising, credit enhancement services, or guarantees by P2P lending platforms.

Following this document, various other rulings came into effect, such as the State Council's No. 21 Document (State Council, 2016) and CBRC's No. 11 Document of the same year (CBRC, 2016a, b). The State Council mandated that, in particular, real estate developers and agents are not allowed to participate P2P lending platforms, equity funding by internet finance is prohibited, and third-party payment platforms cannot join P2P lending platforms (State Council, 2016). Although there has been a lack of conclusive empirical evidence or academic literature on the State Council's focuses, it was alarming to the regulators that P2P lending platforms expanded far beyond reasonable business scopes. Without any formal government policy, China effectively closed down all P2P lending platforms in November 2019.

18.4 China Supports Supply Chain Finance (SCF)

18.4.1 Financialisation of Chinese Firms

Application of Fintech can greatly enhance firm access to financial resources. However, when too many firms are diversified away from their core businesses in real economy, there can be systematic risks (Allen & Carletti, 2013). In addition, sizable financialisation can eventually damage firm innovation and profitability (Orhangazi, 2008). Chinese firms, including SOEs, commonly experience declining profitability in their routine businesses and widely participate in the speculative real estate sector (Xu et al., 2016). Listed firms commonly resort to investment properties to realise profits in their operations (Li, 2018). Coupled with the crypto currency and P2P lending platform issues discussed above, China may risk its "world factory" competitiveness in a fast-changing world market, especially when facing market volatilities following the Trade War in 2018 and the COVID-19 pandemic in 2020 (Xu et al., 2022).

18.4.2 SCF and the Real Economy

As another application of Fintech, SCF has been fast growing in China since the global financial crisis (GFC) in 2008 (Lin & Zhang, 2020; Song et al., 2020). SCF can be particularly meaningful towards digital transformation of the ecosystems of suppliers, manufacturers, distributors, and customers (Danny et al., 2010). Besides designing the SCF, the core firms organically integrate financing activities and business operations in the SCF-based network (Wuttke et al., 2019). In other words, SCF allows better management of material, information, and cash flows (Liebl et al., 2016; Pan et al., 2020).

SCF may sustainably serve the growth of China's real economy. Given the importance of its manufacturing sector, SCF can speed up firm capital structure adjustment, improve firm liquidity, speed up cash turnovers, lower financing costs, and significantly improve firm values (Liebl et al., 2016; Xu et al., 2022; Pan et al., 2022). As an effective short-term financing means and an important dimension of sustainable supply chain management, core firms take advantage of their credit rating, expected cash flows, and bank loans and provide financing to the supply chain. Since upstream and downstream firms in supply chains are often SMEs, which are traditionally biased in their access to vital financial resources for survival and development purposes (Xu & Lin, 2007; Fu et al., 2015; Wu & Xu, 2020), SCF allows efficient allocation of vital resources and continuous investments, collaboration, and contractual relationships (Zhang et al., 2020). Empirical evidence further suggests that SCF contributes to better investment efficiency, rather than overinvestment, enhanced firm values (Pan et al., 2020), reduced firm diversification by private and non-manufacturing firms, lower agency costs, higher production efficiency (Xu et al., 2022), enhanced financial strengths and competitive advantages, lower financing costs, and higher firm values (Pan et al., 2022), which are significantly meaningful for sustainably high-quality economic growth.

18.4.3 Policy Support to SCF

Given that SCF also allows the banks to better support the real economy, the CBIRC mandates that SCF must serve the country's industrial policies (CBIRC, 2019). SCF has recently been expected by policymakers to play an increasing role in consolidating supply chains and serving the real economy (Xu et al., 2022). Similarly, the PBC requires the banks to closely work with firms in supply chains and enhance support to real economy (PBC, 2016, 2020a, b). The State Council also encourages innovations of SCF and supply chains (State Council, 2017). Therefore, further growth and application of SCF may be expected in the foreseeable future.

18.5 Payment Platforms

Fintech has also triggered a bottom-up liberation on market interest rates through payment platforms that bear deposit features, which further expose banks to core deposit drains (Buchak et al., 2021). Fintech has brought competition outside the conventional banking sector. For example, Yu'ebao by AliPay offers much higher rates of return than bank deposits and has been very popular among Chinese households. Similarly, WeChat Pay by Tencent Group has diversified trillions of RMB deposits away from the banks.

Coupled with explosive growth of online products and services, payment platforms, especially AliPay and WeChat Pay, have successfully converted China from a cash-based economy to a cashless one in recent years. Nowadays, AliPay, WeChat Pay, and Union Pay are popular payment means around the world, with over a billion users each. Although the USA initiated a revolution in payments decades ago through stripes and cards, China has taken a lead in digital payments and reshaped the world (PBC, 2018; Klein, 2020). The PBC has experimented digital RMB usage in selected regions (PBC, 2021b) and would further regulate the payment platforms to avoid payment market monopolisation and to facilitate wide implementation, and even internationalisation, of digital RMB in the foreseeable future (PBC, 2021c).

18.6 Banking Enhancement

Chinese banks widely commit to innovative Fintech research and application. The adoption of Fintech may effectively improve SMEs' access to bank loans (Sheng, 2021) and lower the credit risks among Chinese banks (Cheng & Qu, 2020; Katsiampa et al., 2022). Recent empirical evidence suggests that Chinese banks heavily invest into Fintech and achieve patents. Although in the short term, banks may need to report less profits, Fintech capabilities can improve performance in the long term (Zhao et al., 2022). In addition, adoption of Fintech may help the banks better price their green loans, which are further meaningful towards sustainable growth of China's real economy (Dong et al., 2021, 2022; Wu & Xu, 2022).

18.7 Conclusion

Fintech allows China to compete with more advantages in the world market. The fast-evolving technology and its application have brought profound changes to people's life in a short time window. As the largest emerging economy, China has provided rich soil for the development of Fintech. After years of trial and error, China has learnt lessons and achieved noticeable progress in Fintech. Fintech is targeted to serve its real economy rather than financing means for speculative or virtual growth purposes.

Fintech also allows China to develop in its own way, different from other major economies. Aiming at enhanced financial inclusion and greener economy, China would, through its Fintech development blueprints, better achieve its Sustainable Development Goals (SDGs). The organic integration of Fintech and China's SDGs has been embodied in its Fintech Development Plan (2022–2025). Compared to the application of Fintech in the western countries, China seems to have clearer understanding of Fintech targets. Its strengthened regulation, such as that through regulatory technology (Regtech), and active support to Fintech applications can bring meaningful digital changes into the Asian era.

References

Allen, F., & Carletti, E. (2013). What is system risk? *Journal of Money, Credit and Banking, 45*, 121–127.

Allen, F., & Gu, X. (2021). Shadow banking in China compared to other countries. *The Manchester School, 89*(5), 407–419.

Allen, F., Qian, J., & Qian, M. (2005). Law, finance, and economic growth in China. *Journal of Financial Economics, 77*, 57–116.

Allen, F., Qian, Y., Tu, G., & Yu, F. (2019). Entrusted loans: A close look at China's shadow banking system. *Journal of Financial Economics, 133*, 18–41.

Arora, R., & Zhang, Q. (2019). Banking in the shadows: A comparative study of China and India. *Australian Economic History Review, 59*(1), 103–131.

Buchak, G., Hu, J., & Wei, S. (2021). *FinTech as a financial liberator* (NBER working paper 29448). https://www.nber.org/papers/w29448. Accessed 15 Jan 2022.

Central Commission for Discipline Inspection (CCDI). (2022, March 24). *Pay close attention to the corruption and other issues behind virtual currency mining* (in Chinese).

Chen, K., Ren, J., & Zha, T. (2018). The nexus of monetary policy and shadow banking in China. *American Economic Review, 108*(12), 3891–3936.

Cheng, M., & Qu, Y. (2020). Does bank FinTech reduce credit risk? Evidence from China. *Pacific-Basin Finance Journal, 43*, 101398.

China Academy of Information and Communications Technology (CAICT). (2020). *China Fintech ecological white paper*. http://www.caict.ac.cn/kxyj/qwfb/bps/202009/t20200918_347039.htm (in Chinese). Accessed 18 Sept 2020.

China Banking and Insurance Regulatory Commission (CBIRC). (2019). *Guiding opinions on promoting the supply chain finance to serve the real economy*. No. 155 Document. Issued and effective 9 July 2019.

China Banking Regulatory Commission (CBRC). (2016a). *Interim measures for the administration of business activities of online lending information intermediaries*. No. 1 jointly issued with Ministry of Industry and Information Technology, Ministry of Public Security, and State Information Office. Issued and effective on 17 August.

China Banking Regulatory Commission (CBRC). (2016b). *Notice on printing and distributing the "implementation plan for the special rectification of P2P network lending risks"*. No. 11 Document. Issued and effective on 13 October 2016.

Corbet, S., Lucey, B., & Yarovaya, L. (2021). Bitcoin-energy markets interrelationships-new evidence. *Resources Policy, 70*, 101916.

Danny, L., William, F., & Zach, G. (2010). Concentrated supply chain membership and financial performance: Chain- and firm-level perspectives. *Journal of Operations Management, 28*, 1–16.

Dong, S., & Xu, L. (2016). The impact of explicit CSR regulation: Evidence from China's mining firms. *Journal of Applied Accounting Research, 17*(2), 237–258.

Dong, S., Xu, L., & McIver, R. (2021). China's financial sector sustainability and "green finance" disclosures. *Sustainability, Accounting, Management and Policy Journal, 12*(2), 353–384.

Dong, S., Xu, L., & McIver, R. (2022). Sustainability reporting quality and the financial sector: Evidence from China. *Meditari Accountancy Research (Online)*, 1–25.

European Central Bank. (2012). *Virtual currency schemes*. ECB Report.

Financial Stability Board (FSB). https://www.fsb.org/work-of-the-fsb/financial-innovation-and-structural-change/fintech/#:~:text=The%20FSB%20defines%20FinTech%20as,the%20provision%20of%20financial%20services. Accessed 18 Feb 2022.

Fu, Y., Lee, S., Xu, L., & Zurbruegg, R. (2015). The effectiveness of capital regulation on bank behavior in China. *International Review of Finance, 15*, 321–345.

He, Z. (2000). Corruption and anti corruption in reform China. *Communist and Post-Communist Studies, 33*(2), 243–270.

He, Y., Xu, L., & McIver, R. (2019). How does political connection affect firm financial distress and resolution in China? *Applied Economics, 51*(26), 2770–2792.

He, Y., Xu, L., & Yang, M. (2021). The impact of tunnelling on financial distress and resolution: Evidence from listed firms in China. *International Journal of Finance and Economics, 26*(2), 1773–1792.

Huynh, A., Duong, D., Burggraf, T., Luong, H., & Bui, N. (2022). Energy consumption and Bitcoin market. *Asia-Pacific Financial Markets, 29*, 79–93.

Jiang, T., & Nie, H. (2014). The stained China miracle: Corruption, regulation, and firm performance. *Economics Letters, 123*(3), 366–369.

Ju, L., Lu, T., & Tu, Z. (2015). Capital flight and Bitcoin regulation. *International Review of Finance, 16*(3), 445–455.

Kahana, N., & Liu, Q. (2010). Endemic corruption. *European Journal of Political Economy, 26*(1), 82–88.

Katsiampa, P., McGuiness, P., Serbera, J., & Zhao, K. (2022). The financial and prudential performance of Chinese banks and Fintech lenders in the era of digitalization. *Review of Quantitative Finance and Accounting, 58*, 1451–1503.

Klein, A. (2020). China's digital payments revolution. *Brookings*. https://www.brookings.edu/research/chinas-digital-payments-revolution/. Accessed 15 June 2021.

Ko, K., & Weng, C. (2012). Structural changes in Chinese corruption. *The China Quarterly, 211*, 718–740.

Kong, D., Tao, Y., & Wang, Y. (2020). China's anti-corruption campaign and firm productivity: Evidence from a quasi-natural experiment. *China Economic Review, 63*, 101535.

Krause, M., & Tolaymat, T. (2018). Quantification of energy and carbon costs for mining cryptocurrencies. *Nature Sustainability, 1*(11), 711.

Li, G. (2018, December 26). *In order to turn around the loss of listed companies, they are busy selling assets at the end of the year* (in Chinese). Sohu.com. https://www.sohu.com/a/284395632_498715. Accessed 1 Feb 2022.

Li, X., & Lin, J. (2016). Shadow-banking entrusted loan management, deposit insurance premium, and capital regulation. *International Review of Economics and Finance, 41*, 98–109.

Li, J., Hsu, S., & Qin, Y. (2014). Shadow banking in China: Institutional risks. *China Economic Review, 31*, 119–129.

Li, B., Pan, A., Xu, L., Liu, X., & Qin, S. (2020a). Imprinting and peer effects in acquiring state ownership: Evidence from private firms in China. *Pacific-Basin Finance Journal, 61*, 101337.

Li, B., Xu, L., McIver, R., Wu, Q., & Pan, A. (2020b). Green M&A, legitimacy, and risk-taking: Evidence from China's heavy polluters. *Accounting and Finance, 60*, 97–127.

Li, B., Xu, L., McIver, R., Liu, X., & Pan, A. (2022). Mixed-ownership reform and private firms' corporate social responsibility practices: Evidence from China. *Business & Society, 61*(2), 389–691.

Liebl, J., Hartmann, E., & Feisel, E. (2016). Reverse factoring in the supply chain: Objectives, antecedents and implementation barriers. *International Journal of Physical Distribution and Logistics Management, 46*, 393–413.

Lin, Q., & Zhang, T. (2020). Trade credit in economic fluctuations and its impact on corporate performance: A panel data analysis from China. *Applied Economics, 52*, 1–18.

Lin, X., Li, X., & Zheng, Z. (2017). Evaluating borrower's default risk in peer-to-peer lending: Evidence from a lending platform in China. *Applied Economics, 49*(35), 3538–3545.

Liu, A. (2014). The politics of corruption in the People's Republic of China. *American Political Science Review, 77*(3), 602–623.

Lu, Y., Guo, H., Kao, E., & Fung, H. (2015). Shadow banking and firm financing in China. *International Review of Economics and Finance, 36*, 40–53.

Luo, S., Sun, Y., Yang, F., & Zhou, G. (2022). Does fintech innovation promote enterprise transformation? Evidence from China. *Technology in Society, 68*, 101821.

Orhangazi, O. (2008). Financialisation and capital accumulation in the non-financial corporate sector. *Cambridge Journal of Economics, 32*, 863–886.

Pan, X., & Tian, G. (2020). Political connections and corporate investments: Evidence from the recent anti-corruption campaign in China. *Journal of Banking & Finance, 119*, 105108.

Pan, A., Xu, L., Li, B., & Ling, R. (2020). The impact of supply chain finance on firm cash holdings: Evidence from China. *Pacific-Basin Finance Journal, 63*, 101402.

Pan, A., Xu, L., Li, B., Ling, R., & Zheng, L. (2022). The impact of supply chain finance on capital structure adjustment: Evidence from China. *Australian Journal of Management (Online)*, 1–27. https://doi.org/10.1177/03128962221092179

People's Bank of China (PBC). (2016). *Several opinions of the People's Bank of China, the National Development and Reform Commission, the Ministry of Industry and Information Technology, and other authorities on financial support for the industrial sector in stabilizing growth, adjusting structure, and heightening benefits* (in Chinese). No. 42 Document. Issued and effective on 14 February.

People's Bank of China (PBC). (2017). *Announcement of the People's Bank of China, the Office of the Central Leading Group for Cyberspace Affairs, the Ministry of Industry and Information Technology and Other Departments on Preventing the Financing Risks of Initial Coin Offerings*. Effective on 4 September.

People's Bank of China (PBC). (2018). *Payment system report*. http://www.pbc.gov.cn/en/3688259/3689026/3706133/3825632/3793316/2019032515155046000.pdf. Accessed 1 Feb 2020.

People's Bank of China (PBC). (2019). *FinTech development plan (2019–2021)*. No. 209, effective on 23 August.

People's Bank of China (PBC). (2020a). *Guiding opinions on further strengthening financial services for small, medium and micro enterprises, in conjunction with the China Banking and Insurance Regulatory Commission, the National Development and Reform Commission, the Ministry of Industry and Information Technology, the Ministry of Finance, the State Administration for Market Regulation, the China Securities Regulatory Commission, and the State Administration of Foreign Exchange*. No. 120, effective on 26 May.

People's Bank of China (PBC). (2020b). *Opinions of the People's Bank of China, Ministry of Industry and Information Technology, Ministry of Justice, Ministry of Commerce, State-owned Assets Supervision and Administration Commission, State-owned Assets Supervision and Administration Commission, China Banking Regulatory Commission and Foreign Exchange Bureau on Regulating The Development of Supply Chain Finance to Support the Stable Cycle and Optimization and Upgrade of Supply Chain Industry Chains* (in Chinese). No. 226 Document. Issued and effective on 18 September.

People's Bank of China (PBC). (2021a). *FinTech Development Plan (2022–2025)*. No. 335, effective on 29 December.

People's Bank of China (PBC). (2021b). *The research and development progress of China's digital RMB* (in Chinese). Announced on 15 July.

People's Bank of China (PBC). (2021c). *Notice of the People's Bank of China on public comments on the "Regulations on non-bank payment institutions (draft for comment)"*. Announced 20 January.

Shan, Y., & Xu, L. (2012a). Bad debt provisions of financial institutions: Dilemma of China's corporate governance regime. *International Journal of Managerial Finance, 8*, 344–364.

Shan, G., & Xu, L. (2012b). Do internal governance mechanisms impact on firm performance? Empirical evidence from financial sector in China. *Journal of Asia-Pacific Business, 13*(2), 114–142.

Sheng, T. (2021). The effect of Fintech on banks' credit provision to SMEs: Evidence from China. *Finance Research Letters, 39*, 101558.

Song, H., Yang, X., & Yu, K. (2020). How do supply chain network and SMEs' operational capabilities enhance working capital financing? An integrative signaling view. *International Journal of Production Economics, 220*, 107447.

State Council. (2016). *The General Office of the State Council on printing and distributing internet financial risks notice on the implementation plan of special rectification work*. No. 21 Document. Issued and effective on 12 April.

State Council. (2017). *Active guidance on supply chain innovation and application* (in Chinese). No. 84 Document. Issued and effective on 5 October.

Sutton, M., & Taylor, G. (2020, December). *Shadow financing in China*. Reserve Bank of Australia Bulletin. https://www.rba.gov.au/publications/bulletin/2020/dec/shadow-financing-in-china.html. Accessed 20 May 2022.

The Supreme People's Court of the People's Republic of China. (2015, August 6). *Provisions of the Supreme People's Court on Several Issues concerning the application of law in the trial of private lending cases* (in Chinese).

The Supreme People's Court of the People's Republic of China. (2020, August 20). *Decision of the Supreme People's Court on Amending the "Regulations on several issues concerning the application of law in the trial of private lending cases"* (in Chinese).

The Wall Street Journal. (2017, September 12). *China sentences leaders of Ezubo Ponzi Scheme to life in prison.* https://www.wsj.com/articles/china-sentences-leaders-of-ezubo-ponzi-scheme-to-life-in-prison-1505220321. Accessed 1 Oct 2017.

Wang, Y., Lucey, B., Vigne, S., & Yarovaya, L. (2022). An index of cryptocurrency environmental attention (ICEA). *China Finance Review International (Online)*, 1–37. https://doi.org/10.1108/CFRI-09-2021-0191

Wei, W. (2020, December 1). *P2P clearing the game: Who will pay for the 800 billion bad debts?* (in Chinese). Sina Technology. https://finance.sina.com.cn/tech/2020-12-01/doc-iiznezxs4532544.shtml. Accessed 1 Dec 2020.

Wharton Business School. (2019). *Fintech in China: What lies ahead.* https://knowledge.wharton.upenn.edu/article/fintech-china-lies-ahead/. Accessed 18 July 2021.

Wu, L., & Xu, L. (2020). Venture capital certification of small and medium-sized enterprises towards banks: Evidence from China. *Accounting and Finance, 60*, 1601–1633.

Wu, L., & Xu, L. (2022). Bank loans and firm environmental information disclosure: Evidence from China's heavy polluters. *Australian Economic Papers, 61*(1), 42–71.

Wuttke, D., Rosenzweig, E., & Heese, H. (2019). An empirical analysis of supply chain finance adoption. *Journal of Operations Management, 65*, 242–261.

Xinhua. (2018, February 4). *The state will take regulatory measures against the website of the virtual currency overseas trading platform* (in Chinese). http://www.gov.cn/xinwen/2018-02/04/content_5263816.htm. Accessed 8 June 2022.

Xinhua. (2020, December 28). *P2P clears the curtain call and the new policy has repeatedly "blocked the side door" and "opened the main door"* (in Chinese). http://www.xinhuanet.com/fortune/2020-12/28/c_1126914550.htm. Accessed 30 Dec 2020.

Xu, L., & Lin, C. (2007). Can Chinese banks compete after accession to WTO? *Journal of Asian Economics, 18*, 883–903.

Xu, L., & Lin, C. (2008). On the safety and soundness of Chinese banks in the post WTO era. In S. Kim & M. McKenzie (Eds.), *Asia-Pacific financial markets: Integration, innovation and challenges, international finance review* (Vol. 8, pp. 447–470). Elsevier Science.

Xu, N., Xu, X., & Yuan, Q. (2011). Political connections, financing friction, and corporate investment: Evidence from Chinese listed family firms. *European Journal of Finance, 19*(4), 675–702.

Xu, L., Lee, S. C., & Fu, Y. (2015). Impacts of capital regulation and market discipline on capital ratio selection: Evidence from China. *International Journal of Managerial Finance, 11*(3), 270–284.

Xu, L., McIver, R., Shan, G., & Wang, X. (2016). Governance and performance in China's real estate sector. *Managerial Finance, 42*(6), 585–603.

Xu, X., Xu, L., & Li, L. (2021). Domestic heating and China's sustainable energy goals. In K. Wendt (Ed.), *Theories of change, sustainable finance* (pp. 437–451). Springer.

Xu, L., Li, B., Ma, C., & Liu, J. (2022). Supply chain finance and firm diversification: Evidence from China. *Australian Journal of Management (Online)*, 1–28. https://doi.org/10.1177/03128962221075366

Yao, Z., Gu, D., & Cao, W. (2019). SOEs as intermediation: Leakage effect under financial repression. *Pacific-Basin Finance Journal, 53*, 349–361.

Yermack, D. (2014). *Is Bitcoin a real currency? An economic appraisal* (NBER Working Paper No. 19747).

Zade, M., Myklebost, J., Tzscheutschler, P., & Wagner, U. (2019). Is bitcoin the only problem? A scenario model for the power demand of blockchains. *Frontiers in Energy Research, 7*, 1–12.

Zhang, X., Zou, M., Liu, M., & Zhang, Y. (2020). Does a firm's supplier concentration affect its cash holding? *Economic Modelling, 90*, 527–535.

Zhao, J., Li, X., Yu, C., Chen, S., & Lee, C. (2022). Riding the FinTech innovation wave: FinTech, patents and bank performance. *Journal of International Money and Finance, 122*, 102552.

Part V
Financing the Anthropocene

Chapter 19
The Future Wealth of Nations

Stefan Brunnhuber

19.1 Introduction

Until now, our common wealth has primarily been financed through private sector financing, conventional public sector funding and philanthropy. These sources are not sufficient in terms of scale and speed to meet today's pressing finance needs. The global community is too busy repairing, stabilising and refunding the existing system in order to maintain its stability. An adjusted central bank mandate that led to the introduction of an electronic currency specifically designed to finance global commons would provide the necessary resources to achieve the UN SDGs while stabilising the existing monetary system.

The development of cryptocurrencies based on blockchain-distributed ledger technologies has prompted leading central banks around the world to study how this approach could potentially be used to directly inject purchasing power without depending exclusively on the commercial banking system and conventional taxations schemas. In the following we are trying to illustrate on how this approach can be utilised to finance the huge multi-trillion dollar annual investment requirements for achieving the SDGs, the European Green Deal and our common future.[1]

Financing our future requires additional liquidity of approximately 5 trillion USD every year over the next 15–20 years globally, beyond the traditional mechanism of monetary redistribution along the existing value chain. Crowding in private

[1] Brunnhuber, S., and Jacobs, G. (2020). Innovative Financial Engineering to Fund the SDGs: A WAAS Initiative. *Cadmus* 4(2): 141–148. http://cadmusjournal.org/article/volume-4/issue-2-part-2/innovative-financialengineering-fund-sdgs-waas-initiative

S. Brunnhuber (✉)
Trustee World Academy of Arts and Science (WAAS), Full Member Club of Rome, Saxonia, Germany
e-mail: brunnhuber.cor@gmxpro.de

K. Wendt, B. Villhauer (eds.), *Sustainable Wealth Management*, Sustainable Finance,
https://doi.org/10.1007/978-3-031-55505-3_19

sector financing, conventional public sector funding (taxes and fees) and philanthropy will not be enough in terms of scale and speed to accomplish this.[2] The financial system has become more unstable over the last 40 years, with over 425 banking and currency crises that incur costs of over 10% of GDP per event and increase the public debt load globally. These intrinsic limitations of the financial system thwart any technological and political efforts to make the world a better place, because the global community is too busy repairing, stabilising and refunding the system just to maintain a steady status quo or return to business as usual.[3]

To finance our future, we need more financialisation, not less but done in a different way. This can be accomplished by an additional green liquidity system designed to run in a friendly co-existence in parallel to the existing monetary system. This supplementary system would run through different channels and operate with new distributive ledger technology and would provide greater wealth and well-being thanks to multiple positive externalities. Let's look closer to the argument.[4]

19.2 The Indispensable Triad: Friendly Strategic Triangulation

Traditionally, we think of the free market and state intervention as opposites, with the smallest common denominator providing the best possible solutions. But then we end up with over-regulated markets and over-indebted public agencies, ultimately leading to suboptimal results for all of us. As an alternative to approaches focusing on causal relations, such as nudging, voluntary commitments, linear processing, simple stimulus responses, pushbacks or silo solutions, a method of 'strategic friendly triangulation' can offer an additional tool to avoid the smallest common denominator and suboptimal results. It involves introducing a third party that can overcome the polarity and instead unlock the full potential for both parties. Such a strategic friendly triangulation can lead to a more systematic approach to problem-solving and allow us to overcome silo thinking.[5]

Let's consider a specific example. A society decides to spend 40% of its GDP on public goods (hospitals, nurseries, universities, motorways, digital infrastructure, basic needs). If the society has sovereignty over its money creation process (i.e. if it

---

[2] Chenet, H., Ryan-Collins, J., and van Lerven, F. (2021). Finance, Climate-Change and Radical Uncertainty: Towards a Precautionary Approach to Financial Policy. *Ecological Economics* 183. https://doi.org/10.1016/j.ecolecon.2021.106957

[3] Vorisek, D., and Yu, S. (2020). Understanding the Cost of Achieving the Sustainable Development Goals. World Bank Group, Policy Research Working Paper 9146. https://documents1.worldbank.org/curated/en/744701582827333101/pdf/Understanding-the-Cost-of-Achieving-the-Sustainable-Development-Goals.pdf; UNSDG (2018). Unlocking SDG Financing: Good Practices from Early Adopters. https://unsdg.un.org/resources/unlocking-sdg-financing-findings-early-adopters

[4] Brunnhuber, S. (2021). *Financing Our Future*. London: Palgrave Macmillan.

[5] Brunnhuber, S. (2019). Overcoming the Global Trilemma: New Monetary Politics in the Anthropocene: Dani Rodrik Revised. *Cadmus* 4(1): 39–46.

can print money), does not have to rely on external debts nominated in a foreign currency and has the necessary human and natural resources, then it can eventually generate the amount of money needed by itself. Consequently, the subsidies and taxation schemes for the private sector initially brought in to finance these commons will be phased out over time. We would then end up with a free and competitive market system, which makes it possible to allocate goods and services optimally while at the same time having a high-functioning public sector, where the state authorities enable our commons. We can take this argument one step further. The private purse is not the public purse: private households and corporates have to budget carefully so they don't go bankrupt. Private households and corporates cannot spend more than they earn in the first place. The public purse, however, is different. In a situation where there is a sovereign nation state with the ability to issue money, the financing of its public budget follows a fundamentally different logic to the private sector. But both require a third party to be involved to overcome the constraints of any end-of-pipe financing. Central banks and regulators, operating in a proactive, preventive and restorative manner, can serve this role. This means that monetary policy will trump fiscal policy when it comes to financing our commons.

In short, a sovereign state able to issue a currency has only three constraints on the financing of its commons[6]: the amount of natural resources, the amount of human resources and the amount of external debts issued in other currencies. Graph 19.1 illustrates this indispensable triad.

We therefore simultaneously require a stronger enabling state and a stronger competitive fair market system in order to benefit from both institutions.[7] Our challenge is not to privatise the commons but rather to adapt our financial system to the nature of the commons. In short, we need more and better finance. And in fact, this is happening already in a fledgling, experimental form. Monetary regulators and central banks are currently testing what are known as central bank digital currencies (CBDCs) in order to provide additional, targeted liquidity, thereby enhancing their steering capacity, bolstering price stability and generating thousands of new green jobs and public revenues as well as operating in an anti-cyclical manner. If done in the right way, we would have the monetary mechanism in place to finance the UN SDGs and the associated commons. Eventually, we would have the tools available for new, almost unlimited forms of financial engineering to fund and hedge the associated risks. In short, we can wake this sleeping giant.[8] However, the traditional

[6] Davies, G. (2010). *History of Money*. Cardiff: University of Wales Press; Huber, J. (2020). Theory of Dominant Money: Part I: Taxonomy of Money and Monetary Tide Changes. https://sovereignmoney.site/dominant-money-i-taxonomy-and-monetary-tide-changes; Huber, J. (2020). Dominant Money: Part II: The Rise of Sovereign Digital Currency. https://sovereignmoney.site/dominant-money-ii-the-rise-of-sovereign-digital-currency; Huber, J. (2020). Monetary Financing of Helicopter Money. https://sovereignmoney.site/monetary-financing-of-helicopter-money

[7] Mazzucato, M. (2013). *The Entrepreneurial State: Debunking Public* vs *Private Sector Myths*. London: Anthem Press; Mazzucato, M. (2018).

[8] Post-2015 Consensus. https://www.copenhagenconsensus.com/post-2015-consensus; The Economist. https://www.copenhagenconsensus.com/post-2015-consensus/economist

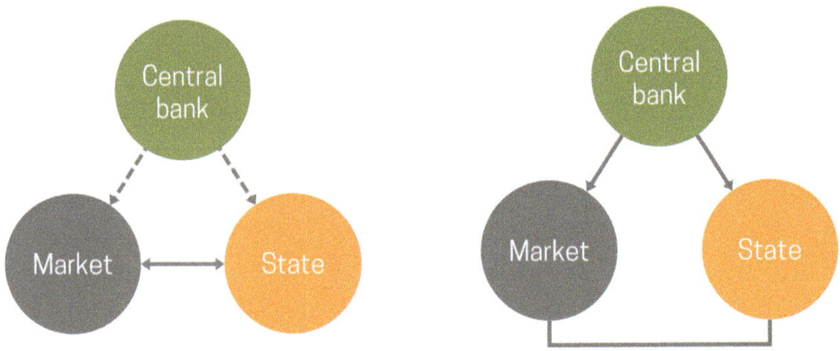

Creating polarities: Traditionally, central banks are passive, neutral, restorative and indirect. Free market and state interventions search for a smallest common denominator. Linear, silo and causal thinking dominates. Welfare remains Pareto inferior.

Overcoming polarities: In the Anthropocene era, central banks are becoming proactive and preventive, and try to facilitate stable and free markets and strong states at the same time. Systems thinking in a complex world dominates. Welfare becomes Pareto superior.

Graph 19.1 Strategic friendly triangulation: the indispensable triad

way to execute our common future follows a different way, which is explained in the next chapter.

19.3 Traditional Approaches: Other Proposal and Beyond the Six Pack

In New York in 2015, world leaders signed up to a future road map with 17 Sustainable Development Goals (SDGs) based on the 5 Ps: people, planet, prosperity, peace and partnerships. Most of the SDGs focus on common goods such as clean air, universal access to healthcare, education and maintaining biodiversity. These goods are not exclusive and should be accessible to and enjoyed by everyone. There is enough scientific evidence, technological expertise and political consensus to achieve each of these goals, and they are valid for the entire planet. But achieving the goals is expensive, requiring around 5 trillion USD/year over the next 15–20 years to finance. Our global GDP, which includes all goods and services, is approximately 80 trillion USD/year. The conventional way to finance social and ecological projects globally has been by redistributing the money remaining at the end of this pipeline.[9]

Historically, the global community has committed to spend 0.7% of global GDP—roughly 500 billion USD/year—to finance common goods. Other than the Scandinavian countries, the vast majority of the world has never attained this 0.7%.

[9] Rich, N. (2018). Losing Earth: The Decade We Almost Stopped Climate Change. *New York Times Magazine*. https://www.nytimes.com/interactive/2018/08/01/magazine/climate-change-losing-earth.html

Currently (2021) the world spent 0.37% on official developments aid (ODA), where less than 20% reach its final targets; the rest is lost somewhere in between. But even if all countries did so, this sum is not realistically enough to finance our future. Approximately eight to ten times more funding—equivalent to 5 trillion out of the global GDP of 80 trillion USD—is required to meet the social and environmental challenges we face. Withdrawing 5 trillion from the economic process, even in a gradual manner, would lead to a global recession. In fact, it is impossible to finance our future solely through monetary redistribution. In addition, the stability of the financial system itself is an impediment to sustainable financing. Over the last 40 years, the financial system has become more unstable, with over 425 banking, monetary or currency crises, and with every consecutive event, we are left with higher debt load and greater expenses, amounting to more than 10% of GDP (Graph 19.2).[10]

Looking closer at this traditional approach reveals at least five steps, including multiple regulatory efforts (taxonomies, ESG standards, equity requirements); taxation schemes (carbon tax), fees and multiple subsidy programmes; the major role of private impact funding (VPCE: seed/early-stage/mature investments, including charity funding); ex-swap strategies (including risk hedging instruments like

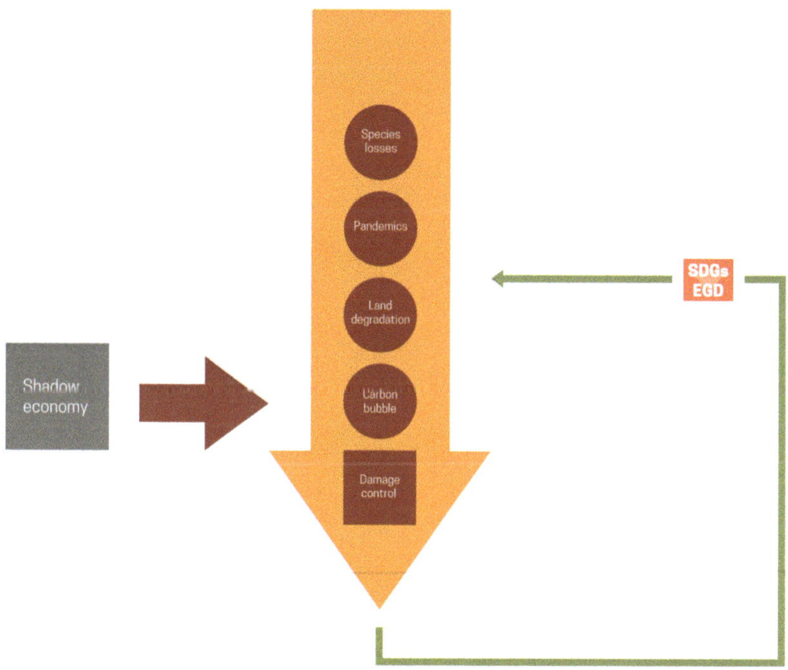

Graph 19.2 The traditional way to do it: end of pipe financing

[10] Brunnhuber, S., 2022, 'The Real Tragedy of the Commons—Garrett Hardin (1968) revised' in: Problems of Sustainable Development (PROBLEMY EKOROZWOJU) 17(2): pp19–23; Hardin, G. (1968). The Tragedy of the Commons. *Science* 162: 1243–1248.

interest swaps and derivatives); and private–public blended finance, state bonds and funds. All these instruments are valid but remain traditional and are not sufficient to finance our common future. There will always be a shortfall that requires a different financial and monetary scheme. Graph 19.3 illustrates this 'six pack'.

Since 2008, central banks have worked on multiple purchasing and accounting programmes. These have included quantitative easing (QE), pandemic emergency purchase programmes (PEPPs), emergency liquidity assistance (ELA), Short-Term European Papers (STEPs), the Agreement on Net Financial Assets (ANFA), long-term repurchasing operations (LTROs), the European Stability Mechanism (ESM), Outright Monetary Transactions (OMTs), Securities Markets Programmes (SMPs), asset purchase programmes (APPs), asset-backed securities (ABSs), non-refundable loans (NRLs), target accounts and differential interest spreads between member states. Despite their legal and technical differences, one factor they usually have in common is that the balance sheets of the regulators have grown substantially over the last decade: starting with 10% of GDP in 2008 up to 60% of GDP in 2020. The ECB alone is already taking on up to 30% of member states' public debts.

Several additional proposals have been discussed in recent years on how to upgrade the existing monetary system, including the modern monetary theory approach, positive money and a central bank stablecoin. None of these proposals are without merit, but we try to provide a different and more advantageous proposal for how to finance our common future. It honours the endeavours but differs in at least two respects from all other proposals made so far, namely, the parallelisation and digitalisation of the current monetary system.

In fact, they reflect a substantial shift in the aggregate of the money supply. Historically, the money supply aggregate was composed of coins and bills only and then shifted to commercial credit lines, which nowadays represent 97% of the entire

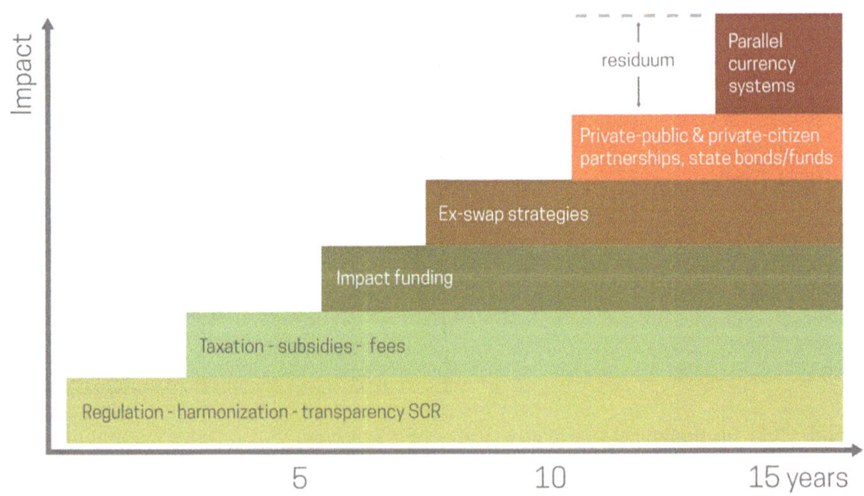

Graph 19.3 The 'six pack' and the remaining shortfall

money creation process through commercial banking credit lines. Now we are witnessing the rise of a new monetary supply aggregate: central bank digital currencies (CBDCs), e-money (e.g. PayPal), cryptocurrencies (e.g. Libra, Bitcoins) regional complementary currencies (e.g. LETS, barter system, local currencies) and money market funds (MMF). Each of them is capitalised differently, and each of them is either private or public, but what they have in common is that they reflect the need for additional liquidity to fund, manage, hedge and finance our common future.[11]

19.4 The Future Wealth of Nations

In order to cover the shortfall described in the previous section, there are mainly three options available: a modified monetary mandate for central bank digital currencies (CBDCs), private cryptocurrencies (e.g. Ripple, Skycoin, Ethereum) or complementary community currencies (e.g. LETS, barter systems, Regiomoney).[12]

Each of these options would stabilise international financial markets, increase monetary regulatory efforts, reduce negative externalities, stabilise consumer pricing, increase welfare and well-being, generate millions of additional jobs and stabilise democracy. This can be started within 6 months, has the potential to end poverty in less than a year and would have a measurable and profound impact on our lives, our society and our planet in less than 2 years. Such a mechanism is the missing link beyond governance, technology, demographics and behavioural changes. In short, we need more, much more financialisation but delivered in a more democratic and humane way in order to increase wealth for the other two thirds of the global population and to protect the planet at the same time.

Is there a different way to finance our future? Based on systems thinking, we propose an outside-the-box solution to generate the funds needed to finance global common goods: (a) Central banks would be given a new monetary mandate to create and issue the 5 trillion USD equivalent of liquidity using blockchain technologies. Alternatively, (b) properly regulated corporate initiatives (cryptocurrencies)[13] or complementary communal currencies (LETS, Regiomoney) would receive a mandate to issue additional liquidity.[14] These funds would be earmarked and used

[11] Huber, J. 2022, Zeitenwende des Geldsystems, Vom Bankengeld zum digitalen Zentralbankgeld, Metropolis, Marburg.

[12] Peneder, M. Digitization and the evolution of money as a social technology of account. *J Evol Econ* **32,** 175–203 (2022). https://doi.org/10.1007/s00191-021-00729-4; Prasad, E. S. (2021). *The Future of Money: How the Digital Revolution Is Transforming Currencies and Finance.* Cambridge, MA: Harvard University Press.

[13] Li, X., Whinston, A.B. Analyzing Cryptocurrencies. *Inf Syst Front* **22,** 17–22 (2020). https://doi.org/10.1007/s10796-019-09966-2; Ryan-Collins, J., et al. (2012). *Where Does Money Come From? A Guide to the UK Monetary and Banking System.* London: New Economics Foundation.

[14] Community Currencies in Action (2015). *People Powered Money: Designing, Developing & Delivering Community Currencies.* London: New Economics Foundation. https://monneta.org/wp-content/uploads/2017/01/CCIA-book-People-Powered-Money.pdf. Lietaer, B., et al. (2012).

exclusively to finance SDG-related projects. This electronic liquidity would run through alternative monetary channels to those of the conventional system. The established commercial banking system and international development finance institutions like the World Bank, IMF, EIB and regional development banks will play a new and crucial role.[15]

We would then have a supplementary currency operating in parallel to the conventional monetary system generating the 5 trillion USD equivalent needed annually for the next 20 years. Research on optional parallel currency systems has shown several dozen positive effects. For example, this new technology could be used to create and channel targeted financial liquidity to millions of African citizens through their mobile phone network. In India, the existing microcredit banking system could be used to transfer additional liquidity to millions of Indian citizens. Any dollar spent and invested through these green, parallel channels has the potential to reduce or even eliminate absolute poverty globally within less than 1 year. The electronic format would prevent corruption and fraud, as each transaction would be transparent and public. Once the currency was accepted for payment of taxes, local authorities would have additional liquidity to rebuild public infrastructure such as nurseries, parks, hospitals and libraries. And the millions of NGOs globally would finally receive the funding they need to do their jobs properly. This targeted added liquidity would enhance education and provide otherwise unachievable access to universal healthcare. It would reduce resource depletion and clean up the air, avoiding the negative effects on our planet and on public health. We would eventually unlock the untapped potential and creativity of millions of unemployed people by creating new jobs, thereby unleashing the creativity of billions more. Graph 19.4 outlines the entire mechanism involved.

19.4.1 Friendly Co-existence: Why Parallel, Digital and Going Direct?

A parallel, special-purpose digital currency based on distributive ledger technology (DLT), accepted as legal tender to pay taxes and wages, convertible into traditional currencies, bearing a higher interest rate (than in the traditional marketplace) and issued by central bank digital currencies (CBDCs) or regulated private agents (cryptocurrencies) could meet these requirements. It is like riding a bike with two wheels rather than a wobbly unicycle.

If we simply inject additional liquidity into the existing value chain, we not only risk consolidating the current track, which still depends on fossil fuels for over 78%

Money and Sustainability: The Missing Link: A Report from the Club of Rome—EU Chapter. Axminster: Triarchy Press.

[15]Chaum, D., Grothoff, C., and Moser, T. (2021). How to Issue a Central Bank Digital Currency. SNB Working Papers 3/2021. https://www.snb.ch/n/mmr/reference/working_paper_2021_03/source/working_paper_2021_03.n.pdf

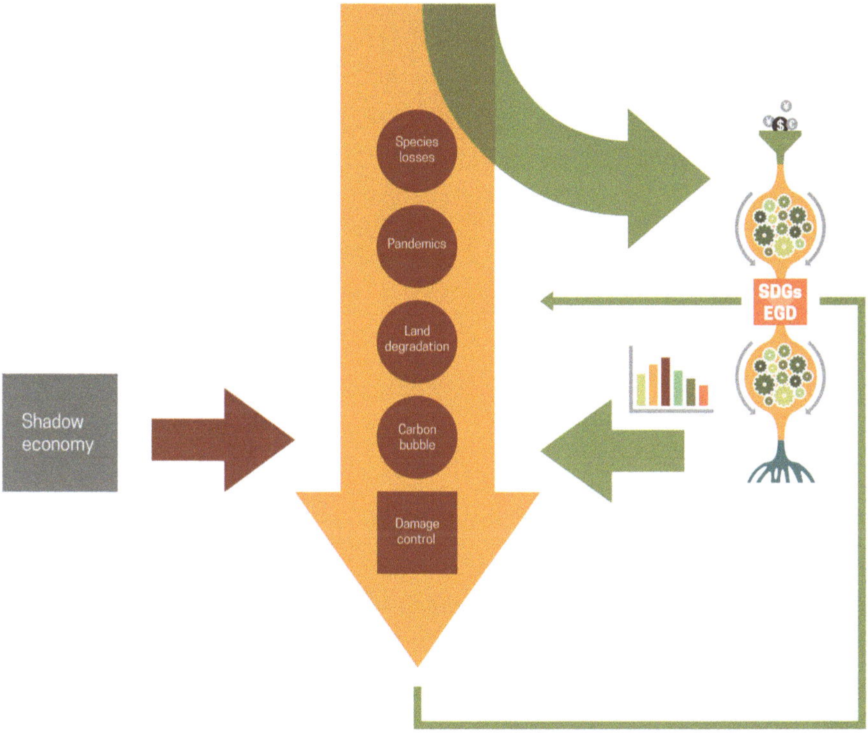

Graph 19.4 Financing our future wealth: riding a bike with two wheels

of its energy needs, but also negating all our efforts or even making things worse. Assuming a multiplier of 1.5–1.8, simply increasing the liquidity could do more harm than good. Any wind turbine or solar panel that is installed would feed back into the existing fossil value chain through multiple second-round and rebound effects. We need a wedge or parallel financial incentive that ensures a shift from the old to the new, from fossil towards a net zero economy (Graph 19.5).

Besides parallelising the currency system,[16] which allows us to create inflation-proof, anti-cyclical and resilient incentives for a new green marketplace, the monetary channels should be digitalised with the support of a distributive ledger technology (DLT). DLT would have significant impacts on all economic activity; the following table summarises some of the major ones (Fig. 19.1).

[16] Rössner, P. R. (2018). Monetary Theory and Cameralist Economic Management, c. 1500–1900 AD. *Journal of the History of Economic Thought* 40(1): 99–134.

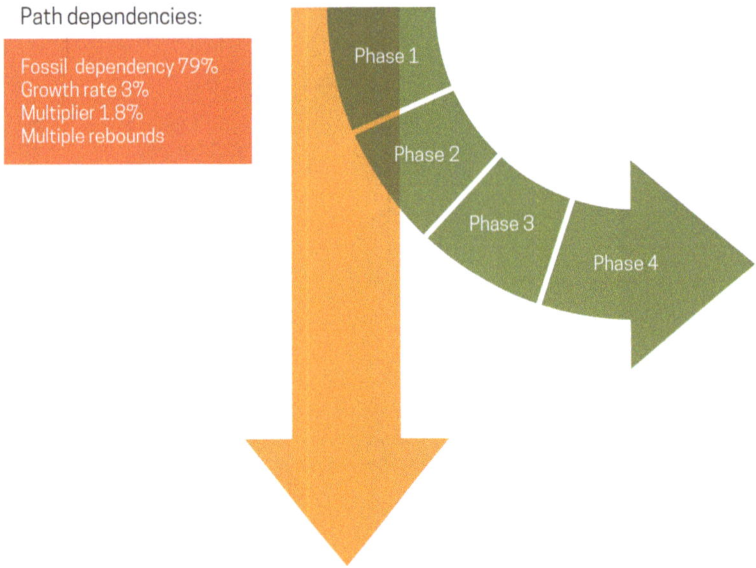

Graph 19.5 Parallelisation is key: lock in effects and how to overcome them

19.4.2 How to Parallelise and Digitalise the Monetary System?

From a practical perspective, we could start with four phases, all ensured by a smart digital contract that prevents some things we don't want (fraud, corruption, fossil dependency) and encourages others (green technology and jobs): What would be the effects on the conventional economy? The annual 5 trillion USD equivalent of added liquidity would not hurt or harm the conventional economy. In fact, the opposite would be true. Corporate and state planning, production and price levels would become more robust and reliable with a longer-term vision. Furthermore, it would stabilise the cyclical economy of booms and busts. Despite arguments to the contrary, we need much more financialisation (finance/GDP) (Fig. 19.1).

However, it must be designed in a more democratic and humane manner, to protect the planet while increasing wealth for the two thirds of the global population currently in poverty. If there is a single most important variable besides technology, governance, behavioural changes and demographics for changing the world, it is a parallel and digital monetary system.

This is the game changer. All this could be started in less than 6 months, if the six largest central banks agreed to create a parallel, optional, complementary currency. A redesign of the financial system would not solve all our problems, but it would allow all our problems to be addressed more easily. This, or a very similar mechanism, is the missing link to achieving better outcomes for the five Ps: people, planet, prosperity, peace and partnerships.

Phase 1	We start by introducing a digital smart contract that prevents fraud, illicit transactions and informal sector activities.
Phase 2	We then introduce additional financial instruments that allow us to hedge planetary and systemic risks, like harvest default swaps.
Phase 3	Next, we accept direct digital cash transfers to affected populations, for purposes such as overcoming poverty and hunger.
Phase 4	We begin to further steer our economic activities towards a more sustainable marketplace, avoiding social and ecological externalities, e.g. alcohol/tobacco ban, pesticides.

Fig. 19.1 The four phases of paralyzing our currency system

19.5 The Top Ten Best Practices

Instead of funding, hedging and managing our global commons using taxpayers' money, private investments or philanthropy alone, we suggest that central banks should become proactive rather than reactive and prevent problems rather than repairing the damage afterwards. A domestic public development bank may be able to manage the necessary financial services. Below, we list the top ten examples of monetary tools and financial engineering that can be used for this purpose (Box 19.1):

Box 19.1 The Top Ten: Better, More, Faster, Different, Targeted, Conditioned, Risk Adjusted and Empirically Tested

- *Harvest default swaps:* Hedging extreme weather and droughts for millions of farmers with an upfront loading of additional, conditioned funding for adverse events. This preventive measure is far cheaper than financing millions of farmers falling below the poverty line.
- *Fossil to commons swaps:* 70% of fossil reserves are public and should remain in the ground. Fossil to commons swaps collateralise lost revenue using green QE, subject to the condition that investment must only be in

(continued)

Box 19.1 (continued)

commons and public goods (the Alaska Nature Reserve Fund is one such preliminary financial contract).

- *Pandemic preparedness fund:* We have to expect further pandemics to come. Fifty billion USD of upfront funding for the WHO is cheaper than repairing the system after the fact and paying for all the damage. (The COVID-19 pandemic has cost 15 trillion USD globally.) This would create a return on investment of >300%.
- *Nature reserve conservation fund:* An additional, conditioned fund (blended or purely public) must be issued to non-governmental organisations (like the WWF) to safeguard the 30% of protected nature reserves globally. The money would be spent on drones, software and rangers. Empirically, the return on investment is between 1:10 and 1:15.
- *Credit default swaps:* In these swaps, the public sector provides an interest derivative to cover part of the additional private capital costs that come from investing in an adverse environment (e.g. a hospital chain in sub-Saharan Africa). The CDS market is highly liquid and provides solutions tailored to customers and projects.
- *Covering capital costs for renewables:* These are measures to cover the differences in capital costs between countries for investments in renewables. The delta is up to ten times higher for developing countries. The project risks remain with the private investors.
- *State guarantees:* Additional money is used to hedge potential risk for VCPE investment in common goods like hospitals or nurseries (e.g. a build–operate–transfer agenda (BOT)), which is commonly used in private–public partnerships (PPPs). Again, the project risks remain private, while the systemic risk is absorbed by green QE.
- *Active state involvement:* This includes preloaded funding of national budgets, tailored and conditioned to national public goods.
- *Advanced commitment strategy (ACS):* This includes a private–public partnership where the public sector guarantees a certain amount/volume of, or price for, a necessary good (e.g. a vaccine).
- *Direct cash transfers:* This includes direct digital transfer of cash to target populations exposed to hunger and poverty.

If we start implementing this green QE procedure using parallel digital (blockchain-based) channels, this will help to prevent fraud, corruption and illicit transactions and create the conditions for a green marketplace. A combination of these top ten monetary tools would allow us to tackle most of the challenges ahead. Part of the funding would need to be front-loaded with additional, conditioned liquidity created by regulators and managed by national public development banks. This can be done whenever an identified risk is systemic or planetary and/or a good/service is defined as a commons and available to everybody. The potential return on investment (1:15) for the stakeholder community far exceeds any that might be expected from private investments.[17] We can take these findings one step further and introduce a general law of economic transformation, which should then apply to any society in transition.

19.6 A General Law of Economic Transformation

Facing future asymmetric shocks in the Anthropocene era, we all caused as humans, we have to admit that our whole society has to transform and not only segments of it. In such a case, a general economic law of transformation comes into play, which comprises of ten general fiscal and monetary laws:

1. Transformation does not come for free but is associated with additional political costs of instability and polarisation and the economic costs of welfare losses.
2. Business as usual (BAU) or wait and see (WAS) strategies are going to be too expensive.
3. Business under transformation (BUT) is expensive too but less than any BAU or WAS scenario.
4. Any BUT comprises always of two costs components: the costs of the shocks and the costs of adapting and mitigating the shock. Both cost components add up.
5. BUT reflects financing multiple trade-offs. This includes trade-offs between regions and between generations, between the private and the public sector, rich and poor households and countries, between economic activities and ecological externalities and economics as a whole versus political costs.
6. Financing such trade-offs will not come for free but require additional liquidity.
7. When these costs of any BUT override the traditional growth corridor significantly, fiscal measures only (austerity, stimulus, fees and taxation) are insufficient and ineffective.
8. Anytime we set a damage/loss/disaster/risk factor/adverse condition now, which will cause additional costs in the future significantly higher than the expected growth corridor, fiscal policy only will remain insufficient and ineffective.
9. Secondary prevention describes an intervention that reduces the expected future costs of a damage/loss/disaster/risk factor/adverse condition which is triggered or unleashed already.
10. In all these cases an augmented, risk-adjusted monetary policy is acting like a secondary preventive measure that can mitigate/reduce the future costs more effectively.

[17] Brunnhuber, S., et al. (2021). Hedging Planetary Risks: From Weapons of Mass Destruction to Tools of Massive Social and Ecological Innovation. *Cadmus* 4(4): 103–114. Lomborg, B. (2020). *False Alarm—How Climate Change Panic Costs Us Trillions, Hurts the Poor, and Fails to Fix the Planet*. New York: Basic Books.

19.7 Conclusion

The indispensable missing link in the debate on sustainability is the monetary system. The existing system is too brittle, slow and low in volume to fund our global commons and to hedge the associated planetary risks. Instead of advocating an abstract, purely theoretical financial framework, we are proposing the single best next step to allow us to finance our common future within the next 15–20 years. This requires additional liquidity of about 5 trillion USD annually and an upgrade of our monetary system into a dual mechanism. And the step recommended here can be started in less than 6 months. Letting go of our current monetary monoculture would in the long run stabilise international financial markets, strengthen monetary regulatory efforts, reduce negative externalities, increase social welfare and well-being and stabilise democracies.[18] This will lead to a multi-stakeholder, non-regret approach for everyone involved. Multiple, empirically evidenced positive impacts can be identified, which would allow us to move past the constraints of a fossil-driven economy, tackle the multiple trade-offs and social/ecological externalities and overcome the dual tragedy of the commons and the horizon at the same time. Instead of further privatising our commons, we can start identifying (almost) unlimited new, innovative financial instruments and forms of financial engineering, including blended finance, derivatives and swaps, direct digital cash transfers and new state guarantees. On this approach, finance would not drive sustainability but the other way round: sustainability would eventually drive finance. Moreover, a general law of economic transformation comprising of ten paragraphs can explain the overall rational.

19.8 Policy Recommendations

1. *Globally, we are in a deflationary situation:* Billions are starving, millions are unemployed, and there are endless infrastructural and environmental challenges but not enough suitable liquidity to meet them.
2. *The traditional way of financing our future is not enough:* Private sector involvement is important, but blended finance is key.
3. *A backstop mechanism that clears up after the fact is not an option:* In fact, it is far too expensive. We need upfront financial loading to cope with the challenges ahead.

[18] Brunnhuber, S., (2021). Open Societies versus Digital Autocratic Experiments. In Macondo, *UN Global Goals Yearbook 2021: The Make or Break Decade Has Begun*, pp. 136–145. https://www.yumpu.com/en/document/read/65831474/the-make-or-break-decade-for-the-sdgs-has-begun

4. *Taxation and borrowing before lending is a myth:* Additional domestic taxation will lead to fiscal exhaustion, and additional borrowing to future liabilities to the private sector, both further deteriorating our common goods.[19]
5. *Digitalisation and parallelisation of the monetary system will be a game changer:* If we start issuing additional digital tokens (CBDCs or private crypto-currencies) that can be used for wages and taxes, this will generate the liquidity that is needed.
6. *A new role for regulators:* Extending the central bank mandate from inflation targets to sustainability will allow central/development banks and the World Bank to be officially involved in financing our future.
7. *Feasibility:* Implementing new technology (DLT), adopting new monetary regulation and allowing new monetary channels to finance our future are politically feasible, fast and fair.
8. *Financialisation and securitisation:* The wisdom and experience from existing, traditional financial engineering can be used and upgraded into blended finance. It is not necessarily a win–win but definitely a non-regret approach.
9. *The real intergenerational conflict is about where the money is spent:* A ravaged planet with no debts and successful austerity will create less prosperity for the next generation than an intact, healthy planet with a large and expanded central bank balance sheet.

References

Brunnhuber, S. (2019). Overcoming the global trilemma: New monetary politics in the Anthropocene: Dani Rodrik revised. *Cadmus, 4*(1), 39–46.

Brunnhuber, S. (2021a). *Financing our future*. Palgrave Macmillan.

Brunnhuber, S. (2021b). Open societies versus digital autocratic experiments. In Macondo (Ed.), *UN global goals yearbook 2021: The make or break decade has begun* (pp. 136–145). https://www.yumpu.com/en/document/read/65831474/the-make-or-break-decade-for-the-sdgs-has-begun

Brunnhuber, S. (2022). The real tragedy of the commons—Garrett Hardin (1968) revised. *Problems of Sustainable Development (PROBLEMY EKOROZWOJU), 17*(2), 19–23.

Brunnhuber, S., & Jacobs, G. (2020). Innovative financial engineering to fund the SDGs: A WAAS initiative. *Cadmus, 4*(2), 141–148. http://cadmusjournal.org/article/volume-4/issue-2-part-2/innovative-financialengineering-fund-sdgs-waas-initiative

Brunnhuber, S., et al. (2021). Hedging planetary risks: From weapons of mass destruction to tools of massive social and ecological innovation. *Cadmus, 4*(4), 103–114.

Chaum, D., Grothoff, C., & Moser, T. (2021). *How to issue a central bank digital currency* (SNB Working Papers 3/2021). https://www.snb.ch/n/mmr/reference/working_paper_2021_03/source/working_paper_2021_03.n.pdf

Chenet, H., Ryan-Collins, J., & van Lerven, F. (2021). Finance, climate-change and radical uncertainty: Towards a precautionary approach to financial policy. *Ecological Economics, 183*. https://doi.org/10.1016/j.ecolecon.2021.106957

[19] Kelton, S. (2020). *The Deficit Myth*. London: John Murray. Randall Wray, L. (2015). *Modern Money Theory: A Primer on Macroeconomics for Sovereign Monetary Systems*. London: Palgrave Macmillan, pp. 137–141, 199–206.

Community Currencies in Action. (2015). *People powered money: Designing, developing & delivering community currencies*. New Economics Foundation. https://monneta.org/wp-content/uploads/2017/01/CCIA-book-People-Powered-Money.pdf

Davies, G. (2010). *History of money*. University of Wales Press.

Hardin, G. (1968). The tragedy of the commons. *Science, 162*, 1243–1248.

Huber, J. (2020a). *Theory of dominant money: Part I: Taxonomy of money and monetary tide changes*. https://sovereignmoney.site/dominant-money-i-taxonomy-and-monetary-tide-changes

Huber, J. (2020b). *Dominant money: Part II: The rise of sovereign digital currency*. https://sovereignmoney.site/dominant-money-ii-the-rise-of-sovereign-digital-currency

Huber, J. (2020c). *Monetary financing of helicopter money*. https://sovereignmoney.site/monetary-financing-of-helicopter-money

Huber, J. (2022). *Zeitenwende des Geldsystems, Vom Bankengeld zum digitalen Zentralbankgeld*. Metropolis.

Kelton, S. (2020). *The deficit myth*. John Murray.

Li, X., & Whinston, A. B. (2020). Analyzing cryptocurrencies. *Information Systems Frontiers, 22*, 17–22. https://doi.org/10.1007/s10796-019-09966-2

Lietaer, B., et al. (2012). *Money and sustainability: The missing link: A report from the Club of Rome—EU chapter*. Triarchy Press.

Lomborg, B. (2020). *False alarm—How climate change panic costs us trillions, hurts the poor, and fails to fix the planet*. Basic Books.

Mazzucato, M. (2013). *The entrepreneurial state: Debunking public vs private sector myths*. Anthem Press. Mazzucato, M. (2018).

Peneder, M. (2022). Digitization and the evolution of money as a social technology of account. *Journal of Evolutionary Economics, 32*, 175–203. https://doi.org/10.1007/s00191-021-00729-4

Post-2015 Consensus. *The Economist*. https://www.copenhagenconsensus.com/post-2015-consensus

Prasad, E. S. (2021). *The future of money: How the digital revolution is transforming currencies and finance*. Harvard University Press.

Randall Wray, L. (2015). *Modern money theory: A primer on macroeconomics for sovereign monetary systems*. Palgrave Macmillan. pp. 137–141, 199–206.

Rich, N. (2018). Losing Earth: The decade we almost stopped climate change. *New York Times Magazine*. https://www.nytimes.com/interactive/2018/08/01/magazine/climate-change-losing-earth.html

Rössner, P. R. (2018). Monetary theory and cameralist economic management, c. 1500–1900 AD. *Journal of the History of Economic Thought, 40*(1), 99–134.

Ryan-Collins, J., et al. (2012). *Where does money come from? A guide to the UK monetary and banking system*. New Economics Foundation.

UNSDG. (2018). *Unlocking SDG financing: Good practices from early adopters*. https://unsdg.un.org/resources/unlocking-sdg-financing-findings-early-adopters

Vorisek, D., & Yu, S. (2020). *Understanding the cost of achieving the sustainable development goals* (World Bank Group, Policy Research Working Paper 9146). https://documents1.worldbank.org/curated/en/744701582827333101/pdf/Understanding-the-Cost-of-Achieving-the-Sustainable-Development-Goals.pdf

Glossary of Terms

A	
Active Ownership	This refers to investors addressing concerns of environmental, social and governance (ESG) issues by voting on such topics or engaging corporate managers and boards of directors on them. Active ownership is utilised to address business strategy and decisions made by the corporation in an effort to reduce risk and enhance sustainable long-term shareholder value.
Asset Overlays	This refers to exclusionary screens that do not just apply to a specific sustainable investment product, but instead to the whole asset base of an asset manager or institutional investor. Often such criteria apply to controversial weapons such as cluster bombs, land mines and nuclear weapons.
B	
Best-in-Class/ Positive Screening	Approach in which a company's or issuer's environmental, social and governance (ESG) performance is compared with the ESG performance of its peers (i.e. of the same sector or category) based on a sustainability rating. All companies or issuers with a rating above a defined threshold are considered as investable. The threshold can be set at different levels (e.g. 30% best performing companies or all companies that reach a minimum ESG score).
Blended Finance	Blended finance refers to the complementary use of grants (usually from public sources) and non-grant financing from private and/or public sources. Such structures are used to make infrastructure and sustainability projects that would otherwise not be financially sustainable and attractive for private investors. The IFC uses the term blended finance to distinguish it from 'concessional finance', which requires a minimum 25% grant element. Although blended finance has a concessional component, the subsidy portion of the investment is minimised in order to avoid crowding out private financing.

K. Wendt, B. Villhauer (eds.), *Sustainable Wealth Management*, Sustainable Finance, https://doi.org/10.1007/978-3-031-55505-3

Broad SI	Sustainability criteria and approaches can be applied to mainstream products or the full asset base of a fund manager or institutional asset owner by integrating them in the investment process. The application of sustainability in these cases relies on a general sustainability policy/approach instead of a product-specific policy referred to in the product prospectus. Usually, such mainstream sustainable investments apply to one of the following approaches or a combination thereof: exclusions, norms-based screening, ESG integration, ESG voting and ESG integration.
C	
Carbon Finance	Generic term for financial services related to mitigation of and adaptation to climate change. It specifically refers to investments in greenhouse gas emission reduction projects and the related creation of CO2 certificates, financial instruments that are tradable on carbon markets.
Carbon Footprint of a Portfolio	A carbon footprint refers to the entire greenhouse gas (GHG) emissions of a portfolio. It is calculated in tons of CO2 equivalents per million USD invested (tCO2e/mUSD). It expresses the amount of annual GHG emissions which can be allocated to the investor per million USD invested in a portfolio and is therefore probably the most intuitive carbon metric available at the portfolio level.
Carbon Neutral	This occurs when an organisation's net carbon emissions are equal to zero. The process requires measuring total CO2 emissions, taking active steps to reduce emissions where the company can, and then purchasing CO2 certificates to offset CO2 emissions that cannot be eliminated from a company's operations. The CO2 certificates contribute to financing projects reducing CO2 emissions (i.e. by replacing fossil power generation with renewable energy projects).
Community Investment	Directing investment capital to communities that are underserved by traditional financial service institutions. Generally it provides access to credit, equity, capital, housing and basic banking products that these communities would otherwise lack. The term usually refers to investments in developed countries.
Core SI	Sustainable investment products (investment funds and discretionary mandates) with a written sustainability investment policy as part of the prospectus or contract are considered core SI. Usually, such sustainable investment products apply multiple approaches (i.e. exclusion criteria in combination with a best-in-class approach or an ESG integration approach in combination with ESG voting and engagement).
Corporate Governance/Governance Factors (G of ESG)	Governance factors within ESG criteria in the context of investing refer to the system of policies and practices by which a company is directed and controlled. They include but are not limited to transparency on board compensation, independence of boards and shareholder rights.
Corporate Social Responsibility (CSR)/Corporate Responsibility (CR)	This term refers to the commitment of an organisation, beyond what is required by law, to ensure that the social, economic and environmental impacts of their actions create a net benefit to communities and society. This is founded on the belief that all corporations have a 'duty of care' to all their stakeholders in every area of their business operations and that being a responsible citizen improves the long-term business success of a company.

D	
Development Finance Institution	DFIs occupy the space between public aid and private investment. They are financial institutions, which provide finance to the private sector for investments that promote development. They focus on developing countries and regions where access to private sector funding is limited. They are usually owned or backed by the governments of one or more developed countries.
Development Finance/Official Development Finance	Official development finance (ODF) describes funds from official development finance institutions to developing nations with the objective of reducing poverty and developing the economy of recipient countries. This includes (a) bilateral official development assistance (ODA), (b) grants and concessional and non-concessional development lending by multilateral financial institutions, and (c) other official flows for development purposes (including refinancing loans) which have too low a grant element to qualify as ODA.
Development Investments/ Investments for Development	Term established by SFF to describe investments with a clear intention to improve the social/environmental/economic situation in developing and emerging markets while targeting market or above-market returns.
E	
Engagement Clearinghouse	Platform offered by the Principles for Responsible Investments (PRI) for institutional investors and asset managers to collaborate on engagement activities with investee companies. An investor posts planned engagement activities and seeks other investors to co-sign letters or actively contribute to engagement activities. Accessible for PRI signatories only.
Engagement Overlay Service	A third-party service that engages investee companies on ESG issues on behalf of shareholder clients.
Environmental Factors (E of ESG)	Environmental factors within ESG criteria in the context of investing include but are not limited to the environmental footprint of a company or country (e.g. energy consumption, water consumption), environmental governance (e.g. environmental management system based on ISO 14 001) and environmental product stewardship (e.g. cars with low fuel consumption).
Environmental Lending	Refers to lending activities for environmental projects or companies often provided by multinational development banks. The term also covers lending activities with clear procedures to assess environmental risks of projects or companies. In some cases, banks provide preferential interest rates for environmental projects (i.e. environmental mortgages for low energy buildings).
Equator Principles	The Equator Principles is a risk management framework, adopted by financial institutions, for determining, assessing and managing environmental and social risk in project finance and is primarily intended to provide a minimum standard for due diligence to support responsible risk decision-making.

ESG Analysis	This analysis includes collecting information on how an investment target manages environmental, social and governance factors. When an investment institution wishes to track how potential investments (i.e. companies, countries and issuers) actively manage ESG risks and opportunities, they carry out an ESG analysis. There is growing evidence suggesting that companies with a strong performance in managing environmental, social and governance factors manage their risks and opportunities more effectively and have lower costs of capital. ESG factors, when integrated into investment analysis and decision-making, may therefore offer investors better insights into opportunities and risks.
ESG Engagement	Engagement is an activity performed by shareholders with the goal of convincing management to take account of environmental, social and governance criteria. This dialogue includes communicating with senior management and/or boards of companies and filing or co-filing shareholder proposals. Successful engagement can lead to changes in a company's strategy and processes so as to improve ESG performance and reduce risks.
ESG Integration	The explicit inclusion by investors of ESG risks and opportunities into traditional financial analysis and investment decisions based on a systematic process and appropriate research sources.
ESG Voting	This refers to investors addressing concerns of environmental, social and governance (ESG) issues by actively exercising their voting rights based on ESG principles or an ESG policy.
ESG—Environmental, Social and Governance	ESG stands for environmental (e.g. energy consumption, water usage), social (e.g. talent attraction, supply chain management) and governance (e.g. remuneration policies, board governance). ESG factors form the basis for the different SI approaches.
Ethical Investment	Investments where the main motivation is aligning the ethical values of an organisation or a person with investments. In comparison to sustainable investments which are based on the conviction that an active management of environmental, social and governance risks and opportunities improves the long-term performance of a company, an ethical investment is mainly guided by ethical codes, religious beliefs or personal values and is often carried out using exclusionary screening.
Eurosif	Eurosif is the European association whose mission is to promote sustainability through European financial markets. It works as a partnership of several Europe-based national Sustainable Investment Forums (SIFs). Eurosif engages in a range of promotional activities such as public events or discussion fora, both with the industry and policymakers (www.eurosif.org).
Exclusion Criteria	Activities on the grounds of which a company, country or issuer is considered as not investable. Exclusion criteria can refer to product categories (i.e. weapons, tobacco) activities (i.e. animal testing) or practices (i.e. severe violation of human rights, corruption). They can also be based on personal values (i.e. gambling) or on risk considerations (i.e. nuclear power).

Exclusionary Screening/Negative Screening	An investment strategy excluding companies, countries or issuers on the grounds of activities considered as not investable. Exclusion criteria can refer to product categories (e.g. weapons, tobacco) activities (e.g. animal testing) or practices (e.g. severe violation of human rights, corruption). They can also be based on personal values (e.g. gambling) or on risk considerations (e.g. nuclear power).
Exclusions	An approach excluding companies, countries or other issuers based on activities considered not investable. Exclusion criteria (based on norms and values) can refer to product categories (e.g. weapons, tobacco), activities (e.g. animal testing) or business practices (e.g. severe violation of human rights, corruption).
F	
Fiduciary Duty/ Responsibility	In the institutional investment context, trustees of pension funds owe fiduciary duties to beneficiaries to exercise reasonable care, skill and caution in pursuing an overall investment strategy suitable to the purpose of the trust and to act prudently and for a proper purpose. The explicit legal nature of fiduciary duty varies depending on the country of origin. While most institutional investment funds strive to create financial benefits for their beneficiaries, it is also possible for trust deeds explicitly to require trustees to consider ESG factors in investments. Given the increasing evidence supporting the materiality of ESG issues, some legal experts conclude that it is part of the fiduciary duty of a trustee to consider such opportunities and risks in investment processes.
Financial Centres for Sustainability	The Financial Centres for Sustainability (FC4S) Network is a partnership between financial centres and the United Nations Environment Programme, with the objective to exchange experience and take common action on shared priorities to accelerate the expansion of green and sustainable finance. The long-term vision of the FC4S Network is rapid global growth of green and sustainable finance across the world's financial centres, supported by strengthened international connectivity and a framework for common approaches (www.fc4s.org).
G	
GEAK	Gebäudeausweis der Kantone (GEAK) is a Swiss tool to measure and indicate the energy consumption of a building. It forms an easy tool to compare the energy efficiency of different buildings both for buyers and investors (www.geak.ch).
Global Impact Investing Network (GIIN)	The GIIN is a not-for-profit organisation that is committed to increasing the scale and effectiveness of impact investing (www.thegiin.org).
Global Impact Investing Rating System (GIIRS)	A system for assessing the social and environmental impact of companies and funds (www.giirs.org).
Global Reporting Initiative (GRI)	The Global Reporting Initiative is the most widely used global framework for the standardised reporting of economic, social and environmental performance. The GRI guidelines are created through a multi-stakeholder, consensus-seeking process that involves an international network of business, civil society, labour and professional institutions (www.globalreporting.org)

Global Sustainable Investment Alliance (GSIA)	A global network of membership-based sustainable investment organisations. GSIA's purpose is to extend the impact and visibility of sustainable investment organisations on a global level. GSIA was founded by Eurosif together with other regional and national SIFs (www.gsi-alliance.org).
Governance/ Corporate Governance Factors (G of ESG)	Governance factors within ESG criteria in the context of investing refer to the system of policies and practices by which a company is directed and controlled. They include, but are not limited to, transparency on board compensation, independence of boards and shareholder rights.
Green Bonds	Green bonds are broadly defined as fixed-income securities that raise capital for a project with specific environmental benefits. The majority of green bonds issued to date have raised money for renewable energy projects, energy efficiency measures, mass transit and water technology. Most green bonds have been either plain vanilla treasury-style retail bonds (with a fixed rate of interest and redeemable in full on maturity) or asset-backed securities tied to specific green infrastructure projects.
Green Investing	Investment in businesses contributing to sustainable solutions in environmental topics including investments in renewable energy, energy efficiency, clean technology, low-carbon transportation infrastructure, water treatment and resource efficiency.
I	
ILO Conventions	ILO conventions encompass international labour standards which are integrated into legally binding international treaties, setting out basic principles and rights at work. Those legal instruments are ratified in all participating countries. The eight fundamental conventions cover the topics of freedom of association and the effective recognition of the right to collective bargaining, the elimination of all forms of forced or compulsory labour, the effective abolition of child labour and the elimination of discrimination in respect of employment and occupation. They are frequently used as the basis for exclusion and engagement approaches.
Impact Investing	Investments intended to generate a measurable, beneficial, social and environmental impact alongside a financial return. Impact investments can be made in both emerging and developed markets and target a range of returns from below-market to above-market rates, depending upon the circumstances. SSF considers impact investments as those having three main characteristics: intentionality, management and measurability.
Institutional Investors Group on Climate Change (IIGCC)	A forum for collaboration on climate change for investors. IIGCC provides investors with a collaborative platform to encourage public policies, investment practices and corporate behaviour that address long-term risks and opportunities associated with climate change (www.iigcc.org).
Integrated Reporting	An integrated report (IR) combines a company's financial report and sustainability report in order to give a concise view about how an organisation's strategy, governance, performance and prospects lead to the creation of value over the short, medium and long term.
Integration/ Mainstreaming	In the context of sustainable investment, this refers to ensuring that environmental, social and governance factors are given full consideration and research support, as an integral part of the investment decision-making process. This analysis therefore becomes fully integrated into the overall financial analysis of standard investment products.

Investments for Development/ Development Investments	Term established by SFF to describe investments with a clear intention to improve the social/environmental/economic situation in developing and emerging markets while targeting market or above-market returns.
IRIS	IRIS is a catalogue of generally accepted performance metrics that impact investors use to measure social, environmental and financial success, evaluate deals and improve the credibility of the impact investing industry. The catalogue is prepared by the Global Impact Investing Network (GIIN), a non-profit organisation dedicated to increasing the scale and effectiveness of impact investing (www.iris.thegiin.org).
M	
Mainstreaming/ Integration	In the context of sustainable investment, this refers to ensuring that environmental, social and governance factors are given full consideration and research support, as an integral part of the investment decision-making process. This analysis therefore becomes fully integrated into the overall financial analysis of standard investment products.
Materiality	In the sustainability context, information is material if there is a clear link to the financial performance of a company.
Microcredit	Refers to small loans from a microfinance institution granted to lower-income entrepreneurs in developing and emerging market countries. These loans contribute to the development of local economies and therewith contribute to creating jobs and reducing poverty.
Microfinance	A range of financial tools (loans, savings, money transfers, etc.) provided by microfinance institutions and designed for people who do not have access to the traditional banking system.
Microfinance Institutions	Organisations that offer microcredits and other microfinance products to companies and individuals in developing and emerging market countries.
Microinsurance	Microinsurance products are designed for individuals in developing and emerging market countries who do not have access to traditional insurance services.
Minder Initiative	Swiss referendum launched by a politician named Minder with the aim to reduce wage levels at Swiss companies. The adoption of the 'Minder Initiative' in March 2013 resulted in an Implementing Ordinance (VegüV), temporarily defining the implementation of this new article of the Swiss Constitution. The main principles are annual mandatory votes for pension funds on board remuneration of Swiss companies and transparent reporting on votes, no severance payments for governing officers, regulation in articles of association of credits and pensions payable to governing officers and custodial sentence for persons violating these principles.
Mission-Based Investing	The incorporation of an organisation's mission into its investment decision-making process. Most often used in reference to foundations and other non-governmental organisations working for social or environmental change. Mission-based investing ensures that organisations' investments are aligned with the overall goals of the organisation itself and are helping, not hindering, the achievement of those goals.
Montreal Carbon Pledge	Launched in September 2014, signatories of the Montreal Carbon Pledge commit to measure and publicly disclose the carbon footprint of their investment portfolios on an annual basis (www.montrealpledge.org).

N	
Natural Capital Finance Alliance	The Alliance and its Secretariat was originally formed to support the signatories of the Natural Capital Declaration (NCD), which was launched at the Rio+20 conference in 2012. The declaration has been signed by the CEOs of more than 40 financial institutions from around the world. It formalises their commitment to the integration of natural capital considerations into financial sector reporting (www.naturalcapital.finance).
Negative Screening/ Exclusionary Screening	An investment strategy excluding companies, countries or issuers on the grounds of activities considered as not investable. Exclusion criteria can refer to product categories (e.g. weapons, tobacco) activities (e.g. animal testing) or practices (e.g. severe violation of human rights, corruption). They can also be based on personal values (e.g. gambling) or on risk considerations (e.g. nuclear power).
Norms-Based Screening	Screening of investments against minimum standards of business practice based on national or international standards and norms such as the ILO conventions, the OECD Guidelines for Multinational Enterprises, the UN Global Compact or the UN Guiding Principles on Business and Human Rights.
O	
OECD Guidelines for Multinational Enterprises	This is a comprehensive set of government-backed recommendations on responsible business. The governments who aim to adhere to the Guidelines intend to encourage and maximise the positive impact multinational enterprises can make to sustainable development and enduring social progress (www.oecd.org/corporate/mne).
Official Development Finance/ Development Finance	Official development finance (ODF) describes funds from official development finance institutions to developing nations with the objective of reducing poverty and developing the economy of recipient countries. This includes (a) bilateral official development assistance (ODA), (b) grants and concessional and non-concessional development lending by multilateral financial institutions and (c) other official flows for development purposes (including refinancing loans) which have too low a grant element to qualify as ODA.
P	
Paris Agreement	Agreed at COP21 in Paris in 2015, the Paris Agreement's central aim is to strengthen the global response to the threat of climate change by keeping a global temperature rise in this century well below 2 °C above pre-industrial levels and to pursue efforts to limit the temperature increase even further to 1.5 °C.
Portfolio Carbon Footprint	An aggregation of the carbon footprint of individual positions within an investment portfolio, relative to the share of the companies held by this portfolio. As a measure to assess the climate risk of an investment portfolio, this key performance indicator is used by institutional investors aiming to offer transparency and reduce the carbon intensity of their portfolios.
Positive Screening/ Best-in-Class	Investment approach based on a sustainability rating in which a company's or issuer's environmental, social and governance (ESG) performance is compared with the ESG performance of its sector pccrs. All companies with a rating above a defined threshold are considered as investable. The threshold can be set at different levels (i.e. 30% best companies eligible).

Principles for Responsible Investment (PRI)	The United Nations-supported Principles for Responsible Investment (PRI) Initiative is an international network of investors and asset managers working together to put the six Principles for Responsible Investment into practice. Its goal is to understand the implications of sustainability for investors and support signatories to incorporate these issues into their investment decision-making and ownership practices. Asset owners, investment managers and service providers can become signatories, which obliges them to annually report on their progress regarding the six principles covering ESG integration, active ownership and promotion of sustainable investments (www.unpri.org).
Principles for Sustainable Insurance (PSI)	Launched by UNEP FI in 2012, the Principles for Sustainable Insurance (PSI) serve as a global framework for the insurance industry to address environmental, social and governance risks and opportunities. The purpose of the PSI Initiative is to better understand, prevent and reduce environmental, social and governance risks and better manage opportunities to provide quality and reliable risk protection (www.unepfi.org/psi/).
Proxy Voting	A ballot cast by one person on behalf of another. One of the benefits of being a shareholder is the right to vote on certain corporate matters. Since most shareholders cannot, or do not want to, attend the annual and special meetings at which the voting occurs, corporations provide shareholders with the option to cast a proxy vote. Shareholders receive a proxy ballot in the mail along with an informational booklet called a proxy statement describing the issues to be voted on. Shareholders return a form by mail agreeing to have their vote cast by proxy.
Public-Private Partnership (PPP)	Typically, medium- to long-term arrangements between the public and private sectors, whereby some of the service obligations of the public sector are provided by the private sector, with clear agreement on shared objectives for delivery of public infrastructure and/or public services. In the finance context, PPPs often form the basis for long-term investments by the private sector in infrastructure or other services of the public domain.
R	
Responsible Investment/ Sustainable Investment	Responsible investment (analogous to sustainable investment) refers to any investment approach, integrating environmental, social and governance factors (ESG) into the selection and management of investments. There are many different forms of responsible investing, such as best-in-class investments, ESG integration, exclusionary screening, thematic investing and impact investing. They are all components of responsible investments and have played a part in its history and evolution.
S	
Science-Based Targets	The term 'science-based targets' is currently mostly applied in the context of climate targets. Such targets provide a clearly defined pathway for companies to reduce greenhouse gas (GHG) emissions. According to the science-based targets initiative, targets are considered 'science-based' if they are in line with what the latest climate science deems necessary to meet the goals of the Paris Agreement—limiting global warming to well below 2 °C above pre-industrial levels and pursuing efforts to limit warming to 1.5 °C. The concept can also be applied to other sustainability targets.

Scope 1, 2, 3	Scope 1: All direct greenhouse gas emissions. Scope 2: Indirect greenhouse gas emissions from consumption of purchased electricity, heat or steam. Scope 3: Other indirect emissions, such as the extraction and production of purchased materials and fuels, transport-related activities in vehicles not owned or controlled by the reporting entity, electricity-related activities (e.g. T and D losses) not covered in Scope 2, outsourced activities, waste disposal, etc. Source Scope 1: Emissions from sources owned or controlled by the company that is measuring emissions. Scope 2: Emissions associated with energy purchased by the company that is measuring emissions. Scope 3: Emissions related to upstream elements of the supply chain (e.g. purchased goods and business travel) and downstream elements (use and end-of-life treatment sold products) of a company that is measuring emissions. Source: SSF Market Study 2021
Shareholder Activism	Investment strategy that employs shareholder power to influence corporate strategy and behaviour. Done by submitting and voting on proxy resolutions that influence a company's policies and practices.
Shareholder Proposal/Resolution	A legal right of shareholders to create a proposal for change in corporate policies and actions. Shareholder proposals are tools of corporate engagement and shareholders reserve the right to circulate proposals and vote on them at the company's Annual General Meeting (AGM). For details on voting, see 'proxy voting'.
Social Factors (S of ESG)	Social factors within ESG criteria in the context of investing include, but are not limited to, worker rights, safety, diversity, education, labour relations, supply chain standards, community relations and human rights.
Socially Responsible Investing (SRI)	Socially responsible investing (SRI) is the term previously used for sustainable or responsible investing. SRI had its origin in the Anglo-Saxon investment world, where it originally referred to investments based on exclusionary screening and later to investments with a best-in-class approach and other forms of sustainable investments. Some players still use it as a generic term for sustainable investing.
Stranded Assets	Stranded assets refer to a scenario in which the value of fossil fuel reserves falls due to rising operational costs associated with carbon prices. Fossil fuel assets could become 'stranded' as production becomes unprofitable. The possibility of increased regulation and public pressure, both domestic and international, poses additional risks. The share price of fossil fuel companies could diminish considerably if political pressure to reduce carbon emissions strengthens. The risk of stranded assets is a growing concern for investors.
Sustainability Index/ Benchmark	A sustainability index/benchmark is a tool to measure the value of a section of the stock market. It is computed from the prices of stocks selected by applying a sustainable investment approach. Investors use this tool to describe the market and to compare the return on specific investments.

Sustainability Ratings	Ratings reflecting a company's/country's/fund's performance with regard to environmental, social and governance (ESG) factors. Sustainability ratings enable investors to gain a quick overview of the sustainability performance of a company/country/fund and are the basis for a best-in-class investment approach.
Sustainability Research Provider/ Sustainability Rating Provider	Organisation providing research and/or ratings on the sustainability performance of companies, issuers, countries or sectors. Most investors and asset managers use such third-party information when preparing sustainable investment products.
Sustainable	Balancing economic, ecological and social goals in such a way that the people living on our planet today can meet their needs without compromising the ability of future generations to meet their own needs (WCED).
Sustainable Assets Under Management	Widely applied key performance indicator referring to the total volume of sustainable investments of an investor, asset manager or country. Often expressed as a percentage of total assets under management.
Sustainable Development Goals (SDGs)	The SDGs are 17 goals aiming to catalyse sustainable development set by the UN in 2015. They include goals such as no poverty, gender equality, decent work, sustainable consumption, climate action and reduced inequalities. The goals were developed to replace the Millennium Development Goals (MDGs) which ended in 2015. Unlike the MDGs, the SDG framework does not distinguish between 'developed' and 'developing' nations.
Sustainable Finance	Sustainable finance refers to any form of financial service with the objective of supporting the transition to a sustainable economy and society by integrating environmental, social and governance (ESG) factors into business and investment decisions. Such finance aims for the lasting benefit to clients, society at large and the planet.
Sustainable Finance Geneva (SFG)	Sustainable Finance Geneva is an association of investment professionals with an interest in sustainable finance. SFG's objectives are to raise key financial players' awareness about sustainable investing through communication, training and networking and to promote the Geneva financial centre with its capacities in sustainable finance. SFG is a network partner of SSF (www.sfgeneva.org).
Sustainable Financial Centre	A sustainable financial centre is a financial marketplace that contributes to sustainable development and value creation in economic, environmental and social terms. In other words, one that increases prosperity and economic competitiveness both today and in the long term, while aiming for the lasting benefit of clients, society at large and the planet.
Sustainable Investment (SI)	Sustainable investment (analogous to responsible investment) refers to any investment approach integrating environmental, social and governance factors (ESG) into the selection and management of investments. There are many different approaches of sustainable investing, including best-in-class, ESG integration, exclusions and impact investing.

Sustainable Investment Forum (SIF)	A sustainable investment forum is an association promoting sustainable investments and finance in a national or multinational financial market. There are many SIFs in Europe, most of which are partners and founders of Eurosif. Eurosif together with other regional and national SIFs has founded the Global Sustainable Investment Alliance (GSIA) to align activities and gain a market overview on sustainable investments globally.
Sustainable Investment Fund	Investment fund based on an investment process integrating ESG criteria in different forms (i.e. best-in-class, ESG integration, exclusionary screening).
Sustainable Investment Mandate	Investment mandate based on an investment process integrating ESG criteria in different forms (i.e. best-in-class, ESG integration, exclusionary screening).
Sustainable Thematic Investments/ Thematic Investing	Investment in businesses contributing to sustainable solutions, both in environmental or social topics. In the environmental segment this includes investments in renewable energy, energy efficiency, clean technology, low-carbon transportation infrastructure, water treatment and resource efficiency. In the social segment this includes investments in education, health systems, poverty reduction and solutions for an ageing society.
SVVK—ASIR	The Swiss Association for Responsible Investments (SVVK—ASIR) is an association of large pension funds aiming to provide services to its members that enable them to invest responsibly. This entails the inclusion of ESG criteria in their investment decisions, where the association supports its members through norms-based and product-based portfolio screening and engagement. The normative standards applied are the Swiss constitution and Swiss law, ILO conventions and the Global Compact. The association was founded in December 2015 and has nine members as of 2018.
Swiss Federal Act on War Material (WMA)	The WMA is a piece of Swiss legislation in force since 1998. This Act focuses on the fulfilment of Switzerland's international obligations and the respect of its foreign policy principles by means of controlling the manufacture and transfer of war material and related technology. At the same time, it aims at maintaining Swiss industrial capacity adapted to the requirements of its national defence. The WMA was amended in 2013 to include the prohibition of the production as well as the direct financing of controversial weapons, encompassing cluster munition, anti-personal mines as well as biological, chemical and nuclear weapons. Switzerland is one of the 13 countries regulating the financing of controversial weapons.
Swiss Sustainable Finance (SSF)	Swiss Sustainable Finance strengthens the position of Switzerland in the global marketplace for sustainable finance by informing, educating and catalysing growth. The association, founded in 2014, has representation in Zurich, Geneva and Lugano. SSF unites over 80 members and network partners from financial service providers, investors, universities and business schools, public sector entities and other interested organisations (www.sustainablefinance.ch).

T	
Thematic Investing/ Sustainable Thematic Investing	Investment in businesses contributing to sustainable solutions both in environmental or social topics. In the environmental segment this includes investments in renewable energy, energy efficiency, clean technology, low-carbon transportation infrastructure, water treatment and resource efficiency. In the social segment this includes investments in education, health systems, poverty reduction and solutions for an ageing society.
Thun Group of Banks	The 'Thun Group of Banks' is an informal group of bank representatives that have been discussing the meaning of the 'Guiding Principles for the implementation of the United Nations "Protect, Respect and Remedy" Framework on Business and Human Rights' ('Guiding Principles') in regard to universal banks and how they could be applied in relation to banking activities (Thun Group Discussion Paper).
Triple Bottom Line	A holistic accounting framework with three parts: environmental, social and financial. These three divisions are also called the three Ps: people, planet and profit, or the 'three pillars of sustainability'.
U	
UN Guiding Principles on Business and Human Rights	The Guiding Principles on Business and Human Rights are meant to support the implementation of the United Nations 'Protect, Respect and Remedy' Framework. This set of guidelines seeks to provide a global standard for preventing and addressing the risk of adverse human rights impacts linked to business activity. They were proposed by the UN Special Representative for Business and Human Rights, John Ruggie, and endorsed by the UN Human Rights Council in June 2011. As they cover all areas of business, they are also applicable to the financial sector.
United Nations Environment Programme Finance Initiative (UNEP FI)	UNEP FI is a global partnership between UNEP and the financial sector founded in 1992. UNEP FI's mission is to bring about systemic change in finance to support a sustainable world and is highlighted in its motto, 'Changing finance, financing change'. Member organisations, representing banking, insurance and investment, recognise sustainability as part of a collective responsibility and support approaches to anticipate and prevent potential negative impacts of the financial industry on the environment and society. UNEP FI develops selective collaborations with other partner organisations, in order to increase awareness and raise support for critical activities (www.unepfi.org).
United Nations Global Compact (UNGC)	This UN initiative aims to encourage businesses worldwide to align their operations and strategies with ten universally accepted principles in the areas of human rights, labour, environment and anti-corruption. Companies signing the UNGC commit to regularly reporting on progress on the ten principles (www.unglobalcompact.org).
V	
Values-Based Exclusions	This refers to exclusions that are based on personal values (as opposed to exclusions based on risk considerations or the violation of international norms). Prominent examples are exclusions of companies involved in gambling, production of weapons or alcohol.

Source: BNP Paribas, FNG, GIIN, pwc, Responsible Investment Association (RIA), RI, SSF, Worldbank, OECD, your SRI, KPMG, WCED

Index

K. Wendt, B. Villhauer (eds.), *Sustainable Wealth Management*, Sustainable Finance, https://doi.org/10.1007/978-3-031-55505-3

Q

R

S

T

V

MIX
Papier aus verantwortungsvollen Quellen
Paper from responsible sources
FSC® C105338

If you have any concerns about our products,
you can contact us on
ProductSafety@springernature.com

In case Publisher is established outside the EU,
the EU authorized representative is:
Springer Nature Customer Service Center GmbH
Europaplatz 3, 69115 Heidelberg, Germany

Printed by Libri Plureos GmbH
in Hamburg, Germany